Madrid

"All you've got to do is decide to go and the hardest part is over.

So go!"

TONY WHEELER, COFOUNDER – LONELY PLANET

D1051840

THIS EDITION WRITTEN AND RESEARCHED BY

Anthony Ham

Contents

(left) **Flamenco dancer, Corral de la Morería (p80)**

....

(above) **Puerta de Alcalá (p110)**

....

(right) **Parque del Buen Retiro (p111)**

....

Parque del Oeste & Northern Madrid
p148

Salamanca
p118

Malasaña & Chueca
p128

Plaza Mayor & Royal Madrid
p50

Sol, Santa Ana & Huertas
p83

El Retiro & the Art Museums
p97

La Latina & Lavapiés
p68

Welcome to Madrid

No city on earth is more alive than Madrid, a beguiling place whose sheer energy carries a simple message: this city really knows how to live.

An Artistic City

Few cities boast an artistic pedigree quite as pure as Madrid's: many art lovers return here again and again. For centuries, Spanish royals showered praise and riches upon the finest artists of the day, from homegrown talents such as Goya and Velázquez to Flemish and Italian greats. Masterpieces by these and other Spanish painters such as Picasso, Dalí and Miró now adorn the walls of the city's world-class galleries. Three in particular are giants – the Museo del Prado, Centro de Arte Reina Sofía and Museo Thyssen-Bornemisza – but in Madrid these are merely good places to start.

A Culinary Capital

Rising above the humble claims of its local cuisine, Madrid has evolved into one of the richest culinary capitals of Europe. The city has wholeheartedly embraced all the creativity and innovation of Spain's gastronomic revolution. But this acceptance of the new is wedded to a passion for the enduring traditions of Spanish cooking, for the conviviality of the eating experience and for showcasing the infinite variety of food from every Spanish region. From tapas in sleek temples to all that's new to sit-down meals beneath centuries-old vaulted ceilings, eating in Madrid is a genuine pleasure.

Killing the Night

Madrid nights are the stuff of legend, and the perfect complement to the more sedate charms of fine arts and fine dining. The city may have more bars than any other city on earth – a collection of storied cocktail bars and nightclubs that combine a hint of glamour with non-stop *marcha* (action). But that only goes some way to explaining the appeal of after-dark Madrid. Step out into the night-time streets of many Madrid neighbourhoods and you'll find yourself swept along on a tide of people, accompanied by a happy crowd intent on dancing until dawn.

Beautiful Architecture

Madrid may lack the cachet of Paris, the monumental history of Rome, or Barcelona's reputation for Modernista masterpieces. And no, there is no equivalent of the Eiffel Tower, Colosseum or La Sagrada Família that you can point to and say 'this is Madrid'. But Madrid has its own particular beauty. Spain's broad sweep of architectural history provides a glorious backdrop to city life, from medieval mansions and royal palaces to the unimagined angles of Spanish contemporary architecture, from the sober brickwork and slate spires of Madrid baroque to the extravagant confections of the belle époque. Put simply, this is one beautiful city.

Why I Love Madrid

By Anthony Ham, Author

More than a decade after I fell for Madrid and decided to call it home, the life that courses relentlessly through the streets here still excites me. Here is a place where the passions of Europe's most passionate country are the fabric of daily life, a city with music in its soul and an unshakeable spring in its step. But Madrid is also one of the most open cities on earth and it doesn't matter where you're from for the oft-heard phrase to ring true: 'If you're in Madrid, you're from Madrid.'

For more about our author, see p256.

Top: Gran Vía (p86)

Madrid's
Top 10

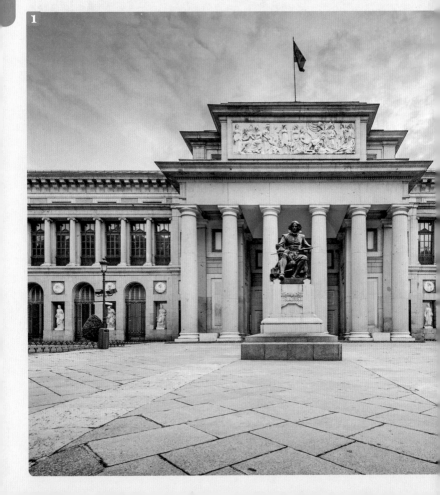

Museo del Prado *(p99)*

1 Spain's premier collection of Spanish and European art belongs among the elite of world art museums. Goya and Velázquez are the stars of the show in the beautiful Museo del Prado that occupies pride of place along the city's grand boulevard, the Paseo del Prado. But the Prado's catalogue has such astonishing depth and breadth, from Rubens and Rembrandt to Botticelli and Bosch, that you'll require more than one visit to take it all in.

⊙ *El Retiro & the Art Museums*

Plaza Mayor *(p52)*

2 Madrid is distinguished by some extraordinarily beautiful plazas (city squares), but Plaza Mayor is easily the king. The plaza's constituent elements are easy to list: uneven cobblestones, perfectly proportioned porticoes, slate spires and facades in deep ochre offset by marvellous frescoes of mythic figures and wrought-iron balconies. But this stately square is the heartbeat of a city, the scene of so many grand events in Madrid's historical story and where the modern city most agreeably throngs with life.

⊙ *Plaza Mayor & Royal Madrid*

Centro de Arte Reina Sofía *(p108)*

3 In a city where world-class art galleries are everywhere, it takes something special for one painting to tower above the rest. But such is the strange and disturbing splendour of Pablo Picasso's *Guernica* that its claim to being Madrid's most extraordinary artwork is unrivalled. After decades of wandering the globe, it looks very much at home in the Centro de Arte Reina Sofía, alongside works by Salvador Dalí and Joan Miró. TOP LEFT: IMAGE COURTESY OF MUSEO NACIONAL CENTRO DE ARTE REINA SOFÍA

⊙ *El Retiro & the Art Museums*

Tapas in La Latina *(p74)*

4 One of the most important gastronomic streets in Spain, La Latina's Calle de la Cava Baja is lined with tapas bars. Some have elevated these tiny morsels into art forms, others serve up specialities in traditional clay pots. Such is Madrid's love affair with tapas and the culture of enjoying them that even this long and graceful thoroughfare cannot contain the neighbourhood's tapas offerings. Nearby you'll find Madrid's best *tortilla de patatas* (potato and onion omelette), a dish beloved by the king...

✕ *La Latina & Lavapiés*

Parque del Buen Retiro *(p111)*

5 The alter ego to Madrid's tableau of sound and movement, the Parque del Buen Retiro is one of our favourite corners of the city. Beautiful by any standards with eye-catching architectural monuments and abundant statues among the trees, El Retiro is where *madrileños* (people from Madrid) come to stroll in great numbers on weekends. As such it's one of the most accessible slices of local culture, at once filled with life and an escape from Madrid's frenetic pace. ABOVE: PALACIO DE CRISTAL

⊙ *El Retiro & the Art Museums*

Palacio Real (p53)

6 Built on the site where Madrid was born in the 9th century, the Palacio Real is one of the city's most significant (and most beautiful) buildings. Watching over a pretty square and shadowed by gorgeous ornamental gardens, the palace is a stately affair, combining grandeur, all the symbolism of an imperial past and unusual accessibility in the city's heart. The interior is as lavish and extravagant as you'd expect, a reminder of the glory days when Spanish royalty ruled the world.

👁 *Plaza Mayor & Royal Madrid*

Malasaña & Chueca Nightlife (p137)

7 The legend of Madrid's hedonistic nights was born in the narrow, inner-city streets of Malasaña and Chueca. In gritty and grungy Malasaña, hard-living rock venues share punters with elegant 19th-century literary cafes. Next door in Chueca, a cool and predominantly gay clientele fills bars and nightclubs to capacity most nights. More than anywhere in the city, this is where locals come for a night out, and the diversity of what's on offer here is representative of a city whose contradictory impulses are legion.

🍷 *Malasaña & Chueca*

Museo Thyssen-Bornemisza *(p104)*

8 Of all Madrid's major art galleries, it is the Museo Thyssen-Bornemisza that most often appeals to the uninitiated. Here beneath one roof are works from seemingly every European painter of distinction, from 13th-century religious art to zany 21st-century creations. There may just be one painting, or a handful of paintings from each artist, but the museum's broad-brushstrokes approach makes a visit here akin to a journey through all that has been refined and masterful during centuries of European art.

◉ El Retiro &
the Art Museums

Ermita de San Antonio de la Florida (p150)

9 One of Madrid's best-kept secrets, the Ermita de San Antonio de la Florida is nonetheless one of the city's most significant artistic landmarks. Here in a small and otherwise nondescript hermitage in 1798, Goya, one of the city's most favoured adopted sons, painted a series of frescoes under royal orders; these extraordinary paintings remain exactly where he first painted them. Breathtaking in their vivid portrayal of Madrid life and the Miracle of St Anthony, they're definitely worth the trip across town to get here.

👁 *Parque del Oeste & Northern Madrid*

Plaza de Santa Ana & Night-Time Huertas (p91)

10 Nights around the Plaza de Santa Ana and neighbouring *barrio* (district) of Huertas are long, loud and filled with variety. The plaza is both epicentre and starting point of so many epic Madrid nights, with outdoor tables a fabulous vantage point from which to take the pulse of the night and plan your journey through it. Within a short radius of the square, live-music venues, old-style sherry bars and sleek rooftop lounge bars for sybarites will get your night going, with legendary Madrid nightclubs nearby.

🍷 *Sol, Santa Ana & Huertas*

What's New

Platea

One of the most exciting developments to occur in Spain in recent years, Platea is a whole new concept in capturing the excitement surrounding Spanish cuisine. Michelin-starred chefs, gourmet food shops and cocktail bars inhabit an artfully converted old cinema, complete with live cabaret. It's a stunning, relentlessly dynamic combination that reinforces Madrid's claims to culinary excellence and innovation. (p123)

Lower Malasaña

Calle del Pez has for years been taking a whole new approach to cool done the Malasaña way. Now it's spreading: visit Maricastaña restaurant to see what we mean. (p133)

Museo de Historia

It took years to get it right, but the stunning renovations at Museo de Historia have brought Madrid's history to life. Step beneath the ornate doorway and lose yourself in this fascinating story. (p130)

Museo Arqueológico Nacional

The renovations here went over time and over budget but they were absolutely worth it – this fabulous exhibition space winningly showcases Spain's ancient history. (p122)

Faro de Madrid

Rising from the city centre's west like an isolated lighthouse, the Faro de Madrid has finally reopened and the views out over western Madrid are as wonderful as ever. (p152)

Spanish Fast Food

Jamón serrano (cured ham), that ultimate Spanish comfort food, is at last taking centre stage for those eating on the run. Small outlets selling rolls filled with *jamón* are exploding into view all across the city.

Rooftop Views

Rooftop bars are old news, but rooftop vantage points for their own sake are suddenly everywhere – from the Mirador de Madrid (p110) at Plaza de la Cibeles to Círculo de Bellas Artes (p88) at Gran Vía.

Capilla del Obispo

One of Madrid's best-kept secrets remained hidden for decades but the Capilla del Obispo has finally opened for guided tours. (p71)

Plaza de Olavide

Although long one of our favourite Madrid plazas, Plaza de Olavide lacked a certain quality when it came to restaurants. The arrival of Mama Campo has changed all that. (p153)

For more recommendations and reviews, see **lonelyplanet.com/madrid**

Need to Know

For more information, see Survival Guide (p203)

Currency
Euro (€)

Language
Spanish (Castellano)

Visas
Generally not required for stays of up to 90 days (not at all for members of EU or Schengen countries). Some nationalities need a Schengen visa.

Money
ATMs are widely available. Credit cards are accepted in most hotels, restaurants and shops.

Mobile Phones
Local SIM cards are widely available and can be used in European and Australian mobile phones. Other phones may need to be set to roaming.

Time
Western European (GMT/UTC plus one hour during winter, plus two hours during daylight-saving period)

Tourist Information
The Centro de Turismo de Madrid (Map p232; ☑010, 91 454 44 10; www.esmadrid.com; Plaza Mayor 27; ☺9.30am-8.30pm; @; Ⓜ Sol) is the main tourist office; there are other branches and information points around the city.

Daily Costs

Budget:
Less than €80
➡ Dorm beds €15–20; *hostal* (budget hotel) doubles €50–70

➡ Three-course *menú del día* (daily set menu) lunches

➡ Plan sightseeing around 'free admission' times

Midrange:
€80–200
➡ Double room in midrange hotel €75–150

➡ Lunch and/or dinner in decent restaurants

➡ Use discount cards to keep costs down

Top End:
More than €200
➡ Double room in top-end hotel from €150

➡ Fine dining for lunch and dinner

Advance Planning

Three months before Reserve your hotel as early as you can and book dinner at DiverXo (p155).

One month before Book a table at La Terraza del Casino (p91) or Viridiana (p114).

One week before Book online entry to the Museo del Prado (p99) and tickets to a Real Madrid game (p154).

Useful Websites

➡ **EsMadrid.com** (www.esmadrid.com) Tourist office's website.

➡ **LeCool** (http://madrid.lecool.com) Alternative, offbeat and avant-garde.

➡ **Lonely Planet** (www.lonelyplanet.com/madrid) An overview of Madrid with hundreds of useful links.

➡ **Turismo Madrid** (www.turismomadrid.es) Regional Comunidad de Madrid tourist office site.

WHEN TO GO

Spring and autumn are the best times to visit. Summer can be fiercely hot although it's a dry heat, while winter can be bitterly cold and snow is possible though rare.

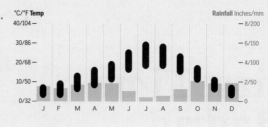

Arriving in Madrid

Aeropuerto de Barajas (Adolfo Suárez Madrid-Barajas Airport) Metro (from 6.05am to 1.30am), bus and minibus (both running 24 hours) to central Madrid; taxis €30.

Estación de Atocha (Atocha Train Station) Close to city centre. Metro and bus to central Madrid from 6.05am to 1.30am; taxi from €8.

Estación de Chamartín (Chamartín Train Station) Metro and bus to central Madrid from 6.05am to 1.30am; taxi around €13.

Estación Sur de Autobuses (Bus Station) Metro and bus to central Madrid from 6.05am to 1.30am; taxi from around €13.

For much more on **arrival**, see p204

Getting Around

Ten-trip Metrobús tickets cost €12.20 and are valid for journeys on Madrid's metro and bus network. Tickets can be bought from most newspaper kiosks and *estancos* (tobacconists), as well as staffed booths and ticket machines in metro stations.

➡ **Metro** The quickest and easiest way to get around. Runs 6.05am to 1.30am.

➡ **Bus** Extensive network but careful planning is needed to make the most of over 200 routes. Runs 6.30am to 11.30pm.

➡ **Taxi** Cheap fares by European standards; plentiful.

➡ **Walking** Compact city centre makes walking a good option, but is hillier than first appears.

For much more on **getting around**, see p206

Sleeping

Madrid is brimful of outstanding hotels, and prices here are often absurdly low when compared to other major European capitals. Advance reservations are always recommended to ensure you get the best deal.

Madrid's midrange and top-end hotels range from tasteful, intimate boutique options to storied palaces of old-fashioned luxury.

Hostales are an excellent budget option, with private bathrooms and rock-bottom prices, while hostels are all about backpacker buzz and dorm-style sleeping.

Useful Websites

➡ **Centro de Turismo de Madrid** (www.esmadrid.com) Tourist office overview of accommodation options.

➡ **Reserva Madrid** (www.reservamadrid.com) Apartment booking service.

➡ **Atrapalo** (www.atrapalo.com) Spanish-language booking service for flights and hotels.

➡ **Lonely Planet** (www.lonelyplanet.com/spain/madrid/hotels) For reviews and bookings online.

For much more on **sleeping**, see p169

A CHEAP LUNCH

Madrid can be expensive for eating out (at least €35 per person in most midrange restaurants), but a great way to sample home-style Spanish cooking is by ordering the weekday lunchtime *menú del día*, a fixed-price, three-course lunch that costs around €12. Lunch is the main meal of the day here; by eating big at lunchtime and ordering tapas in the evening you'll spend surprisingly little on food.

First Time Madrid

For more information, see Survival Guide (p203)

Checklist

➡ Make sure your passport is valid for at least six months past your arrival date

➡ Inform your debit-/credit-card company

➡ Switch off your mobile phone's data roaming unless you want a nasty shock when you get home

➡ Arrange for appropriate travel insurance

➡ Plan your route into the city on the metro

What to Pack

➡ Good walking shoes – Madrid is best appreciated on foot, but is hillier than it looks

➡ A small day pack

➡ As many two-pin continental Europe electrical adaptors as you have devices

➡ Sunscreen in summer, warm clothes in winter

➡ Money belt with emergency cash

➡ Ear plugs to keep out Madrid's night-time noise

Top Tips for Your Trip

➡ Although Madrid does have numerous big-ticket attractions to plan your time around, part of the city's appeal lies in the irresistible energy of its streets. Plan to spend at least part of every day sipping wine in one of Madrid's plazas and watching the world go by.

➡ Madrid is a compact city when compared with other European capitals. Although most of it can be easily explored on foot, if time is tight don't hesitate to make use of the metro as cross-city trips are rarely more than four or five stops.

➡ Try to plan your day around Madrid time – ie lunch after 2pm, dinner after 9pm – with siestas and between-meal tapas to keep you fresh.

What to Wear

Like most Western European cities, Madrid is a fashion-conscious place. Smart casual is considered the bare minimum any time you step outside. For men, that means jeans and T-shirt at least, for women a little more. As a guide, you'd probably dress up more here than you would in London, but it's not quite Paris or Rome.

If you're going out for a meal or to a nightclub, the same rules apply – smart casual is the norm – although it depends on the place. In Malasaña you're more likely to see people dressing down.

Be Forewarned

Madrid is generally safe, but as in any large European city, keep an eye on your belongings and exercise common sense. See p211 for more information.

➡ Favourite pickpocketing haunts include El rastro flea market, around the Museo del Prado, and the metro – and any other areas where tourists congregate in large numbers.

➡ Avoid park areas (such as the Parque del Buen Retiro) after dark.

➡ As a general rule, avoid deserted streets (which are rare in Madrid).

➡ Keep a close eye on your taxi's meter and try to keep track of the route to make sure you're not being taken for a ride.

Tapas

Dive in for one of Madrid's great experiences. There's no big mystery: choose a tapas bar (preferably in La Latina) where the tapas is lined up along the bar, then either point at what you want or take a small plate and help yourself; remember to keep track of what you eat (by holding on to the toothpicks for example). If you really like something, order a *ración* (large plate) from the menu. See p33 for more information.

Taxes & Refunds

In Spain, value-added tax (VAT) is known as IVA. Hotel rooms and restaurant meals attract an additional 10% (usually included in the quoted price but always ask); most other items have 21% added.

If you spend more than €90.16 from any shop, you're entitled to a refund of the 21% IVA on the purchases, provided you will be taking them out of the EU within three months. Ask the shop for a refund form and present it to the customs booth upon leaving the EU.

Tipping

Tipping is not common in Madrid. Locals usually round up taxi fares to the nearest euro, or leave a few coins in restaurants. In better restaurants, 5% is considered ample.

Language

English is generally widely spoken (although sometimes not very well), but Spaniards seem happy to give it a try. Many restaurants have English-language menus. It always helps to learn a few basic phrases (see also the Language chapter, p214).

1 **What time does it open/close?**
¿A qué hora abren/cierran? a ke o·ra ab·ren/thye·ran

The Spanish tend to observe the siesta (midday break), so opening times may surprise you.

2 **Are these complimentary?**
¿Son gratis? son gra·tees

Tapas (bar snacks) are available pretty much around the clock at Spanish bars. You'll find they're free in some places.

3 **When is admission free?**
¿Cuándo es la entrada gratuita?
kwan·do es la en·tra·da gra·twee·ta

Many museums and galleries in Spain have admission-free times, so check before buying tickets.

4 **Where can we go (salsa) dancing?**
¿Dónde podemos ir a bailar (salsa)?
don·de po·de·mos er a bai·lar (sal·sa)

Flamenco may be the authentic viewing experience in Spain, but to actively enjoy the music you'll want to do some dancing.

5 **How do you say this in (Catalan/Galician/Basque)?**
¿Cómo se dice ésto en (catalán/gallego/euskera)?
ko·mo se dee·the es·to en (ka·ta·lan/ga·lye·go/e·oos·ke·ra)

Spain has four official languages, and people in these regions will appreciate it if you try to use their local language.

Etiquette

➡ **Greetings** Greetings should precede even the most casual encounter – *hola, buenos días* is the perfect way to start.

➡ **Bars** Don't be surprised to see people throwing their serviettes and olive stones on the floor – a waiter will come around from time to time to sweep them all up.

➡ **Metro** Stand on the right on escalators in metro stations.

➡ **Churches** Unless you're there for religious reasons, avoid visiting churches (or taking photos) during Mass.

➡ **Bargaining** Haggling is OK at El Rastro, but generally not elsewhere.

Madrid Card

If you want to make the most of your visit, the Madrid Card (p208) can be a good option. It includes free entry to more than 50 museums in and around Madrid, tours and discounts for restaurants, shops and some transport.

Top Itineraries

Day One

Plaza Mayor & Royal Madrid (p50)

 So many Madrid days begin in the **Plaza Mayor**, or perhaps nearby with a breakfast of *chocolate con churros* (chocolate with deep-fried doughnuts) at **Chocolatería de San Ginés**. Drop by the **Plaza de la Villa** and **Plaza de Oriente**, then stop for a coffee or wine at **Cafe de Oriente** and visit the **Palacio Real**.

> **Lunch** Mercado de San Miguel (p61) is one of Madrid's most innovative gastronomic spaces.

El Retiro & the Art Museums (p97)

 Spend as much of the afternoon as you can at the **Museo del Prado**. When this priceless collection of Spanish and European masterpieces gets too much, visit the **Iglesia de San Jerónimo El Real** and **Caixa Forum**.

> **Dinner** Restaurante Sobrino de Botín (p63) is the world's oldest restaurant.

Plaza Mayor & Royal Madrid (p50)

 To kick off the night, perhaps take in a flamenco show at **Las Tablas**, followed by a leisurely drink at **Café del Real** or **Anticafé**. If you're up for a long night, **Teatro Joy Eslava** is an icon of the Madrid night.

Day Two

El Retiro & the Art Museums (p97)

 Get to the **Centro de Arte Reina Sofía** early to beat the crowds, then climb up through sedate streets to spend a couple of hours soaking up the calm of the **Parque del Buen Retiro**. Wander down to admire the **Plaza de la Cibeles**.

> **Lunch** Estado Puro (p114) is one of Madrid's most creative tapas bars.

Parque del Oeste & Northern Madrid (p148)

 After lunch, catch the metro across town to admire the Goya frescoes in the **Ermita de San Antonio de la Florida**. **Templo de Debod** and **Parque del Oeste** are fine places for a stroll.

> **Dinner** Casa Alberto (p89) is one of Madrid's most storied *tabernas* (taverns).

Sol, Santa Ana & Huertas (p83)

 Begin the night at **Plaza de Santa Ana** for a drink or three at an outdoor table if the weather's fine. After another tipple at **La Venencia**, check out if there's live jazz on offer at wonderful **Café Central**, then have an after-show drink at **El Imperfecto**. The night is still young – **Costello Café & Niteclub** is good if you're in the mood to dance, **La Terraza del Urban** if you're in need of more sybaritic pleasures.

Day Three

El Retiro & the Art Museums (p97)

 Begin the morning at the third of Madrid's world-class art galleries, the **Museo Thyssen-Bornemisza**. It's such a rich collection that you could easily spend the whole morning here. If you've time to spare, consider dipping back into the Prado or Reina Sofía.

 Lunch Platea (p123) is one of the city's most exciting culinary experiences.

Salamanca (p118)

 Head out east to take a tour of the **Plaza de Toros** bullring, before dipping into the **Museo Lázaro Galdiano**. Spend the rest of the morning shopping along Calle de Serrano, Calle de José Ortega y Gasset and surrounding streets.

Dinner Naïa Bistro (p76) has a lovely La Latina setting and fresh tastes.

La Latina & Lavapiés (p68)

As dusk approaches, make for La Latina and spend as long as you can picking your way among the tapas bars of **Calle de la Cava Baja** – even if you're not hungry, stop by for a beer or wine to soak up the atmosphere. A wine at **Taberna Tempranillo** and a mojito out on Plaza de la Paja at **Delic** should set you up for the night ahead.

Day Four

Sol, Santa Ana & Huertas (p83)

 Start the day with some souvenir shopping at **Casa de Diego**. If you really love your art, **Real Academia de Bellas Artes de San Fernando** will nicely round out your experience of Madrid's exceptional art scene.

Lunch Opt for Albur (p132) or La Musa (p133) on Calle de Manuela Malasaña.

Malasaña & Chueca (p128)

You've been around almost long enough to be a local and it's therefore worth exploring the laneways of Malasaña between Calle Pez, Plaza del Dos de Mayo and the Glorieta de Bilbao – stop off at **Lolina Vintage Café** along Calle del Espíritu Santo, **Café Manuela** on Calle de San Vincente Ferrer, as well as the **Museo de Historia** or **Museo del Romanticismo** en route.

Dinner La Tasquita de Enfrente (p134) is loved by celebrities and foodies.

Malasaña & Chueca (p128)

Get to know multifaceted Chueca from the dignified calm and boutiques of **Calle de Piamonte**, pass by **Plaza de Chueca** to watch the *barrio* (district) come to life, then get seriously into the cocktail bars along Calle de la Reina, followed by the legendary **Museo Chicote**. **El Junco Jazz Club** will leave you with great memories of the city.

If You Like...

City Squares

Plaza Mayor A perfectly proportioned centrepiece of Madrid life. (p52)

Plaza de Oriente The heart of Royal Madrid, with a royal palace, opera house, statues and gardens. (p55)

Plaza de la Villa Surrounded by impressive examples of Madrid's architectural centuries. (p59)

Plaza de Santa Ana Pretty architecture and a city intent on having a good time. (p87)

Plaza de la Paja On the site of the city's medieval market, it now resembles a ramshackle village square. (p71)

Architecture

Plaza de la Cibeles Madrid's grandest convergence of streets. (p110)

Caixa Forum Central Madrid's most striking symbol of Spain's architectural revolution. (p111)

Convento de la Encarnación Madrid's very own style of baroque architecture close to the Palacio Real. (p57)

Gran Vía Polyglot of facades with the gilded Edificio Metrópolis the pick. (p86)

San Lorenzo de El Escorial Imperial grandeur in the hills surrounding Madrid. (p160)

Centro de Arte Reina Sofía A fitting setting for a premier collection of contemporary art with the architecture a star feature. (p108)

Palacio de Cristal Airy iron-and-glass relic in the Parque del Buen Retiro. (p111)

Caixa Forum (p111)

Art Galleries

Museo del Prado One of the world's best, with Goya, Velázquez and more. (p99)

Centro de Arte Reina Sofía Picasso, Dalí, Miró and other 20th-century masters. (p108)

Museo Thyssen-Bornemisza Astonishing private collection with centuries of European masters. (p104)

Real Academia de Bellas Artes de San Fernando Underrated bastion of Spain's fine artistic tradition. (p85)

Ermita de San Antonio de la Florida Goya's frescoes in their original setting. (p150)

Museo Sorolla Spanish master painter's works in a lovely Chamberí mansion. (p151)

Bastions of Culinary Tradition

Restaurante Sobrino de Botín The world's oldest restaurant and brimful of local specialities. (p63)

Lhardy Much-celebrated Madrid table with impeccable quality and service. (p91)

Posada de la Villa Ancient Madrid inn with reliable cooking and repeat clientele. (p77)

Taberna La Bola Traditional bar-restaurant focused on Madrid specialities. (p61)

Casa Lucio Celebrity clientele and assured cooking of Spanish staples. (p76)

Casa Alberto Historic Huertas *taberna* (tavern) where the

tapas are all about tradition. (p89)

Zalacaín Grand old señor of Madrid restaurants, with an extraordinary wine list. (p155)

Casa Revuelta Essence of the Madrid tapas experience. (p60)

Temples to Innovative Cooking

DiverXo Culinary experimentation with surprising twists in service. (p155)

Estado Puro Tapas from the lab of some of Spain's most innovative chefs. (p114)

Sergi Arola Gastro Overseen by one of Spain's most respected chefs. (p155)

Vi Cool Sergi Arola's foray into reasonably priced tapas. (p89)

La Terraza del Casino Glorious setting and state-of-the-art nouvelle cuisine. (p91)

Green Escapes

Parque del Buen Retiro Madrid's finest city park and scene of so much that's good about Madrid life. (p111)

Parque del Oeste Sloping stand of greenery northwest of the city centre with fine views and scarcely a tourist in sight. (p152)

Real Jardín Botánico An intimate oasis of exotic plants right alongside one of Madrid's busiest boulevards. (p113)

> **For more top Madrid spots, see the following:**
> ➡ Eating (p31)
> ➡ Drinking & Nightlife (p36)
> ➡ Entertainment (p39)
> ➡ Shopping (p44)

PLAN YOUR TRIP IF YOU LIKE…

Casa de Campo Vast expanse of parkland west of downtown Madrid with the city's zoo, an amusement park, and a cable car to get there. (p156)

Madrid Río Kilometres of developed parkland alongside Madrid's long-forgotten river. (p74)

Nightlife

Teatro Joy Eslava Consistently good times every night of the year. (p63)

Kapital Multistorey club with a cross-section of Madrid's dancing public. (p115)

Why Not? Where Chueca gets up close and personal in a quirky, intimate space. (p142)

Ya'sta Get all hot and sweaty at Madrid's best throwback to the heady, rock-fuelled 1980s. (p140)

Charada Move your hips until dawn at this former brothel turned dance palace. (p64)

Museo Chicote One of Europe's most storied cocktail bars, with smooth music and even smoother mojitos. (p140)

1862 Dry Bar Cocktails at their most creative to kick-start a love affair with Malasaña. (p138)

Month by Month

TOP EVENTS

Fiestas de San Isidro Labrador, May

Suma Flamenca, June

Festimad, May

Día del Orgullo de Gays, Lesbianas y Transexuales, June

Festival Jazz Madrid, November

January

Not much happens in Madrid until after 6 January, although the Christmas–New Year period can be high season in some hotels. Temperatures can be bitterly cold, but wonderfully clear, crisp days are also common.

✲ Año Nuevo

Many *madrileños* (people from Madrid) gather in Puerta del Sol on Noche Vieja (New Year's Eve) to wait for the 12 *campanadas* (bell chimes), whereupon they try to stuff 12 grapes (one for each chime) into their mouths to mark Año Nuevo (New Year).

✲ Reyes

On Día de los Reyes Magos (Three Kings' Day), three wise men lead the sweet-distributing frenzy of Cabalgata de Reyes. Horse-drawn carriages and floats make their way from the Parque del Buen Retiro to Plaza Mayor at 6pm on 5 January.

February

Usually the coldest month in Madrid, February always has a chill in the air. In warmer years, late February can be surprisingly mild, heralding the early onset of spring.

✕ Gastro Festival Madrid

All the Spanish chefs who have made it big come to Madrid for this gastronomy summit (www.gastrofestivalmadrid.com), with workshops and events where masters of the Spanish kitchen show off their latest creations. Over 400 bars and restaurants participate with special menus, tapas routes and competitions.

✲ Carnaval

Carnaval spells several days of fancy-dress parades and merrymaking in many *barrios* (districts) across the Comunidad de Madrid, usually ending on the Tuesday 47 days before Easter Sunday. Competitions for the best costume take place in the Círculo de Bellas Artes.

March

Freezing temperatures can occur, but early spring sunshine can prompt restaurants to set up their outdoor tables. *Madrileños* often evacuate the city for Semana Santa (Holy Week), but it can still be high season for some hotels.

✲ Jueves Santo

On Jueves Santo (Holy Thursday), local *cofradías* (lay fraternities) organise colourful yet solemn religious processions. The main procession concludes by crossing Plaza Mayor to the Basílica de Nuestra Señora del Buen Consejo. Iglesia de San Pedro El Viejo is another important focal point.

✿ Viernes Santo

Viernes Santo (Good Friday) and Easter in general are celebrated with greater enthusiasm in some of the surrounding towns. Chinchón, Ávila and Toledo in particular, are known for their lavish Easter processions.

☆ La Noche de los Teatros

On 'The Night of the Theatres' (www.madrid. org/lanochedelosteatros), Madrid's streets become the stage for all manner of performances, with a focus on comedy and children's plays. It usually takes place on the last Saturday of March, and lasts from 5pm to midnight.

May

May is arguably Madrid's biggest month for festivals and with the weather warming up, it's one of our favourite times to be in the city.

✿ Fiestas de San Isidro Labrador

The city's big holiday on 15 May, the Fiestas de San Isidro marks the feast day of its patron saint, San Isidro. Crowds gather in central Madrid to watch the colourful procession, which kicks off a week of cultural events across the city.

☆ Festimad

Festimad (www.festimad. es) is the biggest of Spain's year-round circuit of major music festivals. Bands from all over the country and beyond converge on Móstoles or Leganés (on the MetroSur train network), just outside Madrid, for two days of indie music indulgence. It sometimes begins in April.

▢ Feria del Libro

The northeastern corner of the Parque del Buen Retiro is taken over by the Madrid Book Fair (www. ferialibromadrid.com), with hundreds of stalls. It draws massive crowds with book signings and discounts of around 10%.

June

A select group of festivals usher in the Spanish summer. The city has a real spring in its step with warm weather and summer holidays just around the corner.

☆ Suma Flamenca

A soul-filled flamenco festival (www.madrid.org/ sumaflamenca) in early June that draws some of the biggest names in the genre to Teatros del Canal and some of the better-known *tablaos* (flamenco venues), such as Casa Patas, Villa Rosa and Corral de la Morería.

✿ Día del Orgullo de Gays, Lesbianas y Transexuales

The city's Gay and Lesbian Pride Festival and Parade take place on the last Saturday of the month. The extravagant floats begin on Plaza de la Independencia, passing along Gran Vía to Plaza de España. At all other times, Chueca is the place to be.

July

Madrid can really cook in July and the city's pace slows in response. That may have something to do with the fact that those not at the beach are preparing to head there in August. Hotel prices often drop when things are quiet.

☆ Veranos de la Villa

Half of Madrid evacuates to the beach in July, but those who remain are rewarded with concerts, opera, dance, theatre and exhibitions as part of 'Summers in the City' (www.veranosdelavilla. com). Many events take place at outdoor venues and the program starts in July and runs to the end of August.

August

Temperatures soar and the city can be eerily quiet as locals flock to the cool respite of the coast or mountains. Many restaurants and other businesses close and some museums open reduced hours.

✿ La Asunción

Also known as the Fiesta de la Virgen de la Paloma, 15 August is a solemn date in the city's religious calendar, celebrating the Assumption of the Virgin Mary. La Latina takes a hedonistic approach to it all with street parties.

(Top) Festival Jazz Madrid
(Bottom) Christmastime children's carousel, Plaza Mayor

November

November is when
Madrid's winter chill
usually starts to bite.
The city's jazz festival
headlines an otherwise
quiet month.

☆ Festival Jazz Madrid

Madrid's annual jazz
festival (www.festivaljazz
madrid.com) draws a pres-
tigious cast of performers
from across the globe and
is an increasingly important stop on the European
jazz circuit. Venues vary,
from the city's intimate jazz
clubs to grander theatrical
stages across town.

December

The run-up to Christmas
sees the city brimful of
festive spirit – crowds
throng the city centre
in astonishing numbers,
many of them en route to
Plaza Mayor's Christmas
market. There are high-
season prices in many
hotels.

🎄 Navidad

The main family meal
for Navidad (Christmas)
is served on Nochebuena
(Christmas Eve). Elaborate
nativity scenes are set up
in churches around the city
and an exhibition is held
in Plaza Mayor (otherwise
taken over by a somewhat
tacky, but wildly popular,
Christmas market).

JUAN NAHARRO GIMENEZ / GETTY IMAGES ©

JÖRG HACKEMANN / SHUTTERSTOCK ©

With Kids

Madrid has plenty of child-friendly (and even a handful of excellent child-specific) sights and activities. The city centre is relatively compact and easy to get around on foot (which is just as well because the metro can be a bit of an obstacle course for those with prams).

Child-Friendly Attractions

Art Galleries

Most major art galleries have children's activities (usually in Spanish), and most of the museum bookshops also sell guides to the museums designed specifically for kids.

Museo de Cera

This wax museum (p131) has enough footballers, actresses and international celebrities to get the kids excited. It's a reliable rainy-day option.

Museo del Ferrocarril

Madrid's Railway Museum, the **Museo del Ferrocarril** (☎902 228822; www.museodel ferrocarril.org; Paseo de las Delicias 61; adult/child €6/4; ⏰9.30am-3pm Tue-Fri, 10am-3pm Sat & Sun, closed 2nd half of Aug; Ⓜ Delicias), has around 30 pieces of rolling stock lined up along the platforms, as well as dioramas of train stations, model trains, and tracks in the shop on the way out.

Casa Museo de Ratón Perez

The Spanish version of the tooth fairy is a cute little mouse called 'El Ratón Perez', and this small **museum** (☎91 522 69 68; www.casamuseoratonperez.com; 1st fl, Calle de Arenal 8; admission €3; ⏰5-8pm Mon, 11am-2pm & 5-8pm Tue-Fri, 11am-3pm & 4-8pm Sat; Ⓜ Sol) close to Sol takes you into a re-creation of his home. Entry is by guided tour and the commentary is only in Spanish.

Estadio Santiago Bernabéu

Go to a game, visit the glittering trophy room or take the tour out onto the pitch at the home of Real Madrid (p154).

Parks & Playgrounds

Parque del Buen Retiro

Kids generally love the Parque del Buen Retiro (p111) as much as adults. There's ample lawn space in which they can run free, plus numerous playgrounds dotted around the park. Most get a kick out of the peacocks in the Jardines del Arquitecto Herrero Palacios. Renting a row boat is also a great way to pass the time, while there are occasionally puppet shows at various points around the park on weekends.

ISABEL PAVIS / GETTY IMAGES ©

...sel ride, Madrid

Playgrounds

Beyond the Parque del Buen Retiro, play areas for children are fairly thinly spread in central Madrid and most get pretty busy on weekends and after school. Most (but not all) squares or plazas have at least a small playground.

Primarily for Kids

Zoo Aquarium de Madrid

Madrid's zoo (p156), west of the city centre in the Casa de Campo, is a fine way to spend a day with your kids. Weekends can be busy, so try and visit during the week, although check the opening hours and program online before setting out.

Parque de Atracciones

Rides for all ages are what this old-style amusement park (p156), also out west in the Casa de Campo, are all about. Long queues form on weekends, both at the rides and to get in, so either get here early or come another day if you can.

NEED TO KNOW

➡ **Bars & restaurants** These are smoke-free and children are welcome in most.

➡ **Metro maps** Show (with a wheelchair symbol) which stations have lifts.

➡ **High chairs** Increasingly common in restaurants.

➡ **Guía del Ocio** Available from newspaper kiosks; has a 'Niños' (children) section.

Warner Brothers Movie World

This movie **theme park** (☑902 024100; www.parquewarner.com; San Martín de la Vega; adult/child €39/30; ☉hours vary), 25km south of central Madrid, has much to catch the attention. The park is divided into themes (Cartoon World, the Old West, Hollywood Boulevard, Super Heroes and Warner Brothers Movie World Studios). Opening times are complex and tickets are cheaper if purchased online. See the website for transport details.

Cable Car

The gentle Teleférico cable-car ride (p152) is a worthwhile activity for its own sake, but it can also be a useful way to get out to the Casa de Campo; there's a good playground just below the Casa de Campo station.

Shopping

Models

Model trains, plains and automobiles (for collectors and for kids) from Bazar Matey (p158) are brilliant little tokens to take home. MacChinine (p147) specialises in Matchbox cars and other perfectly proportioned miniatures.

Flamenco

For dancing shoes and genuine polka-dot flamenco dresses, stop by Maty (p65).

Books

In a quiet street in Chamberí, El Dragón Lector (p158) is one of Madrid's best bookshops for kids.

Like a Local

*n Madrid local knowledge is the
ifference between falling in love
vith the city and just passing
hrough. Immerse yourself in
Jalasaña and Chamberí, and
n the local passion for tapas,
hocolate con churros and
utdoor dining. Knowing where
o go on Sundays will transform
our weekend.*

MARK READ / LONELY PLANET ©

:olate con churros, Chocolatería de San Ginés (p63)

A Madrid Sunday

Madrileños (people from Madrid) love
their Sundays and although there are numerous variations on the theme, they usually go something like this. The day begins
in the morning (early or otherwise) at the
flea market of El Rastro (p72). Having
shopped for bargains or simply reasserted
one's right to partake of this age-old tradition, they then fan out into the bars of
La Latina. It is customary at 1pm to order
a vermouth (many of the bars have it on
tap) to accompany the inevitable rounds
of tapas, either as a precursor to lunch
or as the main meal itself. Later, many
gather in Plaza de la Puerta de Moros for
an impromptu street party. But even more
head to Parque del Buen Retiro (p111) to do
everything from taking a boat ride on the
lake, reading the Sunday papers or falling asleep (or all of the above), to having a
picnic or waiting for the drums to start.

Chamberí

Of all the *barrios* (districts) that encircle
Madrid's city centre, Chamberí is the one
where it's easiest to access life as locals
live it away from tourist crowds. Plaza de
Olavide (p151) is the hub of Chamberí life.
Here, old men and women pass the day on
park benches, small children tumble out
into the plaza's playgrounds and queues
form at the outdoor tables of the bars that
encircle the plaza. Inside Bar Méntrida at
No 3 you'll find a stirring photographic
record of the plaza's history. There are
some ageless old shops in the vicinity as
well. Sunday morning is another good time
to be here when they close the Calle de
Fuencarral (between the metro stations of
Bilbao and Quevedo) to cars and the whole
neighbourhood comes out for a stroll.

Cafes of Malasaña

Back in the early 20th century, Malasaña
was an important centre for Madrid's intellectual and cultural life, its cafes providing
a meeting place for the great minds of the
day. A handful of these cafes remain, including Café-Restaurante El Espejo (p142).
But the spirit of that age continues and

the clientele has since broadened out to include a wide cross-section of local society to the extent that the cafes of Malasaña, vintage and otherwise, are the essence of the neighbourhood and the secret of its unmistakable *barrio* feel.

Ir de Tapear

To paraphrase Benito Pérez Galdós, a famous 19th-century Madrid writer, people of Madrid love to go out for a stroll so much that it almost counts as an occupation. That sense of a city unwilling to stay indoors finds its most agreeable expression in the tradition of *ir de tapear* (going out for tapas). Food may be the focal point of this popular tradition (and locals are passionate about their food), but it's also a vehicle (some might call it an excuse) for getting together with friends. Primarily an evening affair, or a lunch-and-afternoon event on weekends, it is one of the core elements of local life, a habit formed over the centuries and one that now is second nature to the vast majority of *madrileños*. Understanding the whole culture behind eating tapas in this way, and following suit, is an important step towards starting to think like a local. See p33 for more information.

The Terraza

An adjunct to the Madrid passion for passing the time with friends over tapas is the local love of the *terraza*, the outdoor tables that fill city squares and footpaths all across the city. Whenever the sun's out, even in winter (although this is generally a warm-weather pastime), bar owners will set out their tables safe in the knowledge that locals will soon come to colonise them. People come and go, but it's not unusual if you're having a good time to begin in the afternoon and still be in residence hours later without really knowing where the time went. Joining them is as easy as grabbing an empty chair as soon as it becomes available and thereafter defending it with your life.

Chocolate con Churros

In most places around the world, chocolate and deep-fried doughnuts would be a dessert. In Madrid this ultimate form of street food is many things, but it's most often breakfast, a hangover cure and/or an early-hours' cure for the munchies. As such it often serves a similar purpose to a 3am kebab in the UK. That's not to say that *madrileños* don't think twice about ordering *chocolate con churros* at other times of the day. It's just that the hours before dawn are when nothing else will do but this iconic street snack. Chocolatería de San Ginés (p63) is the most famous venue for this tradition. Elsewhere, El Brillante (p114) sometimes has queues forming when it opens, while Chocolatería Valor (p64) keeps much more reasonable hours.

For Free

Madrid can be expensive, but with careful planning, the combination of free attractions and specific times when major sights offer free entry enables you to see the best the city has to offer without burning a large hole in your pocket.

DAN MOORE / GETTY IMAGES ©

tro (p72)

Always Free

Most of Madrid's world-class attractions have admission fees, and these have, for the most part, been rising steadily over recent years. Even so, a significant number of attractions – from parks and churches to museums and art galleries – remain free, regardless of when you decide to visit.

➡ **Parque del Buen Retiro** (p111) One of Europe's loveliest city parks.

➡ **El Rastro** (p72) Outstanding Sunday-morning flea market.

➡ **Ermita de San Antonio de la Florida** (p150) Goya frescoes right where he painted them.

➡ **Plaza de Toros & Museo Taurino** (p120) Madrid's bullring and bullfighting museum.

➡ **Museo de Historia** (p130) Wonderful journey through Madrid's history.

➡ **Museo de San Isidro** (p71) Go looking for Madrid's patron saint.

➡ **Iglesia de San Jerónimo El Real** (p111) Church of choice for Spanish royalty.

➡ **Iglesia de San Ginés** (p57) Medieval church with an El Greco painting.

➡ **Caixa Forum** (p111) Fabulous contemporary architecture with hanging garden.

➡ **Campo del Moro** (p55) Expansive gardens below the royal palace.

➡ **Templo de Debod** (p152) Madrid's very own Egyptian temple.

➡ **Catedral de Nuestra Señora de la Almudena** (p55) Madrid's cavernous cathedral.

➡ **Casa de Lope de Vega** (p87) One-time home of Spain's favourite playwright.

➡ **Museo al Aire Libre** (p122) Open-air sculptures by Spain's finest.

➡ **Biblioteca Nacional & Museo del Libro** (p122) Grand architecture and book museum.

➡ **Sociedad General de Autores y Editores** (p130) Madrid's answer to Gaudí.

➡ **Estación de Chamberí** (p153) The metro as it once was.

➡ **Galería Moriarty** (p131) Iconic private art gallery.

➡ **Mercado de Fuencarral** (p144) The soul of grungy Malasaña.

Sometimes Free

Most of Madrid's attractions have times during the week when they offer free admission – sometimes a whole day, sometimes a few hours every day.

Take, for example, Madrid's big three art galleries – the Prado, the Thyssen and the Reina Sofía. Paying the normal admission to visit all three galleries will cost a total of €32 (or €25.60 if you buy the Paseo del Arte ticket). Plan your visits around the free-entry periods, however, and you'll pay nothing.

Although there's something rather appealing about seeing some of the world's best art galleries for nothing, remember that these periods of free entry are usually when the museums are inevitably at their most crowded.

Another way to cut costs is to purchase the Madrid Card (p208), although entry to these museums is, of course, free only once you've forked out for the cost of the card.

➡ **Museo del Prado** (p99) Free 6pm to 8pm Monday to Saturday and 5pm to 7pm Sunday.

➡ **Museo Thyssen-Bornemisza** (p104) Free Monday.

➡ **Centro de Arte Reina Sofía** (p108) Free 1.30pm to 7pm Sunday and 7pm to 9pm Monday and Wednesday to Saturday.

➡ **Real Academia de Bellas Artes de San Fernando** (p85) Free Wednesday.

➡ **Museo Sorolla** (p151) Free Sunday and 2pm to 8pm Saturday.

➡ **Museo de Cerralbo** (p151) Free Sunday, 2pm to 3pm Saturday and 5pm to 8pm Thursday.

➡ **Museo de América** (p151) Free Sunday.

➡ **Museo del Romanticismo** (p130) Free 2.30pm to 8.30pm Saturday.

Free for EU Citizens/Residents

Palaces, convents and other buildings overseen by Spain's heritage authorities have free entry at limited times of the week, but it's only applicable to EU citizens/permanent residents.

➡ **Palacio Real** (p53) Free for EU citizens/residents for last two hours Monday to Thursday.

➡ **Convento de las Descalzas Reales** (p57) Free for EU citizens/residents Wednesday and Thursday afternoons.

➡ **Convento de la Encarnación** (p57) Free for EU citizens/residents Wednesday and Thursday afternoons.

Selection of tapas

Eating

Madrid has transformed itself into one of Europe's culinary capitals, not least because the city has long been a magnet for people (and cuisines) from all over Spain. Travel from one Spanish village to the next and you'll quickly learn that each has its own speciality; travel to Madrid and you'll find them all.

NEED TO KNOW

Price Ranges

The following price ranges are for the cost of a main course:

€	less than €10
€€	€10 to €20
€€€	more than €20

Opening Hours

➡ Lunch: 1pm to 4pm

➡ Dinner: 8.30pm to midnight or later

Tipping

A service charge is generally calculated into most bills in Madrid, so any further tipping is a matter of personal choice. Spaniards often leave no more than €1 per person or nothing more than small change. If you're particularly happy, 5% on top would be fine.

Reservations

Reservations for restaurants (not tapas bars) are strongly recommended on Friday and Saturday nights when many restaurants may have two sittings – one around 9pm, the second around 11pm. Reserving for lunch on Saturday or Sunday is also a good idea.

A Useful Resource

If you read Spanish, watch out for the annual (and indispensable) *Guía Metrópoli – Comer y Beber en Madrid*. It's available from news kiosks for €11.90 and has reviews of over 1800 Madrid restaurants and bars by the food critics of *ABC* newspaper.

The Culture of Eating

Aside from the myriad tastes on offer, it's the buzz that accompanies eating in Madrid that defines the city as a memorable gastronomic experience. Here, eating is not a functional pastime to be squeezed in between other more important tasks; instead, it is one of life's great pleasures, a social event always taken seriously enough to allocate hours for the purpose and to be savoured like all good things in life. Treat it in the same way and you're halfway to understanding why *madrileños* (people from Madrid) are so passionate about their food.

Mercado de San Miguel (p61)

Local Specialities

On the bleak *meseta* (plateau) of inland Spain, food in medieval Madrid was a necessity, good food a luxury, and the dishes that developed were functional and well suited to a climate dominated by interminable, bitterly cold winters. The city's traditional local cuisine is still dominated by these influences to a certain extent. At the same time, Madrid has wholeheartedly embraced dishes from across the country. The city has a thriving tapas culture and has become one of the biggest seafood-consuming cities in the world. Thus it is that Madrid has become an excellent place to understand just why Spanish cuisine has taken the world by storm.

SOUPS & STEWS

When the weather turns chilly, that traditionally means in Madrid *sopa de ajo* (garlic soup) and *legumbres* (legumes) such as *garbanzos* (chickpeas), *judías* (beans) and *lentejas* (lentils). Hearty stews are the order of the day and there are none more hearty than *cocido a la madrileña;* it's a kind of hotpot or stew that starts with a noodle broth and is followed by or combined with carrots, chickpeas, chicken, *morcilla* (blood sausage), beef, lard and possibly other sausage meats – there are as many ways of eating *cocido* as there are *madrileños*. *Repollo* (cabbage) sometimes makes an appearance. *Madrileños* love *cocido*. They dream of it while they're away from home and they wonder why it hasn't caught on elsewhere. There was even a hit song written about it in the 1950s. However, we'll put this as gently as we can: you have to be a *madrileño* to understand what all the fuss is about because it may be filling but it's not Spain's most exciting dish.

ROASTED MEATS

Madrid shares with much of the Spanish interior a love of roasted meats. More specifically, *asado de cordero lechal* (spring lamb roasted in a wood-fired oven) is a winter obsession in Madrid just as it is on much of the surrounding *meseta* of central Spain. Usually served with roasted potatoes (it's customary to also order a green salad to accompany the lamb and lighten things up a little), it's a mainstay in many of Madrid's more traditional restaurants. Less celebrated (it's all relative), is *cochinillo asado* (roast suckling pig) from the Segovia region northwest of Madrid.

SEAFOOD

Every day, tonnes of fish and other seafood are trucked in from Mediterranean and Atlantic ports to satisfy the *madrileño* taste for the sea to the extent that, remarkably for a city so far inland, Madrid is home to the world's second-largest fish market (after Tokyo). There's nothing you can't get here if you know where to look. From Galicia in Spain's Atlantic northwest comes *pulpo gallego* (boiled octopus cooked with oil, paprika and garlic) as well as all manner of weird-and-wonderful shellfish. From Asturias, Cantabria and the Basque Country come a passion for delicious *anchoas* (anchovies) and *bacalao* (cod), while Mediterranean Spain has mastered the art of seafood-laden rice dishes, which *madrileños* have embraced as their own. The lightly fried fish of Andalucía rounds out an extraordinary banquet of seafood choice.

JAMÓN

An essential presence on many a Madrid table, and available from just about any city bar or restaurant, is the cured ham from the high plateau known as *jamón*. The *jamón* from Extremadura or Salamanca is widely considered to be the finest.

Spanish *jamón* is, unlike Italian prosciutto, a bold, deep red and well marbled with buttery fat. At its best, it smells like meat, the forest and the field. Like wines and olive oil, Spanish *jamón* is subject to a strict series of classifications. *Jamón serrano* refers to *jamón* made from white-coated pigs introduced to Spain in the 1950s. Once salted and semidried by the cold, dry winds of the Spanish sierra, most now go through a similar process of curing and drying in a climate-controlled shed for around a year. *Jamón serrano* accounts for approximately 90% of cured ham in Spain.

Jamón ibérico – more expensive and generally regarded as the elite of Spanish hams – comes from a black-coated pig indigenous to the Iberian Peninsula and a descendant of the wild boar. Gastronomically, its star appeal is its ability to infiltrate fat into the muscle tissue, thus producing an especially well-marbled meat. If the pig gains at least 50% of its body weight during the acorn-eating season, it can be classified as *jamón ibérico de bellota,* the most sought-after designation for *jamón.*

OTHER SPECIALITIES

The line between Spain-wide specialities and those from Madrid is often blurred but most *madrileños* aren't too fussed whether the first *tortilla de patatas* (potato and onion omelette) was cooked in Madrid or elsewhere – all that matters is that it has become one of the best-loved dishes in the city. The same could also be said for *croquetas* (croquettes) and *patatas con huevos fritos* (baked potatoes with eggs, also known as *huevos rotos*).

Tapas

Nowhere is the national pastime of *ir de tapear* (going out to eat tapas) so deeply ingrained in local culture as it is in Madrid, where tapas are as much a social event as they are a much-loved culinary form. Anything can be a tapa, from a handful of olives or a slice of *jamón* on bread to a *tortilla de patatas* served in liquefied form. That's because tapas are the canvas upon which Spanish chefs paint the story of a nation's obsession with food, the means by which they show their fidelity to traditional Spanish tastes even as they gently nudge their compatriots in never-before-imagined directions. By making the most of very little, tapas serve as a link to the impoverished Spain of centuries past. By re-imagining even the most sacred Spanish staples, tapas are the culinary trademark of a confident country rushing headlong into the future. La Latina (p74) has Madrid's richest portfolio of tapas bars.

ORDERING TAPAS

Too many travellers miss out on the joys of tapas because, unless you speak Spanish,

MENÚ DEL DÍA

One great way to cap prices at lunchtime Monday to Friday is to order the *menú del día* (daily set menu), a three-course meal with water, bread and wine. These meals start from around €12, although €15 and up is increasingly the norm. You'll be given a menu with five or six entrées, the same number of mains and a handful of desserts – choose one from each category. The philosophy behind the *menú del día* is that, during the working week, few *madrileños* have time to go home to have their lunch. Taking a packed lunch is not the done thing, so the majority of people end up eating in restaurants, and all-inclusive three-course meals are as close as they can get to eating home-style food without breaking the bank.

the art of ordering can seem one of the dark arts of Spanish etiquette. Fear not – it's not as difficult as it first appears.

In many Madrid bars it couldn't be easier. With so many tapas varieties lined up along the bar, you either take a small plate and help yourself or point to the morsel you want. If you do this, it's customary to keep track of what you eat (by holding on to the toothpicks for example) and then tell the bar staff how many you've had when it's time to pay. Otherwise, many places have a list of tapas, either on a menu or posted up behind the bar. If you can't choose, ask for '*la especialidad de la casa*' (the house speciality) and it's hard to go wrong. Another way of eating tapas is to order *raciones* (literally 'rations'; large tapas servings) or *medias raciones* (half-rations; smaller tapas servings). These plates and half-plates of a particular dish are a good way to go if you particularly like something and want more than a mere tapa. Remember, however, that after a couple of *raciones* you'll almost certainly be full; the *media ración* is a good choice if you want to experience a broader range of tastes. In some bars you'll also get a small (free) tapa when you buy a drink.

Vegetarians & Vegans

Pure vegetarianism remains something of an alien concept in most Spanish kitchens; cooked vegetable dishes, for example, often contain ham. That said, Madrid has a growing cast of vegetarian restaurants. Even in those restaurants that serve meat or fish dishes, salads are a Spanish staple and, in some places, can be a meal in themselves. You'll also come across the odd vegetarian paella, as well as dishes such as *verduras a la plancha* (grilled vegetables), *garbanzos con espinacas* (chickpeas and spinach), *patatas bravas* (potato chunks bathed in spicy tomato sauce) and the *tortilla de patatas*. The prevalence of legumes ensures that *lentejas* (lentils) and *judías* (beans) are also easy to track down, while *pan* (bread), *quesos* (cheeses), *alcachofas* (artichokes) and *aceitunas* (olives) are always easy to find. If vegetarianism is rare among Spaniards, vegans will feel as if they've come from another planet. However, some of the established vegetarian restaurants may have certain vegan dishes.

Eating by Neighbourhood

➜ **Plaza Mayor & Royal Madrid** (p60) Reasonable collection of restaurants and tapas bars.

➜ **La Latina & Lavapiés** (p74) Madrid's undisputed home of tapas.

➜ **Sol, Santa Ana & Huertas** (p88) Plenty of restaurants from Spain's regions.

➜ **El Retiro & the Art Museums** (p114) A handful of standout options between the galleries.

➜ **Salamanca** (p123) Terrific tapas and some refined sit-down restaurants.

➜ **Malasaña & Chueca** (p131) Arguably Madrid's widest choice of restaurants.

➜ **Parque del Oeste & Northern Madrid** (p153) Thinly spread but plenty of good places to eat.

Lonely Planet's Top Choices

Restaurante Sobrino de Botín (p63) The world's oldest restaurant and a bastion of tradition.

DiverXo (p155) Three Michelin stars and cutting-edge cooking at its most confronting.

Platea (p123) Dynamic new gastronomic space with fabulous choice.

Estado Puro (p114) Tapas that push the boundaries of nouvelle Spanish cuisine.

Bazaar (p134) Classy cooking in the heart of Chueca.

Mercado de San Miguel (p61) Arguably Madrid's most varied gastronomic space.

Best by Budget

€

Bazaar (p134) Style, substance and celebrities at budget prices.

Casa Revuelta (p60) Classic bar bonhomie and great food.

Casa Julio (p132) Madrid's best croquettes.

La Gloria de Montera (p88) Outstanding food and atmosphere.

€€

Mercado de San Miguel (p61) Madrid's most diverse eating experience.

Taberna Matritum (p74) Tapas, tradition and innovation in La Latina.

Vi Cool (p89) Nouvelle cuisine at its most accessible.

Casa Alberto (p89) Celebrated old *taberna* (tavern) with tapas and sit-down meals.

Albur (p132) Convivial ambience with great rice dishes.

€€€

DiverXo (p155) Experimental cooking in all its glory.

Santceloni (p155) Enduring success story of innovative cooking.

Arriba (p125) Showpiece restaurant of the exceptional new Platea development.

Sergi Arola Gastro (p155) Catalan master chef at the height of his game.

La Terraza del Casino (p91) Brilliant cooking in brilliant surrounds.

Best by Cuisine

Cocido a la Madrileña

Taberna La Bola (p61) Faultless *cocido* in a fine *taberna* setting.

Malacatín (p74) *Cocido* whichever way you like it.

Lhardy (p91) Over 150 years of *cocido* excellence.

Casa Paco (p62) Storied old *taberna* with a fine *cocido* pedigree.

Restaurante Los Galayos (p62) Arguably the best restaurant on the Plaza Mayor.

Roast Lamb or Suckling Pig

Restaurante Sobrino de Botín (p63) Fantastic all-round dining experience.

Posada de la Villa (p77) Lovely setting for this feast of roasted meat.

El Pedrusco (p155) *Cochinillo* direct from its Segovian heartland.

Casa Ciriaco (p63) Roasted meats a speciality for more than a century.

Tortilla de Patatas

Juana La Loca (p77) Our vote for Madrid's best tortilla.

Txirimiri (p77) Just around the corner and not far behind.

Estado Puro (p114) Served in a glass in liquefied form.

Bodega de la Ardosa (p132) No-frills potato omelettes at their best.

José Luis (p124) Consistently ranked among Madrid's best.

Las Tortillas de Gabino (p154) Creative approach to ingredients and it works.

Croquetas

Casa Julio (p132) Madrid's best – just ask U2.

Bar Melo's (p79) Large and late-night comfort food.

La Gastrocroquetería de Chema (p133) New wave croquettes in wonderful variety.

Casa Alberto (p89) Traditional croquettes at their best.

Rice & Paella

Costa Blanca Arrocería (p154) Mediterranean rice and atmosphere.

Casa Perico (p133) Proof that there's more to Spanish rice than paella.

La Paella Real (p62) Assured rice cooking opposite the Teatro Real.

Albur (p132) Casual setting, classy rice dishes.

Drinking & Nightlife

Nights in the Spanish capital are the stuff of legend. They're invariably long and loud most nights of the week, rising to a deafening crescendo as the weekend nears. And what Ernest Hemingway wrote of the city in the 1930s remains true to this day: 'Nobody goes to bed in Madrid until they have killed the night.'

Killing the Night

Madrid has more bars than any other city in the world – six, in fact, for every 100 inhabitants, and, wherever you are in town, there'll be a bar close by. But bars are only half the story. On any night in Madrid, first drinks, tapas and wines then segue easily into cocktail bars and the nightclubs that have brought such renown to Madrid as the unrivalled scene of all-night fiestas.

Cafes

Madrid's thriving cafe culture dates back to the early and mid-20th century, when old-style coffee houses formed the centrepiece of the country's intellectual life. Although many such cafes were torn down in the rush to modernisation, many that recall those times remain, with period architecture and an agreeably formal atmosphere; their clientele long ago broadened to encompass the entire cross-section of modern Madrid society. Added into the mix are some terrific and usually more casual modern cafes, although here, too, the principle remains the same: they're at once social and cultural meeting places, and places to escape from the often frenetic pace of city life.

Cocktail Bars

The mojito (a rum-based drink with sugar, fresh mint, crushed ice and lemon) may have its origins in Cuba, but it has arguably become Madrid's favourite adopted son. As a consequence, the reputation of the city's cocktail bars can rise and fall according to the quality of its mojitos, and those that have lasted the distance have usually done so on the back of a mighty fine mojito. Other cocktails of breathtaking variety are also possible in the city's cocktail bars that range from slick and trendy temples to all that's new to storied bastions of tradition where bow-tied waiters and cocktail makers are as celebrated as the *famosos* (celebrities) who have visited through the decades.

Nightclubs

People here live fully for the moment. Today's encounter can be tomorrow's distant memory, perhaps in part because Madrid's

---

THE SECRET LANGUAGE OF BEER

In the majority of bars you won't have much choice when it comes to beer, but thankfully Madrid's flagship beer, Mahou, goes down well and comes as both draught and bottled. Cruzcampo is a lighter beer. Otherwise, two Catalan companies, Damm and San Miguel, each produce about 15% of all Spain's beer. The most common order is a *caña*, a small glass of *cerveza de barril* (draught beer). A larger beer (about 300mL), more common in the hipper bars and clubs, usually comes in a *tubo* (a long, straight glass). The equivalent of a pint is a *pinta*, while a *jarra* refers to a jug of beer.

GETTING HOME

Madrid's extensive metro system can get you most places, but it grinds to a halt between 1.30am and 6.05am. If you're trying to get back to your hotel at these hours, there are two main options (apart from walking). The first is a taxi – and although these hours attract a higher flag fall (€2.90) and per-kilometre rate (€1.20) than during daylight hours, it should rarely cost you more than €10 to get back to your hotel. The other option is the night buses known as *búhos* (owls), with more than two dozen routes fanning out across the city from Plaza de la Cibeles.

nightclubs (also known as *discotecas*) rival any in the world. The best places are usually the megaclubs, with designer decor, designer people and, sometimes, with enough space for numerous dance floors each with their own musical style to suit your mood. Themed nights are all the rage, so it's always worth checking in advance to see what flavour of the night takes your fancy.

Admission prices vary widely, depending on the time of night you enter, the way you're dressed and the number of people inside. The standard entry fee is €12, which usually includes the first drink, although megaclubs and swankier places charge a few euros more.

Drinking & Nightlife by Neighbourhood

→ **Plaza Mayor & Royal Madrid** (p63) Plenty of nightclubs in the city centre.

→ **La Latina & Lavapiés** (p78) Terrific for wine bars and fortifying tapas.

→ **Sol, Santa Ana & Huertas** (p91) The epicentre of Madrid's night-time action.

→ **El Retiro & the Art Museums** (p115) A daytime *barrio* (district) with little happening after dark.

NEED TO KNOW

Opening Hours

→ Local watering holes that serve as centres of community life usually open throughout the day from breakfast to last drinks.

→ Trendier bars often get going around 8pm and stay open until 1am or 2am during the week, 3am on weekends.

→ Nightclubs don't usually open until midnight or 1am and stay open until 5am or 6am. Some open all week, others from Thursday to Saturday.

Top Tips

→ If you plan to stay out the whole night, sleeping the siesta the afternoon before could be the key to your staying power.

→ Another essential element to surviving the long Madrid night is to never drink on an empty stomach – fill up on tapas or a late dinner wherever possible.

→ Most *madrileños* (people from Madrid) take a localised approach to a night out – once they've begun to drink and otherwise settle into the night, they tend to move from one place to the next within the same *barrio* (district).

→ Even those nightclubs that let you in for free will play catch up with hefty prices for drinks, so don't plan your night around looking for the cheapest entry cost.

→ **Salamanca** (p125) A small collection of nightclubs.

→ **Malasaña & Chueca** (p137) All-night neighbourhoods with terrific cocktail bars (Chueca) and fabulous cafes (Malasaña).

→ **Parque del Oeste & Northern Madrid** (p157) Some nightlife focal points but thinly spread.

PLAN YOUR TRIP DRINKING & NIGHTLIFE

Lonely Planet's Top Choices

La Venencia (p91) Timeless Huertas sherry bar that hasn't changed in decades.

Museo Chicote (p140) One of Europe's most celebrated cocktail bars.

Teatro Joy Eslava (p63) The pick of Madrid's city-centre nightclubs.

Chocolatería de San Ginés (p63) A Madrid institution whatever the hour.

Best Grand Old Cafes

Café-Restaurante El Espejo (p142) A storied echo of another age.

Gran Café de Gijón (p142) Gilded cafe down on Paseo de los Recoletos.

Café del Círculo de Bellas Artes (p92) Bow-tied waiters and stunning decor.

Café Manuela (p138) Magical air with board games.

Cafe de Oriente (p64) Germanic charm with fine views.

Best Mojitos

Café Belén (p140) Long-standing favourite in Chueca.

Delic (p78) Some of Madrid's best on Plaza de la Paja.

Taberna Chica (p79) Exceptional mojitos in La Latina.

Museo Chicote (p140) Mojitos as Hemingway used to like them.

El Eucalipto (p79) Cuban vibe and Cuban know-how.

Dos Gardenias (p92) Secret recipe in this Huertas nook.

Best Rooftop Terrazas (Open-Air Bars)

La Terraza del Urban (p92) Classy summer terrace high above Huertas.

La Terraza de Arriba (p141) Celebrities and fine views above Chueca.

Círculo de Bellas Artes (p88) Lounge chairs and extraordinary views.

The Roof (p92) Sybaritic space atop Plaza de Santa Ana.

Gau&Café (p78) Casual rooftop bar-restaurant in Lavapiés.

Best Cocktail Bars

Museo Chicote (p140) Madrid's top pick for decades.

Del Diego (p141) Some of Madrid's best cocktails.

Le Cabrera (p140) Celebrity mixer and cool clientele.

Bar Cock (p141) Cocktails, *famosos* (celebrities) and bow-tied waiters.

1862 Dry Bar (p138) New kid on the block with a passion for innovation.

José Alfredo (p139) Long-standing cocktail bar off Gran Vía.

Martínez Bar (p139) 1920s atmosphere and 21st-century cocktails.

Best Nightclubs

Kapital (p115) Ibiza megaclub meets Madrid.

Teatro Joy Eslava (p63) Madrid's most diverse nightclub, every night.

Ya'sta (p140) Enduring icon of the Madrid night.

Charada (p64) Excellent downtown dancing till dawn.

Morocco (p140) Consistently full Malasaña club.

Why Not? (p142) Smaller than most but a good time guaranteed.

Best Gay & Lesbian

Café Acuarela (p141) Mellow bar-cafe for any hour.

Why Not? (p142) Hetero-friendly but gay at heart.

Black & White (p142) Anything goes at this club of long standing.

Club 54 Studio (p142) New York–style gay club.

Liquid Madrid (p142) Hot, sweaty and amorous in the best Chueca tradition.

Flamenco performer, Corral de la Morería (p80)

 # Entertainment

Madrid has a happening live-music scene that owes a lot to the city's role as the cultural capital of the Spanish-speaking world. There's flamenco, world-class jazz and a host of performers of whom you may never have heard but who may just be Spain's next big thing. For a dose of high culture, there's opera and zarzuela (satirical musical comedy).

NEED TO KNOW

Reservations

➜ Concert tickets for live music should always be booked in advance – check venue websites for details.

➜ Tickets for most jazz clubs go on sale an hour or two before the scheduled performance start.

➜ Mostly you can buy theatre tickets at the box office on the day of the performance, but for new or weekend shows you should book ahead.

➜ Buy tickets for Real Madrid football matches online. They also usually go on sale the Monday before a game at Gate 42 of the stadium on Calle de Conche de Espina. The all-important telephone number for booking tickets (which you later pick up at Gate 42) is ☑902 324 324 (for calling from within Spain only).

Opening Hours

➜ Theatre box offices are generally open from about 10am until 1pm and again from 5pm until the start of the evening's show.

Useful Websites

➜ In addition to checking the websites of individual live-music venues, check out www.lanocheenvivo.com.

➜ For a history of *zarzuela* in English, translations of *zarzuela* songs and storylines, CD and DVD reviews, and a critical look at current *zarzuela* shows, check out the terrific website www.zarzuela.net.

Flamenco

Madrid has numerous venues with nightly live performances, although seeing flamenco in Madrid can be expensive: at the *tablaos* (restaurants where flamenco is performed) expect to pay at least €35 just to see the show. The admission price usually includes your first drink, but you pay extra for meals (up to €50 per person) that, put simply, are rarely worth the money. For that reason, we suggest you eat elsewhere and just pay for the show (after having bought tickets in advance), on the understanding that you won't have a front-row seat.

Compañía Nacional de Danza

Jazz

Madrid was one of Europe's jazz capitals in the 1920s. It's taken a while, but it's once again among Europe's elite for live jazz. There's only a small number of places devoted exclusively to jazz, but the quality is world-class and the range of styles includes the kind of classic jazz designed to keep the purist happy as well as Latin, nu jazz and countless variations on the theme. Beyond the signature jazz venues, numerous multigenre live-music stages broaden out the experience, often with a weekly jazz jam session. November's Festival Jazz Madrid (p24) is a great time for jazz enthusiasts to be in town.

Other Live Music

Madrid made its name as a live-music city back in the 1980s, when drugs and rock music fuelled the decade-long fiesta known as *la movida madrileña* (the Madrid scene). At the height of *la movida,* an estimated 300 rock bands were performing in the bars of Malasaña alone. While rock remains a Madrid mainstay and the doors of a handful of classic venues remain open, the live-music scene now encompasses every genre imaginable. Many venues double as clubs where DJs follow the live acts, making it possible to start off the night with a great concert and stay on to party until late.

Classical Music & Opera

Madrid loves to party, but scratch beneath the surface and you'll find a thriving city of high culture, with venues dedicated to year-round opera and classical music. Orchestras from all over Europe perform regularly here, but Madrid's own **Orquesta Sinfónica** (www.osm.es) also performs (or accompanies) in the Teatro Real (p56) or Auditorio Nacional de Música (p158). The **Banda Sinfónica Municipal de Madrid** (www.munimadrid.es/bandasinfonica) plays at the Teatro Monumental (p95).

La Zarzuela

What began in the late 17th century as a way to amuse King Felipe IV and his court has become Spain's own unique theatre style. With a light-hearted combination of music and dance, and a focus on everyday people's problems, *zarzuelas* quickly became popular in Madrid, which remains the genre's capital. Although you're likely to have trouble following the storyline (*zarzuelas* are notoriously full of local references and jokes), seeing a *zarzuela* gives an entertaining look into local culture. The best place to catch a show is the Teatro de la Zarzuela (p94).

Dance

Spain's lively **Compañía Nacional de Danza** (http://cndanza.mcu.es) performs worldwide and has won accolades for its marvellous technicality and original choreography. Madrid is also home to the **Ballet Nacional de España** (☑91 517 99 99; http://balletnacional.mcu.es), a classical company known for its unique mix of ballet and traditional Spanish styles, including flamenco and *zarzuela*. When in town, both companies perform at venues that include the Teatro Real (p56) or Teatro de la Zarzuela (p94). One performer who frequently performs in Madrid is **Sara Baras** (www.sarabaras.com), a Cádiz-born performer whose soul-stirring flamenco ballet is unique.

Theatre

Madrid's theatre scene really gets going in autumn. Most shows are in Spanish and tickets cost from €10 to €50.

Film

Plenty of cinemas offer *versión original* (VO; original version) films, which are shown in the original language with Spanish subtitles; otherwise foreign-language films are dubbed in mainstream cinemas. The highest concentrations of Spanish-language cinemas are on Gran Vía and Calle de Fuencarral, between the Glorieta de Bilbao and Glorieta de Quevedo.

Spectator Sports

The Estadio Santiago Bernabéu (p154) is one of the world's great football arenas; watching a game here alongside 80,000 passionate Madridistas (Real Madrid supporters) will send chills down your spine. If you're lucky enough to be in town when **Real Madrid** (www.realmadrdi.com) wins a major trophy, head to Plaza de la Cibeles and wait for the all-night party to begin.

Madrid's other team, **Atlético de Madrid** (www.clubatleticodemadrid.com) has a cult following and attracts passionate support; fans of the *rojiblancos* (red-and-whites) declare theirs to be the real Madrid team.

Bullfighting

Love it or loathe it, bullfighting is a national institution. In the afternoons there are generally six bulls and three star *toreros* (bullfighters) dressed in the dazzling *traje de luces* (suit of lights). Madrid's main bullfighting season begins during the Fiestas de San Isidro, with daily *corridas* (bullfights) from mid-May onwards.

Some regions of Spain, notably Catalonia, have banned bullfighting, and the election of the left-wing Ahora Madrid municipal government in 2015 changed the status quo in the capital. One of the party's policy platforms was to remove all municipal funding for the industry, and Manuela Carmena, the new mayor, ensured that the

---

BOOKING CONCERT & THEATRE TICKETS

Outlets selling tickets online for concerts, theatre and other live performances include the following:

➡ **El Corte Inglés** (www.elcorteingles.es) Click on 'Todos Los Departamentos', then 'Entradas'.

➡ **Entradas.com** (www.entradas.com)

➡ **Fnac** (www.fnac.es) Click on 'Entradas'; mostly modern, big-name music groups.

➡ **Servicaixa** (www.servicaixa.com) You can also get tickets in Servicaixa ATMs.

➡ **Ticketmaster** (www.ticketmaster.es)

Sala El Sol (p93)

box reserved for the mayor and her representatives was empty, for the first time in
decades, during the Fiestas de San Isidro
bullfights in 2015. It remains to be seen
what impact this change in policy will have
on a spectacle that many animal lovers feel
is immoral, and which is vehemently op-
posed by numerous animal-welfare organi-
sations, among them the **World Society for
the Protection of Animals** (www.world
animalprotection.org.uk) and the **League
Against Cruel Sports** (www.league.org.uk).

Entertainment by Neighbourhood
....

➜ **Plaza Mayor & Royal Madrid** (p65) Plenty of
cinemas, theatres and live-music venues.

➜ **La Latina & Lavapiés** (p79) A small handful of
flamenco and live-music venues.

➜ **Sol, Santa Ana & Huertas** (p93) One of
the best *barrios* (districts) for jazz, flamenco,
theatre and live music.

➜ **El Retiro & the Art Museums** (p113)
Football celebrations but not much else.

➜ **Salamanca** (p125) Upmarket nightclubs
scattered thinly.

➜ **Malasaña & Chueca** (p142) Quirky theatres
and grungy live-music stages.

➜ **Parque del Oeste & Northern Madrid** (p157)
A heady mix of football and classical music.

Lonely Planet's Top Choices

Café Central (p93) One of the best jazz clubs on earth.

Sala El Sol (p93) Mythic Madrid stage for rock and other live acts.

Villa Rosa (p94) Top-notch flamenco behind an extravagantly tiled facade.

Estadio Santiago Bernabéu (p154) Legendary home stadium of Real Madrid.

Teatro de la Zarzuela (p94) Home theatre for Spain's home-grown operatic theatre.

Best Flamenco Venues

Corral de la Morería (p80) Prestigious downtown Madrid venue.

Villa Rosa (p94) Iconic flamenco stage on Plaza de Santa Ana.

Café de Chinitas (p65) World-famous flamenco venue.

Cardamomo (p94) Excellent, atmospheric stage in Huertas.

Las Tablas (p65) Top-class performers in a more casual setting.

Las Carboneras (p65) Consistently good flamenco acts.

Casa Patas (p79) Serious flamenco performers.

Best Flamenco Beyond the Tablaos

BarCo (p143) Live flamenco every Sunday at 9pm.

Sala Clamores (p157) Diverse club with regular flamenco.

Sala Juglar (p80) Another live-at-9pm flamenco show.

La Boca Club (p94) Flamenco is often part of the mix here in Huertas.

Galileo Galilei (p157) Occasional flamenco here spices up the mix.

Best Jazz Clubs

Café Central (p93) Spain's best jazz venue.

Populart (p94) Big names and free entry.

El Junco Jazz Club (p143) Live jazz and all-night DJs.

El Despertar (p80) Intimate venue with impeccable jazz cred.

Bogui Jazz (p143) Live jazz Thursday to Saturday.

Best Jazz in Other Venues

Jazz Bar (p93) Non-stop jazz on the sound system.

BarCo (p143) Jazz is a regular at this happening club.

Sala Clamores (p157) Jazz club at heart but with so much more.

Casa Pueblo (p95) Free live jazz in the Barrio de las Letras.

La Boca Club (p94) Occasional live jazz with attitude.

Best Live-Music Venues

Moby Dick (p157) Concerts by almost-superstars.

Café la Palma (p142) Fabulous venue with a number of stages.

Sala Clamores (p157) Nightly concerts across all genres.

Costello Café & Niteclub (p94) New York meets Madrid in cool fashion.

Thundercat (p143) Classic rock in all its glory.

Best for Classical Music & Opera

Teatro Real (p56) Madrid's premier stage for opera, ballet and classical concerts.

Auditorio Nacional de Música (p158) The home stage for Madrid's very own symphony orchestra.

Fundación Juan March (p125) Intimate venue with solo and chamber recitals.

Teatro Monumental (p95) Top-notch auditorium for all things classical.

Teatro de la Zarzuela (p94) Catch Spain's very own operatic form.

Best Theatres

Teatro Español (p95) Gorgeous theatre for Spanish plays on Plaza de Santa Ana.

Teatros del Canal (p157) Diverse modern stage with fine theatre and concerts.

Teatro Pavón (p81) One of the best places in Spain to see classical theatre.

Teatro Valle-Inclán (p81) Stunning theatre complex for Spanish plays.

Shopping

Our favourite aspect of shopping in Madrid is the city's small boutiques and quirky shops. Often run by the same families for generations, they counter the over-commercialisation of mass-produced Spanish culture with everything from fashions to old-style ceramics to rope-soled espadrilles or gourmet Spanish food and wine.

Fashion

The world's most prestigious catwalks are clamouring for Spanish designers and with good reason. Spain's fashion industry, with Madrid as its capital, has a pedigree of bold colours and eye-catching designs born in the creative outpouring of *la movida madrileña* (the Madrid scene) in the 1980s. As such, even a cursory glance in the shop windows of Salamanca, Malasaña and Chueca in particular can be a revelation, confirming that there's so much more to *la moda española* (Spanish fashion) than Zara and Mango.

Souvenirs & Handicrafts

You *could* buy your friends back home a vividly coloured flamenco dress of the kind that hangs from the doorway of many a downtown Madrid souvenir shop. Then again, you could instead opt for a touch more class and take home an artfully designed papier-mâché figurine, a carefully crafted ceramic bowl made by the family potters of central Spain, or an intricately designed Spanish fan. And then there are guitars favoured by everyone from the Beatles to flamenco greats, and dresses from the shops where the flamenco greats get their gear...

Gourmet Foods

Nowhere is Spanish cuisine more accessible than in the city's purveyors of Spanish foods.

At these places – some traditional, some representative of the revolution sweeping Spanish cooking – you can point to your favourite *jamón* (ham) or tub of olives and in no time they'll be packaged up and ready for that Retiro picnic or flight back home. Some are small specialist stores where the packaging is often as exquisite as the tastes on offer. Elsewhere, Madrid's markets have also been transformed into vibrant spaces where you can eat as well as shop.

Shopping by Neighbourhood

➡ **Plaza Mayor & Royal Madrid** (p65) A little bit of everything.

➡ **La Latina & Lavapiés** (p81) Offbeat boutiques and a fabulous Sunday flea market.

➡ **Sol, Santa Ana & Huertas** (p95) Some of Madrid's best souvenirs.

➡ **El Retiro & the Art Museums** (p115) Museum giftshops and bookshops are the main drawcard.

➡ **Salamanca** (p126) The home of Spanish fashion.

➡ **Malasaña & Chueca** (p143) Retro fashions (Malasaña) alongside more upmarket style (Chueca).

➡ **Parque del Oeste & Northern Madrid** (p158) Outposts of tradition aimed at a local market.

Lonely Planet's Top Choices

El Rastro (p72) Europe's largest flea market and Madrid's favourite Sunday pastime.

Mercado de Fuencarral (p144) Icon of retro Malasaña and its passion for down-and-dirty streetwear.

El Arco Artesanía (p65) Modern souvenirs with an art-gallery aesthetic.

Helena Rohner (p81) Designer jewellery from catwalk to casual.

Agatha Ruiz de la Prada (p126) Candy-bright colours from a household name in Madrid fashion.

Antigua Casa Talavera (p65) Handpainted ceramics from small family kilns.

Best Spanish Fashion

Camper (p126) Comfortable, casual footwear for the fashion conscious.

Agatha Ruiz de la Prada (p126) Fun, colourful fashions from a Madrid veteran.

Custo Barcelona (p144) Riotous colours and combinations.

Elisa Bracci (p146) Glamour from one of Madrid's most successful designers.

Loewe (p145) The Louis Vuitton of Spanish fashion.

Manolo Blahnik (p126) World-famous ladies' shoes.

Lurdes Bergada (p145) Natural fibres, warm colours and cutting-edge cuts.

Best Souvenirs & Handicrafts

El Arco Artesanía (p65) Designer flair brought to Spanish themes.

Maty (p65) Authentic flamenco clothes and shoes.

Antigua Casa Talavera (p65) Old-world, hand-crafted ceramics.

Botería Julio Rodríguez (p81) The real deal when it comes to Spanish wineskins.

El Flamenco Vive (p66) Flamenco music and other memorabilia.

Casa de Diego (p95) Ornate Spanish fans and umbrellas.

Best Gourmet Food & Wine

Mantequería Bravo (p127) Madrid's best deli for traditional Spanish foods.

Bombonerías Santa (p126) Individually wrapped Spanish sweets.

Gourmet Experience (p67) One-stop shop for Spanish wines, cheeses etc.

María Cabello (p95) Madrid's most atmospheric wine merchant.

Oriol Balaguer (p126) Designer chocolates from one of Spain's master chefs.

NEED TO KNOW

Opening Hours

➡ 10am to 2pm and 4.30pm to 7.30pm or 5pm to 8pm, or 10am to 8pm, Monday to Saturday. Some shops open on Sundays.

Sales

➡ The peak shopping season is during *las rebajas*, the annual winter and summer sales, when prices are slashed on just about everything. The winter sales begin around 7 January, just after Three Kings' Day, and last well into February. Summer sales begin in early July and last into August.

Taxes & Refunds

➡ Visitors are entitled to a refund of the IVA (value-added tax) on purchases costing more than €90.16 from any shop if the goods are taken out of the EU within three months. Ask the shop for a cash-back refund form at the point of purchase, then present the form at the customs booth for IVA refunds when you depart from Spain (or elsewhere from the EU).

PLAN YOUR TRIP SHOPPING

Explore Madrid

MADRID'S TOP SIGHTS

Neighbourhoods at a Glance

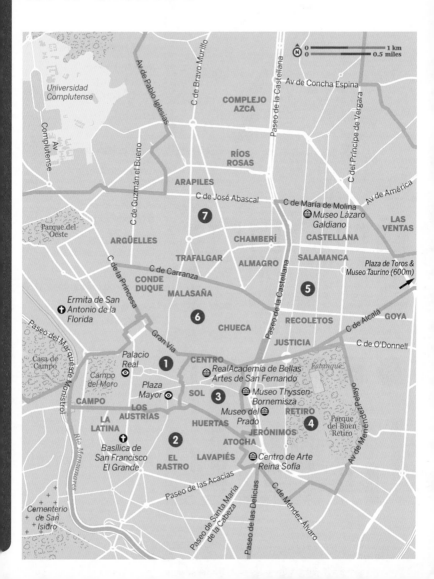

Universidad Complutense

Av de Pablo Iglesias

C de Bravo Murillo

Av de Concha Espina

Paseo de la Castellana

Av del Príncipe de Vergara

COMPLEJO AZCA

RÍOS ROSAS

Av Complutense

C de Guzmán el Bueno

ARAPILES

C de José Abascal

C de María de Molina

Museo Lázaro Galdiano

Av de América

LAS VENTAS

Parque del Oeste

ARGÜELLES

CHAMBERÍ

CASTELLANA

C del Príncipe de Vergara

7

TRAFALGAR

ALMAGRO

SALAMANCA

Plaza de Toros & Museo Taurino (600m)

C de la Princesa

C de Carranza

CONDE DUQUE

MALASAÑA

Paseo de la Castellana

5

Ermita de San Antonio de la Florida

Paseo del Marqués de Monistrol

6

CHUECA

RECOLETOS

C de Alcalá

GOYA

Gran Vía

JUSTICIA

C de O'Donnell

Casa de Campo

Palacio Real

CENTRO

Real Academia de Bellas Artes de San Fernando

Estanque

Campo del Moro

Plaza Mayor

SOL

3

Museo Thyssen-Bornemisza

1

LOS AUSTRIAS

Museo del Prado

RETIRO

4

Parque del Buen Retiro

Av de Menéndez Pelayo

CAMPO

LA LATINA

HUERTAS

2

JERÓNIMOS

ATOCHA

Basílica de San Francisco El Grande

EL RASTRO

LAVAPIÉS

Centro de Arte Reina Sofía

Río Manzanares

Cementerio de San Isidro

Paseo de las Acacias

Paseo de Santa María de la Cabeza

Paseo de las Delicias

C de Méndez Álvaro

N

0   1 km
0   0.5 miles

❶ Plaza Mayor & Royal Madrid (p50)

The bustling, compact and medieval heart of the city is where Madrid's story began and where the city became the seat of royal power. It's also where the splendour of imperial Spain was at its most ostentatious – think palaces, ancient churches, elegant squares and imposing convents. It's an architectural high point of the city, with plenty of fine eating and shopping options thrown in for good measure.

❷ La Latina & Lavapiés (p68)

La Latina combines Madrid's best selection of tapas bars with fine little boutiques and a medieval streetscape studded with elegant churches. Graceful Calle de la Cava Baja could just be our favourite street for tapas in town. Down the hill, Lavapiés is one of the city's oldest *barrios* (districts) and the heart of multicultural Madrid. Spanning the two neighbourhoods is the Sunday flea market of El Rastro.

❸ Sol, Santa Ana & Huertas (p83)

These tightly packed streets are best known for nightlife that never seems to abate once the sun goes down, but there's also the beguiling Plaza de Santa Ana, a stirring literary heritage in the Barrio de las Letras and – at the Sol end of things, Madrid's beating heart – you'll find the sum total of all Madrid's personalities, with fabulous shopping, eating and entertainment options.

❹ El Retiro & the Art Museums (p97)

From the Plaza de la Cibeles in the north, the buildings arrayed along the Paseo del Prado read like a roll-call of Madrid's most popular attractions. Temples to high culture include the Museo del Prado, Museo Thyssen-Bornemisza and Centro de Arte Reina Sofía, which rank among the world's most prestigious art galleries. Up the hill to the east, the marvellous Parque del Buen Retiro helps to make this one of the most attractive areas of Madrid in which to spend your time.

❺ Salamanca (p118)

The *barrio* of Salamanca is Madrid's most exclusive quarter. Like nowhere else in the capital, this is where stately mansions set back from the street share *barrio* space with designer boutiques from the big local and international fashionistas. Salamanca's sprinkling of fine restaurants, designer tapas bars and niche museums are also very much at home here.

❻ Malasaña & Chueca (p128)

The two inner-city *barrios* of Malasaña and Chueca are where Madrid gets up close and personal. Here, it's more an experience of life as it's lived by *madrileños* (people from Madrid) than the traditional traveller experience of ticking off from a list of wonderful, if more static, attractions. These are *barrios* with attitude and personality, *barrios* where Madrid's famed nightlife, shopping and eating choices live and breathe and take you under the skin of the city.

❼ Parque del Oeste & Northern Madrid (p148)

Madrid's north contains some of Madrid's most attractive *barrios,* including Chamberí, which is a wonderful escape from the downtown and offers unique insights into how locals enjoy their city. Parque del Oeste is a gorgeous expanse of green, while a series of fascinating sights – from Goya frescoes to an Egyptian temple – add considerable appeal.

Plaza Mayor & Royal Madrid

Neighbourhood Top Five

❶ Immersing yourself in the street life that courses across the cobblestones or taking up residence at an outdoor table surrounding the **Plaza Mayor** (p52).

❷ Soaking up the grandeur at the **Palacio Real** (p53), Madrid's seat of royal power.

❸ Spending time in **Plaza de la Villa** (p59), one of Madrid's most architecturally rich corners.

❹ Stopping by for Madrid's best *chocolate con churros* (chocolate with deep-fried doughnuts) at the **Chocolatería de San Ginés** (p63).

❺ Learning why locals are obsessed about food at **Mercado de San Miguel** (p61).

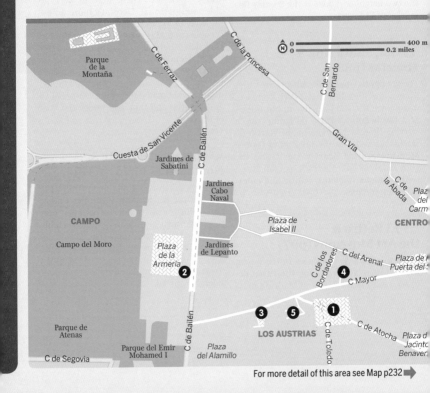

For more detail of this area see Map p232 ➤

Explore: Plaza Mayor & Royal Madrid

The Plaza Mayor is the hub of Madrid's most medieval quarter, an area known as Madrid de los Austrias, in reference to the Habsburg dynasty, which ruled Spain from 1517 to 1700. The plaza is a place both to admire and to get your bearings, the place where so many explorations of the neighbourhood (and wider city) begin. That's because it is at once the hub of neighbourhood life and the topographical high point of the *barrio* (district).

Build your day exploring this neighbourhood around this and other squares, which are lovely and quiet in the morning, and lively and pretty in the soft light of late afternoon. Running close to its northern edge, Calle Mayor connects Plaza Mayor with the rest of the neighbourhood, running down the hill past the wonderful Mercado de San Miguel to Plaza de la Villa with tangled lanes of medieval origin twisting away on either side. Away to the north is the Plaza de Oriente, royal palace and cathedral.

Although it's no hard-and-fast rule, the shops, restaurants, bars and nightclubs tend to be concentrated at the eastern end of the neighbourhood, close to the Plaza Mayor, while the architectural highlights are more evenly spread.

Local Life

➡ **Hang out** The broad appeal of the neighbourhood is summed up by two of its favourite meeting places: the stunningly converted Mercado de San Miguel (p61) and the timeless Chocolatería de San Ginés (p63).

➡ **Meeting points** The equestrian statue of Felipe III in the centre of Plaza Mayor was moved here in 1848 and has ever since been a favoured meeting point for locals who arrange to meet 'under the balls of the horse'.

➡ **Shopping** Ignore the tacky souvenir shops that overflow from shopfronts across the centre: small artisan shops abound across the neighbourhood and are well worth tracking down.

➡ **Nightclubs** Watch out for themed nights that might make Monday a better night to dance than the weekend.

Getting There & Away

➡ **Metro** A short step from Plaza Mayor, Sol metro station is one of the most useful in Madrid, with lines 1, 2 and 3 all passing through.

➡ **Metro** Ópera (lines 2 and 5) is another useful neighbourhood station – line 2 can carry you to the Paseo del Prado (leaving a short walk to the galleries), Parque del Buen Retiro or Salamanca in no time.

Lonely Planet's Top Tip

Treat Plaza Mayor as a place to soak up the atmosphere, and order a coffee or wine to justify your presence at one of the outdoor tables. Come in the morning when the pressure to order something more substantial is minimal. For a meal you're better off heading to the Mercado de San Miguel.

Best Places to Eat

➡ Mercado de San Miguel (p61)
➡ Restaurante Sobrino de Botín (p63)
➡ Taberna La Bola (p61)
➡ Casa Revuelta (p60)
➡ Casa Paco (p62)

For reviews, see p60

Best Places to Drink

➡ Chocolatería de San Ginés (p63)
➡ The Sherry Corner (p63)
➡ Teatro Joy Eslava (p63)
➡ Café del Real (p63)
➡ Cafe de Oriente (p64)

For reviews, see p63

Best Shopping

➡ Antigua Casa Talavera (p65)
➡ El Arco Artesanía (p65)
➡ Maty (p65)
➡ Convento del Corpus Cristi (p66)
➡ Casa Hernanz (p66)

For reviews, see p65

TOP SIGHT
PLAZA MAYOR

It's easy to fall in love with Madrid in the Plaza Mayor. This is the monumental heart of the city and the grand stage for so many of the city's most important historical events. Here, Madrid's relentless energy courses across its cobblestones beneath ochre-hued apartments, wrought-iron balconies, frescoes and stately spires. This juxtaposition of endlessly moving city life and more static architectural attractions is Madrid in microcosm.

DON'T MISS...

➡ A Sense of History
➡ Spires & Slate Roofs
➡ Real Casa de la Panadería
➡ Markets

PRACTICALITIES

➡ Map p232
➡ Ⓜ Sol

A Grand History

Ah, the history the plaza has seen! Inaugurated in 1619, its first public ceremony was suitably auspicious – the beatification of San Isidro Labrador (St Isidro the Farm Labourer), Madrid's patron saint. Thereafter it was as if all that was controversial about Spain took place in this square. Bullfights, often in celebration of royal weddings or births, with royalty watching on from the balconies and up to 50,000 people crammed into the plaza, were a recurring theme until 1878. Far more notorious were the *autos-da-fé* (the ritual condemnations of heretics during the Spanish Inquisition), followed by executions – burnings at the stake and deaths by garrotte on the north side of the square, hangings to the south. To see the plaza's epic history told in pictures, check out the carvings on the circular seats beneath the lamp posts.

A Less-Grand History

Not all the plaza's activities were grand events and, just as it is now surrounded by shops, it was once filled with food vendors. In 1673, King Carlos II issued an edict allowing the vendors to raise tarpaulins above their stalls to protect their wares and themselves from the refuse and raw sewage that people habitually tossed out of the windows above! Well into the 20th century, trams ran through Plaza Mayor.

Spires & Slate Roofs

The plaza was designed in the 17th century by Juan Gómez de Mora who, following the dominant style of the day, adopted a Herrerian style (named after Juan de Herrera, one of the towering architectural figures of the Spanish Renaissance). The slate spires and roofs are the most obvious expression of this pleasing and distinctively Madrid style, and their sombre hues are nicely offset by the warm colours of the uniformly ochre apartments and their 237 wrought-iron balconies.

Real Casa de la Panadería

The exquisite frescoes of the 17th-century Real Casa de la Panadería (Royal Bakery) rank among Madrid's more eye-catching sights. The present frescoes date to just 1992 and are the work of artist Carlos Franco, who chose images from the signs of the zodiac and gods (eg Cybele) to provide a stunning backdrop for the plaza. The frescoes were inaugurated to coincide with Madrid's 1992 spell as European Capital of Culture. The building now houses the city's main tourist office.

Markets

On Sunday mornings the plaza's arcaded perimeter is taken over by traders in old coins, banknotes and stamps. In December and early January the plaza is occupied by a hugely popular Christmas market selling fairground kitsch and nativity scenes of real quality.

⊙ TOP SIGHT
PALACIO REAL

You can almost imagine how the eyes of Felipe V, the first of the Bourbon kings, lit up when the *alcázar* (Muslim-era fortress) burned down in 1734 on Madrid's most exclusive perch of real estate. His plan? Build a palace that would dwarf all its European counterparts. The resulting 2800-room royal palace never quite attained such a scale, but it's still an Italianate baroque architectural landmark of arresting beauty, an intriguing mix of the extravagant, restrained and unmistakably elegant.

History's Tale

A little understanding of the Palacio Real's genesis and subsequent development will enhance your appreciation of what you see. The Italian architect Filippo Juvara (1678–1736), who had made his name building the Basilica di Superga and the Palazzo di Stupinigi in Turin, was called in to try and fulfil Felipe V's dream, but, like Felipe, he died without bringing the project to fruition. Upon Juvara's death, another Italian, Giovanni Battista Sacchetti, took over, finishing the job in 1764.

Farmacia Real

The Farmacia Real (Royal Pharmacy), the first set of rooms to the right at the southern end of the Plaza de la Armería courtyard, contains a formidable collection of medicine jars and stills for mixing royal concoctions; the royals were either paranoid or decidedly sickly. At the time of research, there was talk of moving the pharmacy to new premises; we hope it's only talk.

DON'T MISS...

➡ History's Tale
➡ Farmacia Real
➡ Plaza de la Armería
➡ Salón del Trono
➡ Gasparini & Porcelana
➡ Comedor de Gala
➡ Jardines de Sabatini

PRACTICALITIES

➡ Map p232
➡ ☎ 91 454 88 00
➡ www.patrimonio nacional.es
➡ Calle de Bailén
➡ adult/concession €11/6, guide/audioguide €4/4, EU citizens free last two hours Mon-Thu
➡ ⊙10am-8pm Apr-Sep, 10am-6pm Oct-Mar
➡ Ⓜ Ópera

PART-TIME PALACE

The Palacio Real is occasionally closed for state ceremonies and official receptions (the only way you'll know is if you turn up and it's closed), but the present king is rarely in residence – he and his family live in the smaller, less ostentatious Palacio de la Zarzuela just outside Madrid.

There are numerous places to have a drink close to the Palacio Real, among them La Mar del Alabardero (p62), Taberna del Alabardero (p62) and Taberna La Bola (p61). If you're after a coffee, there's no finer perch in Madrid than the outdoor tables of Cafe de Oriente (p64) that look out towards the palace. Not far away, Café del Real (p63) is one of our favourite places in Madrid for coffee, cake or a mojito.

BEST VIEWS

Some of the best views of the Palacio Real are through the trees from the northern end of the Plaza de Oriente, but less well known are the superlative views from the western side, the lush ornamental gardens of Campo del Moro.

Plaza de la Armería

The Plaza de la Armería (Plaza de Armas; Plaza of the Armoury) courtyard puts the sheer scale of the palace into perspective, and it's from here that Madrid's cathedral (Catedral de Nuestra Señora de la Almudena) takes on its most pleasing aspect. The colourful changing of the guard in full parade dress takes place at noon on the first Wednesday of every month (except August and September) between the palace and the cathedral, with a less extravagant changing of the guard inside the palace compound at the Puerta del Príncipe every Wednesday from 11am to 2pm. The plaza also provides access to the Armería Real (Royal Armoury), a hoard of weapons and striking suits of armour, mostly dating from the 16th and 17th centuries.

Salón del Trono

From the northern end of the Plaza de la Armería, the main stairway, a grand statement of imperial power, leads to the royal apartments and eventually to the Salón del Trono (Throne Room). The room is nauseatingly lavish with its crimson-velvet wall coverings complemented by a ceiling painted by the dramatic Venetian baroque master, Tiepolo, who was a favourite of Carlos III.

Gasparini & Porcelana

Close to the Throne Room, the Salón de Gasparini (Gasparini Room) has an exquisite stucco ceiling and walls resplendent with embroidered silks. The aesthetic may be different in the Sala de Porcelana (Porcelain Room), but the aura of extravagance continues with myriad pieces from the one-time Retiro porcelain factory screwed into the walls.

Comedor de Gala

In the midst of such extravagance, the spacious Comedor de Gala (Gala Dining Room) is where grand ceremonial occasions were once (and are still occasionally) held. The stately air is enhanced by the extravagant chandeliers, hoary old artworks on the walls and lavishly adorned archway.

Jardines de Sabatini

The French-inspired Jardines de Sabatini lie along the northern flank of the Palacio Real. They were laid out in the 1930s to replace the royal stables that once stood on the site. These quite formal gardens with fountains and small labyrinths offer a fine alternative view of the palace's northern facade.

◉ SIGHTS

PLAZA MAYOR SQUARE
See p52.

PALACIO REAL PALACE
See p53.

PLAZA DE ORIENTE SQUARE
Map p232 (Ⓜ Ópera) A royal palace that once
had aspirations to be the Spanish Versailles.
Sophisticated cafes watched over by apartments that cost the equivalent of a royal salary. The **Teatro Real**, Madrid's opera house
and one of Spain's temples to high culture.
Some of the finest sunset views in Madrid...
Welcome to Plaza de Oriente, a living,
breathing monument to imperial Madrid.

At the centre of the plaza, which the palace overlooks, is an equestrian **statue of
Felipe IV**) designed by Velázquez. It's the
perfect place to take it all in, with marvellous views wherever you look. If you're
wondering how a heavy bronze statue of a
rider and his horse rearing up can actually
maintain that stance, the answer is simple:
the hind legs are solid, while the front ones
are hollow. That idea was Galileo Galilei's.
Nearby are some 20 marble statues, mostly
of ancient monarchs. Local legend has it
that these ageing royals get down off their
pedestals at night to stretch their legs.

The adjacent **Jardines Cabo Naval**, a
great place to watch the sunset, adds to the
sense of a sophisticated oasis of green in the
heart of Madrid.

**CATEDRAL DE NUESTRA SEÑORA
DE LA ALMUDENA** CATHEDRAL
Map p232 (☎91 542 22 00; www.museocatedral.
archimadrid.es; Calle de Bailén; cathedral & crypt
by donation, museum adult/child €6/4; ⊙9am-
8.30pm Mon-Sat, for Mass Sun, museum 10am-
2.30pm Mon-Sat; Ⓜ Ópera) Paris has Notre
Dame and Rome has St Peter's Basilica. In
fact, almost every European city of stat-
ure has its signature cathedral, a standout
monument to a glorious Christian past. Not
Madrid. Although the exterior of the Catedral de Nuestra Señora de la Almudena
sits in harmony with the adjacent Palacio
Real, Madrid's cathedral is cavernous and
largely charmless within; its colourful,
modern ceilings do little to make up for
the lack of old-world gravitas that so distin-
guishes great cathedrals.

Carlos I first proposed building a cathedral here back in 1518, but building didn't

actually begin until 1879. It was finally finished in 1992 and its pristine, bright-white
neo-Gothic interior holds no pride of place
in the affections of *madrileños* (people
from Madrid).

It's possible to climb to the cathedral's
summit, with fine views. En route you
climb up through the cathedral's museum;
follow the signs to the **Museo de la Catedral y Cúpola** on the northern facade, opposite the Palacio Real.

Just around the corner in Calle Mayor,
the low-lying **ruins of Santa María de la
Almudena** are all that remain of Madrid's
first church, which was built on the site of
Mayrit's Great Mosque when the Christians
arrived in the 11th century.

And just down the hill beneath the cathedral's southern wall on Calle Mayor is
the neo-Romanesque **crypt**, with more
than 400 columns, 20 chapels and fine
stained-glass windows.

MURALLA ÁRABE LANDMARK
Map p232 (Cuesta de la Vega; Ⓜ Ópera) Behind the
cathedral apse and down Cuesta de la Vega
is a short stretch of the original 'Arab Wall',
the city wall built by Madrid's early-medieval
Muslim rulers. Some of it dates as far back
as the 9th century, when the initial Muslim
fort was raised. Other sections date from the
12th and 13th centuries, by which time the
city had been taken by the Christians.

The earliest sections were ingeniously
conceived – the outside of the wall was made
to look dauntingly sturdy, while the inside
was put together with cheap materials to
save on cost. It must have worked, as the
town was rarely taken by force. In summer
the city council organises open-air theatre
and music performances here. Just above
the wall on Cuesta de la Vega, information
panels show the original extent of the city
walls superimposed on a modern map.

CAMPO DEL MORO GARDENS
Map p232 (☎91 454 88 00; www.patrimoniona-
cional.es; Paseo de la Virgen del Puerto; ⊙10am-
8pm Apr-Sep, 10am-6pm Oct-Mar; Ⓜ Príncipe Pío)
These gardens beneath the Palacio Real
were designed to mimic the gardens surrounding the palace at Versailles; nowhere
is this more in evidence than along the
east–west **Pradera**, a lush lawn with the
Palacio Real as its backdrop. The gardens'
centrepiece, which stands halfway along the
Pradera, is the elegant **Fuente de las Conchas** (Fountain of the Shells) designed by

Ventura Rodríguez, the Goya of Madrid's 18th-century architecture scene. The entrance is from Paseo de la Virgen del Puerto.

From the park you can also gain an appreciation of Madrid in its earliest days – it was from here, in what would become known as Campo del Moro (Moor's Field), that an Almoravid army laid siege to the city in 1110. The troops occupied all but the fortress (where the Palacio Real now stands), but the Christian garrison held on until the Almoravid fury abated and their forces retired south.

The 20 hectares of gardens that now adorn the site were first laid in the 18th century, with major overhauls in 1844 and 1890.

PLAZA DE RAMALES   SQUARE

Map p232 (MÓpera) This pleasant little triangle of open space is not without historical intrigue. Joseph Bonaparte ordered the destruction of the Iglesia de San Juanito to open up a pocket of fresh air in the then-crowded streets. It is believed Velázquez was buried in the church; a small monument announces this as the last resting place of the master painter who died on 6 August 1660.

On the west side of the plaza is the **Escuela Superior de Música Reina Sofía** (☑91 523 04 19; www.escuelasuperiordemusica-reinasofia.es; Calle de Requena 1), a prestigious musical conservatory that sometimes hosts concerts and organises open-air recitals in the adjacent Plaza de Oriente – check the monthly program listed on the wall outside for details.

The decadent building on the plaza's northeastern corner, where Calle de la Amnistía and Calle de Vergara meet the plaza, is one of downtown Madrid's more attractive apartment complexes.

TEATRO REAL   NOTABLE BUILDING

Map p232 (☑91 516 06 96; www.teatro-real.com; Plaza de Oriente; guided tours adult/child under 7yr €8/free; ⊙10.30am-1pm; MÓpera) Backing onto the Plaza de Oriente, Madrid's signature opera house took on its present neoclassical form in 1997 and, viewed from Plaza de Isabel II, it's a fine addition to the central Madrid cityscape; in Plaza de Oriente, however, it's somewhat overshadowed by the splendour of its surrounds. The 1997 renovations combined the latest in theatre and acoustic technology with a remake of the most splendid of its 19th-century decor. The 50-minute guided tours (in Spanish) leave every half-hour.

For all such modern magnificence, the Teatro Real does not have the most distinguished of histories. The first theatre, built in 1708 on the site of public wash houses, was torn down in 1816. Its successor was built in 1850 under the reign of Isabel II, whereafter it burned down and was later blown up in the civil war (when it was used

---

WHERE ARE THEY BURIED?

While other countries have turned cemeteries and the graves of famous locals into tourist attractions, Spain has been slow to do the same. But that may be because mystery surrounds the final resting places of some of Spain's most towering historical figures.

➡ **Diego Velázquez** (1599–1660) According to historical records, Spain's master painter was buried in the Iglesia de San Juanito, but the church was destroyed in the early 19th century by Joseph Bonaparte to make way for what would later become the Plaza de Ramales. Excavations in 2000 revealed the crypt of the former church, but Velázquez was nowhere to be found.

➡ **Francisco Goya** (1746–1828) In 1919, 91 years after Goya's death in Bordeaux, France, his remains were entombed in the Ermita de San Antonio de la Florida (p150), the small chapel still adorned by some of Goya's most celebrated frescoes. But his head was never found.

➡ **Miguel de Cervantes Saavedra** (1547–1616) Cervantes, the author of *Don Quijote*, lived much of his life in Madrid and upon his death his body was buried at the Convento de las Trinitarias (p89), in the Barrio de las Letras. In the centuries that followed, his body was somehow misplaced until, in early 2015, forensic archaeologists announced that they had discovered the bones of Cervantes in a crypt in the convent. Still home to cloistered nuns, the convent is closed to the public, but authorities are considering opening part of the convent to the public to mark Cervantes' last resting place.

as a powder store, resulting in the inevitable fireworks)...

PLAZA DE ESPAÑA   SQUARE

Map p232 (Ⓜ Plaza de España) It's hard to know what to make of this curiously unprepossessing square. The square's centrepiece is a 1927 statue of Cervantes with, at the writer's feet, a bronze statue of his immortal characters Don Quijote and Sancho Panza. The 1953 **Edificio de España** (Spain Building) on the northeast side clearly sprang from the totalitarian recesses of Franco's imagination such is its resemblance to austere Soviet monumentalism. To the north stands the 35-storey **Torre de Madrid** (Madrid Tower).

CONVENTO DE LA ENCARNACIÓN CONVENT

Map p232 (www.patrimonionacional.es; Plaza de la Encarnación 1; admission €6, incl Convento de las Descalzas Reales €8, EU citizens free Wed & Thu afternoon; ⊘10am-2pm & 4-6.30pm Tue-Sat, 10am-3pm Sun; Ⓜ Ópera) Founded by Empress Margarita de Austria, this 17th-century mansion built in the Madrid baroque style (a pleasing amalgam of brick, exposed stone and wrought iron) is still inhabited by nuns of the Augustine order. The large art collection dates mostly from the 17th century and among the many gold and silver reliquaries is one that contains the blood of San Pantaleón, which purportedly liquefies each year on 27 July. The convent also sits on a pretty plaza close to the Palacio Real.

CONVENTO DE LAS
DESCALZAS REALES   CONVENT

Map p232 (Convent of the Barefoot Royals; www. patrimonionacional.es; Plaza de las Descalzas 3; admission €6, incl Convento de la Encarnación €8, EU citizens free Wed & Thu afternoon; ⊘10am-2pm & 4-6.30pm Tue-Sat, 10am-3pm Sun; Ⓜ Ópera, Sol) The grim plateresque walls of the Convento de las Descalzas Reales offer no hint that behind the facade lies a sumptuous stronghold of the faith. The compulsory guided tour (in Spanish) leads you up a gaudily frescoed Renaissance stairway to the upper level of the cloister. The vault was painted by Claudio Coello, one of the most important artists of the Madrid School of the 17th century and whose works adorn San Lorenzo de El Escorial.

You then pass several of the convent's 33 chapels – a maximum of 33 Franciscan nuns is allowed to live here (perhaps because Christ is said to have been 33 when he died) as part of a closed order. These

LOCAL KNOWLEDGE

CHILDREN'S PLAYGROUNDS

There aren't many children's play areas in this part of Madrid, although the Jardines de Sabatini (p54) and Campo del Moro (p55) have some areas where kids can stretch their legs a little. The most important dedicated children's play area is the large playground at the southern end of Plaza de Oriente (p55).

nuns follow in the tradition of the Descalzas Reales (Barefooted Royals), a group of illustrious women who cloistered themselves when the convent was founded in the 16th century.

The first of these chapels contains a remarkable carved figure of a dead, reclining Christ, which is paraded in a Good Friday procession each year. At the end of the passage is the antechoir, then the choir stalls themselves. Buried here is Doña Juana, Carlos I's widowed daughter who, in a typical piece of 16th-century collusion between royalty and the Catholic Church, commandeered the palace and had it converted into a convent. A *Virgen la Dolorosa* by Pedro de la Mena is seated in one of the 33 oak stalls.

In the former sleeping quarters of the nuns are some of the most extraordinary tapestries you're ever likely to see. Woven in the 17th century in Brussels, they include four based on drawings by Rubens. To produce works of this quality, four or five artisans could take up to a year to weave just 1 sq metre of tapestry.

IGLESIA DE SAN GINÉS   CHURCH

Map p232 (Calle del Arenal 13; ⊘8.45am-1pm & 6-9pm Mon-Sat, 9.45am-2pm & 6-9pm Sun; Ⓜ Sol, Ópera) Due north of Plaza Mayor, San Ginés is one of Madrid's oldest churches: it has been here in one form or another since at least the 14th century. What you see today was built in 1645 but largely reconstructed after a fire in 1824. The church houses some fine paintings, including El Greco's *Expulsion of the Money-changers from the Temple* (1614), which is beautifully displayed; the glass is just 6mm from the canvas to avoid reflections.

The church has stood at the centre of Madrid life for centuries. It is speculated that, prior to the arrival of the Christians in 1085, a Mozarabic community (Christians in Muslim territory) lived around the

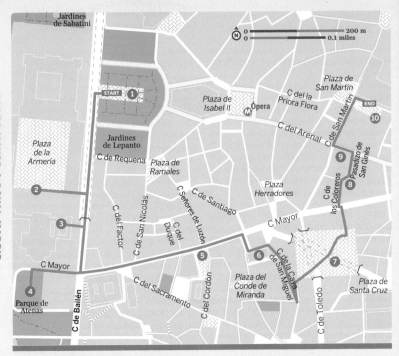

Neighbourhood Walk
Old Madrid

START PLAZA DE ORIENTE
END CONVENTO DE LAS DESCALZAS REALES
LENGTH 2KM; TWO HOURS

Start in **1 Plaza de Oriente** (p55), a splendid arc of greenery and graceful architecture that could be Madrid's most agreeable plaza. You'll find yourself surrounded by gardens, the Palacio Real and the Teatro Real, and an ever-changing cast of *madrileños* at play. Overlooking the plaza, the **2 Palacio Real** (p53) was Spain's seat of royal power for centuries. Almost next door is the **3 Catedral de Nuestra Señora de la Almudena** (p55); it may lack the old-world gravitas of other Spanish cathedrals, but it's a beautiful part of the skyline.

From the cathedral, drop down to the **4 Muralla Árabe** (p55), then climb gently up Calle Mayor, pausing to admire the last remaining ruins of Madrid's first cathedral, Santa María de la Almudena, then on to **5 Plaza de la Villa** (p59), a cosy square surrounded on three sides by some of the

best examples of Madrid baroque architecture. A little further up the hill and just off Calle Mayor, the **6 Mercado de San Miguel** (p61), one of Madrid's oldest markets, has become one of the coolest places to eat and mingle with locals in downtown Madrid.

Head down the hill along Cava de San Miguel, then climb up through the Arco de Cuchilleros to **7 Plaza Mayor** (p52), one of Spain's grandest and most beautiful plazas. Down a narrow lane north of the plaza, **8 Chocolatería de San Ginés** (p63) is justifiably famous for its *chocolate con churros*, the ideal Madrid indulgence at any hour of the day. Almost next door, along pedestrianised Calle del Arenal, there's the pleasing brick-and-stone **9 Iglesia de San Ginés** (p57), one of the longest-standing relics of Christian Madrid.

A short climb to the north, the **10 Convento de las Descalzas Reales** (p57) is an austere convent with an extraordinarily rich interior. In the heart of downtown Madrid, it's a great place to finish up.

stream that later became Calle del Arenal and that their parish church stood on this site. Spain's premier playwright Lope de Vega was married here and novelist Francisco de Quevedo was baptised in its font.

PLAZA DE LA VILLA & AROUND SQUARE

(ⓂÓpera) There are grander plazas in Madrid, but this intimate little square is one of the prettiest. Enclosed on three sides by wonderfully preserved examples of 17th-century Madrid-style baroque architecture *(barroco madrileño)*, it was the permanent seat of Madrid's city government from the Middle Ages until recent years when Madrid's city council relocated to the grand Palacio de Comunicaciones on Plaza de la Cibeles.

The 17th-century **Casa de la Villa** (old town hall), on the western side of the square, is a typical Habsburg edifice with Herrerian slate-tiled spires. First planned as a prison in 1644 by Juan Gómez de Mora, who also designed the Convento de la Encarnación, its granite and brick facade is a study in sobriety. The final touches to the Casa de la Villa were made in 1693, although Juan de Villanueva, of Museo del Prado fame, made some alterations a century later. The **Salón del Pleno** (council chambers) were restored in the 1890s and again in 1986; the decoration is sumptuous neoclassical with late 17th-century ceiling frescoes. Ask at the Centro de Turismo de Madrid (p208) about guided tours to the Casa de la Villa. Look for the ceramic copy of Pedro Teixeira's landmark 1656 map of Madrid just outside the chambers.

On the opposite side of the square, the 15th-century **Casa de los Lujanes** is more Gothic in conception with a clear Mudéjar (a Moorish architectural style) influence. The brickwork tower was 'home' to the imprisoned French monarch François I and his sons after their capture during the Battle of Pavia (1525). As the star prisoner was paraded down Calle Mayor, locals are said to have been more impressed by the splendidly attired Frenchman than they were by his more drab captor, the Spanish Habsburg emperor Carlos I. The tower's wooden door is a wonderful original.

Closed to the public at the time of research, the **Casa de Cisneros**, built in 1537 by the nephew of Cardinal Cisneros, a key adviser to Queen Isabel, is plateresque in inspiration, although it was much restored and altered at the beginning of the 20th century. The main door and window above it are what remains of the Renaissance-era building. It's now home to the Salón de Tapices (Tapestries Hall), adorned with exquisite 15th-century Flemish tapestries.

The section of Calle Mayor that runs past the plaza witnessed one of the most dramatic moments in the history of early 20th-century Madrid. On 31 May 1906, on the wedding day of King Alfonso XIII and Britain's Victoria Eugenia, a Catalan anarchist Mateu Morral threw a bomb concealed in a bouquet of flowers at the royal couple. Several bystanders died, but the monarch and his new wife survived, save for her blood-spattered dress. During the Spanish Civil War, Madrid's republican government briefly renamed the street Calle Mateu Morral.

Just down the hill from the plaza are the 18th-century baroque remakes of the **Iglesia del Sacramento** (☑91 547 36 24; Calle del Sacramento 11), the central church of the Spanish army, and the **Palacio del Duque de Uceda** (Calle Mayor 79), which is now used as a military headquarters (the Capitanía General), but is a classic of the Madrid baroque architectural style and was designed by Juan Gómez de Mora in 1608.

CONVENTO DEL CORPUS CRISTI CONVENT

Map p232 (Las Carboneras; ☑91 548 37 01; Plaza del Conde de Miranda; ⊙9.30am-1pm & 4-6.30pm; ⓂÓpera) FREE Architecturally nondescript but culturally curious, this church hides behind sober brickwork on the western end of a quiet square. A closed order of nuns occupies the convent building and, when Mass is held, the nuns gather in a separate area at the rear of the church. They maintain a centuries-old tradition of making sweet biscuits that can be purchased from the entrance just off the square on Calle del Codo (p66).

BASÍLICA DE SAN MIGUEL CHURCH

Map p232 (☑91 548 40 11; www.bsmiguel.es; Calle de San Justo 4; ⊙10.15am-1.15pm & 6-9pm Mon-Fri; ⓂLa Latina, Sol) Hidden away off Calle de Segovia, this basilica is something of a surprise. Its convex, late-baroque facade sits in harmony with the surrounding buildings of old Madrid. Among its fine features are statues representing the four virtues, and the reliefs of Justo and Pastor, the saints to whom the church was originally dedicated. The rococo and Italianate interior, completed by Italian architects in 1745, is another world altogether with gilded flourishes and dark, sombre domes.

IGLESIA DE SAN NICOLÁS DE LOS SERVITAS
CHURCH

Map p232 (☑91 548 83 14; Plaza de San Nicolás 6; ⊘8am-1.30pm & 5.30-8.30pm Mon, 8-9.30am & 6.30-8.30pm Tue-Sat, 9.30am-2pm & 6.30-9pm Sun & holidays; Ⓜ Ópera) Tucked away up the hill from Calle Mayor, this intimate little church is Madrid's oldest surviving building of worship; it is believed to have been built on the site of Muslim Mayrit's second mosque. The most striking feature is the restored 12th-century Mudéjar bell tower, although much of the remainder dates in part from the 15th century. The vaulting is late Gothic while the fine timber ceiling, which survived a fire in 1936, dates from about the same period.

Despite plateresque and baroque touches, much of the interior is a study in simplicity. The architect Juan de Herrera, one of the great architects of Renaissance Spain, was buried in the crypt in 1597.

PALACIO DE SANTA CRUZ
HISTORIC BUILDING

Map p232 (Plaza de la Provincia; Ⓜ Sol) Just off the southeastern corner of Plaza Mayor and dominating Plaza de Santa Cruz is this baroque edifice, which houses the **Ministerio de Asuntos Exteriores** (Ministry of Foreign Affairs) and hence can only be admired from the outside. A landmark with its grey slate spires, it was built in 1643 and initially served as the court prison.

EATING

★ CASA REVUELTA
TAPAS €

Map p232 (☑91 366 33 32; Calle de Latoneros 3; tapas from €2.80; ⊘10.30am-4pm & 7-11pm Tue-Sat, 10.30am-4pm Sun, closed Aug; Ⓜ Sol, La Latina) Casa Revuelta puts out some of Madrid's finest tapas of *bacalao* (cod) bar none – unlike elsewhere, *tajadas de bacalao* don't have bones in them and slide down the throat with the greatest of ease. Early on a Sunday afternoon, as the Rastro crowd gathers here, it's filled to the rafters. It's also famous for its *callos* (tripe), *torreznos* (bacon bits) and *albóndigas* (meatballs).

MUSEO DEL PAN GALLEGO
GALICIAN, BAKERY €

Map p232 (☑91 542 51 60; www.museodelpangallego.com; Plaza Herradores 9; pastries from €12.50 per kg; ⊘8.30am-3pm & 5.30-9pm Mon-Fri, 8.30am-3.30pm & 5.30-9pm Sat, 8.30am-3.30pm Sun; Ⓜ Ópera) Part bakery, part temple to a handful of Galician staples, this simple

---

MADRID'S OLD-STYLE PASTRY SHOPS

Horno de Santiguesa (Map p232; ☑91 559 62 14; Calle Mayor 73; pastries from €2.50; ⊘8am-9pm; Ⓜ Ópera) Everything's a speciality at this wonderful old *pastelería*, from cakes and pastries to bite-sized sweets and Christmas *turrón* (a nougat-like sweet).

Confitería El Riojano (☑91 366 44 82; www.confiteriaelriojano.com; Calle Mayor 10; pastries from €3; ⊘10am-2pm & 5-9pm Mon-Fri, 10am-2.30pm & 5.30-9pm Sat & Sun; Ⓜ Sol) Founded in 1855, this place serves the usual suspects, as well as traditional Madrid offerings such as *azucarillos* (meringue-like sugar bombs) of lemon, coffee or strawberry and *bartolillos* (sweet filled pastries).

La Mallorquina (☑91 521 12 01; www.pasterialamallorquina.es; Plaza de la Puerta del Sol 8; pastries from €2; ⊘9am-9.15pm; Ⓜ Sol) A classic pastry shop that's packed to the rafters by *madrileños* who just couldn't pass by without stopping. Treat yourself to a takeaway *ensaimada* (a light pastry dusted with icing sugar) from Mallorca.

La Duquesita (☑91 308 02 31; www.laduquesita.es; Calle de Fernando VI 2; pastries from €2.50; ⊘9.30am-2.30pm & 5-9pm Tue-Sun; Ⓜ Alonso Martínez) A lavish step back in time with wonderful traditional pastries.

Antigua Pastelería del Pozo (☑91 522 38 94; Calle del Pozo 8; pastries from €1.50; ⊘9.30am-2pm & 5-8pm Tue-Sun; Ⓜ Sol) Antigua Pastelería del Pozo has lost none of its old charm in turning out all sorts of great pastries. It has been in operation since 1830, making it the city's oldest pastry shop.

Casa Mira (☑91 429 88 95; www.casamira.es; Carrera de San Jerónimo 30; pastries from €2.50; ⊘10am-2pm & 5-9pm Mon-Sat; Ⓜ Sol) The turning, wedding-cake-like display in the window is laden with sweets, cakes, fat pastries and candied fruits. The shop is especially known for its *turrónes*.

bakery with a wood-fired oven is one of Madrid's oldest, dating back to the 18th century. It's an institution for its mix of salty and sweet – *empanadas* (pastries) filled with tuna/cod (€12.50/17 per kilo) and even baby clams or octopus, and the *tarta de Santiago* (sweet Galician almond cake).

TAQUERÍA MI CIUDAD   MEXICAN €

Map p232 (☑91 559 87 11; www.taqueriamiciudad.com; Calle de las Hileras 5; tacos €1.50; ⊙1.30-4.30pm & 8pm-1.30am; MÓpera) This family-run Mexican bar has something of a cult following, serving up bite-sized tacos (the *cochinita pibil* is our favourite) washed down by fabulous margaritas (including those flavoured with tamarind). It's wildly popular on weekend nights. If you get the munchies between meals, try its tiny **sister outlet** (☑608 621096; Calle de las Fuentes 11; ⊙11.30am-2am Sun-Thu, 11.30am-2.30am Fri & Sat) around the corner.

MUSEO DEL JAMÓN   SPANISH €

Map p232 (☑91 531 45 50; www.museodeljamon.com; Calle Mayor 7; raciónes from €2.50; ⊙8am-midnight; MSol) Famous for having appeared in Pedro Almodóvar's 1997 film *Carne Trémula* (Live Flesh), and equally beloved by first-time visitors to Spain for the sight of hundreds of hams hanging from the ceiling, Museo del Jamón is definitely a local landmark. Prices for a *ración/bocadillo* (large tapas serving/filled roll) start at €2.50/1.50 and can go much higher depending on the quality of the *jamón* (cured ham).

BANGKOK THAI RESTAURANT   THAI €

Map p232 (☑91 559 16 96; 1st fl, Calle de los Bordadores 15; mains €8-14; ⊙noon-4pm & 8pm-midnight; MSol, Ópera) Good Thai food, reasonable prices, attentive service and a Thai-style dining area make for a terrific meal in the heart of town. In addition to its à la carte choices, there's a well-priced *menú del día* (daily set menu; €12) that's available for lunch seven days a week, a *menú de noche* (evening set menu; €15) and a *menú de degustación* (€20). If you're lucky, you'll get one of the tables overlooking the busy pedestrian thoroughfare of Calle del Arenal. Its opening hours are particularly friendly to non-Spanish stomachs.

VIANDAS DE SALAMANCA   SPANISH €

(☑91 521 27 74; www.viandasdesalamanca.es; Calle del Carmen 27; bocadillos €3.90;

ⓘ MERCADO DE SAN MIGUEL

The Mercado de San Miguel has become almost too popular for its own good and, as a consequence, lunchtime and evenings can be uncomfortably crowded. Although it's always busy and snaffling a table or a bar stool is invariably a game of chance, we recommend coming for a late lunch or early dinner from 5pm to 7pm when there's usually far more room to move.

⊙10.30am-10.30pm Sun-Thu, 10.30am-11pm Fri & Sat; MCallao, Sol) Viandas de Salamanca sells cured meats from Salamanca, one of Spain's finest *jamón*-producing regions. It sells *bocadillos de jamón*, little paper cones filled with *jamón* and *jamón*-filled pastries and vacuum-sealed cured meats.

★MERCADO DE SAN MIGUEL   TAPAS €€

Map p232 (www.mercadodesanmiguel.es; Plaza de San Miguel; tapas from €1; ⊙10am-midnight Sun-Wed, 10am-2am Thu-Sat; MSol) One of Madrid's oldest and most beautiful markets, the Mercado de San Miguel has undergone a stunning major renovation. Within the early 20th-century glass walls, the market has become an inviting space strewn with tables. You can order tapas and sometimes more substantial plates at most of the counter-bars, and everything here (from caviar to chocolate) is as tempting as the market is alive.

All the stalls are outstanding, but you could begin with the fine fishy *pintxos* atop mini toasts at **La Casa de Bacalao** (Stalls 16–17), follow it up with some *jamón* or other cured meats at **Carrasco Guijuelo** (Stall 18), cheeses at Stalls 20–21, all manner of pickled goodies at Stall 22, or the gourmet tapas of **Lhardy** (Stalls 61–62). There are also plenty of places to buy wine, Asturian cider and the like; at Stall 24, the Sherry Corner (p63) has sherry tastings with tapas.

TABERNA LA BOLA   MADRILEÑO €€

Map p232 (☑91 547 69 30; www.labola.es; Calle de la Bola 5; mains €16-24; ⊙1.30-4.30pm & 8.30-11pm Mon-Sat, 1.30-4.30pm Sun, closed Aug; MSanto Domingo) Taberna La Bola (going strong since 1870 and run by the sixth generation of the Verdasco family) is a much-loved bastion of traditional Madrid cuisine.

If you're going to try *cocido a la madrileña* (meat-and-chickpea stew; €21) while in Madrid, this is a good place to do so. It's busy and noisy and very Madrid.

CASA PACO SPANISH €€
Map p232 (☑91 366 31 66; Plaza de Puerta Cerrada 11; mains €12-20; ⊙1-4pm & 8pm-midnight Mon-Sat, 1-4pm Sun; ⓜLa Latina, Tirso de Molina) The gaily painted exterior of this old Madrid tavern, which opened in 1933, is hard to miss and the food is even harder to resist, especially in winter when the local Madrid specialities – *callos, cocido* and succulent steaks – come into their own. The bar area, its walls lined with celebrity visitors past and present, is also a good place for tapas or a wine.

LA PAELLA REAL SPANISH €€
Map p232 (☑91 542 09 42; www.lapaellareal. es; Calle de Arrieta 2; mains €15-34, 3-course set menu €30; ⊙1-4pm & 7.30-10pm; ⓜÓpera) Finding a good paella in Madrid can be surprisingly difficult, but it's almost guaranteed at this august place opposite the Teatro Real. *Paella de marisco* (seafood paella), *paella de bogavante* (lobster paella) and *arroz negro* (black rice, cooked in squid ink) are the house specialities, but there are plenty of rice dishes to choose from. You'll need a minimum of two for an order.

CASA MARÍA SPANISH €€
Map p232 (☑91 559 10 07; www.casamariaplazamayor.com; Plaza Mayor 23; tapas from €2.90, 4/6 tapas €11/16, mains €9-18; ⊙noon-11pm; ⓜSol) A rare exception to the generally pricey and mediocre options that surround Plaza Mayor, Casa María combines professional service and a menu that effortlessly spans the modern and traditional. There's something for most tastes, with carefully chosen tapas, lunchtime stews and dishes such as sticky rice with lobster.

TABERNA DEL ALABARDERO SPANISH €€
Map p232 (☑91 547 25 77; www.grupolezama.es; Calle de Felipe V 6; bar raciónes €6-25, restaurant mains €17-30; ⊙noon-1am; ⓜÓpera) This fine old Madrid *taberna* (tavern) is famous for its croquettes, fine *jamón, montaditos de jamón* (small rolls of cured ham) and *montaditos de bonito* (small rolls of cured tuna) in the bar, while out the back the more classic cuisine includes *rabo de toro estofado* (bull's tail, served with honey, cinnamon, mashed potato and pastry with herbs; €21).

Madrid's notoriously fussy diners generally accept that the prices here are worth it. The sister restaurant around the corner in Plaza de Oriente, **La Mar del Alabardero** (☑91 541 33 33; Plaza de Oriente 6; mains €12-24; ⊙1.30-4pm & 8.30-11pm), is renowned for its high-quality seafood and rice dishes.

RESTAURANTE LOS GALAYOS SPANISH €€
Map p232 (☑91 366 30 28; www.losgalayos. net; Calle de Botoneros 5; mains €14-25; ⊙1pm-12.30am; ⓜSol) Most of the restaurants surrounding Plaza Mayor are tourist traps, but Los Galayos, a few steps off the plaza's southeastern corner and open for a mere 120 years, is an exception. Renowned for its *cocido* (€19; lunch only), it's a good place to sample traditional local cooking from around Spain.

There are two *terrazas* (open-air areas) for restaurants and bars): a quieter one on Calle de Botoneras, and another on Plaza Mayor. Inside check out the wooden bar, which was handcrafted in the 17th century.

GOURMET EXPERIENCE FOOD COURT €€
Map p232 (9th fl, Plaza del Callao 2; mains €8-20; ⊙10am-10pm; ⓜCallao) Ride the elevator to the 9th floor of El Corte Inglés department store for one of downtown Madrid's best eating experiences. The views here are fab, especially those that look down over Plaza del Callao and down Gran Vía, but the food is also excellent, with everything from top-notch tapas to gourmet hamburgers.

EL BISTRO DE LA CENTRAL BISTRO €€
Map p232 (☑91 790 99 30; www.lacentral.com; Postigo de San Martín 8; mains €11-16; ⊙9am-midnight Mon-Wed, 9am-1am Thu & Fri, 9.30am-1am Sat, 9.30am-midnight Sun; ⓜCallao) Housed on the ground floor of one of Madrid's coolest bookstores, this highly recommended cafe-bistro serves up breakfast, brunch and dishes that include bull's-tail lasagne or black rice with squid and saffron. The desserts (including Ferrero Rocher brownies) are very hard to resist and there's an excellent three-course lunch menu (€12) from Monday to Friday.

ALGARABÍA SPANISH €€
Map p232 (☑91 542 41 31; www.restaurantealgarabia.com; Calle de la Unión 8; mains €11-18, set menu €35; ⊙2-4pm & 9.30-11.30pm Mon-Fri, 9.30-11.30pm Sat, closed Aug; ☎; ⓜÓpera) You know the wines of La Rioja, but the food of this northern Spanish region is also filled with flavour. The La Rioja cuisine here is all about

home-cooking, and choosing the *menú de degustación* is a great way to get an overview of regional specialities. The *croquetas* (croquettes) have a loyal following and, not surprisingly, the wine list is excellent.

CASA CIRIACO   MADRILEÑO €€

Map p232 (⏺91 548 06 20; Calle Mayor 84; mains from €12; ⏲1-4pm & 8pm-midnight Thu-Tue, closed Aug; ⏺⏺; ⓂÓpera) One of the *grande dames* of the Madrid restaurant scene, Casa Ciriaco has witnessed attempted assassinations (of King Alfonso XIII in 1906) and was immortalised by the Spanish writer Valle-Inclán who set part of his novel *Luces de Bohemia* here. Its legend made, it now puts all its energies into fine Madrileño cooking.

Offerings range from seafood and hearty meat dishes such as roast suckling pig to *cocido a la madrileña*.

YERBABUENA   VEGETARIAN €€

Map p232 (⏺91 548 08 11; www.yerbabuena.ws; Calle de los Bordadores 3; mains €8-13; ⏲1-4.30pm & 8pm-midnight; ⏺; ⓂSol, Ópera) Cheerful bright colours, a full range of vegetarian staples (soya-bean burgers, biological rice and homemade yoghurt) and plenty of creatively conceived salads add up to one of central Madrid's best restaurants for vegetarians and vegans.

★RESTAURANTE SOBRINO DE BOTÍN   CASTILIAN €€€

Map p232 (⏺91 366 42 17; www.botin.es; Calle de los Cuchilleros 17; mains €19-27; ⏲1-4pm & 8pm-midnight; ⓂLa Latina, Sol) It's not every day that you can eat in the oldest restaurant in the world (the *Guinness Book of Records* has recognised it as the oldest – established in 1725). The secret of its staying power is fine *cochinillo asado* (roast suckling pig; €25) and *cordero asado* (roast lamb; €25) cooked in wood-fired ovens. Eating in the vaulted cellar is a treat.

Yes, it's filled with tourists. And yes, staff are keen to keep things ticking over and there's little chance to linger. But the novelty value is high and the food excellent.

The restaurant has also appeared in many novels about Madrid, most notably Hemingway's *The Sun Also Rises* and Frederick Forsyth's *Icon* and *The Cobra*. Much of this history is told in tours run by Insider's Madrid (p207). The tours (€75) run for 45 minutes from 12.15pm and 7pm, and include a six-course lunch or dinner and a small ceramic gift.

🍷 DRINKING & ♟ NIGHTLIFE

★CHOCOLATERÍA DE SAN GINÉS   CAFE

Map p232 (⏺91 365 65 46; www.chocolateria-sangines.com; Pasadizo de San Ginés 5; ⏲24hr; ⓂSol) One of the grand icons of the Madrid night, this *chocolate con churros* cafe sees a sprinkling of tourists throughout the day, but locals pack it out in their search for sustenance on their way home from a nightclub somewhere close to dawn. Only in Madrid...

★THE SHERRY CORNER   WINE BAR

Map p232 (⏺681 007700; www.sherry-corner.com; Stall 24, Mercado de San Miguel, Plaza de San Miguel; ⏲10am-9pm; ⓂSol) The Sherry Corner, inside the Mercado de San Miguel, has found an excellent way to give a crash course in sherry. For €25, you get six small glasses of top-quality sherry to taste, each of which is matched to a different tapa. Guiding you through the process is an audioguide in eight languages (Spanish, English, German, French, Italian, Portuguese, Russian and Japanese). Advance bookings are recommended for groups of three or more people.

★TEATRO JOY ESLAVA   CLUB

Map p232 (Joy Madrid; ⏺91 366 37 33; www.joy-eslava.com; Calle del Arenal 11; ⏲11.30pm-6am; ⓂSol) The only things guaranteed at this grand old Madrid dance club (housed in a 19th-century theatre) are a crowd and the fact that it'll be open (it claims to have operated every single day for the past 29 years). The music and the crowd are a mixed bag, but queues are long and invariably include locals and tourists, and even the occasional *famoso* (celebrity). Every night's a little different. Tuesday is about glamour and house music, Wednesday's R&B and hip hop, Thursday is Epic with an international focus while the weekend is all about the best Madrid has to offer. There's even the no-alcohol, no-smoking 'Joy Light' on Saturday evenings (5.30pm to 10pm) for those aged between 14 and 17. Throw in occasional live acts and cabaret-style performances on stage and it's a point of reference for Madrid's professional party crowd. Admission is €12 to €15.

CAFÉ DEL REAL   BAR

Map p232 (⏺91 547 21 24; Plaza de Isabel II 2; ⏲8am-1am Mon-Thu, 8am-2.30am Fri, 9am-2.30am Sat, 10am-11.30pm Sun; ⓂÓpera) A cafe and cocktail bar in equal parts, this intimate little place serves up creative coffees

---

ℹ️ SPANISH FAST FOOD & WHERE TO EAT BETWEEN MEALS

If you're still adjusting to Spanish restaurant hours and need a meal in between, there are a number of options in the centre.

When it comes to local fast food, one of the lesser-known culinary specialities of Madrid is a *bocadillo de calamares* (a small baguette-style roll filled to bursting with deep-fried calamari). You'll find them in many bars in the streets surrounding Plaza Mayor and neighbouring bars along Calle de Botoneras off Plaza Mayor's southeastern corner. At around €2.70, it's the perfect snack.

➡ **Mercado de San Miguel** (p61) All-day tapas.

➡ **Taquería Mi Ciudad** (p61) Budget tacos.

➡ **La Campana** (Map p232; ☑91 364 29 84; www.calamareslacampana.com; Calle de Botoneras 6; bocadillos €2.70; ☺9am-11pm Sun-Thu, to midnight Fri & Sat; Ⓜ Sol) *Bocadillo de calamares.*

➡ **La Ideal** (Map p232; ☑91 365 72 78; Calle de Botoneras 4; bocadillos €2.70; ☺9am-11pm Sun-Thu, 9am-midnight Fri & Sat; Ⓜ Sol) Filled calamari rolls.

➡ **Viandas de Salamanca** (p61) *Jamón* rolls.

➡ **Cervecería 100 Montaditos** (Map p232; www.100montaditos.com; Calle Mayor 22; montaditos €0.50-3; ☺noon-midnight; Ⓜ Sol) Tiny *bocadillos.*

---

and a few cocktails to the soundtrack of chill-out music. The best seats are upstairs, where the low ceilings, wooden beams and leather chairs make for a great place to pass an afternoon with friends.

CAFE DE ORIENTE
CAFE

Map p232 (☑91 541 39 74; Plaza de Oriente 2; ☺8.30am-1.30am Mon-Thu, 9am-2.30am Fri & Sat, 9am-1.30am Sun; Ⓜ Ópera) The outdoor tables of this distinguished old cafe are among the most sought-after in central Madrid, providing as they do a front-row seat for the beautiful Plaza de Oriente, with the Palacio Real as a backdrop. The building itself was once part of a long-gone, 17th-century convent and the interior feels a little like a set out of Mitteleuropa. It's the perfect spot for a coffee when the weather's fine.

ANTICAFÉ
CAFE

Map p232 (Calle de la Unión 2; ☺5pm-2am Tue-Sun; Ⓜ Ópera) Bohemian kitsch in the best sense is the prevailing theme here and it runs right through the decor, regular cultural events (poetry readings and concerts) and, of course, the clientele. As such, it won't be to everyone's taste, but we think that it adds some much-needed variety to the downtown drinking scene. Coffees are as popular as the alcohol, although that rather strange predilection wears off as the night progresses.

EL CAFÉ DE LA OPERA
CAFE

Map p232 (☑91 542 63 82; www.elcafedela opera.com; Calle de Arrieta 6; ☺8am-midnight;

Ⓜ Ópera) Opposite the Teatro Real, this classic before-performance cafe has one unusual requirement for some of its would-be waiters – they have to be able to sing opera. They break into song from around 9.30pm on Friday and Saturday evenings, when you'll fork out a minimum €45 for a meal – not bad value if you don't have tickets for the show across the road.

CHOCOLATERÍA VALOR
CAFE

Map p232 (www.chocolateriasvalor.es; Postigo de San Martín; ☺8am-10.30pm Mon-Thu, 8am-1am Fri, 9am-1am Sat, 9am-10.30pm Sun; Ⓜ Callao) It may be Madrid tradition to indulge in *chocolate con churros* around sunrise on your way home from a nightclub, but for everyone else who prefers a more reasonable hour, this is one of the best *chocolaterías* in town. Our favourite chocolate variety among many has to be *cuatro sentidos de chocolate* (four senses of chocolate; €7.95), but we'd happily try everything on the menu to make sure.

OBA OBA
CLUB, LIVE MUSIC

Map p232 (Calle de Jacometrezo 4; ☺9pm-5.30am Wed-Sun; Ⓜ Callao) This nightclub is one of the best places for salsa in Madrid, with Thursday especially good – there's a bit of jazz and other genres thrown in for good measure and live music mixes with DJs most nights. Admission ranges from free to €10.

CHARADA
CLUB

Map p232 (☑663 230504; www.charada.es; Calle de la Bola 13; ☺midnight-6am Wed-Sun; Ⓜ Santo

Domingo) Charada is a reliable regular on the Madrid clubbing scene. Its two rooms (one red, the other black) are New York chic with no hint of the building's former existence as a brothel. The cocktails are original and we especially like it when they turn their attention to electronica, but there's also disco and house. Admission is €12.

ENTERTAINMENT

CINESA CAPITOL
CINEMA

Map p232 (☑902 333231; www.cinesa.es; Gran Vía 41; ⓂCallao) One of the stalwarts of the Madrid cinema scene – expect Hollywood more than art house.

CAFÉ DE CHINITAS
FLAMENCO

Map p232 (☑91 547 15 02; www.chinitas.com; Calle de Torija 7; admission incl drink/meal €36/48; ⓉShows 8pm & 10.30pm Mon-Sat; ⓂSanto Domingo) One of the most distinguished *tablaos* (flamenco venues) in Madrid, drawing in everyone from the Spanish royal family to Bill Clinton, Café de Chinitas has an elegant setting and top-notch performers. It may attract loads of tourists, but flamenco aficionados also give it top marks. Reservations are highly recommended.

LAS TABLAS
FLAMENCO

Map p232 (☑91 542 05 20; www.lastablasmadrid.com; Plaza de España 9; ⓉShows 8pm & 10pm; ⓂPlaza de España) Las Tablas has a reputation for quality flamenco and reasonable prices (admission including drink is €27); it could just be the best choice in town. Most nights you'll see a classic flamenco show, with plenty of throaty singing and soul-baring dancing. Antonia Moya and Marisol Navarro, leading lights in the flamenco world, are regular performers here.

LAS CARBONERAS
FLAMENCO

Map p232 (☑91 542 86 77; www.tablaolascarboneras.com; Plaza del Conde de Miranda 1; ⓉShows 8.30pm & 10.30pm Mon-Thu, 8.30pm & 11pm Fri & Sat; ⓂÓpera, Sol, La Latina) Like most of the *tablaos* around town, this place sees far more tourists than locals, but the quality is nonetheless excellent. It's not the place for gritty, soul-moving spontaneity, but it's still an excellent introduction and one of the few places that flamenco aficionados seem to have no complaints about. Admission including drink/tapas/meal costs €34/66/71.

LA COQUETTE BLUES
LIVE MUSIC

Map p232 (☑91 530 80 95; Calle de las Hileras 14; Ⓣ8pm-3am Tue-Thu, 8pm-3.30am Fri & Sat, 7pm-3am Sun; ⓂÓpera) Madrid's best blues bar has been around since the 1980s and its 8pm Sunday jam session is legendary. Live acts perform Tuesday to Thursday at 10.30pm and the atmosphere is very cool at any time.

CAFÉ BERLIN
JAZZ

Map p232 (☑91 521 57 52; www.berlincafe.es; Calle de Jacometrezo 4; Ⓣ9pm-3am Tue-Thu, 9pm-5am Fri & Sat; ⓂCallao, Santo Domingo) El Berlín has been something of a Madrid jazz stalwart since the 1950s, although a recent makeover has brought flamenco, R&B, soul, funk and fusion into the mix. The art-deco interior ads to the charm. Headline acts play at 11pm, although check the website as some can begin as early as 9pm (admission from €5 to €14).

SHOPPING

★ANTIGUA CASA TALAVERA
CERAMICS

Map p232 (☑91 547 34 17; www.antiguacasatalavera.com; Calle de Isabel la Católica 2; Ⓣ10am-1.30pm & 5-8pm Mon-Fri, 10am-1.30pm Sat; ⓂSanto Domingo) The extraordinary tiled facade of this wonderful old shop conceals an Aladdin's cave of ceramics from all over Spain. This is not the mass-produced stuff aimed at a tourist market, but comes from the small family potters of Andalucía and Toledo, ranging from the decorative (tiles) to the useful (plates, jugs and other kitchen items). The old couple who run the place are delightful.

★EL ARCO ARTESANÍA
HANDICRAFTS

Map p232 (☑913 65 26 80; www.artesaniaelarco.com; Plaza Mayor 9; Ⓣ10am-9pm Mon-Sat, 10am-5pm Sun; ⓂSol, La Latina) This original shop in the southwestern corner of Plaza Mayor sells an outstanding array of homemade designer souvenirs, from stone, ceramic and glass work to jewellery and home fittings. The papier-mâché figures are gorgeous, but there's so much else here to turn your head.

MATY
FLAMENCO

Map p232 (☑91 531 32 91; www.maty.es; Calle del Maestro Victoria 2; Ⓣ10am-1.45pm & 4.30-8pm Mon-Fri, 10am-2pm & 4.30-8pm Sat & 1st Sun of month; ⓂSol) Wandering around central Madrid, it's easy to imagine that flamenco

FLEA MARKETS OF MADRID

In addition to **El Rastro** (p72), Madrid has a number of fine, if little-known flea markets, including the following:

➡ **Art Market** (Map p232; Plaza del Conde de Barajas; ⊙10am-2pm Sun; ⓂSol) Local art and prints of the greats.

➡ **Cuesta de Moyano Bookstalls** (p115) Madrid's answer to the bookstalls on Paris' Left Bank.

➡ **Mercadillo Marqués de Viana** (p158) A calmer version of El Rastro in northern Madrid.

➡ **Mercado de Monedas y Sellos** (Map p232; Plaza Mayor; ⊙9am-2pm Sun; ⓂSol) Old coins and stamps.

outfits have been reduced to imitation dresses sold as souvenirs to tourists. That's why places like Maty matter. Here you'll find dresses, shoes and all the accessories that go with the genre, with sizes for children and adults. These are the real deal, with prices to match, but they make brilliant gifts. Maty also does quality disguises for Carnaval.

CONVENTO DEL CORPUS CRISTI
FOOD & DRINK

Map p232 (Las Carboneras; ☑91 548 37 01; Plaza del Conde de Miranda; ⊙9.30am-1pm & 4-6.30pm; ⓂÓpera) The cloistered nuns at this convent (p59) also happen to be fine pastry chefs. You make your request through a door, then a grille on Calle del Codo, and the products (sweet biscuits) are delivered through a little revolving door that allows the nuns to remain unseen by the outside world.

EL JARDÍN DEL CONVENTO
FOOD

Map p232 (☑91 541 22 99; www.eljardindelconvento.net; Calle del Cordón 1; ⊙11am-3pm & 5.30-9pm Tue-Sun; ⓂÓpera) In a quiet lane just south of Plaza de la Villa, this appealing little shop sells homemade sweets baked by nuns in abbeys, convents and monasteries all across Spain.

CASA HERNANZ
SHOES

Map p232 (☑91 366 545 0; www.alpargateriahernanz.com; Calle de Toledo 18; ⊙9am-1.30pm & 4.30-8pm Mon-Fri, 10am-2pm Sat; ⓂLa Latina, Sol) Comfy, rope-soled *alpargatas* (espadrilles), Spain's traditional summer footwear, are worn by everyone from the King of Spain down, and you can buy your own pair at this humble workshop, which has been hand-making the shoes for five generations; you can even get them made to order. Prices range from €5 to €40 and queues form whenever the weather starts to warm up.

EL FLAMENCO VIVE
FLAMENCO

Map p232 (☑91 547 39 17; www.elflamencovive.es; Calle Conde de Lemos 7; ⊙10am-1.45pm & 5-9pm Mon-Fri, 10am-1.45pm & 5-9pm Sat & 1st Sun of month; ⓂÓpera) This ˙temple to flamenco has it all, from guitars and songbooks to well-priced CDs, polka-dotted dancing costumes, shoes, colourful plastic jewellery and literature about flamenco. It's the sort of place that will appeal as much to curious first timers as to serious students of the art. It also organises classes in flamenco guitar.

SOMBRERERÍA MEDRANO
ACCESSORIES

Map p232 (☑91 366 42 34; www.sombrereriamedrano.com; Calle Imperial 12; ⊙10am-2.30pm & 4.30-8pm Mon-Fri, 10am-2.30pm Sat; ⓂSol) They've been making hats at this place since 1832 and while concessions have been made to modern fashions, the look here is reassuringly rather a classic one. It's a marvellous old shop/workshop where the quality is unimpeachable, and there are hats and gloves for men, women and children.

LA CHINATA
FOOD

Map p232 (☑91 152 20 08; www.lachinata.es; Calle Mayor 44; ⊙10.30am-9pm Mon-Sat, noon-3.30pm & 4.30-8pm Sun; ⓂSol, Ópera) Olive oil is the centrepiece of this gourmet *'oleoteca'* just across from the Plaza Mayor. You can buy bottles of the stuff, as well as olive-oil-based cosmetics and carefully selected gourmet food products.

CODO 3
JEWELLERY

Map p232 (☑91 548 09 48; www.codo3.com; Calle del Codo 3; ⊙5.30-8pm Mon, 11am-2pm & 5.30-8pm Tue-Sun; ⓂÓpera) Classy designer jewellery handcrafted in Barcelona from silver, pewter and other natural products are a real find down this quiet pedestrian lane off the back of Plaza de la Villa. Necklaces, bracelets, rings and earrings range from the understated to those calculated to make a bold statement.

ARTELEMA
ARTS, SOUVENIRS

Map p232 (☑91 559 7817; www.artelema.com; Calle Mayor 74; ☺10.30am-2pm & 5-8pm Mon-Fri, 10.30am-2pm Sat; MÓpera) High-quality prints and old photos of Madrid dominate this quiet store just down the hill from Plaza de la Villa. It also sells old Madrid maps, bronze sculptures, etchings, pens and other classy gifts and wall hangings.

SALVADOR BACHILLER
ACCESSORIES

Map p232 (☑91 559 83 21; www.salvadorbachiller. com; Gran Vía 65; ☺10am-9pm Mon-Sat, 11am-9pm Sun; MPlaza de España, Santo Domingo) The stylish and high-quality leather bags, wallets, suitcases and other accessories of Salvador Bachiller are a staple of Spanish shopping aficionados. This is leather with a typically Spanish twist – the colours are dazzling in bright pinks, yellows and greens. Sound garish? You'll change your mind once you step inside. It also has an **outlet** (☑91 523 30 37; Calle de Gravina 11; ☺10.30am-9.30pm Mon-Thu, 10.30am-11pm Fri & Sat, noon-9pm Sun; MChueca) in Chueca for superseded stock.

FRANSEN ET LAFITE
HOMEWARES, FLOWERS

Map p232 (☑91 142 85 25; www.fransenetlafite. com; Calle del Espejo 5; ☺10am-8pm Tue-Sat, noon-3pm Sun; MÓpera) A stunning collection of flowers from all over Europe is the main business here, but that's not why we include it. Spread over three floors and with a tranquil outdoor patio, this charming space also has carefully selected homewares, antiques, candles and all manner of decorative pieces. But even more than what it sells, it's the just-rightness of the space that means we'd happily spend time here just for the sheer pleasure of the experience.

LA GRAMOLA
MUSIC

Map p232 (☑91 559 25 12; Postigo de San Martín 4; ☺10am-2pm & 5-9pm Mon-Sat; MÓpera) In this era of music downloads, illegal and otherwise, stores like La Gramola are cause for nostalgia and strangely reassuring. Don't come here looking for something in particular (you could take all day to find it as things are a little all over the shop), but do come to spend a blissful hour thumbing your way through CDs and vinyl just like in the old days.

CHOCOLALABELGA
FOOD

Map p232 (☑91 843 77 57; www.chocolalabelga. com; Calle de Bonetillo 1; ☺10am-2.30pm & 5-8.30pm Tue-Sun; MÓpera) Madrid's love affair with chocolate keeps rolling on. The chocolates from the Belgian homeland of chocolatier Paul-Hector Bossier are, as you would expect, sinfully delicious, with plenty of modern flavours blended in.

LA LIBRERÍA
BOOKS

Map p232 (☑91 454 00 18; Calle Mayor 80; ☺10am-2pm & 5-8pm Mon-Fri, 11am-2pm Sat; MÓpera, Sol) This bookshop may be small, but it's the place to find books (mostly in Spanish) covering everything to do with Madrid, from coffee-table books to histories of every *barrio* (district) in the capital.

GOURMET EXPERIENCE
FOOD & DRINK

Map p232 (☑91 379 80 00; www.elcorteingles.es; 9th fl, Plaza del Callao 9; ☺10am-10pm Mon-Sat; MCallao) On a winning perch high above the Plaza del Callao and with stunning views down Gran Vía is a food court and this fabulous store for foodies looking for Spanish products, including cheeses, wines, cured meats and craft Spanish beers.

LIBRERÍA DE SAN GINÉS
BOOKS

Map p232 (☑91 366 46 86; Pasadizo de San Ginés 2; ☺10am-8.30pm; MSol) With its wooden shutters and old-style clutter, this second-hand bookshop is an utterly charming little corner of old Madrid. Most books are in Spanish but there are a few English titles and bibliophiles will love the atmosphere as much as what's for sale.

LA CENTRAL DE CALLAO
BOOKS, SOUVENIRS

Map p232 (☑917 90 99 30; www.lacentral.com; Postigo de San Martín 8; ☺9.30am-10pm Mon-Fri, 10am-10pm Sat, 10am-9.30pm Sun; MCallao) Inhabiting an old palace, La Central is a fabulous multistorey bookstore, cafe and purveyor of better-than-average Madrid souvenirs.

FNAC
DEPARTMENT STORE

Map p232 (☑91 595 61 00; www.fnac.es; Calle de Preciados 28; ☺10am-9.30pm Mon-Sat, 11.30-9.30pm Sun; MCallao) This four-storey megastore has a terrific range of CDs, as well as DVDs, video games, electronic equipment and books (including English-and other foreign-language titles); there's a large children's section on the 4th floor.

La Latina & Lavapiés

Neighbourhood Top Five

1 Moving from bar to bar ordering wine and tapas along **Calle de la Cava Baja** (p74), one of the world's great culinary streets.

2 Looking for Goya under the fourth-largest church dome in the world at the **Basílica de San Francisco El Grande** (p70).

3 Joining the local crowds on Sunday mornings for **El Rastro** (p72), one of Europe's busiest flea markets and a Madrid institution.

4 Getting to the heart of medieval Madrid in the delightfully sloping **Plaza de la Paja** (p71), the gateway to Madrid's Moorish Quarter, La Morería.

5 Letting flamenco fill your soul with a live performance at **Corral de la Morería** (p80).

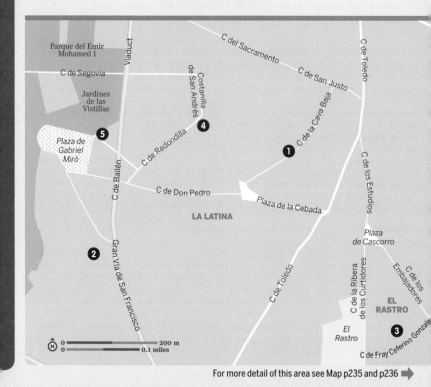

For more detail of this area see Map p235 and p236 ➡

Explore: La Latina & Lavapiés

La Latina's proximity to Plaza Mayor and the downtown area make it an easy area to dip into. Need a break nursing a mojito on a warm afternoon? Head for Plaza de la Paja and linger for as much time as you can spare. Eager to understand the buzz surrounding tapas and the local passion for going on a tapas crawl? Most evenings of the week are busy along Calle de la Cava Baja, but early Sunday lunchtime when the Rastro crowds pour into La Latina is when you'll most appreciate being here.

With few sights to speak of, Lavapiés is a good place for an afternoon stroll or an evening spent catching the sights and sounds of Madrid's most multicultural corner. Access to Lavapiés is either a steep downhill walk from La Latina or an easy stroll along Calle de Argumosa from near the lower end of the Paseo del Prado.

Belonging to and connecting both neighbourhoods is El Rastro, which centres on Calle de la Ribera de los Curtidores. Quiet and really rather pretty for six days of the week, it gets overwhelmed on Sundays when market stalls spill out onto the surrounding streets. To make the most of your El Rastro experience, get here early to avoid the crowds, or stay long enough to join the post-market dispersal into La Latina's tapas bars.

Local Life

→ **Hang out** On Sunday afternoons after El Rastro's clamour has faded and the tapas crowds are thinning, head for the Plaza de la Puerta de Moros for an infectious street party.

→ **Mojitos** Many people in Madrid reckon the mojitos at Delic (p78) are the city's best. The other half of the population might just vote for Taberna Chica (p79), just around the corner. Why not try both?

→ **Local tradition** In Madrid 1pm Sunday is *la hora del vermut* (vermouth hour), when friends and families head out for a quick aperitif before Sunday lunch. Calle de la Cava Baja is the epicentre of this long-standing, civilised tradition.

Getting There & Away

→ **Metro** Unless you're walking from Plaza Mayor (an easy, agreeable stroll), La Latina metro station (line 5) is the best metro station both for the tapas bars of La Latina and El Rastro; Tirso de Molina station (line 1) is also OK.

→ **Metro** If you're only visiting Lavapiés or don't mind a steep uphill climb to La Latina, Lavapiés station (line 3) is your best bet.

Lonely Planet's Top Tip

If you can't stomach an entire meal of *cocido* (meat-and-chickpea stew), or if you just want to see what all the fuss is about, head to Malacatín (p74) where the *degustación de cocido* (taste of *cocido;* €5) at the bar is a great way to try Madrid's favourite dish without going all the way – although locals might say it's a bit like smoking without inhaling.

LA LATINA & LAVAPIÉS

✕ Best Places to Eat

→ Casa Lucio (p76)
→ Taberna Matritum (p74)
→ Txirimiri (p77)
→ Juana La Loca (p77)
→ Almendro 13 (p77)
→ Posada de la Villa (p77)

For reviews, see p74 →

🍷 Best Places to Drink

→ Delic (p78)
→ Taberna Tempranillo (p78)
→ Gau&Café (p78)
→ Café del Nuncio (p79)
→ El Eucalipto (p79)
→ El Viajero (p79)

For reviews, see p78 →

◎ Best Churches

→ Basílica de San Francisco El Grande (p70)
→ Iglesia de San Andrés (p71)
→ Basílica de Nuestra Señora del Buen Consejo (p73)
→ Capilla del Obispo (p71)

For reviews, see p70 →

BASÍLICA DE SAN FRANCISCO EL GRANDE

The recently restored Basílica de San Francisco El Grande is a leading candidate for the title of Madrid's favourite church. Its imposing scale, artworks by master painters and the presence of St Francis de Assisi in the story of the church's origins add both a whiff of legend and an unmistakable sense of gravitas.

The Dome

You could easily spend an hour admiring the basilica's frescoed dome whose eight main panels are devoted to the Virgin Mary. This is the largest-diameter dome in Spain and the fourth largest in the world, with a height of 56m (or 72m above the church's floor) and diameter of 33m.

St Francis & Sabatini

Legend has it that St Francis of Assisi built a chapel on this site in 1217. The current version was designed by Francesco Sabatini in the 18th century. He also designed the Puerta de Alcalá and finished off the Palacio Real, and his unusual floor plan has a circular nave surrounded by chapels.

Goya

Of all the basilica's chapels, most people rush to the Capilla de San Bernardino, where the central fresco was painted by Goya in the early stages of his career. Unusually, Goya has painted himself into the scene (he's the one in the yellow shirt on the right).

Museum Artworks

A series of corridors behind the high altar (accessible only as part of the guided visit) is lined with works of art from the 17th to 19th centuries; highlights include a painting by Francisco de Zurbarán, and another by Francisco Pacheco, the father-in-law and teacher of Velázquez. In the sacristy, watch out for the fine Renaissance *sillería* (the sculpted walnut seats where the church's superiors would meet).

DON'T MISS...

➡ The Dome
➡ St Francis & Sabatini
➡ Goya
➡ Museum artworks

PRACTICALITIES

➡ Map p236
➡ Plaza de San Francisco 1
➡ adult/concession €3/2
➡ ⊘ mass 8-10.30am Mon-Sat, museum 10.30am-12.30pm & 4-6pm Tue-Sun Sep-Jun, 10.30am-12.30pm & 5-7pm Tue-Sun Jul & Aug
➡ Ⓜ La Latina, Puerta de Toledo

SIGHTS

BASÍLICA DE SAN
FRANCISCO EL GRANDE　　CHURCH
See p70.

MUSEO DE SAN ISIDRO　　MUSEUM
Map p236 (Museo de los Orígenes; ☑91 366
74 15; www.madrid.es; Plaza de San Andrés 2;
⊙9.30am-8pm Tue-Sun Sep-Jul, 9.30am-2.30pm
Tue-Fri & 9.30am-8pm Sat & Sun Aug; ⓂLa Latina)
FREE This engaging museum occupies the
spot where San Isidro Labrador ended his
days around 1172. A particular highlight is
the large model based on Pedro Teixeira's
famous 1656 map of Madrid. Of great historical interest (though not much to look
at) is the 'miraculous well', where the saint
called forth water to slake his master's
thirst. In another miracle, the son of the
saint's master fell into a well, whereupon
Isidro prayed and prayed until the water
rose and lifted his son to safety.

The museum is housed in a largely new
building with a 16th-century Renaissance
courtyard and a 17th-century chapel. Apart
from the focus on San Isidro, the collection
has archaeological finds from the Roman
period, including a 4th-century mosaic
found on the site of a Roman villa in the
barrio (district) of Carabanchel, maps, scale
models, paintings and photos of Madrid
down through the ages.

IGLESIA DE SAN ANDRÉS　　CHURCH
Map p236 (Plaza de San Andrés 1; ⊙8am-1pm
& 6-8pm Mon-Sat, 8am-1pm Sun; ⓂLa Latina)
This proud church is more imposing than
beautiful and what you see today is the
result of restoration work completed after
the church was gutted during the civil war.
Stern, dark columns with gold-leaf capitals
against the rear wall lead your eyes up into
the dome – all rose, yellow and green, and
rich with sculpted floral fantasies and cherubs poking out of every nook and cranny.

CAPILLA DEL OBISPO　　CHURCH
Map p236 (☑91 559 28 74; reservascapilladel
obispo@archimadrid.es; Plaza de la Paja; admission €2; ⊙10am-12.30pm Tue, 4-5.30pm Thu;
ⓂLa Latina) The Capilla del Obispo is a
hugely important site on the historical map
of Madrid. It was here that San Isidro Labrador, patron saint of Madrid, was first buried. When the saint's body was discovered
there in the late 13th century, two centuries
after his death, decomposition had not yet

set in. Thus it was that King Alfonso XI
ordered the construction in San Andrés of
an ark to hold his remains and a chapel in
which to venerate his memory.

In 1669 (47 years after the saint was canonised) the last of many chapels was built
on the site and that's what you see today.
Don't go looking for the saint's remains
though – San Isidro made his last move
to the Basílica de Nuestra Señora del Buen
Consejo (p73) in the 18th century. From
Tuesday to Friday at 12.30pm, stop by for
the sung service 'Oficio del Mediodía'.

Visits are by 40-minute guided tour only,
and advance reservations must be made at
the Museo de la Catedral y Cúpula in the
Catedral de Nuestra Señora de la Almudena
(p55).

PLAZA DE LA PAJA　　SQUARE
Map p236 (Straw Square; ⓂLa Latina) Around
the back of the Iglesia de San Andrés, the
delightful Plaza de la Paja slopes down into
the tangle of lanes that once made up Madrid's Muslim quarter. In the 12th and 13th
centuries, the city's main market occupied
the square. At the top of the square is the
Capilla del Obispo, while down the bottom
of Plaza de la Paja, the walled 18th-century
Jardín del Príncipe Anglona (⊙10am-10pm
Apr-Oct, 10am-6.30pm Nov-Mar) is a peaceful
garden.

LA MORERÍA　　HISTORIC SITE
Map p236 (ⓂLa Latina) The area stretching northwest from the Iglesia de San
Andrés to the viaduct was the heart of
the *morería* (Moorish Quarter). Strain
the imagination a little and the maze
of winding and hilly lanes even now retains a whiff of the North African *medina*.

ⓘ VISITING BASÍLICA DE SAN FRANCISCO EL GRANDE

Entry to the Basílica de San Francisco
El Grande is free during morning Mass
times, but there is no access to the
museum and the lights in the Capilla
de San Bernardino won't be on to illuminate the Goya. The same problem
applies Friday afternoons or Saturday
when there are often weddings. At
all other times, visit is by Spanish-
language guided tour (included in the
admission price).

LA LATINA & LAVAPIÉS SIGHTS

TOP SIGHT
EL RASTRO

On Sunday mornings this is the place to be, with all of Madrid converging on El Rastro in search of a bargain or simply to soak up the atmosphere. Back in the 17th and 18th centuries, El Rastro was largely dedicated to a meat market (*rastro* means 'stain', in reference to the trail of blood left behind by animals dragged down the hill). The road leading through the market, Calle de la Ribera de los Curtidores, translates as Tanners' Alley.

You could easily spend an entire morning inching your way down the hill and the maze of streets that hosts El Rastro. Cheap clothes, luggage, old flamenco records, even older photos of Madrid, faux designer purses, grungy T-shirts, household goods and electronics are the main fare. For every 10 pieces of junk, there's a real gem (a lost masterpiece, an Underwood typewriter) waiting to be found. Antiques are also a major drawcard with a concentration of stores at Nuevas Galerías and Galerías Piquer; Plaza General Vara del Rey also has some curious bric-a-brac.

A word of warning: pickpockets love El Rastro as much as everyone else, so keep a tight hold on your belongings and don't keep valuables in easy-to-reach pockets.

DON'T MISS...

➡ Antiques
➡ Sense of history
➡ Treasure hunt

PRACTICALITIES

➡ Map p235
➡ Calle de la Ribera de los Curtidores
➡ ⏰8am-3pm Sun
➡ Ⓜ La Latina

This is where the Muslim population of Mayrit was concentrated in the wake of the 11th-century Christian takeover of the town.

VIADUCT &
CALLE DE SEGOVIA   HISTORIC SITE
Map p236 (ⓂÓpera) High above Calle de Segovia, Madrid's viaduct, which connects La Morería with the cathedral and royal palace, was built in the 19th century and replaced by a newer version in 1942; the plastic barriers were erected in the late 1990s to prevent suicide jumps. Before the viaduct was built, anyone wanting to cross from one side of the road or river to the other was obliged to make their way down to Calle de Segovia and back up the other side.

If you feel like re-enacting the journey, head down to Calle de Segovia and cross to the southern side. Just east of the viaduct, on a characterless apartment block wall (No 21), is a **coat of arms**, one of the city's oldest. The site once belonged to Madrid's Ayuntamiento.

A punt would ferry people across what was then a trickling tributary of the Río Manzanares. You could follow that former trickle's path west, down to the banks of the Manzanares and a nine-arched bridge, the **Puente de Segovia**, which Juan de Herrera built in 1584.

JARDINES DE LAS VISTILLAS   GARDENS
Map p236 (ⓂÓpera) West across Calle de Bailén from La Morería are the *terrazas* (open-air cafes) of Jardines de Las Vistillas, which offer one of the best vantage points in Madrid for a drink, with views towards the Sierra de Guadarrama. During the civil war, Las Vistillas was heavily bombarded by nationalist troops from the Casa de Campo, and they in turn were shelled from a republican bunker here.

IGLESIA DE SAN PEDRO EL VIEJO   CHURCH
Map p236 (☎91 365 12 84; Costanilla de San Pedro; ⓂLa Latina) This fine old church is one of the few remaining windows on post-Muslim Madrid, most notably its clearly Mudéjar (a Moorish architectural style) brick bell tower, which dates from the 14th century. The church is generally closed to the public, but it's arguably more impressive from the outside; the Renaissance doorway has stood since 1525. If you can peek inside, the nave dates from the 15th century, although the interior largely owes its appearance to 17th-century renovations.

The church is the focus of important Good Friday celebrations. Along with the Iglesia de San Nicolás de los Servitas (p60), the Iglesia de San Pedro El Viejo is one of very few sites where traces of Mudéjar Madrid remain in situ. Otherwise, you need to visit Toledo, 70km south of Madrid, to visualise what Madrid once was like.

BASÍLICA DE NUESTRA SEÑORA DEL BUEN CONSEJO
CHURCH

Map p236 (☑91 369 20 37; Calle de Toledo 37; ◷7.30am-1pm & 6-9pm; Ⓜ Tirso de Molina, La Latina) Towering above the northern end of bustling Calle de Toledo, and visible through the arches from Plaza Mayor, this imposing church long served as the city's de facto cathedral until the Catedral de Nuestra Señora de la Almudena (p55) was completed in 1992. Still known to locals as the Catedral de San Isidro, the austere baroque basilica was founded in the 17th century as the headquarters for the Jesuits.

The basilica is today home to the remains of the city's main patron saint, San Isidro (in the third chapel on your left after you walk in). His body, apparently remarkably well preserved, is only removed from here on rare occasions, such as in 1896 and 1947 when he was paraded about town in the hope he would bring rain (he did, at least in 1947). Official opening hours aren't always to be relied upon.

INSTITUTO DE SAN ISIDRO
HISTORIC BUILDING

Map p236 (☑91 365 12 71; Calle de Toledo 39; Ⓜ Tirso de Molina, La Latina) Next door to the Basílica de San Isidro, the Instituto de San Isidro once went by the name of Colegio Imperial and, from the 16th century on, was where many of the country's leading figures were schooled by the Jesuits. You can wander in and look at the elegant courtyard.

PLAZA DE LAVAPIÉS
SQUARE

Map p235 (Ⓜ Lavapiés) The triangular Plaza de Lavapiés is one of the few open spaces in Lavapiés and is a magnet for all that's good (a thriving cultural life) and bad (drugs and a high police presence) about the *barrio*. It's been cleaned up a little in recent years and the Teatro Valle-Inclán (p81), on the southern edge of the plaza, is a stunning contemporary addition to the eclectic Lavapiés streetscape.

To find out what makes this *barrio* tick, consider dropping into the **Asociación de Vecinos La Corrala** (☑91 467 05 09; www.lavapiesdiaynoche.org; Calle de Lavapiés 38), the local neighbours' association just up the hill from the plaza, where staff are happy to highlight all that's good about Lavapiés without dismissing its problems.

LA CORRALA
HISTORIC BUILDING

Map p235 (cnr Calles de Mesón de Paredes & del Tribulete; Ⓜ Lavapiés) One building that catches the community spirit of the lively *barrio* of Lavapiés is La Corrala, an example of an intriguing traditional (if much tidied up) tenement block, with long communal balconies built around a central courtyard; working-class Madrid was once strewn with buildings like this and very few survive. Almost opposite are the ruins of an old church, now converted into a library and the stunning Gau&Café (p78).

LA CASA ENCENDIDA
CULTURAL CENTRE

(☑902 430322; www.lacasaencendida.es; Ronda de Valencia 2; ◷10am-10pm Tue-Sun; Ⓜ Embajadores) This cultural centre is utterly unpredictable, if only because of the quantity and scope of its activities – everything from exhibitions and cinema sessions to workshops and more. The focus is often on international artists or environmental themes and, if it has an overarching theme, it's the alternative slant it takes on the world.

LA LATINA & LAVAPIÉS SIGHTS

MADRID'S OLDEST STREET?

There are numerous candidates for the title of Madrid's oldest street. Calle del Arenal stakes a strong claim, although the date when it ceased to be a small river and became a street remains unresolved by historical records. According to the historian Rafael Fraguas, the oldest street in Madrid is Calle de Grafal, which dates back to 1190 when it was called Calle del Santo Grial. But not that you'd notice: in the midst of La Latina's medieval streets, Calle de Grafal is not the prettiest thoroughfare in the *barrio* (district), with largely modern brick apartment blocks. It runs southwest off Plaza de Segovia Nueva between Calle de Toledo and Calle de la Cava Baja.

WORTH A DETOUR

MADRID RÍO

For decades, nay centuries, Madrid's Río Manzanares (Manzanares River) was a laughing stock. In the 17th century, renowned Madrid playwright Lope de Vega described the beautiful Puente de Segovia over the river to be a little too grand for the 'apprentice river'. He suggested the city buy a bigger river or sell the bridge. Thus it remained until the 21st century, when Madrid's town hall decided to bring the river up to scratch.

Planned before the economic crisis swung a wrecking ball through the city's long list of planned infrastructure projects, the Madrid Río development saw the M-30 motorway driven underground and vast areas – up to 500,000 sq metres by some estimates – of abandoned riverside land turned into parkland that one former mayor described as 'a giant green carpet'. A summer beach à la Paris, bike paths, outdoor cafes and children's playgrounds are all part of the mix in this attractive 10km-long stretch of parkland. It has also made more accessible a number of appealing sights.

Contemporary arts centre **Matadero Madrid** (☑91 252 52 53; www.mataderomadrid. com; Paseo de la Chopera 14; ⓂLegazpi), opened in 2007, is a stunning multipurpose space south of the centre. Occupying the converted buildings of the old Arganzuela livestock market and slaughterhouse, Matadero Madrid covers almost 15 hectares and hosts cutting-edge drama, musical and dance performances and exhibitions on architecture, fashion, literature and cinema. It's a dynamic space and its proximity to the newly landscaped riverbank makes for a non-touristy alternative to sightseeing in Madrid, not to mention a brilliant opportunity to see the latest avant-garde theatre or exhibitions.

Atlético de Madrid's home, **Estadio Vicente Calderón** (☑902 530500, 91 366 47 07; www.clubatleticodemadrid.com; Paseo de la Virgin del Puerto; ⓂPirámides) isn't as large as Real Madrid's (Vicente Calderón seats a mere 60,000), but what it lacks in size it makes up for in raw energy. To see a game try phoning, but you're most likely to manage a ticket if you turn up at the ground a few days before the match.

The three easiest ways to access Madrid Río:

➡ Walk down the hill from La Latina to the western end of Calle de Segovia.

➡ Follow the signs from Matadero Madrid.

➡ Catch the metro to the Estadio Vicente Calderón.

EATING

La Latina is Madrid's best *barrio* (district) for tapas, complemented by a fine selection of sit-down restaurants. If you're planning only one tapas crawl while in town, do it here in Calle de la Cava Baja and the surrounding streets. Lavapiés is more eclectic and multicultural and, generally speaking, the further down the hill you go, the better it gets, especially along Calle de Argumosa.

BAR SANTURCE SPANISH €

Map p235 (☑646 238303; www.barsanturce. com; Plaza General Vara del Rey 14; bocadillos from €2.50, raciónes from €3.90; ⓗ9am-3pm Tue-Sun; ⓂLa Latina) This basic bar is famous for its *sardinas a la plancha* (sardines cooked on the grill) and *pimientos de padrón* (fiery green peppers). It's wildly popular on Sundays during El Rastro when it can be difficult to even get near the bar. The

media ración (half-serve) of six sardines for €2 is Madrid's best bargain.

★**TABERNA MATRITUM** MODERN SPANISH €€

Map p236 (☑91 365 82 37; Calle de la Cava Alta 17; mains €12-22; ⓗ1.30-4pm & 8.30pm-midnight Wed-Sun, 8.30pm-midnight Mon & Tue; ⓂLa Latina) This little gem is reason enough to detour from the more popular Calle de la Cava Baja next door. The seasonal menu here encompasses terrific tapas, salads and generally creative cooking – try the *cocido* croquettes or the winter *calçots* (large spring onions) from Catalonia. The wine list runs into the hundreds and it's sophisticated without being pretentious. Highly recommended.

MALACATÍN MADRILEÑO €€

Map p235 (☑91 365 52 41; www.malacatin.com; Calle de Ruda 5; mains €11-15; ⓗ11am-5.30pm Mon-Wed & Sat, 11am-5.30pm Thu & Fri, closed

Aug; Ⓜ La Latina) If you want to see *madrile-ños* (people from Madrid) enjoying their favourite local food, this is one of the best places to do so. The clamour of conversation bounces off the tiled walls of the cramped dining area adorned with bullfighting memorabilia. The speciality is as much *co-cido* as you can eat (€20). The *degustación de cocido* (taste of *cocido;* €5) at the bar is a great way to try Madrid's favourite dish.

OLIVEROS
MADRILEÑO €€

Map p236 (☑91 354 62 52; Calle de San Milán 4; mains €12-18; ⊙1-4pm & 8.30pm-midnight Tue-Sat, noon-6pm Sun mid-Sep–mid-Aug; Ⓜ La Latina) This famous old *taberna* (tavern) has been in the Oliveros family since 1921 and nothing seems to have changed much since it opened. It's a tiny, warm, bottle-lined den that doesn't disappoint with its local dishes of *cocido a la madrileña* (meat-and-chickpea stew) or dishes like *solomillo ibérico al Cabrales* (sirloin with blue cheese).

ENE RESTAURANTE
MODERN SPANISH €€

Map p236 (☑91 366 25 91; www.enerestaurante. com; Calle del Nuncio 19; mains €9-18, brunch €22; ⊙1-4pm & 8.30pm-midnight daily, brunch 12.30-4.30pm Sat & Sun; Ⓜ La Latina) Just across from Iglesia de San Pedro El Viejo, one of Madrid's oldest churches, Ene is anything but old world. The design is contemporary if a little worn, awash with reds and purples, while the young and friendly waiters circulate to the tune of lounge music. The food is Span-ish-Asian fusion (try the peeled aubergine with tahini, peppermint sauce and yoghurt).

ENOTABERNA DEL LEÓN DE ORO
SPANISH €€

Map p236 (☑91 119 14 94; www.posadadelle-ondeoro.com; Calle de la Cava Baja 12; tapas from €3.50, mains €14-20; ⊙1-4pm & 8pm-midnight; Ⓜ La Latina) The stunning restoration work that brought to life the Posada del León de Oro (p173) also bequeathed to La Latina a fine new bar-restaurant. The emphasis is on matching carefully chosen wines with creative dishes (such as baby squid with po-tato emulsion and rucula pesto) in a casual atmosphere. There are also plenty of gins to choose from. It's a winning combination.

CASA CURRO
ANDALUCIAN €€

Map p236 (☑91 364 22 59; www.tabernacasacurro. com; Calle de la Cava Baja 23; raciónes €6-12; ⊙noon-4.30pm & 6.30pm-1.30am Wed & Thu, noon-1.30am Fri-Sun, 7pm-1.30am Tue; Ⓜ La Latina) This fine An-dalucian bar serves tasty salted prawns from Huelva and all manner of other dishes from Spain's south – the emphasis is on seafood, but there are a few token meat dishes as well. The look is modern and they have a passion for good food without too many elaborations.

LA ANTOÑITA
MODERN SPANISH €€

Map p236 (☑91 119 14 24; www.posadadeldragon. com; Calle de la Cava Baja 14; tapas from €5.90, mains from €13; ⊙2-11pm; Ⓜ La Latina) The res-taurant of the stunning new hotel Posada del Dragón (p173), this fine place retains

---

THE ORIGIN OF TAPAS

There are many stories concerning the origin of tapas.

One of the most common explanations derives from the fact that medieval Spain was a land of isolated settlements and people on the move – traders, pilgrims, emigrants and journeymen – who had to cross the lonely high plateau of Spain en route elsewhere. All along the way, travellers holed up in inns where the keepers, concerned about drunk-en men on horseback setting out from their village, developed a tradition of putting a 'lid' (*tapa*) of food atop a glass of wine or beer. The purpose was partly to keep the bugs out, but primarily to encourage people not to drink on an empty stomach.

Another story holds that in the 13th century, doctors to King Alfonso X advised him to accompany his small sips of wine between meals with small morsels of food. So enamoured with the idea was the monarch that he passed a law requiring all bars in Castilla to follow suit.

In Andalucía in particular, it is also claimed that the name 'tapa' attained wide-spread usage in the early 20th century when King Alfonso XIII stopped at a beachside bar in Cádiz province. When a strong gust of wind blew sand in the king's direction, a quick-witted waiter rushed to place a slice of *jamón* (ham) atop the king's glass of sherry. The king so much enjoyed the idea (and the *jamón*) that, wind or no wind, he ordered another and the name stuck.

LOCAL KNOWLEDGE

CHILDREN'S PLAYGROUNDS

There are very few open spaces or areas for children to run free in La Latina and even fewer in Lavapiés. The only dedicated children's playground is in Plaza de Tirso de Molina, while Plaza de la Paja (p71) and Jardines de Las Vistillas (p72) have at least some space to stretch little legs.

some features (exposed wooden beams, heavy stonework) of the original inn. There's tapas at the bar and a range of creative dishes ('fun market cooking') in the rear sit-down restaurant, such as *secreto ibérico con guacamole* (pork fillet with guacamole) or the five types of marinated tomatoes.

LA BUGA DEL LOBO   SPANISH €€

Map p235 (☑91 467 61 51; www.labocadellobo. com; Calle de Argumosa 11; mains €12-21; ☺11am-2am Wed-Mon; ⓜLavapiés) La Buga del Lobo has been one of those 'in' places in cool and gritty Lavapiés for years now and it's still hard to get a table. The atmosphere is bohemian and inclusive, with funky, swirling murals, contemporary art exhibitions and jazz or lounge music. The food's traditional with a few creative detours.

SANLÚCAR   ANDALUCIAN €€

Map p236 (☑91 354 00 52; www.latabernasanlucar. com; Calle de San Isidro Labrador 14; mains €12-20; ☺1-5pm&8.30pm-midnightTue-Sat,1-5pmSun; ⓜLa Latina) The seafood-dominated cooking of the Andalucian province of Cádiz is what this place is all about, with every imaginable sea creature (usually lightly fried) sharing the menu with gazpacho served in a tall drinking glass. Quiet at lunchtimes (except on Sundays), it can be hard to find a place in the evenings.

LA MUSA LATINA   MODERN SPANISH €€

Map p236 (☑91 354 02 55; www.grupolamusa. com/restaurante-lamusalatina; Costanilla de San Andrés 1; cold/hot tapas from €4/6, mains €4.50-12; ☺10am-1am Mon-Wed, 10am-1.30am Thu, 10am-2am Fri & Sat, 10am-1am Sun; ⓜLa Latina) Laid-back La Musa Latina has an ever-popular dining area and food that's designed to bring a smile to your face – the hanging kebabs have achieved something close to legendary status. The outdoor tables are lovely when the weather's warm, while the downstairs bar in the former wine cellar,

complete with table tennis and table football, is also charming.

EL ESTRAGÓN   VEGETARIAN €€

Map p236 (☑91 365 89 82; www.elestragonvegetariano.com; Plaza de la Paja 10; mains €8-15; ☺11.30am-midnight; ⓩ; ⓜLa Latina) A delightful spot for crêpes, veggie burgers and other vegetarian specialities, El Estragón is undoubtedly one of Madrid's best vegetarian restaurants, although attentive vegans won't appreciate the use of butter. Apart from that, we're yet to hear a bad word about it, and the *menú del día* (daily set menu; from €9) is one of Madrid's best bargains.

VIVA BURGER   VEGETARIAN €€

Map p236 (☑91 366 33 49; www.vivaburger.es; Costanilla de San Andrés 16; mains €9-13; ☺11am-midnight Sun-Thu, 11am-2am Fri & Sat; ⓩ; ⓜLa Latina) With a terrace that spills over onto Plaza de la Paja, Viva Burger does veggie burgers of the highest order – the patties are made from soya beans, nuts and fruit, and come with all manner of options, from blue cheese and mushrooms to seaweed, ginger, asparagus and red onions.

NAÏA BISTRO   FUSION €€

Map p236 (☑91 366 27 83; www.naiabistro.com; Plaza de la Paja 3; mains €10-19; ☺1.30-4.30pm & 8.30-11.30pm Tue-Sun; ⓜLa Latina) Naïa has a real buzz about it, with modern Spanish cuisine, a chill-out lounge downstairs and outdoor tables on lovely Plaza de la Paja. The emphasis throughout is on natural ingredients, healthy food and exciting tastes.

★CASA LUCIO   SPANISH €€€

Map p236 (☑91 365 82 17, 91 365 32 52; www. casalucio.es; Calle de la Cava Baja 35; mains €18-28; ☺1-4pm&8.30pm-midnight, closed Aug; ⓜLa Latina) Lucio has been wowing *madrileños* with his light touch, quality ingredients and home-style local cooking since 1974 – think eggs (a Lucio speciality) and roasted meats in abundance. There's also *rabo de toro* (bull's tail) during the Fiestas de San Isidro Labrador and plenty of *rioja* (red wine) to wash away the mere thought of it.

The lunchtime *guisos del día* (stews of the day), including *cocido* on Wednesdays, are also popular. Casa Lucio draws an august, well-dressed crowd, which has included the former king of Spain, former US president Bill Clinton and Penélope Cruz.

POSADA DE LA VILLA MADRILEÑO €€€
Map p236 (☑91 366 18 80; www.posadadelavilla. com; Calle de la Cava Baja 9; mains €19-28; ◷1-4pm & 8pm-midnight Mon-Sat, 1-4pm Sun, closed Aug; Ⓜ La Latina) This wonderfully restored 17th-century *posada* (inn) is something of a local landmark. The atmosphere is formal, the decoration sombre and traditional (heavy timber and brickwork), and the cuisine decidedly local – roast meats, *cocido*, *callos* (tripe) and *sopa de ajo* (garlic soup).

RESTAURANTE JULIÁN DE TOLOSA NAVARRAN €€€
Map p236 (☑91 365 82 10; www.casajuliandetolosa.com; Calle de la Cava Baja 18; mains €23-30;

LA LATINA TAPAS

Almendro 13 (Map p236; ☑91 365 42 52; Calle del Almendro 13; mains €7-15; ◷1-4pm & 7.30pm-midnight Sun-Thu, 1-5pm & 8pm-1am Fri & Sat; Ⓜ La Latina) Almendro 13 is a charming *taberna* (tavern) where you come for traditional Spanish tapas with an emphasis on quality rather than frilly elaborations. Cured meats, cheeses, omelettes and variations on these themes dominate the menu. It serves both *raciónes* and half-sized plates – a full *ración* of the famously good *huevos rotos* ('broken eggs') served with *jamón* (ham) and thin potato slices is a meal in itself. The only problem is that the wait for a table requires the patience of a saint, so order a wine or *manzanilla* (dry sherry) and soak up the buzz.

Taberna Txakolina (Map p236; ☑91 366 48 77; www.tabernatxakolinamadrid.com; Calle de la Cava Baja 26; tapas from €4; ◷8pm-midnight Tue, 1-4pm & 8pm-midnight Wed-Sat, 1-4pm Sun; Ⓜ La Latina) Taberna Txakolina calls its *pintxos* 'high cuisine in miniature'. If ordering tapas makes you nervous because you don't speak Spanish or you're not quite sure how it works, it couldn't be easier here – they're lined up on the bar, Basque style, in all their glory, and you can simply point. Whatever you order, wash it down with a *txacoli*, a sharp Basque white.

Txirimiri (Map p236; ☑91 364 11 96; www.txirimiri.es; Calle del Humilladero 6; tapas from €4; ◷noon-4.30pm & 8.30pm-midnight Mon-Sat, closed Aug; Ⓜ La Latina) This *pintxos* (Basque tapas) bar is a great little discovery just down from the main La Latina tapas circuit. Wonderful wines, gorgeous *pinchos* (tapas; the *tortilla de patatas* – potato and onion omelette – is superb) and fine risottos add up to a pretty special combination.

Juana La Loca (Map p236; ☑91 364 05 25; Plaza de la Puerta de Moros 4; tapas from €5, mains €8-19; ◷noon-1am Tue-Sun, 8pm-1am Mon; Ⓜ La Latina) Juana La Loca does a range of creative tapas with tempting options lined up along the bar, and more on the menu that they prepare to order. But we love it above all for its *tortilla de patatas*, which is distinguished from others of its kind by the caramelised onions – simply wonderful.

La Chata (Map p236; ☑91 366 14 58; Calle de la Cava Baja 24; mains €10-23, tapas from €3; ◷1-4pm & 8.30pm-midnight Thu-Mon, 8.30pm-midnight Tue & Wed; Ⓜ La Latina) Behind the lavishly tiled facade, La Chata looks for all the world like a neglected outpost of the past. The decor may be rundown and the bullfighting memorabilia not to everyone's taste, but this is an essential stop on a tapas tour of La Latina. Don't come here without ordering a *cazuela* (stew cooked and served in a ceramic pot, including wild mushrooms with clams).

Lamiak (Map p236; ☑91 365 52 12; Calle de la Cava Baja 42; raciónes €5-11; ◷1-4pm & 8pm-midnight Tue-Sat, 1-4pm Sun; Ⓜ La Latina) Another casual La Latina tapas bar, Lamiak is filled to the rafters on Sundays and busy at other times, thanks to its contemporary exhibitions, laid-back atmosphere, good wines and tapas dishes such as tomato with goat's cheese and caramelised onion, or red pepper stuffed with seafood.

Taberna de Antonio Sánchez (Map p235; ☑91 539 78 26; www.tabernaantoniosanchez. com; Calle de Mesón des Paredes 13; tapas from €4.50; ◷noon-4pm & 8pm-midnight Mon-Sat, noon-4.30pm Sun; 🛜; Ⓜ Tirso de Molina) Behind one of the best-preserved old *taberna* facades in Madrid hides this gem of a traditional tapas bar famous for its Madrid specialities – *tortilla de san isidro*, *callos* (tripe), *morcilla* (blood sausage), *huevos estrellados* (fried eggs) and a host of other excellent local favourites.

ℹ SPANISH FAST FOOD & WHERE TO EAT BETWEEN MEALS

If you just can't wait until lunch- and/or dinner-time ticks around, there are a number of options scattered around La Latina in particular.

➡ **La Antoñita** (p75) Creative tapas.

➡ **La Buga del Lobo** (p76) Traditional tapas.

➡ **La Musa Latina** (p76) Fun tapas.

➡ **El Estragón** (p76) All-day vegetarian.

➡ **Alma de Ibérico** (p82) *Jamón* rolls.

➡ **Cervecería 100 Montaditos** (Map p236; www.100montaditos.com; Calle del Nuncio; montaditos €0.50-3; ☺noon-midnight; ⓂLa Latina) Mini-rolls.

☺noon-4pm & 9pm-midnight Tue-Sun, noon-4pm Mon; ⓂLa Latina) Navarran cuisine is treated with respect at this classy place that's popular with celebrities and well-regarded by food critics. There are only four main dishes to choose from – two fish and two meat – and they haven't changed in years, but there's still a contemporary feel, and why change the *chuletón* (T-bone steak) when it's already close to perfection?

🍷 DRINKING & NIGHTLIFE

For those whose idea of a night out reaches its limit at the sensible hour of 3am, La Latina and Lavapiés are ideal. Both have memorable cafes and bars that you could spend more than a single night exploring, but few stay open until dawn. Most nights (and Sunday afternoons), crowds of happy *madrileños* hop from bar to bar across La Latina. This is a *barrio* beloved by a discerning crowd of twenty- and thirty-something urban sophisticates who ensure that there's little room to move in the good places and that the bad ones don't survive long; the scene is a little more diverse on Sundays as crowds fan out from El Rastro. Most of the action takes place along Calle de la Cava Baja, the western end of Calle del Almendro and Plaza de la Paja. Many of these places are better known for their tapas, but they're equally great for a drink. Lavapiés is a completely different kettle of fish altogether – working-class and multicultural, with an alternative, often bohemian crowd and quirky bars brimful of personality. Not everyone loves Lavapiés, but we do.

⭐**DELIC** BAR

Map p236 (📞91 364 54 50; www.delic.es; Costanilla de San Andrés 14; ☺11am-2am Sun & Tue-Thu, 11am-2.30am Fri & Sat; ⓂLa Latina) We could go on for hours about this long-standing cafe-bar, but we'll reduce it to its most basic elements: nursing an exceptionally good mojito (€8) or three on a warm summer's evening at Delic's outdoor tables on one of Madrid's prettiest plazas is one of life's great pleasures. Bliss. Due to local licensing restrictions, the outdoor tables close two hours before closing time, whereafter the intimate interior is almost as good. It also has an especially wide range of gin and tonics.

⭐**TABERNA TEMPRANILLO** WINE BAR

Map p236 (Calle de la Cava Baja 38; ☺1-3.30pm & 8pm-midnight Tue-Sun, 8pm-midnight Mon; ⓂLa Latina) You could come here for the tapas, but we recommend Taberna Tempranillo primarily for its wines, of which it has a selection that puts numerous Spanish bars to shame; many wines are sold by the glass. It's not a late-night place, but it's always packed in the early evening and on Sundays after El Rastro.

GAU&CAFÉ CAFE

Map p235 (www.gaucafe.com; 4th fl, Calle de Tribulete 14; ☺11am-midnight Mon-Fri, 1.30pm-midnight Sat; ⓂLavapiés) Decoration that's light and airy, with pop-art posters of Audrey Hepburn and James Bond. A large terrace with views over the Lavapiés rooftops. A stunning backdrop of a ruined church atop which the cafe sits. With so much else going for it, it almost seems incidental that it also serves great teas, coffees and snacks (as well as meals). The cafe is around 300m southwest of Plaza de Lavapiés along Calle de Tribulete; look for the glass doors (which close at 11.30pm).

CAFÉ DEL NUNCIO
BAR

Map p236 (✆91 366 08 53; Calle de Segovia 9; ⏰12.30pm-2.30am Sun-Thu, 12.30pm-3am Fri & Sat; Ⓜ️La Latina) Café del Nuncio straggles down a laneway to Calle de Segovia. You can drink on one of several cosy levels inside or, better still in summer, enjoy the outdoor seating that one local reviewer likened to a slice of Rome. By day it's an old-world cafe, but by night it's one of the best no-frills bars in the *barrio*.

EL EUCALIPTO
COCKTAIL BAR

Map p235 (Calle de Argumosa 4; ⏰5pm-2am Sun-Thu, 5pm-3am Fri & Sat; Ⓜ️Lavapiés) This fine little bar is devoted to all things Cuban – from the music to the clientele and the Caribbean cocktails (including non-alcoholic), it's a sexy, laid-back place. Not surprisingly, the mojitos are a cut above average, but the juices and daiquiris also have a loyal following.

EL VIAJERO
BAR

Map p236 (✆91 366 90 64; www.elviajeromadrid. com; Plaza de la Cebada 11; ⏰5pm-2am Tue-Fri, noon-2.30am Sat, noon-midnight Sun; Ⓜ️La Latina) The undoubted highlight of this landmark of La Latina nights is the rooftop *terraza*, which boasts fine views down onto the thronging streets. When the weather's warm, it's nigh on impossible to get a table. Our secret? It often closes the *terraza* around 8pm to spruce it up a little; be ready to pounce when it reopens and thereafter guard your table with your life.

LA INQUILINA
BAR

Map p235 (✆91 468 25 33; www.lainquilina.es; Calle del Ave María 39; ⏰7pm-2.30am Tue-Thu, 7pm-3am Fri, 1pm-2.30am Sat & Sun; Ⓜ️Lavapiés) One of our favourite *barrio* bars, La Inquilina has a cool-and-casual vibe and deep roots in the Lavapiés soil. Contemporary artworks by budding local artists adorn the walls and you can either gather around the bar or have a table out the back. It's a small slice of sophistication in a *barrio* not known for such characteristics.

NUEVO CAFÉ DE BARBIERI
CAFE

Map p235 (✆91 527 36 58; Calle del Ave María 45; ⏰4pm-1am Tue-Thu, 4pm-2am Fri & Sat, 4-11pm Sun; Ⓜ️Lavapiés) This *barrio* classic is Lavapiés' grandest old cafe, the sort of place for quiet conversation amid the columns and marble-topped tables right on the Plaza de Lavapiés. It does everything from coffees and cakes to cocktails and it's

always been an intellectual hub of *barrio* life. If it all sounds a bit staid, it gets busy with a younger crowd on weekend nights.

TABERNA CHICA
BAR

Map p236 (✆683 269114; Costanilla de San Pedro 7; ⏰8pm-2am Mon-Thu, 5pm-2am Fri, 1pm-2am Sat & Sun; Ⓜ️La Latina) Most of those who come to this narrow little bar are after one of two things, the famous Santa Teresa rum that comes served in an extra-large mug, or some of the finest mojitos in Madrid. The music is chill-out with a nod to lounge, which makes it an ideal pit-stop if you're hoping for conversation.

BONANNO
WINE BAR

Map p236 (✆91 366 68 86; www.elbonanno.com; Plaza del Humilladero 4; ⏰noon-2am; Ⓜ️La Latina) If much of Madrid's nightlife starts too late for your liking, Bonanno could be for you. It made its name as a cocktail bar, but many people come here for the great wines and it's usually full of young professionals from early evening onwards. Be prepared to snuggle up close to those around you if you want a spot at the bar.

⭐ ENTERTAINMENT

⭐ CASA PATAS
FLAMENCO

Map p235 (✆91 369 04 96; www.casapatas.com; Calle de Cañizares 10; ⏰shows 10.30pm Mon-Thu, 9pm & midnight Fri & Sat; Ⓜ️Antón Martín, Tirso de Molina) One of the top flamenco stages in Madrid, this *tablao* (flamenco venue) always offers flawless quality that serves as a good introduction to the art. It's not the friendliest place in town, especially if

DISAPPEARED LA LATINA LANDMARKS

The narrow streets of **Calle de la Cava Alta** and **Calle de la Cava Baja** delineate where the second line of medieval Christian city walls ran from the 13th century onwards. They continued north along what is now **Calle de los Cuchilleros** (Knifemakers St) and along the **Calle de la Cava de San Miguel**, and were superseded by the third circuit of walls, which was raised in the 15th century. The *cavas* (caves or cellars) were initially ditches dug in front of the walls, later used as refuse dumps and finally given over to housing when the walls no longer served any defensive purpose.

Just west of La Latina metro station, the busy and bar-strewn corner of Madrid marked by the ill-defined **Plaza de la Cebada** (Barley Square) occupies an important historical space. In the wake of the Christian conquest, the square was, for a time, the site of a Muslim cemetery, and the nearby **Plaza de la Puerta de Moros** (Moors' Gate) underscores that this area was long home to the city's Muslim population. Plaza de la Cebada later became a popular spot for public executions – until well into the 19th century, the condemned would be paraded along Calle de Toledo, before turning into the square and mounting the gallows. Later the plaza was the site of one of the largest markets in Madrid.

you're only here for the show, and you're likely to be crammed in a little, but no one complains about the standard of the performances (admission including drink €36).

★**CORRAL DE LA MORERÍA**   FLAMENCO
Map p236 (☑91 365 84 46; www.corraldelamoreria.com; Calle de la Morería 17; ☺7pm-12.15am, shows 9pm & 10.55pm; ⓂÓpera) This is one of the most prestigious flamenco stages in Madrid, with 50 years' experience as a leading venue and top performers most nights. The stage area has a rustic feel, and tables are pushed up close. Admission including drink costs from €39; set menus from €40.

MARULA CAFÉ   LIVE MUSIC
Map p236 (☑91 366 15 96; www.marulacafe.com; Calle de Caños Viejos 3; ☺11pm-5am Sun-Thu, 11.30pm-6am Fri & Sat; ⓂLa Latina) An Afro hairstyle would be the perfect look here, where the music (concerts at 11.30pm, DJs until sunrise) is all about funk, soul, jazz, music from the American South, Afrobeat and even a little hip hop. It's a club with attitude and always has a great rhythm. Admission ranges from free to €10. It's a little hard to find – it's almost under the viaduct just down the hill from Calle de la Morería.

CONTRACLUB   LIVE MUSIC
Map p236 (☑91 365 55 45; www.contraclub.es; Calle de Bailén 16; ☺10pm-6am Wed-Sat; ⓂLa Latina) ContraClub is a crossover live-music venue and nightclub, with an eclectic mix of live music (pop, rock, indie, singer-songwriter, blues...). After the live acts (from 10pm), the resident DJs serve up equally diverse beats (indie, pop, funk and soul) to make sure you don't move elsewhere. Admission €6 to €15.

SALA JUGLAR   LIVE MUSIC
Map p235 (☑91 528 43 81; www.salajuglar.com; Calle de Lavapiés 37; ☺9.30pm-3am Sun-Wed, to 3.30am Thu-Sat; ⓂLavapiés) One of the hottest spots in Lavapiés, this great venue hosts a largely bohemian crowd who come from all over the city for a fine roster leavened with flamenco (9pm Sunday), rock and fusion. Admission from €5 to €15. After the live acts leave the stage around midnight, it's DJ-spun tunes.

EL DESPERTAR   JAZZ
Map p235 (☑91 530 80 95; www.cafeeldespertar.com; Calle de la Torrecilla del Leal 18; ☺7.30pm-late Wed-Mon; ⓂAntón Martín) El Despertar is all about jazz down to its roots. Everything about this place harks back to the 1920s, with a commitment to old-style jazz and decor to match from its days as a meeting point for the *barrio*'s intelligentsia. There are live performances every Friday and Saturday, as well as most Thursdays, Sundays and many other nights. Concerts start between 8.30pm and 11pm; check the website for details. Admission ranges from free to €6.

EL RINCÓN DEL ARTE NUEVO   LIVE MUSIC
Map p236 (☑91 365 50 45; www.elrincondelartenuevo.com; Calle de Segovia 17; ☺8.30pm-5am Sun-Thu, 8.30pm-6am Fri & Sat; ⓂLa Latina) With more than 30 years in the business, this small venue knows what its punters

like and serves up a nightly feast of singer-songwriters, blues, rock and '70s, '80s and '90s tunes for an appreciative crowd. The acts are as diverse as the genre itself, with Melendi, Fran Postigo and Diego El Negro among those to have taken the stage here. Concerts start between 9.30pm and 12.30am and sometimes stray into flamenco or pop. Admission from €5 to €10.

LA ESCALERA DE JACOB THEATRE
Map p235 (☑625 721745; www.teatro laescaleradejacob.com; Calle de Lavapiés 9; ☺6.30pm-midnight Mon-Thu, 6.30pm-2am Fri, 10.30am-2am Sat, 10.30am-midnight Sun; ⓂAntón Martín, Tirso de Molina) As much a cocktail bar as a live-music venue or theatre, 'Jacob's Ladder' is one of Madrid's most original stages. Magicians, storytellers, children's theatre, live jazz and other genres are all part of the mix. This alternative slant on life makes for some terrific live performances (concerts from €6). Regardless of what's on, it's worth stopping by here for creative cocktails that you won't find anywhere else – the *fray aguacate* (Frangelico, vodka, honey, avocado and vanilla) should give you an idea of how far they go.

CINE DORÉ CINEMA
Map p235 (☑91 369 11 25; www.mecd.gob.es/cultura-mecd/areas-cultura/cine/mc/fe/cinedore/programacion.html; Calle de Santa Isabel 3; ☺Tue-Sun; ⓂAntón Martín) The National Film Library offers fantastic classic and vanguard films for just €2.50.

TEATRO CIRCO PRICE THEATRE
(☑91 528 98 65; www.teatrocircoprice.es; Ronda de Atocha 35; ⓂLavapiés, Embajadores, Atocha) Just south of Lavapiés, this modern theatre does a little bit of everything from concerts and circuses to dance performances.

TEATRO PAVÓN THEATRE
Map p235 (☑91 528 28 19; http://teatroclasico.mcu.es; Calle de los Embajadores 9; ⓂLa Latina, Tirso de Molina) The home of the National Classical Theatre Company, this theatre has a regular calendar of classical shows by Spanish and European playwrights.

TEATRO VALLE-INCLÁN THEATRE
Map p235 (☑91 505 88 01; http://cdn.mcu.es; Plaza de Lavapiés; ⓂLavapiés) The stunning refurbishment of this theatre has brought new life (and quality plays) to this once run-down corner of Lavapiés. Located on the southern end of the Plaza de Lavapiés, it is now the headquarters for the Centro Dramático Nacional (National Drama Centre) and puts on landmark plays by (mostly) Spanish playwrights such as Valle-Inclán and Fernando Arrabal. Tickets from €15.

 SHOPPING

La Latina may be a largely after-dark and weekend affair, but its appeal to a hip, well-to-do urban crowd has attracted small boutiques, especially those specialising in designer jewellery, to the narrow streets. This is also the *barrio* that throngs with Sunday bargain hunters, drawn here by El Rastro (which tumbles down into Lavapiés), and you'll also come across curio shops so specialised that you'll wonder how they ever keep going.

★**HELENA ROHNER** JEWELLERY
Map p236 (☑91 365 79 06; www.helenarohner.com.es; Calle del Almendro 4; ☺9am-8.30pm Mon-Fri, noon-2.30pm & 3.30-8pm Sat, noon-3pm Sun; ⓂLa Latina, Tirso de Molina) One of Europe's most creative jewellery designers, Helena Rohner has a spacious boutique in La Latina. Working with silver, stone, porcelain, wood and Murano glass, she makes inventive pieces and her work is a regular feature of Paris fashion shows. In her own words, she seeks to recreate 'the magic of Florence, the vitality of London and the luminosity of Madrid'.

★**BOTERÍA JULIO RODRÍGUEZ** HANDICRAFTS
(☑91 365 66 29; www.boteriajuliorodriguez.es; Calle del Águila 12; ☺9.30am-2pm & 4.30-8pm Mon-Fri, 10am-1.30pm Sat; ⓂLa Latina) One of the last makers of traditional Spanish wineskins left in Madrid, Botería Julio Rodríguez is like a window on a fast-disappearing world. They make a great gift and, as you'd expect, they're in a different league from the cheap wineskins found in souvenir shops across downtown Madrid.

DE PIEDRA JEWELLERY
Map p236 (☑91 365 96 20; www.depiedracreaciones.com; Calle del Almendro 10; ☺11am-2pm & 5-8pm Mon-Fri, 11am-7pm Sat, noon-3pm Sun; ⓂLa Latina) Necklaces, earrings, bracelets and home decorations fill this lovely showroom. Silver and semiprecious stones are the mainstays.

ALMA DE IBÉRICO
FOOD & DRINK

Map p236 (☎91 366 15 24; www.julianbecerro. com; Calle de la Cava Baja 41; ☺10am-10pm; Ⓜ La Latina) This purveyor of some of the finest *embutidos* (cured meats) is perfectly at home on this, one of Madrid's most important culinary streets. The *jamón* comes from the renowned Salamanca region of Castilla y León, with cheeses and other products from around Spain.

CARAMELOS PACO
FOOD

Map p236 (☎91 365 42 58, 91 354 06 70; www. caramelospaco.com; Calle de Toledo 53-55; ☺9.30am-2pm & 5-8.30pm Mon-Fri, 9.30am-2pm Sat, 11am-3pm Sun; Ⓜ La Latina) A sweet shop that needs to be seen to be believed, Caramelos Paco has been indulging children and adults alike since 1934 and it remains unrivalled when it comes to variety. There's almost nothing you can't find here and even the shop window is a work of art.

ACEITUNAS JIMÉNEZ
FOOD

Map p235 (☎91 365 46 23; Plaza del General Vara del Rey 14; ☺10.30am-2.30pm & 3.30-8pm Mon-Thu, 10.30am-2.30pm Fri & Sat, 10.30am-3pm Sun; Ⓜ La Latina) An institution during a Sunday stroll in El Rastro, this tiny shop serves up pickled olives in plastic cups and in all manner of varieties, as well as aubergines, garlics and anything else they've decided to soak in lashings of oil and/or vinegar.

🏃 SPORTS & ACTIVITIES

ACADEMIA AMOR DE DIOS
DANCE COURSE

Map p235 (Centro de Arte Flamenco y Danza Española; ☎91 360 04 34; www.amordedios.com; 1st fl, Calle de Santa Isabel 5; Ⓜ Antón Martín) This is the best-known course for flamenco dancing (and probably the hardest to get into). Although it's more for budding professionals (as the list of past graduates attests to) than casual visitors, it does have the odd Spanish-language '*cursillo*' (little course) that runs for a day or more. It's on the top floor of the Mercado de Antón Martín.

Even if you've no plans to enrol, if you're keen to immerse yourself in the flamenco world, it may be worth stopping by just for a look.

FUNDACIÓN CONSERVATORIO CASA PATAS
DANCE COURSE

Map p235 (www.conservatorioflamenco.org; Calle de Cañizares 10; one-hour class from €17, per month €40-75, joining fee €3; Ⓜ Antón Martín, Tirso de Molina) There's every conceivable type of flamenco instruction here, including dance, guitar, singing and much more. It's upstairs from the Casa Patas flamenco venue.

Sol, Santa Ana & Huertas

Neighbourhood Top Five

1 Discovering the little-known artistic riches of the **Real Academia de Bellas Artes de San Fernando** (p85).

2 Spending a lazy afternoon watching the world go by from one of the outdoor tables on **Plaza de Santa Ana** (p87).

3 Stepping back in time at **La Venencia** (p91), an old-style sherry bar that captures the spirit of a Spain that long ago disappeared elsewhere.

4 Getting into the swing at **Café Central** (p93), an art-deco salon that's internationally recognised as one of the world's finest jazz clubs.

5 Losing yourself in the lanes of the **Barrio de las Letras** (p89), with its echoes of Cervantes and Madrid's literary past.

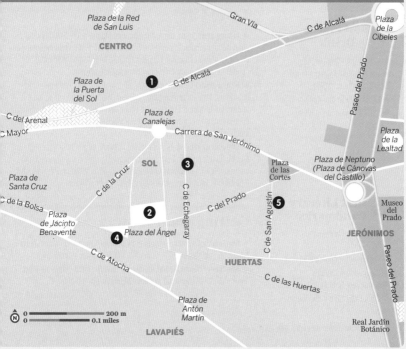

For more detail of this area see Map p238 ➡

Lonely Planet's Top Tip

The Real Academia de Bellas Artes de San Fernando may have a collection the envy of many a European gallery but it's free if you come on a Wednesday. And unlike free days at other better-known Madrid art galleries, you'll see no discernible rise in visitor numbers on the day, allowing you to enjoy it both for free and in peace.

 Best Places to Eat

→ Casa Alberto (p89)

→ La Terraza del Casino (p91)

→ Casa Labra (p88)

→ Lhardy (p91)

→ Vi Cool (p89)

For reviews, see p88 ➡

🍷 **Best Places to Drink**

→ La Venencia (p91)

→ La Azotea (Círculo de Bellas Artes; p88)

→ El Imperfecto (p92)

→ La Terraza del Urban (p92)

→ Taberna La Dolores (p92)

For reviews, see p91 ➡

👁 **Best Literary Landmarks**

→ Calle de Cervantes 2 (p89)

→ Casa Alberto (p89)

→ Convento de las Trinitarias (p89)

→ Casa de Lope de Vega (p87)

For reviews, see p87 ➡

Explore: Sol, Santa Ana & Huertas

Sol, Santa Ana and Huertas together make up Madrid's most clamorous corner. So many explorations of this neighbourhood begin in the Plaza de la Puerta del Sol, the pulsing heart of downtown Madrid, then move on to nearby Plaza de Santa Ana and the tangle of laneways that tumble down the hillside to the east.

And yet, there are subtle differences between the two squares. Sol is above all a crossroads, a place for people to meet before fanning out across the city. There are reasons to linger, but for the most part a sense of transience is what prevails. And Sol is always busy, no matter the hour.

Plaza de Santa Ana, on the other hand, is a destination in its own right, a stirringly beautiful square that has become emblematic of a city intent on living the good life. It is also a place of many moods. On a sunny weekday afternoon, it can be quiet (by its own rather noisy standards), a place to nurse a wine as you plot your path through the city. This is when the Barrio de las Letras is also at its most accessible, its streets suitably sedate for a *barrio* (district) rich in literary resonance. But come most nights of the week, Santa Ana and the surrounding streets crescendo into life, an explosion of noise and revelry that ripples out across the city.

Local Life

→ **Hang out** 1pm on a Sunday is known in Madrid as *la hora del vermut* (vermouth hour). Mostly this resonates in neighbouring La Latina (p69), but Casa Alberto (p89) is arguably the real star of the hour.

→ **Flamenco** One of the great flamenco venues of Old Madrid, the extravagantly tiled Villa Rosa (p94) has mercifully shed its recent past as a fairly run-of-the-mill nightclub and returned to its roots. It even starred in a Pedro Almodóvar movie.

→ **Meeting point** It's a cliché whose time has passed for the in-crowd, but meeting at the paving stone that marks Spain's Kilometre Zero on Plaza de la Puerta del Sol (p86) is a time-honoured local tradition.

Getting There & Away

→ **Metro** Sol metro station is one of the most useful in Madrid, with lines 1, 2 and 3 all passing through.

→ **Metro** Other useful stations are Sevilla (line 2) and Tirso de Molina and Antón Martín (both line 1).

TOP SIGHT
REAL ACADEMIA DE BELLAS ARTES DE SAN FERNANDO

Madrid's 'other' art gallery, the Real Academia de Bellas Artes has for centuries played a pivotal role in the artistic life of the city. As the royal fine arts academy, it has nurtured local talent, thereby complementing the royal penchant for drawing the great international artists of the day into their realm. The pantheon of former alumni reads like a who's who of Spanish art, and the collection that now hangs on the academy's walls is a suitably rich one.

DON'T MISS...

➡ Zurbarán & El Greco
➡ 1st-Floor Masters
➡ Picasso, Sorolla & Gris

PRACTICALITIES

➡ Map p238
➡ ☎91 524 08 64
➡ www.realacademia bellasartessanfernando. com
➡ Calle de Alcalá 13
➡ adult/child €6/free, free Wed
➡ ⊙10am-3pm Tue-Sun Sep-Jul
➡ ⓂSol, Sevilla

Bastion of Tradition

In any other city, this gallery would be a standout attraction, but in Madrid it often gets forgotten in the rush to the Prado, Thyssen or Reina Sofía. Nonetheless a visit here is a fascinating journey into another age of art; when we tell you that Picasso and Dalí studied at this academy, but found it far too stuffy for their liking, you'll get an idea of what to expect. A centre of excellence since Fernando VI founded the academy in the 18th century, it remains a stunning repository of works by some of the best-loved old masters.

Zurbarán & El Greco

The 1st floor, mainly devoted to 16th- to 19th-century paintings, is the most noteworthy of those in the academic gallery. Among relative unknowns, you come across a hall of works by Zurbarán (especially arresting is the series of full-length portraits of white-cloaked friars) and a *San Jerónimo* by El Greco.

Other 1st-Floor Masters

At a 'fork' in the exhibition, a sign points right to rooms 11 to 16, the main one showcasing Alonso Cano (1601–67) and José de Ribera (1591–1652). In the others a couple of minor portraits by Velázquez hang alongside the occasional Rubens, Tintoretto and Bellini, which have somehow been smuggled in. Rooms 17 to 22 offer a space full of Bravo Murillo and last, but most captivating, 13 pieces by Goya, including self-portraits, portraits of King Fernando VII and the infamous minister Manuel Godoy, along with one on bullfighting.

Modern Art

The 19th and 20th centuries are the themes upstairs. It's not the most extensive or engaging modern collection, but you'll find drawings by Picasso as well as works by Joaquín Sorolla, Juan Gris, Eduardo Chillida and Ignacio Zuloaga, in most cases with only one or two items each.

◉ SIGHTS

REAL ACADEMIA DE BELLAS
ARTES DE SAN FERNANDO
MUSEUM

See p85.

PLAZA DE LA PUERTA DEL SOL
SQUARE

Map p238 (Ⓜ Sol) The official centre point of Spain is a gracious, crowded hemisphere of elegant facades. It is, above all, a crossroads: people here are forever heading somewhere else, on foot, by metro (three lines cross here) or by bus (many lines terminate and start nearby). Hard as it is to believe now, in Madrid's earliest days, the Puerta del Sol (Gate of the Sun) was the eastern gate of the city.

The main building on the square houses the regional government of the Comunidad de Madrid. The **Casa de Correos**, as it is called, was built as the city's main post office in 1768. The clock was added in 1856 and on New Year's Eve people throng the square to wait impatiently for the clock to strike midnight, and at each gong swallow a grape – not as easy as it sounds! On the footpath outside the Casa de Correos is a plaque marking Spain's **Kilometre Zero**, the point from which Spain's network of roads is measured.

The semicircular junction owes its present appearance in part to the Bourbon king Carlos III (r 1759–88), whose **equestrian statue** (complete with his unmistakable nose) stands in the middle. Look out for the **statue of a bear** nuzzling a *madroño* (strawberry tree) at the plaza's eastern end; this is the official symbol of the city.

GRAN VÍA
STREET

(Ⓜ Gran Vía, Callao) It's difficult to imagine Madrid without Gran Vía, the grand boulevard lined with towering belle-époque facades that climbs up through the centre of Madrid from Plaza de España then down to Calle de Alcalá. But it has only existed since 1910, when it was bulldozed through what was then a labyrinth of old streets. Fourteen streets disappeared off the map, as did 311 houses, including one where Goya had once lived.

Plans for the boulevard were first announced in 1862 and so interminable were the delays that a famous *zarzuela* (satirical musical comedy), *La Gran Vía*, first performed in 1886, was penned to mock the city authorities. It may have destroyed whole *barrios* (districts), but Gran Vía is still considered one of the most successful examples of urban planning in central Madrid since the late 19th century.

One eye-catching building, the **Edificio Carrión** (Ⓜ Callao), on the corner of Gran Vía and Calle de Jacometrezo, was Madrid's first pre-WWI tower-block apartment hotel. Also dominating the skyline about one-third of the way along Gran Vía is the 1920s-era **Telefónica Building**, which was for years the highest building in the city. During the civil war, when Madrid was besieged by Franco's forces and the boulevard became known as 'Howitzer Alley' due to the artillery shells that rained down upon it, the Telefónica building was a favoured target.

Among the more interesting buildings is the stunning, French-designed **Edificio Metrópolis** (Map p238; Ⓜ Banco de España), built in 1905, which marks the southern end of Gran Vía. The winged victory statue atop its dome was added in 1975 and is best seen from Calle de Alcalá or Plaza de la Cibeles. A little up the boulevard is the **Edificio Grassy** (Map p238; Ⓜ Banco de España), with the Rolex sign and built in 1916. With its circular 'temple' as a crown, and profusion of arcs and slender columns,

---

THINGS THEY SAID ABOUT...PUERTA DEL SOL

During the first days I could not tear myself away from the square of the Puerta del Sol. I stayed there by the hour, and amused myself so much that I should like to have passed the day there. It is a square worthy of its fame; not so much on account of its size and beauty as for the people, life and variety of spectacle which it presents at every hour of the day. It is not a square like the others; it is a mingling of salon, promenade, theatre, academy, garden, a square of arms, and a market. From daybreak until one o'clock at night, there is an immovable crowd, a crowd that comes and goes through the 10 streets leading into it, and a passing and mingling of carriages which makes one giddy.

Edmondo De Amicis, Spain & the Spaniards (1885)

TOP SIGHT
PLAZA DE SANTA ANA

The Plaza de Santa Ana is a delightful confluence of elegant architecture and irresistible energy. Situated in the heart of Huertas, it was laid out in 1810 during the controversial reign of Joseph Bonaparte, giving breathing space to what had hitherto been one of Madrid's most claustrophobic *barrios* (districts). The plaza became a focal point for the intellectual life of the day, and the cafes surrounding the plaza thronged with writers, poets and artists engaging in endless *tertulias* (literary and philosophical discussions).

Echoes of this literary history survive in the statues of the 17th-century writer Calderón de la Barca and **Federíco García Lorca** (added in 1998 on the 100th anniversary of his birth), and in the **Teatro Español** (p95; formerly the Teatro del Príncipe) at the plaza's eastern end, and continue down into the Barrio de las Letras (p89). Culture of a very different kind – bullfighting – also took centre stage here, with many a (long-since-disappeared) bullfighting bar nearby and the Gran Victoria Hotel (now Me by Meliá; p175) the hotel of choice for Spain's best *toreros* (bullfighters). Apart from anything else, the plaza is the starting point for many a long Huertas night.

DON'T MISS...

➡ Outdoor Tables
➡ Lorca Statue
➡ Teatro Español

PRACTICALITIES

➡ Map p238
➡ Plaza de Santa Ana
➡ M Sevilla, Sol, Antón Martín

SOL, SANTA ANA & HUERTAS SIGHTS

it's one of the most elegant buildings along Gran Vía.

Otherwise Gran Vía is home to around twice as many businesses (over 1050 at last count) as homes (nearly 600); over 13,000 people work along the street; and up to 55,000 vehicles pass through every day (including almost 185 buses an hour during peak periods). There are over 40 hotels on Gran Vía, but sadly just three of the 15 cinemas for which Gran Vía was famous remain.

CASA DE LOPE DE VEGA   MUSEUM

Map p238 (📞91 429 92 16; www.casamuseolopedevega.org; Calle de Cervantes 11; ⊙guided tours every 30min 10am-6pm Tue-Sun; Mantón Martín) **FREE** Lope de Vega may be little known outside the Spanish-speaking world, but he was one of the greatest playwrights ever to write in Spanish, not to mention one of Madrid's favourite and most colourful literary sons. The house, which was restored in the 1950s, is filled with memorabilia related to his life and times. Out the back is a tranquil garden, a rare haven of birdsong.

Scandalously, he shared the house, where he lived and wrote for 25 years until his death in 1635, with a mistress and four children by three different women; Lope de Vega's house was a typical *casa de malicia* (house of ill repute).

ATENEO CIENTÍFICO, LITERARIO Y ARTÍSTICO DE MADRID   BUILDING

Map p238 (📞91 429 17 50, ext 124; www.ateneodemadrid.com; Calle del Prado 21; guided visits €3; ⊙guided visits 10am-1pm Mon-Fri Sep-Jul; MSevilla) This venerable club of learned types was founded in 1821, although the building took on its present form in 1884. Its library prompted Benito Pérez Galdós to describe it as the most important 'intellectual temple' in Madrid and a reference point for the thriving cultural life of the Barrio de las Letras. Guided visits take you into the foyer and the upstairs library, a jewel of another age, with dark timber stacks, weighty tomes and creakily quiet reading rooms dimly lit with desk lamps.

CONGRESO DE LOS DIPUTADOS   LANDMARK

Map p238 (📞91 390 65 25; www.congreso.es; Plaza de las Cortes; ⊙guided tours 10.30am-12.30pm Sat Sep-Jul; MSevilla) **FREE** Spain's lower house of parliament was originally a Renaissance building, but it was completely revamped in

1850 and given a facade with a neoclassical portal. The imposing lions watching over the entrance were smelted from cannons used in Spain's African wars during the mid-19th century. On the day that they were mounted outside the parliament building, one irreverent Madrid newspaper wrote 'And what mouths they have! One might imagine them to be parliamentarians!'

It was here, on 11 February 1981, that renegade members of Spain's Guardia Civil launched a failed coup attempt. Be sure to bring your passport if you want to visit.

CÍRCULO DE BELLAS ARTES
ARTS CENTRE, VIEWPOINT

Map p238 (La Azotea; ☑91360 54 00; www.circulo bellasartes.com; Calle de Alcalá 42; admission to centre/roof terrace €1/4; ☺roof terrace 9am-2am Mon-Thu, 9am-2.30am Fri, 11am-2.30am Sat & Sun; Ⓜ Banco de España) For some of Madrid's best views, take the lift to the 7th floor of the 'Fine Arts Circle'. You can almost reach out and touch the glorious dome of the Edificio Metrópolis and otherwise take in Madrid in all its finery, including the distant mountains. Two bars, lounge music and places to recline add to the experience. Downstairs, the centre has exhibitions, concerts, short films and book readings. There's also a fine belle-époque cafe (p92) on the ground floor.

EATING

Sol has something for everyone, but the noise surrounding Huertas nightlife can obscure the fact that the *barrio* is a terrific place to eat out. Its culinary appeal lies in a hotchpotch of styles rather than any overarching personality. There are bastions of traditional cooking with restaurants serving Basque, Galician, Andalucian and Italian cuisine. When you factor in the fine bars and pulsing nightlife, it's difficult to find a good reason to leave the *barrio* once the sun goes down.

CASA LABRA
TAPAS €

Map p238 (☑91 532 14 05; www.casalabra.es; Calle de Tetuán 11; tapas from €1.25; ☺11.30am-3.30pm & 6-11pm; Ⓜ Sol) Casa Labra has been going strong since 1860, an era that the decor strongly evokes. Locals love their *bacalao* (cod) and ordering it here – either as deep-fried tapas (*una tajada de bacalao*

goes for €1.30) or as *una croqueta de bacalao* – is a Madrid rite of initiation. As the lunchtime queues attest, they go through more than 700kg of cod every week.

This is also a bar with history – it was where the Partido Socialista Obrero Español (PSOE; Spanish Socialist Party) was formed on 2 May 1879. It was a favourite of Lorca, the poet, as well as appearing in Pío Baroja's novel *La Busca*. It's the sort of place that fathers bring their sons, just as their fathers did before them.

LA GLORIA DE MONTERA
SPANISH €

Map p238 (www.grupandilana.com; Calle del Caballero de Gracia 10; mains €7-13; ☺1.15-4pm & 8.30-11.30pm; Ⓜ Gran Vía) From the same stable as La Finca de Susana, La Gloria de Montera combines classy decor with eminently reasonable prices. It's not that the food is especially creative, but rather the tastes are fresh and the surroundings sophisticated. You'll get a good initiation into Spanish cooking without paying over the odds.

It doesn't take reservations, so turn up early or be prepared to wait.

LA FINCA DE SUSANA
SPANISH €

Map p238 (☑91 369 35 57; www.grupandilana. com/es/restaurantes/la-finca-de-susana; Calle de Arlabán 4; mains €7-12; ☺1-3.45pm & 8.30-11.30pm Sun-Wed, 1-3.45pm & 8.15pm-midnight Thu-Sat; Ⓜ Sevilla) It's difficult to find a better combination of price, quality cooking and classy atmosphere anywhere in Huertas. The softly lit dining area is bathed in greenery and the sometimes innovative, sometimes traditional food draws a hip young crowd. The duck confit with plums, turnips and couscous is a fine choice. No reservations.

LAS BRAVAS
TAPAS €

Map p238 (☑91 522 85 81; www.lasbravas.com; Callejón de Álvarez Gato 3; raciónes €3.75-12; ☺12.30-4.30pm & 7.30pm-12.30am; Ⓜ Sol, Sevilla) Las Bravas has long been the place for a *caña* (small glass of beer) and some of the best *patatas bravas* (fried potatoes with a spicy tomato sauce; €3.75) in town. In fact, their version of the *bravas* sauce is so famous that they patented it. Other good orders include *calamares* (calamari) and *oreja a la plancha* (grilled pig's ear).

The antics of the bar staff are enough to merit a stop, and the distorting mirrors are a minor Madrid landmark. Elbow your way to the bar and be snappy about your orders.

BARRIO DE LAS LETRAS

In medieval Madrid, the Barrio de las Letras – bordered by Plaza de Santa Ana (west), Carrera de San Jerónimo (north), Paseo del Prado (east) and Calle de Atocha (south) – was one of Madrid's most important cultural hubs.

At Calle de Cervantes 11, Lope de Vega (1562–1635), arguably Spain's premier playwright, lived and died, and his house is now a **museum** (p87). But the street on which Lope de Vega's house sits owes its name to an even more famous former resident, Miguel de Cervantes Saavedra (1547–1616). Cervantes, the author of *Don Quijote,* spent much of his adult life in Madrid and lived and died at **Calle de Cervantes 2** (Map p238; MAntón Martín); a plaque (dating from 1834) sits above the door. Sadly, the original building was torn down in the early 19th century despite a plea from King Fernando VII.

When Cervantes died, his body was interred around the corner at the **Convento de las Trinitarias** (Map p238; Calle de Lope de Vega 16; MAntón Martín), which is marked by another plaque. After centuries of mystery, his body was discovered in 2015, although the convent (which is still home to cloistered nuns) remains closed to casual visitors; pass by to see if this has changed.

A **statue of Cervantes** stands in the Plaza de las Cortes, opposite the parliament building.

SOL, SANTA ANA & HUERTAS EATING

VINOS GONZALEZ
TAPAS, DELI €

Map p238 (Calle de León 12; tapas from €3.50; ⏰9.30am-midnight Mon-Thu, 9am-1am Fri & Sat, 11am-6pm Sun; MAntón Martín) Ever dreamed of a deli where you could choose a tasty morsel and sit down and eat it right there? Well, here you can. On offer is a tempting array of cheeses, cured meats and other typically Spanish delicacies. The tables are informal, cafe style and it also does takeaway, but we recommend lingering.

LA PIOLA
ITALIAN €

Map p238 (Calle de León 9; mains from €8; ⏰10am-1am Mon-Thu, 10.30am-2am Fri, 11am-2.30am Sat; MAntón Martín) This charming Italian place is part cafe and part bar. The small range of pasta on offer is well priced and filled with subtle flavours. In addition to the rustic tables and bar stools, there's a sofa that has to be the best seat in the house.

You're likely to find it full most nights of the week, which has as much to do with the atmosphere and cocktails as the food.

ENRIQUE TOMAS
SPANISH €

Map p238 (☎91 299 20 70; www.enriquetomas. com; Calle de la Cruz 25; bocadillos €2.20-3.60; ⏰9am-midnight Mon-Thu, 9am-1am Fri & Sat; MSol) It took far longer than it should but the *jamón*-as-fast-food potential has finally taken hold. This fine example of the genre (which has two shops in London) has all the usual suspects – cheap filled rolls stuffed with *jamón serrano,* paper cones filled with the same and all manner of cured

meats. The welcome addition of a few tables allows you to enjoy it all in-shop.

★CASA ALBERTO
SPANISH, TAPAS €€

Map p238 (☎91 429 93 56; www.casaalberto. es; Calle de las Huertas 18; tapas €4-10, raciónes €6.50-16, mains €14-21; ⏰restaurant 1.30-4pm & 8pm-midnight Tue-Sat, 1.30-4pm Sun, bar 12.30pm-1.30am Tue-Sat & 12.30-4pm Sun, closed Sun Jul & Aug; MAntón Martín) One of the most atmospheric old *tabernas* (taverns) in Madrid, Casa Alberto has been around since 1827 and occupies a building where Cervantes is said to have written one of his books. The secret to its staying power is vermouth on tap, excellent tapas at the bar and fine sit-down meals. Casa Alberto's *rabo de toro* (bull's tail) is famous among aficionados, but it's also known for its pig's trotters, snails, meatballs, croquettes and cod.

★VI COOL
MODERN SPANISH €€

Map p238 (☎91 429 49 13; www.vi-cool.com; Calle de las Huertas 12; mains €8-19; ⏰1.30-4.15pm & 8.30pm-12.15am Tue-Sun; MAntón Martín) Catalan master chef Sergi Arola is one of the most restless and relentlessly creative culinary talents in the country. Aside from his showpiece Sergi Arola Gastro (p155), he has dabbled in numerous new restaurants around the capital and in Barcelona, and this is one of his most interesting yet.

In a modern bar-style space with prices that enable the average mortal to sample his formidable gastronomic skill, dishes might include sardines marinated in oil

LOCAL KNOWLEDGE

CHILDREN'S PLAYGROUNDS

The tight tangle of streets and laneways of these inner-city *barrios* (districts) don't leave a whole lot of space for kids to run free in safety, although some of the streets (including Calle de las Huertas) are partially pedestrianised. The only dedicated play area around here is one of Madrid's smallest, on Plaza de Santa Ana (p87). Otherwise, if you're down the hill, your best bet is to cross the Paseo del Prado and head for the Real Jardín Botánico (p113) or, better still, continue on to the Parque del Buen Retiro (p111).

from sun-dried tomatoes and fresh oregano, or fried prawns with curry and mint. There's another branch in Salamanca.

⭐**RAMIRO'S TAPAS WINE BAR**   TAPAS €€

Map p238 (📞91 843 73 47; Calle de Atocha 51; tapas from €4.50, raciónes from €10; ⏰1-4.30pm & 8-11.30pm Mon-Sat, 1-4.30pm Sun; Ⓜ Antón Martín) One of the best tapas bars to open in Madrid in recent years, this fine gastrobar offers up traditional tapas with subtle but original touches. Most of the cooking comes from Castilla y León but they do exceptional things with cured meats, foie gras and prawns. Highly recommended.

LOS GATOS   TAPAS €€

Map p238 (📞91 429 30 67; Calle de Jesús 2; tapas from €3.50; ⏰11am-2am; Ⓜ Antón Martín) Tapas you can point to without deciphering the menu and eclectic old-world decor (from bullfighting memorabilia to a fresco of skeletons at the bar) make this a popular choice down the bottom end of Huertas. The most popular orders are the *canapés* (tapas on toast), which, we have to say, are rather delicious.

MORATÍN VINOTECA   SPANISH, BISTRO €€

Map p238 (📞91 127 60 85; www.vinotecamoratin. com; Calle de Moratín 36; mains €12-15; ⏰1.30-4pm & 7.30pm-midnight Tue-Sat; Ⓜ Antón Martín) We're yet to hear a bad word about this engaging little bistro down in the Paseo del Prado hinterland. Service is both warm and knowledgable, the food is outstanding (we liked the octopus in olive oil with paprika and coriander on potato parmentier), and the wines are perfectly matched.

EL TRICICLO   MODERN SPANISH €€

Map p238 (📞91 024 47 98; www.eltriciclo.es; Calle de Santa María 28; raciónes €6-21; ⏰1-4pm & 8pm-12.30am Mon-Sat; Ⓜ Antón Martín) A relative newcomer on Madrid's culinary scene, 'The Tricycle' has quickly earned plaudits for its assured fusion cooking that places seasonal ingredients at the centre of everything it does. The approach is also a broad church – with some traditional staples, innovative diversions and international dishes all given space on the menu. You can order full-, half- and even one-third-sized dishes – nice idea.

LA CASA DEL ABUELO   TAPAS €€

Map p238 (📞902 027334; www.lacasadelabuelo. es; Calle de la Victoria 12; raciónes from €9.50; ⏰noon-midnight Sun-Thu, noon-1am Fri & Sat; Ⓜ Sol) The 'House of the Grandfather' is an ageless, popular place, which recently passed its centenary. The traditional order here is a *chato* (small glass) of the heavy, sweet El Abuelo red wine (made in Toledo province) and the heavenly *gambas a la plancha* (grilled prawns) or *gambas al ajillo* (prawns sizzling in garlic on little ceramic plates). They cook more than 200kg of prawns here on a good day. There's another branch over in Salamanca.

MACEIRAS   GALICIAN €€

Map p238 (📞91 429 15 84; Calle de las Huertas 66; mains €7-14; ⏰1.15-4.15pm & 8.30pm-midnight Mon-Wed & Sat, to 1am Thu & Fri, to 11.30pm Sun; Ⓜ Antón Martín) Galician tapas (think octopus, green peppers etc) never tasted so good as in this agreeably rustic bar down the bottom of the Huertas hill, especially when washed down with a crisp white Ribeiro. The simple wooden tables, loyal customers and handy location make this a fine place to rest after (or en route to) the museums along the Paseo del Prado.

Galician music plays in the background and there's another **branch** (Map p238; Calle de Jesús 7; Ⓜ Antón Martín) with similar hours around the corner.

LA HUERTA DE TUDELA   NAVARRAN €€

Map p238 (📞91 420 44 18; www.lahuertade tudela.com; Calle del Prado 15; mains €14-22, set menus €36-44; ⏰1.30-4pm & 8.30-11.30pm Mon-Sat, 1.30-3.30pm Sun; Ⓜ Antón Martín) A bastion of fine cooking from the northern Spanish region of Navarra, La Huerta de Tudela and its chef Ricardo Gil do excellent seasonal vegetable dishes, as well as some outstanding steaks and stews. The superb range of set menus includes one for coeliacs and another for vegetarians and vegans – typical of the thought that goes into this place. The atmosphere is formal, so dress well.

RESTAURANTE INTEGRAL
ARTEMISA   VEGETARIAN €€

Map p238 (☑91 429 50 92; www.restaurantes-vegetarianosartemisa.com; Calle de Ventura de la Vega 4; meals €9-14; ◷1.30-4pm & 9pm-midnight; ☑; ⓂSevilla) With a couple of options for meat eaters, this mostly vegetarian restaurant does a brisk trade with its salads, moussaka and rice dishes. The decor is simple, the service is no-nonsense and the salads are what marks this place out as worthy of a visit. Alternatively, try the *plato degustación* (from €26) for a range of tastes.

★LA TERRAZA DEL
CASINO   MODERN SPANISH €€€

Map p238 (☑91 532 12 75; www.casinodemadrid.es; Calle de Alcalá 15; mains €35-45, lunch set menu €69; ◷1-4pm & 9pm-midnight Mon-Sat; ⓂSevilla) Perched atop the lavish Casino de Madrid building, this temple of haute cuisine is presided over by celebrity chef Paco Roncero and is the proud bearer of two Michelin stars. It's all about culinary experimentation, with a menu that changes as each new idea emerges from the laboratory and moves into the kitchen. The *menú de degustación* (€135) is a fabulous avalanche of tastes.

★LHARDY   SPANISH €€€

Map p238 (☑91 521 33 85; www.lhardy.com; Carrera de San Jerónimo 8; mains €19-38; ◷1-3.30pm & 8.30-11pm Mon-Sat, 1-3.30pm Sun, closed Aug; ⓂSol, Sevilla) This Madrid landmark (from 1839) is an elegant treasure trove of takeaway gourmet tapas downstairs, while the six upstairs dining areas are the upmarket preserve of traditional Madrid dishes with an occasional hint of French influence. House specialities include *cocido a la madrileña* (meat-and-chickpea stew; €36), pheasant and wild duck in an orange perfume.

The quality and service are unimpeachable. A favourite haunt of royalty in the 19th century, Lhardy has drawn the great and good of Madrid ever since.

A TASCA DO BACALHAU
PORTUGÊS   PORTUGUESE €€€

Map p238 (☑91 429 56 75; Calle de Lope de Vega 14; mains from €25; ◷1.30-4pm & 8.30pm-midnight Tue-Sat, 1.30-4pm Sun, closed 1st half Aug; ⓂAntón Martín) One of the few authentic Portuguese restaurants in Madrid, A Tasca do Bacalhau doesn't have a particularly extensive menu, but it's dominated by excellent *bacalhau* (cod) and rice dishes. It claims to have 412 different recipes for cod, although thankfully only a handful of these appear on the menu. If you're not familiar with Portuguese cooking, this is a good place to have your first taste.

SIDRERÍA VASCA ZERAÍN   BASQUE €€€

Map p238 (☑91 429 79 09; www.restaurante-vasco-zerain-sidreria.es; Calle Quevedo 3; mains €14-38; ◷1.30-4pm & 7.30pm-midnight Mon-Sat, 1.30-4pm Sun, closed Aug; ⓂAntón Martín) In the heart of the Barrio de las Letras, this sophisticated restaurant is one of the best places in town to sample Basque cuisine. The essential staples include cider, *bacalao* and wonderful steaks, while there are also a few splashes of creativity thrown in (the secret's in the sauce). We highly recommend the *menú sidrería* (cider-house menu; €36.30).

🍷 DRINKING &
🍸 NIGHTLIFE

Huertas comes into its own after dark and stays that way until close to sunrise – this is one of the iconic neighbourhoods of the Madrid night. Bars are everywhere, from Sol down to the Paseo del Prado hinterland, but it's in Plaza de Santa Ana and along Calle de las Huertas that most of the action is concentrated. Huertas is good at any time of the night, but it's in the live jazz (and other music) venues and nightclubs that it really comes into its own.

★LA VENENCIA   BAR

Map p238 (☑91 429 73 13; Calle de Echegaray 7; ◷12.30-3.30pm & 7.30pm-1.30am; ⓂSol, Sevilla) La Venencia is a *barrio* classic, with fine sherry from Sanlúcar and *manzanilla* from Jeréz poured straight from the dusty wooden barrels, accompanied by a small selection of tapas with an Andalucian bent. Otherwise, there's no music, no flashy decorations; it's all about you, your *fino* (sherry) and your friends. As one reviewer put it, it's 'a classic among classics'.

EL IMPERFECTO
COCKTAIL BAR

Map p238 (Plaza de Matute 2; ⊙5pm-2.30am Mon-Thu, 3pm-2.30am Fri & Sat; Ⓜ Antón Martín) Its name notwithstanding, the 'Imperfect One' is our ideal Huertas bar, with occasional live jazz and a drinks menu as long as a saxophone, ranging from cocktails (€7, or two *mojitos* for €10) and spirits to milkshakes, teas and creative coffees. Its pina colada is one of the best we've tasted and the atmosphere is agreeably buzzy yet chilled.

LA TERRAZA DEL URBAN
COCKTAIL BAR

Map p238 (Ⓙ91 787 77 70; Carrera de San Jerónimo 34; ⊙noon-8pm Sun & Mon, noon-3am Tue-Sat mid-May–Sep; Ⓜ Sevilla) A strong contender with the Roof and Splash Óscar (La Terraza de Arriba; p141) for the prize for best rooftop bar in Madrid, this indulgent terrace sits atop the five-star Urban Hotel and has five-star views with five-star prices. Worth every euro, but it's only open while the weather's warm, usually from sometime in May to latish September. In case you get vertigo, head downstairs to the similarly high-class **Glass Bar** (⊙noon-3am).

THE ROOF
COCKTAIL BAR

Map p238 (Ⓙ91 701 60 20; www.memadrid.com; Plaza de Santa Ana 14; ⊙9pm-1.30am Mon-Thu, 8pm-3am Fri & Sat; Ⓜ Antón Martín, Sol) High above the Plaza de Santa Ana, this sybaritic open-air (7th floor) cocktail bar has terrific views over Madrid's rooftops. The high admission price (€25) announces straight away that riff-raff are not welcome and it's a place for sophisticates, with chill-out areas strewn with cushions, funky DJs and a dress policy designed to sort out the classy from the wannabes. If you don't like heights, consider the equally classy **Midnight Rose** on the ground floor.

CAFÉ DEL CÍRCULO DE BELLAS ARTES
CAFE

Map p238 (Ⓙ91 521 69 42; Calle de Alcalá 42; ⊙9am-1am Sun-Thu, to 3am Fri & Sat; Ⓜ Sevilla) This wonderful belle-époque cafe was designed by Antonio Palacios in 1919 and boasts chandeliers and the charm of a bygone era. Unless you're here between 1.30pm and 4.30pm or after 9pm (when dinners are served), you have to buy a token temporary club membership (€1) to drink here.

It does, however, include access to the centre's exhibitions and it's worth every cent, even if the waiters are not averse to looking aggrieved if you put them out. The entrance is on Calle de Marqués de Casa Riera.

CERVECERÍA ALEMANA
BAR

Map p238 (Ⓙ91 429 70 33; www.cerveceriaalemana.com; Plaza de Santa Ana 6; ⊙11am-12.30am Sun-Thu, to 2am Fri & Sat, closed Aug; Ⓜ Antón Martín, Sol) If you've only got time to stop at one bar on Plaza de Santa Ana, let it be this classic *cervecería* (beer bar), renowned for its cold, frothy beers and a wider selection of Spanish beers than is the norm. It's fine inside, but snaffle a table outside in the plaza on a summer's evening and you won't be giving it up without a fight.

The bar opened in 1904 and this was one of Hemingway's haunts – neither the wood-lined bar nor the bow-tied waiters have changed much since his day.

DOS GARDENIAS
BAR

Map p238 (Ⓙ627 003571; Calle de Santa María 13; ⊙9.30pm-2.30am Tue-Sat; Ⓜ Antón Martín) When Huertas starts to overwhelm, this tranquil little bar is the perfect antidote. The flamenco and chill-out music ensure a relaxed vibe, while sofas, softly lit colours and some of the best mojitos (and exotic teas) in the *barrio* make this the perfect spot to ease yourself into or out of the night.

TABERNA LA DOLORES
BAR

Map p238 (Ⓙ91 429 22 43; Plaza de Jesús 4; ⊙11am-1am; Ⓜ Antón Martín) Old bottles and beer mugs line the shelves behind the bar at this Madrid institution (1908), known for its blue-and-white-tiled exterior and for a thirty-something crowd that often includes the odd *famoso* (celebrity) or two. It claims

---

ⓘ SPANISH FAST FOOD & WHERE TO EAT BETWEEN MEALS

If your tummy starts to rumble at a very un-Spanish hour, there are options from *bocadillos* (filled rolls) to tapas.

➜ **Vinos Gonzalez** (p89) Deli tapas.

➜ **Enrique Tomas** (p89) *Jamón* rolls.

➜ **Casa Alberto** (p89) Traditional tapas.

➜ **Los Gatos** (p90) Tapas in Huertas.

➜ **La Casa del Abuelo** (p90) Grilled prawns.

to be 'the most famous bar in Madrid' – that's pushing it, but it's invariably full most nights of the week, so who are we to argue?

It serves good house wine, great anchovies and what Spaniards like to call 'well-poured beer'.

TABERNA ALHAMBRA BAR
Map p238 (☎91 521 07 08; Calle de la Victoria 9; ⏱11am-1.30am Sun-Wed, 11am-2am Thu, 11am-2.30am Fri & Sat; MSol) There can be a certain sameness about the bars between Sol and Huertas, which is why this fine old *taberna* stands out. The striking facade and exquisite tile-work of the interior are quite beautiful; however, this place is anything but stuffy and the feel is cool, casual and busy. It serves tapas and, later at night, there are some fine flamenco tunes.

JAZZ BAR BAR
Map p238 (☎91 429 70 31; Calle de Moratín 35; ⏱3pm-2.30am; MAntón Martín) Jazz aficionados will love this place for its endless jazz soundtrack and discreet leather booths (at last, a bar that has gone for privacy instead of trying to cram too many people in), and there's plenty of greenery to keep you cheerful. If you want live jazz, head elsewhere, but this place is like a mellow after-party for aficionados in the know.

MALASPINA BAR
Map p238 (☎91 523 40 24; Calle de Cádiz 9; ⏱11am-2am Sun-Thu, to 2.30am Fri & Sat; ☎; MSol) Although it serves inviting tapas, we like this cosy bar, with its wooden tables and semirustic decor, as a mellow place for a quiet drink before heading home for an early night. Many of the bars in this area lack character or have sold their soul to the god of tourism. This place is different.

LA NEGRA TOMASA BAR
Map p238 (☎91 523 58 30; www.lanegratomasa.com; Calle de Cádiz 9; ⏱1.30pm-4am Sun-Thu, 1.30pm-5.30am Fri & Sat; MSol) Bar, live-music venue, restaurant and magnet for all things Cuban, La Negra Tomasa is a boisterous meeting place for the Havana set, with waitresses dressed in traditional Cuban outfits (definitely pre-Castro) and Cuban musicians playing deep into the night. Groups start at 1.30pm every night of the week, with additional performances at 2.30am on Fridays and Saturdays and 3pm on Sundays.

Some nights there's even a tarot card reader tucked away in the corner.

> ### ⓘ DRINKING DRESS CODE
> Going out for a drink in Madrid is generally a pretty casual affair, but to visit The Roof (p92) or La Terraza del Urban (p92) you should dress well. No running shoes should go without saying, while a button-up shirt for men is close to obligatory. You might get away with jeans depending on the day and who's at the door.

VIVA MADRID BAR
Map p238 (☎91 420 35 96; www.restaurante-vivamadrid.com; Calle de Manuel Fernández y González 7; ⏱noon-midnight Mon-Thu, noon-2am Fri & Sat; MAntón Martín, Sol) The tiled facade of Viva Madrid is one of Madrid's most recognisable and it's an essential landmark on the Huertas nightlife scene. It's packed to the rafters on weekends and you come here for fine mojitos and the casual, friendly atmosphere. The recently improved tapas offerings are another reason to pass by.

 # ENTERTAINMENT

★CAFÉ CENTRAL JAZZ
Map p238 (☎91 369 41 43; www.cafecentralmadrid.com; Plaza del Ángel 10; ⏱12.30pm-2.30am Sun-Thu, 12.30pm-3.30am Fri & Sat, performances 9pm; MAntón Martín, Sol) In 2011 the respected jazz magazine *Down Beat* included this art-deco bar on the list of the world's best jazz clubs, the only place in Spain to earn the prestigious accolade (said by some to be the jazz equivalent of earning a Michelin star). With well over 9000 gigs under its belt, it rarely misses a beat. Admission costs from €12 to €18.

Big international names like Chano Domínguez, Tal Farlow and Wynton Marsalis have all played here and you'll hear everything from Latin jazz and fusion to tango and classical jazz. Performers usually play here for a week and then move on, so getting tickets shouldn't be a problem, except on weekends. Shows start at 9pm and tickets go on sale from 6pm before the set starts.

★SALA EL SOL LIVE MUSIC
Map p238 (☎91 532 64 90; www.elsolmad.com; Calle de los Jardines 3; ⏱midnight-5.30am Tue-Sat Jul-Sep; MGran Vía) Madrid institutions

don't come any more beloved than Sala El Sol. It opened in 1979, just in time for *la movida madrileña* (the Madrid scene), and quickly established itself as a leading stage for all the icons of the era, such as Nacha Pop and Alaska y los Pegamoides.

La movida may have mostly faded into history, but it lives on at El Sol, where the music rocks and rolls and usually resurrects the '70s and '80s, while soul and funk also get a run. It's a terrific venue, and although most concerts start at 11pm and despite the official opening hours, some acts take to the stage as early as 10pm. After the show, DJs spin rock, fusion and electronica from the awesome sound system. Check the website (which also allows you to book online) for upcoming acts. Admission including a drink is €10; concert tickets are €8 to €25.

⭐ **VILLA ROSA**　　　FLAMENCO

Map p238 (☑91 521 36 89; www.tablaoflamenco villarosa.com; Plaza de Santa Ana 15; ⊙11pm-6am Mon-Sat, shows 8.30pm & 10.45pm Sun-Thu, 8.30pm, 10.45pm & 12.15am Fri & Sat; Ⓜ Sol) Villa Rosa has been going strong since 1914 and has seen many manifestations – it made its name as a flamenco venue and has recently returned to its roots with well-priced shows and meals that won't break the bank. Admission (show and drink) costs from €32/17 per adult/child.

The extraordinary tiled facade (1928) is the work of Alfonso Romero, who was also responsible for the tile-work in the Plaza de Toros – the facade is a tourist attraction in itself. This longstanding nightclub even appeared in the Pedro Almodóvar film *Tacones lejanos* (High Heels; 1991).

⭐ **TEATRO DE LA ZARZUELA**　　THEATRE

Map p238 (☑91 524 54 00; http://teatrodelazar zuela.mcu.es; Calle de Jovellanos 4; tickets €5-50; ⊙box office noon-6pm Mon-Fri, 3-6pm Sat & Sun; Ⓜ Banco de España, Sevilla) This theatre, built in 1856, is the premier place to see *zarzuela* (satirical music comedies). It also hosts a smattering of classical music and opera, as well as the cutting-edge Compañía Nacional de Danza. Tickets range from €5 to €50.

TORRES BERMEJAS　　　FLAMENCO

(☑91 532 33 22; www.torresbermejas.com; Calle de los Mesoneros Romanos 11; ⊙shows 9pm-midnight, doors open 8pm; Ⓜ Callao) For decades this was the Madrid stage for flamenco legend Camarón de la Isla, and it's once again a good place to see flamenco. The

atmosphere is aided by the extravagantly tiled interior. Admission including drink is €41.

COSTELLO CAFÉ & NITECLUB　　LIVE MUSIC

Map p238 (☑91 522 18 15; www.costelloclub. com; Calle del Caballero de Gracia 10; ⊙8pm-3am Sun-Wed, 6pm-3.30am Thu-Sat; Ⓜ Gran Vía) Very cool. Costello Café & Niteclub weds smooth-as-silk ambience to an innovative mix of pop, rock and fusion in Warholesque surrounds. There's live music (pop and rock, often of the indie variety) at 9.30pm every night except Sundays, with resident and visiting DJs keeping you on your feet until closing time from Thursday to Saturday. Admission costs €5 to €10.

POPULART　　　JAZZ

Map p238 (☑91 429 84 07; www.populart.es; Calle de las Huertas 22; ⊙6pm-2.30am Sun-Thu, to 3.30am Fri & Sat, concerts 10pm; Ⓜ Antón Martín, Sol) **FREE** One of Madrid's classic jazz clubs, this place offers a low-key atmosphere and top-quality music, which is mostly jazz with occasional blues, swing and even flamenco thrown into the mix. Compay Segundo, Sonny Fortune and the Canal Street Jazz Band have all played here. Shows start at 10pm but, if you want a seat, get here early.

LA BOCA CLUB　　　LIVE MUSIC

Map p238 (☑91 429 70 13; www.labocaclub.com; Calle de Echegaray 11; ⊙9.30pm-3am Tue-Thu, 9.30pm-3.30am Fri & Sat; Ⓜ Sol, Sevilla) Known for offering mostly rock and alternative concerts, La Boca Club has broadened its horizons to include just about anything – roots, reggae, jazz, soul, ska, flamenco, funk and fusion. Amid all the variety are some mainstays – Wednesdays and Thursdays at 11pm are set aside for a four-hour funk, soul and blues jam session, for example.

Concerts usually start at 11pm (check the website). Fridays and Saturdays and DJs take over until closing time. Admission varies from free to €10.

CARDAMOMO　　　FLAMENCO

Map p238 (☑91 805 10 38; www.cardamomo. es; Calle de Echegaray 15; ⊙10pm-3.30am & live shows 8pm & 10pm Wed-Mon; Ⓜ Sol, Sevilla) One of the better flamenco stages in town, Cardamomo draws more tourists than aficionados, but the flamenco is top-notch. The early show lasts just 50 minutes, the latter 90 minutes. Admission including a drink for early/late sessions costs €25/39.

CASA PUEBLO   LIVE MUSIC
Map p238 91 420 20 38; Calle de León 3; 5pm-2am Mon-Thu, 5pm-3am Fri, 3pm-3am Sat, 3pm-2am Sun; Antón Martín, Banco de España) A storied Huertas bar that prides itself on free live jazz, a bohemian outlook and (according to the owners) political conspiracies, Casa Pueblo is an agreeable bar serving up a winning combination of cakes and cocktails that draws a discerning thirty-something crowd.

TEATRO ESPAÑOL   THEATRE
Map p238 (91 360 14 84; www.teatroespanol.es; Calle del Príncipe 25; Sevilla, Sol, Antón Martín) This theatre, which fronts onto the Plaza de Santa Ana, has been here in one form or another since the 16th century and is still one of the best places to catch mainstream Spanish drama, from the works of Lope de Vega to more recent playwrights.

TEATRO MONUMENTAL   CLASSICAL MUSIC
Map p238 91 429 12 81, 91 429 10 55; www.rtve.es/orquesta-coro; Calle de Atocha 65; ticket office 11am-2pm & 5-7pm Mon-Fri; Antón Martín) The main concert season runs from October to March each year, when performances include those of the Banda Sinfónica Municipal Madrid, the Orquesta Sinfónica de RTVE, and occasional operas, ballets or *zarzuelas* (tickets €10 to €22). It's a modern theatre with fabulous acoustics.

 SHOPPING

The shops in the streets surrounding Sol range from department stores and chain-clothing shops to some real gems. Shopping in Huertas is akin to being on a treasure hunt. Small, quirky shops – some run by the same family for generations, others devoted to the most specialised of niches – pop up in the most unlikely places, with especially rich pickings in the tangle of lanes that make up the Barrio de las Letras.

CASA DE DIEGO   ACCESSORIES
Map p238 (www.casadediego.com; Plaza de la Puerta del Sol 12; 9.30am-8pm Mon-Sat; Sol) This classic shop has been around since 1858, making, selling and repairing Spanish fans, shawls, umbrellas and canes. Service is old style and occasionally grumpy, but the fans are works of antique art. There's another **branch** (Map p238; 91

531 02 23; Calle del los Mesoneros Romanos 4; 9.30am-1.30pm & 4.45-8pm Mon-Sat; Callao, Sol) nearby.

JOSÉ RAMÍREZ   MUSIC
Map p238 (91 531 42 29; www.guitarrasramirez.com; Calle de la Paz 8; 10am-2pm & 4.30-8pm Mon-Fri, 10.30am-2pm Sat; Sol) José Ramírez is one of Spain's best guitar makers and his guitars have been strummed by a host of flamenco greats and international musicians (including the Beatles). Using Honduran cedar, Cameroonian ebony and Indian or Madagascan rosewood, among other materials, and based on traditions dating back over generations, this is craftsmanship of the highest order.

Out the back there's a little museum with guitars dating to 1830. Ask here about guitar classes.

JUAN ALVAREZ   MUSIC
Map p238 (91 429 20 33; www.guitarrasjuanalvarez.com; Calle de San Pedro 7; 5-8pm Mon, 10am-1.30pm & 5-8pm Tue-Fri, 10am-1.30pm Sat; Antón Martín) The shop and workshop (located off Calle de Moratín) may be tiny, but Juan Alvarez is one of the most celebrated guitar makers in Spain. The family business dates back to 1945 and former clients include Eric Clapton, Compay Segundo and a host of flamenco greats. Prices start from €150 and don't stop until they reach €12,000.

MARÍA CABELLO   WINE
Map p238 (91 429 60 88; Calle de Echegaray 19; 9.30am-2.30pm & 5.30-9pm Mon-Fri, 10am-2.30pm & 6.30-9.30pm Sat; Sevilla, Antón Martín) All wine shops should be like this. This family-run corner shop really knows its wines and the interior has scarcely changed since 1913, with wooden shelves and even a faded ceiling fresco. There are fine wines in abundance (mostly Spanish, and a few foreign bottles), with some 500 labels on show or tucked away out the back.

SANTARRUFINA   RELIGIOUS
Map p238 (91 522 23 83; www.santarrufina.com; Calle de la Paz 4; 10am-2pm & 4.30-8pm Mon-Fri, 10am-2pm Sat; Sol) This gilded outpost of Spanish Catholicism has to be seen to be believed. Churches, priests and monasteries are some of the patrons of this overwhelming three-storey shop full of everything from simple rosaries to imposing statues of saints and even a litter used to carry the Virgin in processions. Head

downstairs for a peek at the extravagant chapel.

JUSTO ALGABA
GIFTS

Map p238 (☑91 523 37 17; www.justoalgaba.com; Calle de la Paz 4; ⊙10am-2pm & 5-8pm Mon-Fri, 10am-2pm Sat; MSol) This is where Spain's *toreros* (bullfighters) come to have their *traje de luces* (suit of lights, the traditional glittering bullfighting suit) made in all its intricate excess.

ALMACÉN DE PONTEJOS
CLOTHING

Map p238 (☑91 521 55 94; www.almacendepontejos.com; Plaza de Pontejos 2; ⊙9.30am-2pm & 4.30-8.15pm Mon-Fri, 9.30am-2pm Sat; MSol) Describing what this shop sells – fabrics, buttons, all manner of knicks and knacks for dressmakers – only tells half the story. It's one of many such stores on the square and in the surrounding streets, an intriguing hidden subculture that dates back decades, a stone's throw from the Puerta del Sol. And it's very much alive – these shops can throng with people.

MÉXICO
ANTIQUES

Map p238 (☑91 429 94 76; Calle de las Huertas 20; ⊙10.30am-2pm & 5-8pm Mon-Fri, 10.30am-2pm Sat; MAntón Martín) A treasure chest of original old maps and drawings, this is a great place to find a unique souvenir of Spain. Some 160 folders hold antique maps of Madrid, Spain and the rest of the world. These are all originals or antique copies, not modern reprints, so prices range from a few hundred to thousands of euros.

SECRETOS DE LEÓN
FOOD & DRINK

Map p238 (☑91 061 81 15; www.secretosdeleon.com; Calle de Lope de Vega 1; ⊙10.30am-2.30pm & 4-8.30pm Tue-Sat, noon-3.30pm Sun; MAntón Martín) The focus here is on the province of León in Spain's inner north, and that means cheeses, cured meats, speciality sweets and other products. It's a lovely, intimate space and they also organise tastings of craft beers – quite an unusual occurrence in Madrid.

LA VIOLETA
FOOD

Map p238 (☑91 522 55 22; www.lavioletaonline.es; Plaza de Canalejas 6; ⊙10am-2pm & 4.30-8.30pm Mon-Sat Sep-Jul; MSevilla, Antón Martín) In the early 20th century, *violetas* (small violet-coloured sweets and frosted petals from the violet flower) took on an iconic status and remain one of the city's most typical sweets. This tiny shop evokes that era in its decor and it doesn't serve much else other than the elegantly wrapped sweets.

TIENDA REAL MADRID
SPORTS

Map p238 (☑91 755 45 38; www.realmadrid.com; Gran Vía 31; ⊙10am-9pm Mon-Sat, 11am-9pm Sun; MGran Vía, Callao) The Real Madrid club shop sells replica shirts, posters, caps and just about everything else under the sun to which it could attach a club logo. In the centre of town there's a smaller **branch** (☑915 21 79 50; Calle del Carmen 3; ⊙10am-9pm Mon-Sat, 11am-8pm Sun; MSol), and, in the city's north, the stadium branch (p158).

LIBRERÍA DESNIVEL
BOOKS

Map p238 (☑91 429 12 81; www.libreriadesnivel.com; Plaza de Matute 6; ⊙10am-8.30pm Mon-Fri, 11am-8pm Sat; MAntón Martín) Although focused on mountaineering and rock-climbing, this fine bookshop has an excellent range of maps, travel books and even a small kids section.

🏃 SPORTS & ACTIVITIES

HAMMAM AL-ANDALUS
SPA

Map p238 (☑91 429 90 20; www.madrid.hammamalandalus.com; Calle de Atocha 14; treatments €30-73; ⊙10am-midnight; MSol) Housed in the excavated cellars of old Madrid, this imitation of a traditional Arab bath offers massages and aromatherapy beneath graceful arches, accompanied by the sound of trickling water. Prices are cheapest from 10am to 4pm Monday to Friday; reservations are required. There's also a Moroccan-style tea room and restaurant upstairs.

El Retiro & the Art Museums

Neighbourhood Top Five

1 Taking a journey through the richest centuries of Spanish and European art, beginning with Goya and Velázquez, at the **Museo del Prado** (p99).

2 Marvelling at the sheer genius of Picasso as you ponder the many dimensions of *Guernica* at the **Centro de Arte Reina Sofía** (p108).

3 Ticking off just about every European master under one roof at the **Museo Thyssen-Bornemisza** (p104).

4 Enjoying the peace and beauty of the **Parque del Buen Retiro** (p111), one of the most beautiful city parks in Europe.

5 Sampling all that's innovative about the Spanish food revolution at **Estado Puro** (p114), one of Madrid's premier tapas bars.

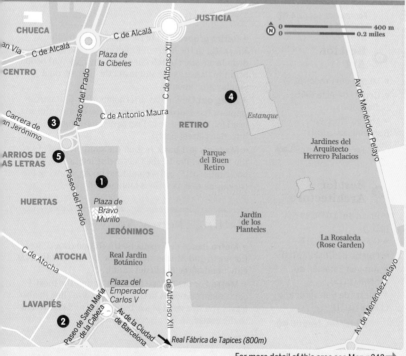

For more detail of this area see Map p242 ➡

Lonely Planet's Top Tip

Avoid the free opening hours at the Museo del Prado, when crowds can really spoil your visit. First thing in the morning is the best time and if you've purchased your ticket online and in advance, you'll skip the queues. The Prado is worth two visits to take it all in; its 'Two Visits in a Year' ticket for €20 saves you €8.

If you're visiting the Reina Sofía and Thyssen as well, you'll save €6.40 with the 'Paseo del Arte' combined ticket – it gets you into all three galleries for €25.60.

Best Places to Eat

➜ Estado Puro (p114)
➜ Viridiana (p114)
➜ El Brillante (p114)

For reviews, see p114 ➜

Best for Art

➜ Museo del Prado (p99)
➜ Centro de Arte Reina Sofía (p108)
➜ Museo Thyssen-Bornemisza (p104)

For reviews, see p99 ➜

Best for Architecture

➜ Plaza de la Cibeles (p110)
➜ Caixa Forum (p111)
➜ Palacio de Cristal (p111)
➜ Antigua Estación de Atocha (p113)
➜ Iglesia de San Jerónimo El Real (p111)

For reviews, see p110 ➜

EL RETIRO & THE ART MUSEUMS

Explore: El Retiro & the Art Museums

The Paseo del Prado, a former river and now one of Europe's grandest boulevards, is all about the fabulous art galleries arrayed along or close to its shores. With other grand monuments and the city's botanical gardens also in residence, it's very much a daytime neighbourhood, one that all but shuts down – at least by Madrid standards – after dark. Metro stations sit at either end of the Paseo del Prado with none in between – when walking from one end to the other, take the footpaths under the trees down the centre of the Paseo, not those on the outer extremities. The *barrio* (district) of Huertas climbs up the hill to the west.

Behind the Museo del Prado and Real Jardín Botánico to the east, a gentle rise of tranquil and refined residential streets leads towards the Parque del Buen Retiro. The park is even more of a daytime experience (the gates close soon after sunset), but its moods vary with the days. On weekdays, the park is quiet and sleepy, sprinkled with enough people to feel alive but peaceful in a way that serves as an antidote to the clamour of downtown Madrid nearby. Come Saturday and Sunday, locals stream into the park – when the weather's fine on a Sunday afternoon, it can seem as if the whole city has come here to play.

Local Life

➜ **Retiro groove** East of the Monument to Alfonso XII (p112) in the heart of El Retiro, crowds gather, drumbeats start to roll out across the park and people begin to dance as the sun nears the horizon on a Sunday afternoon.

➜ **Hang out** On Sunday afternoons after El Rastro's clamour has faded and the tapas crowds are thinning, head for the Plaza de la Puerta de Moros for an infectious street party.

➜ **Madrid's left bank** Just off the southern end of the Paseo del Prado, the Cuesta de Claudio Moyano bookstalls (p115) sell secondhand books, drawing the curious as well as serious bibliophiles.

Getting There & Away

➜ **Metro** Banco de España metro station (line 2) to the north and Atocha station (line 1) to the south sit at either end of the Paseo del Prado.

➜ **Metro** For the Parque del Buen Retiro, the most convenient station is Retiro (line 2). Ibiza (line 9) also leaves you in a good place, but isn't as well connected to the centre.

MUSEO DEL PRADO

Welcome to one of the world's premier art galleries. The more than 7000 paintings held in the Museo del Prado's collection (although only around 1500 are on display at any one time) are like a window onto the historical vagaries of the Spanish soul, at once grand and imperious in the royal paintings of Velázquez, darkly tumultuous in Goya's *Pinturas negras* (Black Paintings) and outward looking with sophisticated works of art from all across Europe.

Goya in the Prado

Goya is sometimes described as the first of the great Spanish masters and his work is found on all three floors of the Prado. Begin at the southern end of the ground or lower level where, in Rooms 64 and 65, Goya's *El dos de mayo* and *El tres de mayo* rank among Madrid's most emblematic paintings. In the adjacent rooms (66 and 67), his disturbing *Pinturas negras* (Black Paintings) are so named for the distorted animalesque appearance of their characters. The *Saturno devorando a su hijo* (Saturn Devouring His Son) is utterly disturbing, while *La romería de San Isidro* and *Aquelarre* (El Gran Cabrón) are dominated by the compelling individual faces of the condemned souls. An interesting footnote to *Pinturas negras* is *El coloso,* a Goyaesque work hanging next to the Black Paintings that was long considered part of the master's portfolio until the Prado's experts decided otherwise in 2008.

Up on the 1st floor, other masterful works include the intriguing *La família de Carlos IV,* which portrays the Spanish royal family in 1800; Goya portrayed himself in the background just as Velázquez did in *Las meninas*. Also present are *La maja vestida* (The Young

DON'T MISS...

➡ Goya
➡ Velázquez
➡ Flemish Collection
➡ *The Garden of Earthly Delights*
➡ El Greco

PRACTICALITIES

➡ Map p242
➡ www.museodelprado.es
➡ Paseo del Prado
➡ adult/child €14/free, free 6-8pm Mon-Sat & 5-7pm Sun, audioguides €3.50, admission plus official guidebook €23
➡ ⊘10am-8pm Mon-Sat, 10am-7pm Sun
➡ ☎
➡ Ⓜ Banco de España

Entrance to the Prado is via the northern Puerta de Goya or the eastern Puerta de los Jerónimos. Tickets must first be purchased from the ticket office at the northern end of the building, opposite the Hotel Ritz and beneath the Puerta de Goya. Better still, buy your tickets online and skip the queues. Once inside, pick up the free plan from the ticket office or information desk just inside the entrance – it lists the locations of 50 of the Prado's most famous works and gives room numbers for all major artists; PDF versions are available on the website to help you plan your visit.

Lady Dressed) and *La maja desnuda* (The Young Lady Undressed). These portraits of an unknown woman, commonly believed to be the Duquesa de Alba (who some think may have been Goya's lover), are identical save for the lack of clothing in the latter.

Velázquez

Velázquez' role as court painter means that his works provide a fascinating insight into 17th-century royal life and the Prado holds the richest collection of his works. Of all the works by Velázquez, *Las meninas* (The Maids of Honour; Room 12) is what most people come to see. Completed in 1656, it is more properly known as *La família de Felipe IV* (The Family of Felipe IV). It depicts Velázquez himself on the left and, in the centre, the infant Margarita. There's more to it than that: the artist in fact portrays himself painting the king and queen, whose images appear, according to some experts, in mirrors behind Velázquez. His mastery of light and colour is never more apparent than here. An interesting detail of the painting, aside from the extraordinary cheek of painting himself in royal company, is the presence of the cross of the Order of Santiago on his vest. The artist was apparently obsessed with being given a noble title. He got it shortly before his death, but in this oil painting he has awarded himself the order years before it would in fact be his!

The rooms surrounding *Las meninas* (Rooms 14 and 15) contain more fine paintings of various members of royalty who seem to spring off the canvas, many of them on horseback. Also nearby is his *La rendición de Breda* (The Surrender of Breda), while other Spanish painters worth tracking down in the neighbouring rooms include Bartolomé Esteban Murillo, José de Ribera and the stark figures of Francisco de Zurbarán.

The Flemish Collection

The Prado's outstanding collection of Flemish art includes the fulsome figures and bulbous cherubs of Peter Paul Rubens (1577–1640). His signature works are *Las tres gracias* and *Adoración de los reyes magos*. Other fine works in the vicinity include *The Triumph of Death* by Pieter Bruegel and those by Anton Van Dyck.

Van Der Weyden's 1435 painting *El descendimiento* is unusual, both for its size and for the recurring crossbow shapes in the painting's upper corners, which are echoed in the bodies of Mary and Christ (the painting was commissioned by a Crossbow Manufacturers Brotherhood). Once the central part of a triptych, the painting is filled with drama and luminous colours.

On no account miss the weird and wonderful *The Garden of Earthly Delights* (Room 56A) by Hieronymus Bosch (c 1450–1516). No one has yet been able to provide a definitive explanation for this hallucinatory work, although many have tried. The closer you look, the harder it is to escape the feeling that he must have been doing some extraordinary drugs.

Judith at the Banquet of Holofernes, the only painting by Rembrandt in the Prado's collection, was completed in 1634; note the artist's signature and date on the arm of the chair. The painting shows a master at the peak of his powers, with a masterly use of the chiaroscuro style, and the astonishing detail in the subject's clothing and face.

El Greco

This Greek-born artist (hence the name) is considered the finest of the Prado's Spanish Renaissance painters. The vivid, almost surreal works by this 16th-century master and adopted Spaniard, whose figures are characteristically slender and tortured, are perfectly executed. Two of his more than 30 paintings in the collection – *The Annunciation* and *The Flight into Egypt* – were painted in Italy before the artist arrived in Spain, while *The Trinity* and *Knight with His Hand on his Breast* are considered his most important works.

Emperor Carlos V on Horseback (Titian)

Considered one of the finest equestrian and royal portraits in art history, this 16th-century work is said to be the forerunner to similar paintings by Velázquez a century later. One of the great masters of the Renaissance, Titian (1488–1576) was entering his most celebrated period as a painter when he created this, and it is widely recognised as one of his masterpieces.

The Best of the Rest

No matter how long you spend in the Prado, there's always more to discover, such as the paintings by Dürer, Rafael, Tintoretto, Sorolla, Gainsborough, Fra Angelico, Tiepolo...

Edificio Villanueva

The Prado's western wing (Edificio Villanueva) was completed in 1785 as the neoclassical Palacio de Villanueva. It served as a cavalry barracks for Napoleon's troops between 1808 and 1813. In 1814 King Fernando VII decided to use the palace as a museum. Five years later the Museo del Prado opened with 311 Spanish paintings on display.

Edificio Jerónimos

The Prado's eastern wing (Edificio Jerónimos) is part of the Prado's stunning modern extension. Dedicated to temporary exhibitions (usually to display Prado masterpieces held in storage for decades for lack of wall space), its main attraction is the 2nd-floor cloisters. Built in 1672 with local granite, the cloisters were until recently attached to the adjacent Iglesia de San Jerónimo El Real (p111).

Nearby: Casón del Buen Retiro

This **building** (☑90 210 70 77; Calle de Alfonso XII 28; ⊘guided visits 11am & 12.30pm Sun; ⓂRetiro) overlooking the Parque del Buen Retiro is run as an academic library by the Museo del Prado. The Prado runs guided visits to the stunning Hall of the Ambassadors, which is crowned by the astonishing 1697 ceiling fresco *The Apotheosis of the Spanish Monarchy* by Luca Giordano.

EL RETIRO & THE ART MUSEUMS MUSEO DEL PRADO

Museo del Prado

PLAN OF ATTACK

Begin on the 1st floor with **Las meninas ①** by Velázquez. Although it alone is worth the entry price, it's a fine introduction to the 17th-century golden age of Spanish art; nearby are more of Velázquez' royal paintings and works by Zurbarán and Murillo. While on the 1st floor, seek out Goya's **La maja vestida and La maja desnuda ②** with more of Goya's early works in neighbouring rooms. Downstairs at the southern end of the Prado, Goya's anger is evident in the searing **El dos de mayo and El tres de mayo ③**, and the torment of Goya's later years finds expression in the adjacent rooms with his **Las pinturas negras ④**, or Black Paintings. Also on the lower floor, Hieronymus Bosch's weird and wonderful **The Garden of Earthly Delights ⑤** is one of the Prado's signature masterpieces. Returning to the 1st floor, El Greco's **Adoration of the Shepherds ⑥** is an extraordinary work, as is Peter Paul Rubens' **Las tres gracias ⑦** which forms the centrepiece of the Prado's gathering of Flemish masters. (Note: this painting may be moved to the 2nd floor.) A detour to the 2nd floor takes in some lesser-known Goyas, but finish in the **Edificio Jerónimos ⑧** with a visit to the cloisters and the outstanding bookshop.

ALSO VISIT:

Nearby are Museo Thyssen-Bornemisza and Centro de Arte Reina Sofía. They form an extraordinary trio of galleries.

TOP TIPS

» **Book online** Purchase your ticket online (www.museodelprado.es) and avoid the queues.

» **Best time to visit** As soon after opening time as possible.

» **Free tours** The website (www.museo delprado.es/coleccion/que-ver/) has self-guided tours for one- to three-hour visits.

Las meninas (Velázquez)
This masterpiece depicts Velázquez and the Infanta Margarita with the king and queen whose images appear, according to some experts, in mirrors behind Velázquez.

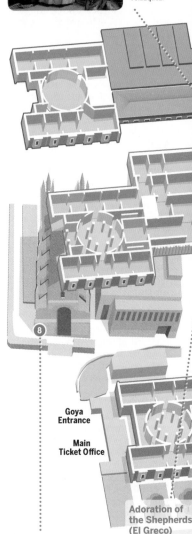

Goya Entrance

Main Ticket Office

Edificio Jerónimos
Opened in 2007, this state-of-the-art extension has rotating exhibitions of Prado masterpieces held in storage for decades for lack of wall space, and stunning 2nd-floor granite cloisters that date back to 1672.

Adoration of the Shepherds (El Greco)
There's an ecstatic quality to this intense painting. El Greco's distorted rendering of bodily forms came to characterise much of his later work.

as tres gracias (Rubens)

late Rubens asterpiece, *The Three races* is a classical and asterly expression of ubens' preoccupation ith sensuality, here ortraying Aglaia, uphrosyne and Thalia, he daughters of Zeus.

La maja vestida & La maja desnuda (Goya)

These enigmatic works scandalised early 19th-century Madrid society, fuelling the rumour mill as to the woman's identity and drawing the ire of the Spanish Inquisition.

Edificio Villanueva

①

⑦

②

El dos de mayo & El tres de mayo (Goya)

Few paintings evoke a city's sense of self quite like Goya's portrayal of Madrid's valiant but ultimately unsuccessful uprising against French rule in 1808.

Las pinturas negras (Goya)

Las pinturas negras are Goya's darkest works. *Saturno devorando a su hijo* evokes a writhing mass of tortured humanity, while *La romería de San Isidro* and *El aquelarre* are profoundly unsettling.

Information Counter & Audioguides

ónimos Entrance (Main Entrance)

Gift Shop

Cafeteria

⑤

③ **④**

Murillo Entrance

Velázquez Entrance

The Garden of Earthly Delights (Bosch)

A fantastical painting in triptych form, this overwhelming work depicts the Garden of Eden and what the Prado describes as 'the lugubrious precincts of Hell' in exquisitely bizarre detail.

TOP SIGHT
MUSEO THYSSEN-BORNEMISZA

One of the most extraordinary private collections of predominantly European art in the world, the Museo Thyssen-Bornemisza is a worthy member of Madrid's 'Golden Triangle' of art. Where the Museo del Prado or Centro de Arte Reina Sofía enable you to study the body of work of a particular artist in depth, the Thyssen is a place to immerse yourself in a breathtaking breadth of artistic styles.

Religious Art

The 2nd floor, which is home to medieval art, includes some real gems hidden among the mostly 13th- and 14th-century and predominantly Italian, German and Flemish religious paintings and triptychs. Much of it is sacred art that won't appeal to everyone, but it somehow captures the essence of medieval Europe.

Rooms 5 to 10

Unless you've a specialist's eye for the paintings that fill the first four rooms, pause for the first time in Room 5 where you'll find one work by Italy's Piero della Francesca (1410–92) and the instantly recognisable *Portrait of King Henry VIII* by Holbein the Younger (1497–1543). In Room 8 *Jesus Among the Doctors* by Albrecht Dürer, a leading figure in the German Renaissance, is an exceptional, vaguely disturbing work; note Dürer's anagram on the slip of paper emerging from the book in the painting's foreground. Continue on to Room 10 for the evocative 1586 *Massacre of the Innocents* by Lucas Van Valckenborch.

DON'T MISS...

➡ Religious Art
➡ El Greco & Tintoretto
➡ 2nd-Floor European Masters
➡ Dutch & Flemish Masters
➡ Rooms 31 to 35
➡ The Baroness Collection
➡ Cubism & Surrealism
➡ Contemporary Icons

PRACTICALITIES

➡ Map p242
➡ ☎902 760511
➡ www.museothyssen.org
➡ Paseo del Prado 8
➡ adult/child €10/free, free Mon
➡ ⏰10am-7pm Tue-Sun, noon-4pm Mon
➡ Ⓜ Banco de España

Spain & Venice

Room 11 is dedicated to El Greco (with three pieces) and his Venetian contemporaries Tintoretto and Titian, while Caravaggio and the Spaniard José de Ribera dominate Room 12. A single painting each by Murillo and Zurbarán add further Spanish flavour in the two rooms that follow, while the exceptionally rendered views of Venice by Canaletto (1697–1768) should on no account be missed. Few paintings have come to be the iconic image of a city quite like Canaletto's *View of Piazza San Marco* – the painter's use of line and angle, and the intense detail in even the smallest of the painting's figures give a powerful sense of atmosphere and movement.

The Baroness Collection I

Best of all on the top floor is the extension (Rooms A to H) that houses the collection of Carmen Thyssen-Bornemisza; the rest belonged to Baron Thyssen-Bornemisza, a German-Hungarian magnate and her late husband. Room C houses paintings by Canaletto, Constable and Van Gogh, while the stunning Room H includes works by Monet, Sisley, Renoir, Pissarro and Degas.

Rooms 28 to 35

If all that sounds impressive, the 1st floor is where the Thyssen really shines. There's a Gainsborough in Room 28 and a Goya in Room 31. The latter's *Asensio Julià* is believed to be dedicated to Goya's friend and fellow artist, the eponymous Valencian painter who worked with Goya on the frescoes in the Ermita de San Antonio de la Florida (p150). Art historians also single out this painting's confident brushstrokes as a forerunner to the Romantic movement. Also in Room 31, one of the Thyssen's lesser-known masterpieces, the 19th-century *Dresden Easter Morning* by Caspar David Friedrich, is a haunting study in light and texture by one of the leading figures in the German Romantic movement. The painting is rich in symbolism – the moon and dawn evoke death and resurrection – and the shades of colour portray shifts of extraordinary subtlety.

If you've been skimming the surface, Room 32 is the place to linger over every painting. The astonishing texture of Van Gogh's *Les Vessenots* is a masterpiece, but the same applies to Manet's *Woman in Riding Habit,* Monet's *The Thaw at Véthueil,* Renoir's *Woman with a Parasol in a Garden* and Pissarro's *Rue Saint-Honoré in the Afternoon.* Simply extraordinary.

There's no time to catch your breath, because Room 33 is similarly something special with Cézanne, Gauguin, Toulouse-Lautrec and Degas all

For decades there was nowhere decent to take a break from all the galleries with a quick and enjoyable snack. That all changed with the opening of Estado Puro (p114), a sophisticated, creative tapas bar just around the roundabout within sight of the museum entrance. If you're still hungry and willing to stray a tiny bit further in search of something a little more earthy and eclectic, Los Gatos (p90) also does tapas but with a more traditional slant. Then again, for a casual sit-down meal it's hard to ignore Maceiras (p90), the purveyors of fine Galician cooking just up the hill in Huertas in the Paseo del Prado hinterland.

EL RETIRO & THE ART MUSEUMS MUSEO THYSSEN-BORNEMISZA

on show. The big names continue in Room 34 (Picasso, Matisse and Modigliani) and 35 (Edvard Munch and Egon Schiele).

The Baroness Collection II

In the 1st floor's extension (Rooms I to P), Room K has works by Monet, Pissarro, Sorolla and Sisley, while Room L is the domain of Gauguin (including his iconic *Mata Mua*), Degas and Toulouse-Lautrec. Rooms M (Munch), N (Kandinsky), O (Matisse and Georges Braque) and P (Picasso, Matisse, Edward Hopper and Juan Gris) round out an outrageously rich journey.

Cubism & Surrealism

Down on the ground floor, in Room 41 you'll see a nice mix of the big three of cubism, Picasso, Georges Braque and Madrid's own Juan Gris, along with several other contemporaries. Kandinsky is the main drawcard in Room 43, while there's an early Salvador Dalí alongside Max Ernst and Paul Klee in Room 44.

Twentieth-Century Icons

Picasso appears again in Room 45, another one of the gallery's standout rooms; it includes works by Marc Chagall and Dalí's hallucinatory *Dream Caused by the Flight of a Bee Around a Pomegranate, One Second Before Waking up*.

There's no let-up as the Thyssen builds to a stirring climax. Room 46 has Joan Miró's *Catalan Peasant with a Guitar*, Jackson Pollock's *Brown and Silver I* and the deceptively simple but strangely pleasing *Untitled (Green on Maroon)* by Mark Rothko. In Rooms 47 and 48, Francis Bacon, Roy Lichtenstein, Henry Moore and Lucian Freud, Sigmund's Berlin-born grandson, are all represented.

The Thyssen-Bornemisza Legend

The story behind the museum's collection is almost as interesting as the paintings themselves. And it is a very Spanish story that has a celebrity love affair at its heart. The paintings held in the museum are the legacy of Baron Thyssen-Bornemisza, a German-Hungarian magnate. Madrid managed to acquire the prestigious collection when the baron married Carmen Tita Cervera, a former Miss España and ex-wife of Lex Barker (of *Tarzan* fame). The deal was sealed when the Spanish government offered to overhaul the neoclassical Palacio de Villahermosa specifically to house the collection. Although the baron died in 2002, his glamorous wife has shown that she has learned much from the collecting nous of her late husband. In early 2000 the museum acquired two adjoining buildings, which have been joined to the museum to house approximately half of the collection of Carmen Thyssen-Bornemisza. She remains an important figure in the cultural life of the city – when the city authorities threatened in 2006 to tear down some 18th-century trees outside the museum to facilitate the re-routing of the Paseo del Prado, the Baroness threatened to chain herself to one of the trees in protest. The plan was quietly shelved.

MUSEO THYSSEN-BORNEMISZA

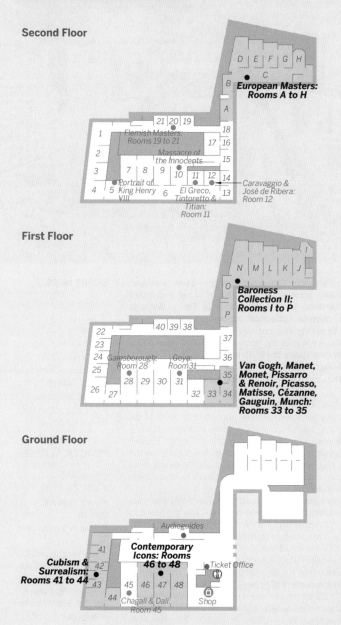

Second Floor

D E F G H

B
C
European Masters: Rooms A to H

A

21 20 19

1
Flemish Masters: Rooms 19 to 21

18

2

17 16

Massacre of the Innocents

15

3

7 8 9
10
11 12

14

Portrait of King Henry VIII

6
El Greco, Tintoretto & Titian: Room 11

13 — *Caravaggio & José de Ribera: Room 12*

4 5

First Floor

I

N M L K J

O
Baroness Collection II: Rooms I to P

P

40 39 38

22

37

23

24
Gainsborough: Room 28
Goya: Room 31

36

25

28 29 30 31

35
Van Gogh, Manet, Monet, Pissarro & Renoir, Picasso, Matisse, Cézanne, Gauguin, Munch: Rooms 33 to 35

26

27

32 33 34

Ground Floor

Audioguides

41
Cubism & Surrealism: Rooms 41 to 44

Contemporary Icons: Rooms 46 to 48
Ticket Office

42

45 46 47 48

43

44 *Chagall & Dalí: Room 45*

Shop

Home to Picasso's *Guernica*, arguably Spain's single-most famous artwork, and a host of other important Spanish artists, the Centro de Arte Reina Sofía is Madrid's premier collection of contemporary art. In addition to plenty of paintings by Picasso, other major drawcards are works by Salvador Dalí and Joan Miró. The collection spans the 20th century up to the 1980s, and although some non-Spaniard artists make an appearance, most of the collection is strictly peninsular.

Guernica (Picasso)

Claimed by some to be the most important artwork of the 20th century, Pablo Picasso's *Guernica* measures 3.5m by 7.8m and is an icon of the cubist style for which Picasso became famous. You could easily spend hours studying the painting; take the time to both examine the detail of its various constituent elements and step back to get an overview of this extraordinary canvas.

To deepen your understanding of *Guernica*, don't neglect the sketches that Picasso painted as he prepared to execute his masterpiece. They're in the rooms surrounding Room 206. They offer an intriguing insight into the development of this seminal work.

Guernica was Picasso's response to the bombing of Gernika (Guernica) in the Basque Country by Hitler's Legión Condor, at the request of Franco, on 26 April 1937. At least 200 died in the attack and much of the town was destroyed. The painting subsequently migrated to the USA and only returned to Spain in 1981, in keeping with Picasso's wish that the painting return to Spanish shores (first to Picasso's

DON'T MISS...

➡ Picasso's *Guernica*
➡ Juan Gris & Georges Braque
➡ Joan Miró
➡ Salvador Dalí
➡ Contemporary Spanish Art Collection
➡ Edificio Nouvel
➡ Librería la Central Bookshop (p115)

PRACTICALITIES

➡ Map p242
➡ ☎91 774 10 00
➡ www.museoreinasofia.es
➡ Calle de Santa Isabel 52
➡ adult/concession €8/free, free 1.30-7pm Sun, 7-9pm Mon & Wed-Sat
➡ ⊙10am-9pm Mon & Wed-Sat, 10am-7pm Sun
➡ Ⓜ Atocha

preferred choice, the Museo del Prado, then to its current home) once democracy had been restored.

Other Cubist Masters

Picasso may have been the brainchild behind the cubist form, but he was soon joined by others who saw its potential. Picasso is said to have been influenced by the mask traditions of Africa, and these elements can also be discerned in the work of Madrid-born Juan Gris (1887–1927) or Georges Braque (1882–1963), two of the masters of the genre.

Joan Miró

The work of Joan Miró (1893–1983) is defined by often delightfully bright primary colours. Since his paintings became a symbol of the Barcelona Olympics in 1992, his work has begun to receive the international acclaim it so richly deserves and the museum is a fine place to get a representative sample of his innovative work.

Salvador Dalí

The Reina Sofía is also home to around 20 canvases by Salvador Dalí, of which the most famous is perhaps the surrealist extravaganza *El gran masturbador* (1929); at once disturbing and utterly compelling, this is one of the museum's standout paintings. Look also for a strange bust of a certain *Joelle* done by Dalí and his friend Man Ray.

Contemporary Spanish Artists

Reina Sofía offers a terrific opportunity to learn more about lesser-known 20th-century Spanish artists. Among these: Miquel Barceló (b 1957); *madrileño* artist José Gutiérrez Solana (1886–1945); the renowned Basque painter Ignazio Zuloaga (1870–1945); and Benjamín Palencia (1894–1980), whose paintings capture the turbulence of Spain in the 1930s. The late Barcelona painter Antoni Tàpies (1923–2012), for years one of Spain's most creative talents, is represented, as are the pop art of Eduardo Arroyo (b 1937), abstract painters such as Eusebio Sempere (1923–85) and members of the Equipo 57 group (founded in 1957 by a group of Spanish artists in exile in Paris), including Pablo Palazuelo (1916–2007).

Sculptures

Of the sculptors, watch for Pablo Gargallo (1881–1934), whose work in bronze includes a bust of Picasso, and the renowned Basque sculptors Jorge Oteiza (1908–2003) and Eduardo Chillida (1924–2002); Chillida's forms rendered in rusted wrought iron are among Spanish art's most intriguing forms.

EDIFICIO NOUVEL

Beyond its artwork, the Reina Sofía is an important architectural landmark, adapted from the shell of an 18th-century hospital with eye-catching external glass lifts. The stunning extension (the Edificio Nouvel), which spreads along the western tip of the Plaza del Emperador Carlos V, hosts temporary exhibitions, auditoriums, the bookshop, a cafe and the museum's library.

TOP TIPS

➡ The permanent collection is on the 2nd and 4th floors of the museum's main wing, the Edificio Sabatini.

➡ *Guernica's* location (Room 206, 2nd floor) never changes.

➡ The Reina Sofía's paintings are grouped together by theme rather than artist – pick up a copy of the *Planos de Museo* (Museum Floorplans).

➡ The museum's *Guide to the Collection* (€22), available from the gift shop, takes a closer look at 80 of the museum's signature works.

EL RETIRO & THE ART MUSEUMS CENTRO DE ARTE REINA SOFÍA

◉ SIGHTS

MUSEO DEL PRADO   MUSEUM
See p99.

MUSEO THYSSEN-BORNEMISZA   MUSEUM
See p104.

CENTRO DE ARTE REINA SOFÍA   MUSEUM
See p108.

PLAZA DE LA CIBELES   SQUARE
Map p242 (ⓂBanco de España) Of all the grand
roundabouts that punctuate the Paseo del
Prado, Plaza de la Cibeles most evokes the
splendour of imperial Madrid. The jewel
in the crown is the astonishing **Palacio de
Comunicaciones**. Other landmark buildings around the plaza's perimeter include
the Palacio de Linares and Casa de América (p122), the **Palacio Buenavista** (1769)
and the national **Banco de España** (1891).
The spectacular **fountain of the goddess
Cybele** at the centre of the plaza is one of
Madrid's most beautiful.

Ever since it was erected in 1780 by
Ventura Rodríguez, the fountain has been
a Madrid favourite. Carlos III liked it so
much that he tried to have it moved to the
royal gardens of the Granja de San Ildefonso, on the road to Segovia, but *madrileños*
(people from Madrid) kicked up such a fuss
that he let it be.

There are fine views east from the Plaza
de la Cibeles towards the Puerta de Alcalá
or, even better, west towards the Edificio
Metrópolis (p86).

CENTROCENTRO   ARTS CENTRE
Map p242 (☏91 480 00 08; www.centrocentro.
org; Plaza de la Cibeles 1; ◷10am-8pm Tue-Sun;
ⓂPlaza de España) **FREE** One of Madrid's
more surprising and diverse cultural spaces,
CentroCentro is housed in the grand Palacio

LOCAL KNOWLEDGE

CHILDREN'S PLAYGROUNDS

Playgrounds in this area are largely
restricted to the Parque del Buen
Retiro (p111), but it does have quite a
few, including one close to the park's
entrance on Plaza de la Independencia and another at the eastern
end of the park, just off (and visible
from) the Paseo del Duque de Fernán
Nuñez.

---

de Comunicaciones. It has cutting-edge exhibitions covering 5000 sq metres over four
floors (floors 1, 3, 4 and 5), as well as quiet
reading rooms and some stunning architecture, especially in the soaring Antiguo Patio
de Operaciones on the 2nd floor. Up on the
8th floor is the Mirador de Madrid.

MIRADOR DE MADRID   VIEWPOINT
Map p242 (www.centrocentro.org; 8th fl, Palacio
de Comunicaciones, Plaza de la Cibeles; adult/
child €2/0.50; ◷10.30am-1.30pm & 4-7pm Tue-
Sun; ⓂBanco de España) The views from the
summit of the Palacio de Comunicaciones
are arguably Madrid's best, sweeping west
down over the Plaza de la Cibeles, up the
hill towards the sublime Edificio Metrópolis and out to the mountains. But the views
are splendid whichever way you look. Take
the lift up to the 6th floor, from where the
gates are opened every half-hour. From
there you can either take another lift or
climb the stairs up to the 8th floor.

PUERTA DE ALCALÁ   MONUMENT
Map p242 (Plaza de la Independencia; ⓂRetiro)
This imposing triumphal gate was once the
main entrance to the city (its name derives
from the fact that the road that passed under it led to Alcalá de Henares) and was surrounded by the city's walls. It was here that
the city authorities controlled access to the
capital and levied customs duties.

The first gate to bear this name was built
in 1599, but Carlos III was singularly unim-
pressed and had it demolished in 1764 to be
replaced by another, the one you see today.
It's best appreciated from the east for fine
views through the arch down towards central Madrid. Our only complaint? It could
do with a clean.

Twice a year, in autumn and spring, cars
abandon the roundabout and are replaced
by flocks of sheep being transferred in an
age-old ritual from their summer to winter
pastures (and vice versa). And the Puerta
de Alcalá was immortalised in the cultural
lexicon in 1986 when Ana Belén and Victor
Manuel's strangely catchy song 'La Puerta
de Alcalá' became an unlikely smash hit.

PLAZA DE NEPTUNO   SQUARE
Map p242 (Plaza de Cánovas del Castillo; ⓂBanco
de España) Officially known as Plaza de
Cánovas del Castillo, the next roundabout
south of Cibeles is something of a crossroads of Spanish nobility. The Ritz and
the Palace, two of Madrid's most exclusive

TOP SIGHT
PARQUE DEL BUEN RETIRO

The glorious gardens of El Retiro are as beautiful as any you'll find in a European city. Littered with marble monuments, landscaped lawns, the occasional elegant building and abundant greenery, it's quiet and contemplative during the week but comes to life on weekends. Put simply, this is one of our favourite places in Madrid.

El Retiro wasn't always so accessible. Laid out in the 17th century by Felipe IV as the preserve of royalty, the park was opened to the public in 1868 and ever since, *madrileños* (people from Madrid) gather here to stroll, read the Sunday papers in the shade, take a boat ride or nurse a cool drink at the numerous outdoor *terrazas* (open-air cafes). Weekend buskers, Chinese masseurs and tarot readers ply their trades, while art and photo exhibitions are sometimes held around the park.

Hidden among the trees south of the lake is the **Palacio de Cristal** (Map p242; ☑91 574 66 14; www.museoreinasofia.es; ☉10am-10pm Apr-Sep, 10am-6pm Oct-Mar; ⓂRetiro), a magnificent metal-and-glass structure that is arguably El Retiro's most beautiful architectural monument. It was built in 1887 as a winter garden for exotic flowers and is now used for temporary exhibitions organised by the Centro de Arte Reina Sofía.

DON'T MISS...

→ El Estanque & Monument to Alfonso XII

→ Palacio de Cristal

→ La Rosaleda

→ El Ángel Caído

→ Boat Ride

PRACTICALITIES

→ Map p242

→ ☉6am-midnight May-Sep, to 11pm Oct-Apr

→ ⓂRetiro, Príncipe de Vergara, Ibiza, Atocha

---

hotels, glower at each other across the plaza with self-righteous grandeur, while the Museo Thyssen-Bornemisza and the Prado do likewise in competition for the title of Madrid's best-loved repository of fine art. The centrepiece is an ornate fountain and 18th-century sculpture of Neptune, the sea god, by Juan Pascual de Mena.

CAIXA FORUM
MUSEUM, ARCHITECTURE

Map p242 (☑91 330 73 00; www.obrasocial.lacaixa.es; Paseo del Prado 36; admission free, exhibitions from €4; ☉10am-8pm; ⓂAtocha) This extraordinary structure is one of Madrid's most eye-catching landmarks. Seeming to hover above the street, this brick edifice is topped by an intriguing summit of rusted iron. On an adjacent wall is the *jardín colgante* (hanging garden), a lush (if thinning) vertical wall of greenery almost four storeys high. Inside there are four floors of exhibition and performance space awash in stainless steel and with soaring ceilings. The exhibitions here are always worth checking out and include photography, contemporary painting and multimedia shows.

Caixa Forum's shop is outstanding.

IGLESIA DE JESÚS DE MEDINACELI
CHURCH

Map p242 (☑91 429 93 75; Plaza de Jesús 2; ☉7am-1.30pm & 5-9pm Mon-Thu, 6.30am-11pm Fri, 8.30am-1.30pm & 5-9pm Sat, 8.30am-2pm & 5-9pm Sun; ⓂBanco de España) Up to 100,000 people crowd the Iglesia de Jesús de Medinaceli on the first Friday of Lent to kiss the right foot of a wooden sculpture of Christ (*besapié;* kissing of the foot). Pilgrims make three wishes to Jesus, of which he is said to grant one.

IGLESIA DE SAN JERÓNIMO EL REAL
CHURCH

Map p242 (☑91 420 35 78; Calle de Ruiz de Alarcón; ☉10am-1pm & 5-8.30pm Mon-Sat Oct-Jun, hours vary Jul-Sep; ⓂAtocha, Banco de España) Tucked away behind the Museo del Prado, this chapel was traditionally favoured by the Spanish royal family, and King Juan Carlos I was crowned here in 1975 upon the death of Franco. The sometimes sober, sometimes splendid mock-Isabelline interior is actually a 19th-century reconstruction that took its cues from the Iglesia de San Juan de los Reyes in Toledo; the original was largely destroyed during the Peninsular War. What

EL RETIRO & THE ART MUSEUMS SIGHTS

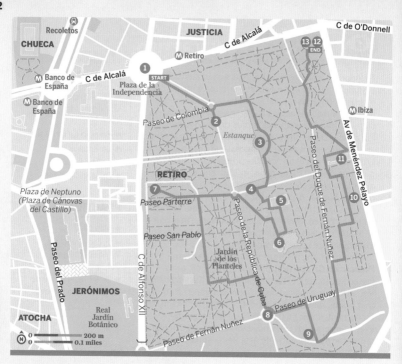

Neighbourhood Walk
Parque del Buen Retiro

START PUERTA DE ALCALÁ
END CASITA DEL PESCADOR
DURATION 4KM; TWO TO THREE HOURS

Start at the ❶ **Puerta de Alcalá**, one of Madrid's grand monumental gates and right next to the park's northwestern gate. Once inside the park, a gentle climb leads past postcard-pretty flower beds to a lovely fountain from where the ❷ **estanque** (artificial lake) is visible. Around the lake's eastern shore is the stunning ❸ **Monument to Alfonso XII**, with its soaring columns and carved lions overlooking the water.

On the lake's southern shore, the ❹ **Fuente Egipcia** (Egyptian Fountain), legend has it, is where Felipe IV buried an enormous fortune in the mid-18th century. Down the hill to the southeast, the brick ❺ **Palacio de Velázquez** hosts temporary exhibitions. Even better, among the trees further south is the ❻ **Palacio de Cristal**, a magnificent metal-and-glass structure built in 1887 as a winter garden for exotic flowers and now used for temporary exhibitions.

Away to the northwest, just inside the Puerta de Felipe IV, stands what is thought to be ❼ **Madrid's oldest tree**, a Mexican conifer (ahuehuete). Planted in 1633 and with a trunk circumference of 52m, it was used by French soldiers during the Napoleonic Wars in the early 19th century as a cannon mount. Returning southeast, seek out ❽ **El Ángel Caído** (Fallen Angel, aka Lucifer), one of few statues to the devil anywhere in the world. It sits 666m above sea level. Nearby is ❾ **La Rosaleda** (Rose Garden) with more than 4000 roses, while a short walk east brings you to the sculpted hedgerows, peacocks and lily ponds of the ❿ **Jardines del Arquitecto Herrero Palacios**. Beyond these gardens are the enclosures of the former ⓫ **Casa de Fieras** (Madrid's zoo until 1972), then the pleasing ruins of the 13th-century ⓬ **Ermita de San Isidro**, one of the few examples of Romanesque architecture in Madrid. Almost next door is the cute ⓭ **Casita del Pescador**, a former royal fishing lodge and now an information office.

remained of the former cloisters has been incorporated into the Museo del Prado.

REAL JARDÍN BOTÁNICO   GARDENS

Map p242 (Royal Botanical Garden; ☑91 420 04 38; www.rjb.csic.es; Plaza de Bravo Murillo 2; adult/child €3/free; ⊙10am-9pm May-Aug, to 8pm Apr & Sep, to 7pm Mar & Oct, to 6pm Nov-Feb; Ⓜ Atocha) Although not as expansive or as popular as the Parque del Buen Retiro, Madrid's botanical gardens are another leafy oasis in the centre of town. With some 30,000 species crammed into a relatively small 8-hectare area, it's more a place to wander at leisure than laze under a tree, although there are benches dotted throughout the gardens where you can sit.

In the centre stands a statue of Carlos III, who in 1781 moved the gardens here from their original location at El Huerto de Migas Calientes, on the banks of the Río Manzanares, while in the **Pabellón Villanueva**, on the eastern flank of the gardens, art exhibitions are frequently staged – the opening hours are the same as for the park and the exhibitions are usually free.

There are Spanish-language **guided visits** to the gardens; reservations by phone are essential.

MUSEO NAVAL   MUSEUM

Map p242 (☑91 523 87 89; Paseo del Prado 5; admission €3; ⊙10am-7pm Tue-Sun Sep-Jul, 10am-3pm Tue-Sun Aug; Ⓜ Banco de España) A block south of Plaza de la Cibeles, this museum will appeal to those who always wondered what the Spanish Armada really looked like. On display are quite extraordinary models of ships from the earliest days of Spain's maritime history to the 20th century. Lovers of antique maps will also find plenty of interest, especially Juan de la Cosa's parchment map of the known world, put together in 1500. The accuracy of Europe and Africa is astounding, and it's supposedly the first map to show the Americas.

Also of interest is the wall-sized map showing Spanish maritime journeys of discovery from the 15th to 18th centuries. Littered throughout this pleasant exhibition space are dozens of uniforms, weapons, flags and other naval paraphernalia.

MUSEO DE ARTES DECORATIVAS   MUSEUM

Map p242 (☑91 532 64 99; http://mnartesdecorativas.mcu.es; Calle de Montalbán 12; adult/child, student & senior €3/1.50, free Sun & 5-8pm Thu Sep-Jun; ⊙9.30am-3pm Tue, Wed, Fri & Sat,

FOOTBALL PLAZA CELEBRATIONS

The battle for football supremacy in Madrid is rarely confined to the stadiums. Whenever Real Madrid wins a major trophy, crowds head for the Plaza de la Cibeles (p110) to celebrate in their hundreds and thousands. To protect the fountain, the city council boards up the statue and surrounds it with police on the eve of important matches. A little further down the Paseo del Prado, Plaza de Neptuno (p110) is where fans of Atlético de Madrid hold equally popular (and every bit as destructive) celebrations.

9.30am-3pm & 5-8pm Thu, 10am-3pm Sun, closed Mon year-round & Thu Jul & Aug; Ⓜ Retiro) Those who love sumptuous period furniture, ceramics, carpets, tapestries and the like will find themselves passing a worthwhile hour or two here. There's plenty to catch your eye and the ceramics from around Spain are a definite feature, while the re-creations of kitchens from several regions are curiosities. Reconstructions of regal bedrooms, women's drawing rooms and 19th-century salons also help shed light on how the privileged classes of Spain have lived through the centuries.

ANTIGUA ESTACIÓN
DE ATOCHA   NOTABLE BUILDING

Map p242 (Plaza del Emperador Carlos V; Ⓜ Atocha Renfe) In 1992 the northwestern wing of the Antigua Estación de Atocha (old Atocha train station) was given a stunning overhaul. The structure of this grand iron-and-glass relic from the 19th century was preserved, while its interior was artfully converted into a light-filled tropical garden with more than 500 plant species. The project was the work of architect Rafael Moneo and his landmark achievement was to create a thoroughly modern space that resonates with the stately European train stations of another age.

In the modern northeastern corner of the station, on the 1st floor, the **11 March 2004 Memorial** (Map p242; ⊙11am-2pm & 5-7pm Tue-Sun Apr-Feb, 10am-8pm daily March) is a moving monument to the victims of the 2004 terrorist attack at the station. Although partially visible from the Paseo de la Infanta Isabel, the memorial is best viewed from below. A glass panel shows the names of those killed, while the airy glass-and-perspex dome is inscribed with the messages of condolence and solidarity left by well-wishers in a number of languages in the immediate aftermath of the attack. The 12m-high dome is designed so that the sun highlights different messages at different times of the day, while the effect at night is akin to flickering candles.

REAL FÁBRICA DE TAPICES
LANDMARK

Map p242 (☑91 434 05 50; www.realfabricadetapices.com; Calle de Fuenterrabía 2; adult/child €4/3; ⏰10am-2pm Mon-Fri Sep-Jul, guided tours every half-hour; Ⓜ Atocha Renfe, Menéndez Pelayo) If a wealthy Madrid nobleman wanted to impress, he came here to the Real Fábrica de Tapices (Royal Tapestry Workshop) where royalty commissioned the pieces that adorned their palaces and private residences. The Spanish government, Spanish royal family and the Vatican were the biggest patrons of the tapestry business: Spain alone is said to have collected four million tapestries. With such an exclusive clientele, it was a lucrative business and remains so, 300 years after the factory was founded.

Goya began his career here, first as a cartoonist and later as a tapestry designer. Given such an illustrious history, it is, therefore, somewhat surprising that coming here today feels like visiting a carpet shop, with small showrooms strewn with fine tapestries. There is a permanent exhibition on show and a sales area. If you're lucky, you'll get to see how they're made.

ⓘ SPANISH FAST FOOD & WHERE TO EAT BETWEEN MEALS

There aren't many options for eating outside normal Spanish dining hours around here, but you could try the following:

➜ **El Brillante** (p114) *Churros* and bar food.

➜ **Estado Puro** (p114) For 21st-century tapas.

➜ **Mallorca** (p123) For Parque del Buen Retiro picnics.

➜ **Cafeteria of the Museo del Prado** (p99) Opens 10am to 7.30pm.

EATING

In the discreet residential enclave between the Parque del Buen Retiro and the Paseo del Prado you'll find a handful of exclusive restaurants where eating is taken seriously, classic charm is the pervasive atmosphere, and limousines wait outside to ferry the well-heeled back home. On the western shore of the *paseo* is one of Madrid's most exciting tapas bars.

EL BRILLANTE
SPANISH €

Map p242 (☑91 528 69 66; Plaza del Emperador Carlos V; bocadillos €4.50-7, raciónes €7.50-12; ⏰7.30am-2.30am Sep-Jul; Ⓜ Atocha) Just by the Centro de Arte Reina Sofía, this breezy, no-frills bar-eatery is a Madrid institution for its *bocadillos* (filled rolls) – the *bocadillo de calamares* has been a favourite for more than half a century – and no-nonsense *raciónes* (large tapas servings).

It's also famous for *chocolate con churros* or *porras* (chocolate with deep-fried doughnuts) in the wee hours after a hard night on the tiles.

★ ESTADO PURO
TAPAS €€

Map p242 (☑91 330 24 00; www.tapasenestadopuro.com; Plaza Neptuno/Plaza de Cánovas del Castillo 4; tapas €5-16, mains €13-22; ⏰noon-midnight Mon-Sat, noon-4pm Sun; Ⓜ Banco de España, Atocha) A slick but casual tapas bar, Estado Puro serves up fantastic tapas, such as the *tortilla española siglo XXI* (21st-century Spanish omelette, served in a glass...), lobster gazpacho and parmesan ice cream. The kitchen here is overseen by Paco Roncero, the head chef at La Terraza del Casino (p91), who learned his trade with master chef Ferran Adrià.

Most of the tapas involve spectacular riffs on traditional Spanish themes. The outdoor tables are often reserved and have higher prices, and the long opening hours are a treat for those whose appetites don't conform to Spanish eating hours.

VIRIDIANA
MODERN SPANISH €€€

Map p242 (☑91 523 44 78; www.restauranteviridiana.com; Calle de Juan de Mena 14; mains €28-38, menú de degustación €100; ⏰1.30-4pm & 8pm-midnight; Ⓜ Banco de España) The chef here, Abraham García, is a much-celebrated Madrid figure and his larger-than-life personality is reflected in Viridiana's menu. Many influences are brought to bear on the cooking here, among them international innovations and ingredients and well-considered seasonal variations.

This place was doing fusion cooking long before it became fashionable and has developed a fiercely loyal clientele as a result. In short, it's one of Madrid's best restaurants.

 DRINKING & NIGHTLIFE

KAPITAL CLUB

Map p242 (☑91 420 29 06; www.grupo-kapital.com; Calle de Atocha 125; ⊙5.30-10.30pm & midnight-6am Fri & Sat, midnight-6am Thu & Sun; Ⓜ Atocha) One of the most famous megaclubs in Madrid, this seven-storey venue has something for everyone: from cocktail bars and dance music to karaoke, salsa, hip hop and chilled spaces. There's even a 'Kissing Room'. Admission from €15.

It's such a big place that a cross-section of Madrid society (VIPs and the Real Madrid set love this place) hangs out here without ever getting in each other's way.

 SHOPPING

CUESTA DE CLAUDIO MOYANO BOOKSTALLS BOOKS

Map p242 (Cuesta de Claudio Moyano; ⊙hours vary; Ⓜ Atocha) Madrid's answer to the booksellers that line the Seine in Paris, these secondhand bookstalls are an enduring

---

> **ⓘ GETTING ACTIVE IN EL RETIRO**
>
> Most visitors are content to explore El Retiro on foot, but there are plenty of alternatives on offer.
>
> Renting a **row boat** (Map p242; per boat per 45min weekdays/weekends €5.80/7.50; ⊙10am-8.30pm Apr-Sep, to 5.45pm Oct-Mar) on the lake is a very Madrid thing to do. **Cycling** and **in-line skating** are terrific ways to range far and wide across El Retiro; the north–south **Paseo del Duque Fernán Nuñez** on the park's eastern side is the favoured haunt of in-line skaters. **Bike & Roll** (p206) rents out bikes just off the northeastern corner of El Retiro.

Madrid landmark. Most titles are in Spanish, but there's a handful of offerings in other languages. Opening hours vary from stall to stall, and some of the stalls close at lunchtime.

LIBRERÍA LA CENTRAL BOOKS

Map p242 (☑91 787 87 82; www.lacentral.com; Ronda de Atocha 2; ⊙10am-9pm Mon & Wed-Sat, to 2.30pm Sun; Ⓜ Atocha) Part of the stunning extension to the Centro de Arte Reina Sofía, La Central is Madrid's best gallery bookshop, with a range of posters, postcards and artistic stationery items as well as extensive sections on contemporary art, design, architecture and photography. Most, but by no means all, books are in Spanish.

1. *El tres de mayo* (Goya) 2. *El jardín de las delicias* (Bosch)
3. *La rendición de Breda* (Velázquez)

Masterpieces in Madrid

See the following grand materpieces of Spanish painting and you've drawn near to greatness. All except *Guernica* are in the Museo del Prado (p99).

El jardín de las delicias (Bosch)

Amid the Prado's accumulation of dark and sometimes brooding paintings, Hieronymus Bosch's *The Garden of Earthly Delights* seems to spring from an entirely different place. Weird, wonderful and unforgettable, it's a surreal work of art that rewards lengthy inspection.

El tres de mayo (Goya)

Goya's genius for capturing human drama is nowhere more evident than in *El tres de mayo,* with all the intensity and despair of Madrid's failed 1808 rebellion against Napoleon laid bare on canvas.

Guernica (Picasso)

Epic in scale, compelling in its original detail, *Guernica* is the spectacular symbol of the cubist style perfected by Picasso and arguably the most famous painting of the 20th century. It can be found in the Centro de Arte Reina Sofía (p108).

La rendición de Breda (Velázquez)

Best known for the intimacy of his royal portraits, Velázquez takes on the drama of a city's surrender in this piece (The Surrender of Breda). In doing so he brings to the canvas his perfect understanding of light, colour and the individuality of human faces.

Las meninas (Velázquez)

This intriguing royal scene (The Maids of Honour) is Velázquez' most recognisable painting, a marriage of a painter at the peak of his powers and a subject matter (royal life) that he made his own.

Salamanca

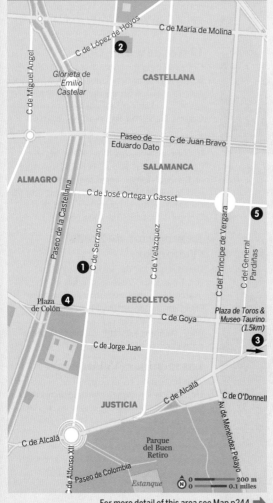

Neighbourhood Top Five

❶ Shopping for Spanish fashions along Calle de Serrano, one of the most prestigious shopping boulevards in Europe, beginning with **Agatha Ruiz de la Prada** (p126).

❷ Gaining an insight into the old-money Salamanca world by visiting the extraordinary art collection at the **Museo Lázaro Galdiano** (p121).

❸ Finding out more about bullfighting by taking a tour at the **Plaza de Toros Monumental de Las Ventas** (p120).

❹ Catching the buzz of Spanish culinary innovation in stunning new **Platea** (p123).

❺ Discovering a whole new world of chocolates in the boutique of master chocolatier **Oriol Balaguer** (p126).

For more detail of this area see Map p244 ➡

Explore: Salamanca

One of the larger *barrios* (districts) that we cover in this book, Salamanca can look daunting on a map, but it's easily navigated for the most part on foot. Calle de Serrano and Calle de José Ortega y Gasset are the two main shopping strips, and if you're in town to shop then there's very little of interest that's more than a short detour from these two main axes. For the Museo Lázaro Galdiano, it's a stiff uphill climb from the rest of the neighbourhood, while the Plaza de Toros, out in the east of the neighbourhood, is a 30-minute walk from Calle de Serrano, also uphill for much of the way. For both of these major attractions, consider hopping on the metro.

Although you will find bars and nightclubs here, Salamanca is very much a daytime *barrio*. Salamanca's tapas bars and restaurants overflow with a busy lunchtime crowd during the week when eating is often a pit stop on part of a shopping itinerary. We suggest you do likewise to really get under Salamanca's skin. By evening, things are much quieter, with many people coming specifically to eat before heading elsewhere in Madrid to continue their night.

Local Life

➡ **Hang out** José Luis (p124), close to the Museo Lázaro Galdiano, is beloved by a wealthy crowd, its outdoor tables invariably inhabited by suits lingering over bottled mineral water.

➡ **Picnic** Mallorca (p123) has some fantastic takeaway foods, and it's ideal if you're planning a picnic in the Parque del Buen Retiro, which borders Salamanca to the south.

➡ **Slice of Andalucía** At El Nuevo Rincón de Jerez (p125) they sing *La Salve Rociera,* a song with deep roots in the flamenco and Catholic traditions of the south. Breathtaking.

Getting There & Away

➡ **Metro** Serrano and Velázquez (both line 4) or Núñez de Balboa (lines 4 and 5) are the most convenient metro stations; the last means a downhill walk to most of the *barrio*.

➡ **Metro** Gregorio Marañon (lines 7 and 10) is best for the Museo Lázaro Galdiano. Ventas (lines 2 and 5) is the station for the Plaza de Toros.

Lonely Planet's Top Tip

María Luisa Banzo, the owner of **La Cocina de María Luisa** (p124), was formerly a prominent figure in the government of conservative Popular Party Prime Minister José María Aznar – keep an eye out for the former PM (also from Castilla y León) and other prominent politicians in her restaurant.

 Best Places to Eat

➡ Platea (p123)

➡ Biotza (p123)

➡ La Colonial de Goya (p123)

➡ La Cocina de María Luisa (p124)

For reviews, see p123 ➡

 Best Places to Drink

➡ El Lateral (p123)

➡ Geographic Club (p125)

➡ Almonte (p125)

For reviews, see p125 ➡

 Best Shopping

➡ Agatha Ruiz de la Prada (p126)

➡ Manolo Blahnik (p126)

➡ Oriol Balaguer (p126)

➡ Gallery (p126)

➡ Calle de José Ortega y Gasset (p126)

For reviews, see p126 ➡

TOP SIGHT
PLAZA DE TOROS & MUSEO TAURINO

Madrid's Plaza de Toros Monumental de Las Ventas (Las Ventas) is the heart and soul of Spain's bullfighting tradition and the most prestigious bullring in the world. A visit here is a good way to gain an insight into this very Spanish tradition, but the architecture also makes it worth visiting for those with no interest in *la corridas* (bullfights).

Architecture

One of the largest rings in the bullfighting world, Las Ventas can hold 25,000 spectators, and has a grand Mudéjar (a Moorish architectural style) exterior and a suitably coliseum-like arena surrounding the broad sandy ring.

Puerta de Madrid

The grand and decidedly Moorish Puerta de Madrid symbolises the aspiration of all bullfighters and, suitably, it's known colloquially as the 'gate of glory'. Madrid's bullfighting crowd is known as the most demanding in Spain – if they carry a *torero* (bullfighter) out through the gate (usually clutching an ear or a tail – other trophies awarded to an elite few), it's because he has performed exceptionally.

Guided Tour

Although you can visit the ring without taking a tour, we strongly recommend that you take one of the **guided visits** (📞687 739032; www.lasventastour.com; adult/child €14/8; ⏲10am-5.30pm, days of bullfight 10am-1.30pm) – these are in English and Spanish and must be booked in advance. The tours take you out onto the sand and into the royal box.

Museo Taurino

The Museo Taurino was closed for renovations and expansion at the time of research. Once it reopens, expect a new space dedicated to bullfighting legend Manolete, as well as a curious collection of paraphernalia, costumes (the *traje de luces* or suit of lights, is one of bullfighting's most recognisable props), photos and other memorabilia on the top floor above one of the two courtyards by the ring.

DON'T MISS...

→ Architecture
→ Puerta de Madrid
→ Museo Taurino

PRACTICALITIES

→ off Map p244
→ 📞91 356 22 00
→ www.las-ventas.com
→ Calle de Alcalá 237
→ ⏲10am-5.30pm
→ Ⓜ Ventas

TOP SIGHT
MUSEO LÁZARO GALDIANO

This imposing early-20th-century Italianate stone mansion, set discreetly back from the street, belonged to Don José Lázaro Galdiano (1862–1947), a successful businessman and passionate patron of the arts. His astonishing private collection, which he bequeathed to the city upon his death, contains 13,000 works of art and objets d'art (including paintings by some of Europe's grand masters), a quarter of which are on show at any time.

DON'T MISS...

➡ Old Masters
➡ Goya Paintings
➡ Curio Collection
➡ Frescoes & Textiles

PRACTICALITIES

➡ Map p244
➡ ☎ 91 561 60 84
➡ www.flg.es
➡ Calle de Serrano 122
➡ adult/concession/child €6/3/free, last hour free
➡ ⊙10am-4.30pm Mon & Wed-Sat, 10am-3pm Sun
➡ Ⓜ Gregorio Marañón

Old Masters

It can be difficult to believe the breadth of masterpieces that Galdiano gathered during his lifetime, and there's enough here to merit this museum's inclusion among Madrid's best art galleries. The highlights include works by Zurbarán, Claudio Coello, Hieronymus Bosch, Esteban Murillo, El Greco, Lucas Cranach and Constable, and there's even a painting in room 11 attributed to Velázquez.

Goya

As is often the case, Goya belongs in a class of his own. He dominates room 13, while the ceiling of the adjoining room 14 features a collage from some of Goya's more famous works. Some that are easy to recognise include *La maja desnuda*, *La maja vestida* and the frescoes of the Ermita de San Antonio de la Florida.

Curio Collection

This remarkable collection ranges beyond paintings to sculptures, bronzes, miniature figures, jewellery, ceramics, furniture, weapons...clearly Lázaro Galdiano was a man of wide interests. The ground floor is largely given over to a display setting the social context in which Galdiano lived, with hundreds of curios from all around the world on show. There are more on the top floor.

Frescoes & Textiles

The lovely 1st floor, which contains many of the Spanish artworks, is arrayed around the centrepiece of the former ballroom and beneath lavishly frescoed ceilings. And on no account miss the top floor's room 24, which contains some exquisite textiles. As you wander from room to room and from floor to floor, seek out the information panels in each room – most include photos of each room as they appeared in Galdiano's prime.

The Man Behind the Collection

Born in Navarra in northeastern Spain, José Lázaro Galdiano moved to Madrid as a young man. He would later become a hugely significant figure in the cultural life of the city. During WWI he was an important supporter of the Museo del Prado, and later built his own private collection by buying up Spanish artworks in danger of being sold overseas and bringing home those that had already left. He lived in exile during the Spanish Civil War, but continued to collect and upon his return he set up a respected artistic foundation in his former palace that would ultimately house the museum.

◉ SIGHTS

PLAZA DE TOROS &
MUSEO TAURINO STADIUM
See p120.

MUSEO LÁZARO GALDIANO MUSEUM
See p121.

PALACIO DE LINARES &
CASA DE AMÉRICA NOTABLE BUILDING
Map p244 (☑91 595 48 00; www.casamerica.
es; Plaza de la Cibeles 2; adult/child/student &
senior €8/free/5; ☺guided tours 11am, noon &
1pm Sat & Sun Sep-Jul, shorter hours Aug, ticket
office 10am-3pm & 4-8pm Mon-Fri, 11am-1pm Sat
& Sun; ⓜBanco de España) So extraordinary is
the Palacio de Comunicaciones on Plaza de
la Cibeles (p110) that many visitors fail to
notice this fine 19th-century pleasure dome
that stands watch over the northeastern
corner of the plaza. Built in 1873, the Palacio de Linares is a worthy member of the
line-up of grand facades on the plaza, while
its interior is notable for the copious use of
Carrara marble. Tours take an hour and you
can purchase tickets at the ticket office.

Tickets can also be reserved on ☑902
221 424 or booked online at www.entradas.
com; they often sell out in advance, so don't
leave it until the last minute. In the palace's
grounds is the Casa de América, a modern
exhibition centre, which also hosts all sorts
of events and concerts.

MUSEO ARQUEOLÓGICO
NACIONAL MUSEUM
Map p244 (man.mcu.es; Calle de Serrano 13; admission €3, 2-8pm Sat & 9.30am-noon Sun free;
☺9.30am-8pm Tue-Sat, 9.30am-3pm Sun; ⓜSer-
rano) Reopened after a massive overhaul of

the building, the showpiece National Ar-
chaeology Museum contains a sweeping accumulation of artefacts behind its towering
facade. Daringly redesigned within, the museum ranges across Spain's ancient history
and the large collection includes stunning
mosaics taken from Roman villas across
Spain, intricate Muslim-era and Mudéjar
handiwork, sculpted figures such as the
Dama de Ibiza and *Dama de Elche,* examples of Romanesque and Gothic architectural styles and a partial copy of the prehistoric
cave paintings of Altamira (Cantabria).

BIBLIOTECA NACIONAL &
MUSEO DEL LIBRO LIBRARY, MUSEUM
Map p244 (☑91 580 78 05; www.bne.es; Paseo
de los Recoletos 20; ☺library 9am-9pm Mon-Fri,
9am-2pm Sat mid-Sep–mid-Jun, 9am-7.30pm
Mon-Fri mid-Jun–mid-Sep; museum 10am-8pm
Tue-Sat, 10am-2pm Sun; ⓜColón) **FREE** Perhaps
the most impressive of the grand edifices
erected along the Paseo de los Recoletos
in the 19th century, the 1892 Biblioteca
Nacional (National Library) dominates
the southern end of Plaza de Colón. Downstairs, and entered via a separate entrance,
the fascinating and recently overhauled
museum is a must for bibliophiles, with in-
teractive displays on printing presses and
other materials, illuminated manuscripts,
the history of the library, and literary cafes.

Our favourite exhibits are the 1626 map
of Spain and Picasso's *Mademoiselle Léo-
nie en un sillón* in the Sala de las Musas.
There's not an e-book in sight.

MUSEO AL AIRE LIBRE SCULPTURE
Map p244 (Paseo de la Castellana; ☺24hr;
ⓜRubén Darío) **FREE** This fascinating open-
air collection of 17 abstract sculptures

SALAMANCA'S DIFFICULT BIRTH

When Madrid's authorities were looking to expand beyond the newly inadequate con-
fines of the medieval capital, the Marqués de Salamanca, a 19th-century aristocrat
and general with enormous political clout, heard the call. He threw everything he had
into the promotion of his *barrio* (district) in the 1870s, buying up land cheaply, which he
hoped to sell later for a profit. He was ahead of his time: the houses he built contained
Madrid's first water closets, the latest in domestic plumbing and water heating for
bathrooms and kitchens, while he also inaugurated horse-drawn tramways. In the year
of his death, 1883, the streets got electric lighting. Hard as it is now to imagine, there
was little enthusiasm for the project and the *marqués* quickly went bankrupt. Towards
the end of his life, he wrote 'I have managed to create the most comfortable *barrio* in
Madrid and find myself the owner of 50 houses, 13 hotels and 18 million feet of land.
And I owe more than 36 million reales on all of this. The task is completed but I am
ruined.' It was only later that *madrileños* (people of Madrid) saw the error of their ways.

PLATEA

Platea (Map p244; ☑91 577 00 25; www.plateamadrid.com; Calle de Goya 5-7; ⊙12.30pm-12.30am Sun-Wed, 12.30pm-2.30am Thu-Sat; Ⓜ Serrano, Colón) is one of the most exciting things to happen in Madrid's eating scene in years. The ornate cinema named Carlos III opposite the Plaza de Colón has been artfully transformed into a dynamic culinary scene with more than a hint of burlesque. Working with the original theatre-style layout, the developers have used the multilevel seating to array a series of restaurants that seem at once self-contained yet connected to the whole through the soaring open central space, with all of them in some way facing the stage area where cabaret-style or 1930s-era performances or live cooking shows provide a rather glamorous backdrop. It's where food court meets haute cuisine, a daring combination of lunch or dinner with floor show without the formality that usually infuses such places. The chefs to have opened up here boast six Michelin stars among them, and there are 12 restaurants (among them the outstanding Arriba, p125), three gourmet food stores and cocktail bars.

includes works by the renowned Basque artist Eduardo Chillida, the Catalan master Joan Miró, as well as Eusebio Sempere and Alberto Sánchez, the latter one of Spain's foremost sculptors of the 20th century. The sculptures are beneath the overpass where Paseo de Eduardo Dato crosses Paseo de la Castellana, but somehow the hint of traffic grime and pigeon shit only adds to the appeal. All but one are on the eastern side of Paseo de la Castellana.

EATING

Eating out in Salamanca is generally a suave affair and restaurants here invite you to rub shoulders with the young, the beautiful and the very well dressed – in most places you'll need to dress accordingly – while celebrity chefs occasionally tug the city's most conservative *barrio* in new culinary directions.

EL LATERAL   TAPAS €

Map p244 (☑91 435 06 04; www.lateral.com; Calle de Velázquez 57; tapas €1.55-7.65; ⊙noon-1am Sun-Wed, noon-2am Thu-Sat; Ⓜ Velázquez, Núñez de Balboa) El Lateral does terrific *pinchos* (tapas), which serve as the ideal accompaniment to the fine wines on offer. Tapas are creative without being over the top (wild mushroom croquettes or sirloin with foie gras). This being Salamanca, they draw a pretty upmarket crowd, but you'd be surprised how rapidly the ties loosen up after work.

Service is restaurant standard, rather than your average tapas-bar brusqueness.

There's another branch in **Malasaña** (☑91 531 68 77; Calle de Fuencarral 43; ⊙noon-midnight Sun-Wed, noon-2am Thu-Sat; Ⓜ Tribunal), with a further bar-restaurant in **Huertas** (☑91 420 15 82; Plaza de Santa Ana 12; ⊙noon-midnight Sun-Wed, noon-2am Thu-Sat; Ⓜ Antón Martín, Sol).

MALLORCA   SELF-CATERING €

Map p244 (☑915771859; www.pasteleria-mallorca.com; Calle de Serrano 6; mains €7-12; ⊙9am-9pm; Ⓜ Retiro) For fine takeaway food, head to Mallorca, a Madrid institution. Everything here, from gourmet mains to snacks and sweets, is delicious.

BIOTZA   TAPAS, BASQUE €€

Map p244 (☑91 781 03 13; Calle de Claudio Coello 27; cold/hot pintxos €2.80/3.40, raciónes from €6, set menus from €18; ⊙1-5pm & 8pm-midnight Mon-Sat; Ⓜ Serrano) This breezy Basque tapas bar is one of the best places in Madrid to sample the creativity of bite-sized *pintxos* (Basque tapas) as only the Basques can make them. It's the perfect combination of San Sebastián–style tapas, Madrid-style pale-green/red-black decoration and unusual angular benches. The prices quickly add up, but it's highly recommended nonetheless. There's also a more formal Basque restaurant out the back.

LA COLONIAL DE GOYA   TAPAS €€

Map p244 (☑91 575 63 06; www.lacolonialdegoya.com; Calle de Jorge Juan 34; mains €11-22; ⊙1-4pm & 8pm-midnight; Ⓜ Velázquez) Other better-known places have come and gone around here, but La Colonial de Goya has stood the test of time. The food ranges across the creative (prawn and beef meatballs or broad-bean

🛈 SPANISH FAST FOOD & WHERE TO EAT BETWEEN MEALS

If your body clock is not quite operating on Spanish time, the following offer food outside of traditional meal times:

➡ **El Lateral** (p123) Gourmet tapas.

➡ **Platea** (p123) Gourmet food stores and tapas.

➡ **Viandas de Salamanca** (Map p244; ☑91 577 99 12; www.viandasdesalamanca.es; Calle de Goya 43; bocadillos from €3.60; ◔9.30am-9.30pm Mon-Sat, 9.30am-8pm Sun; Ⓜ Velázquez) *Jamón* (cured ham) rolls.

➡ **Restaurante Estay** (p124) Cool tapas.

and octopus risotto, for example) to the more traditional (such as canapés and *croquetas*). The atmosphere is casual, while the all-white decor of wood and exposed brick walls is as classy as the neighbourhood.

LA COCINA DE MARÍA LUISA   CASTILIAN €€

Map p244 (☑91 781 01 80; www.lacocinademarialuisa.es; Calle de Jorge Juan 42; mains €17-27; ◔1.30-4pm & 9pm-midnight Mon-Sat Sep-Jul; Ⓜ Velázquez) The home kitchen of former parliamentarian María Luisa Banzo has one of Salamanca's most loyal followings. The cooking is a carefully charted culinary journey through Castilla y León, accompanied by well-chosen regional wines and rustic decor that add much warmth to this welcoming place. The house speciality comes from María Luisa's mother – pigs' trotters filled with meat and black truffles

from Soria. The chance to choose half-sized versions of most dishes will appeal to many.

JOSÉ LUIS   SPANISH €€

Map p244 (☑91 563 09 58; www.joseluis.es; Calle de Serrano 89; tapas from €5; ◔8.30am-1am Mon-Fri, 9am-1am Sat, 12.30pm-1am Sun; Ⓜ Gregorio Marañón) With numerous branches around Madrid, José Luis is famous for its fidelity to traditional Spanish recipes. It wins many people's vote for Madrid's best *tortilla de patatas* (Spanish potato omelette), but it's also good for *croquetas* and *ensaladilla rusa* (Russian salad). This outpost along Calle de Serrano has a slightly stuffy, young-men-in-suits feel to it, which is, after all, *very* Salamanca.

LA MARUCA   CANTABRIAN €€

Map p244 (☑91 781 49 69; www.restaurantelamaruca.com; Calle de Velázquez 54; mains €12-20; ◔11am-1am; Ⓜ Velázquez) This classy and fresh space is dedicated to the cooking of Spain's northern Cantabria region and it's extremely popular among Salamanca's young and wealthy. While Cantabria means the best *anchoas* (anchovies) in the country and other fruits of the sea, La Maruca is unusual in that it focuses as much on the Cantabrian interior – think meatballs and hearty stews.

RESTAURANTE ESTAY   TAPAS €€

Map p244 (☑91 578 04 70; www.estayrestaurante.com; Calle de Hermosilla 46; tapas €1.75-5, 6-tapas set menu from €13.25; ◔8am-midnight Mon-Thu, 8am-1am Fri & Sat; Ⓜ Velázquez) Restaurante Estay is partly a standard Spanish bar, where besuited waiters serve *café con leche* (coffee with milk) at breakfast, and also one of the best-loved tapas bars in this part of town. The long list of hot and cold tapas concentrates mostly on Spanish sta-

SPANISH WINES

Spanish wine is subject to a complicated system of wine classification with a range of designations marked on the bottle. Most importantly, they are labelled according to region or classificatory status rather than grape variety. If an area meets certain strict standards for a given period and covers all aspects of planting, cultivating and ageing, it receives Denominación de Origen (DO; Denomination of Origin) status. There are currently over 60 DO-recognised wine-producing areas in Spain.

An outstanding wine region gets the much-coveted Denominación de Origen Calificada (DOC). At present, the only DOC wines come from La Rioja in northern Spain and the small Priorat area in Catalonia. Other important indications of quality depend on the length of time a wine has been aged, especially if in oak barrels. The best wines are often, therefore, *crianza* (aged for one year in oak barrels), *reserva* (two years ageing, at least one of which is in oak barrels) and *gran reserva* (two years in oak and three in the bottle).

ples, with a selection of more adventurous combinations, such as quail with onion and chocolate. Like this dish, it all seems rather an odd mix, but it somehow works.

ARRIBA
MODERN SPANISH €€€

Map p244 (☑91 219 23 05; www.restaurantearriba. com; 1st fl, Calle de Goya 5; mains €17-32; ⊙1.30-4.30pm & 8.30pm-midnight; Ⓜ Serrano, Colón) Up on the 1st floor of the exciting Platea development, just off Plaza de Colón, this exciting restaurant by the two-Michelin-starred celebrity chef Ramón Freixa has a bistro feel, with a what's-fresh-in-the-market approach to cooking and dishes whose origins range from Catalonia all the way down to Andalucía. The cooking is assured, dominated by that reliable mantra of nouvelle cuisine – don't fiddle too much with traditional tastes, but make it worth it when you do. The sticky rice with cod, mushrooms and black Catalan sausage or the octopus carpaccio are two examples of the approach.

DRINKING & NIGHTLIFE

Salamanca is the land of the beautiful people and it's all about gloss and glamour: heels for her and hair gel for him. As you glide through the *pijos* (beautiful people or yuppies), keep your eyes peeled for Real Madrid players and celebrities. Although places do exist in Salamanca's otherwise quiet streets that enable you to spend the whole night here, we're of the view that there are far better *barrios* to get a feel for Madrid's famous nightlife. And many of Salamanca's celebrities would appear to agree – the clubs and cocktail bars of Malasaña, Chueca and elsewhere are where they're more likely to show up.

GEOGRAPHIC CLUB
BAR

Map p244 (☑91 578 08 62; www.thegeographic-club.es; Calle de Alcalá 141; ⊙1pm-2am Sun-Thu, to 3am Fri & Sat; Ⓜ Goya) With its elaborate stained-glass windows, ethno-chic from all over the world and laid-back atmosphere, the Geographic Club is an excellent choice in Salamanca for an early-evening drink – try one of the 30-plus tropical cocktails. We like the table built around an old hot-air-balloon basket almost as much as the cavernlike pub downstairs.

EL NUEVO RINCÓN DE JEREZ

Out in the eastern reaches of Salamanca, the Andalucian bar **El Nuevo Rincón de Jerez** (☑91 112 30 80; www.elnuevorincondejerez.es; Calle de Rufino Blanco 5; raciónes €7-13; ⊙1-4.30pm & 7pm-midnight Tue-Sat, 1-4.30pm Sun Sep-Jul; Ⓜ Manuel Bacerra) is utterly unlike anywhere else in Madrid. At 11pm on Friday and Saturday, they turn off the lights, light the candles and sing as one *La Salve Rociera*, a near-mythical song with deep roots in the flamenco and Catholic traditions of the south. It will send chills down your spine.

ALMONTE
CLUB

Map p244 (☑91 563 25 04; www.almontesalaro-ciera.com; Calle de Juan Bravo 35; ⊙10pm-5am Sun-Fri, 10pm-6am Sat; Ⓜ Núñez de Balboa, Diego de León) If flamenco has captured your soul, but you're keen to do more than watch, head to Almonte. Live acts kick the night off, paying homage to the flamenco roots of Almonte in Andalucía's deep south. The young and the beautiful who come here have *sevillanas* (a flamenco dance style) in their soul and in their feet. So head downstairs to see the best dancing. Dance if you dare.

SERRANO 41
CLUB

Map p244 (☑687 871045; www.serrano41.com; Calle de Serrano 41; ⊙11pm-5.30am Wed-Sun; Ⓜ Serrano) If bullfighters, Real Madrid stars and other A-listers can't drag themselves away from Salamanca, chances are that you'll find them here, although the glamour has waned a little of late. Danceable pop and house dominate Friday and Saturday nights, funk gets a turn on Sunday (Funk Kombat night) and it's indie night on Thursday. Admission from €12. Its outdoor terrace opens in late May and is very cool until it closes in mid-September.

☆ ENTERTAINMENT

FUNDACIÓN JUAN MARCH
CONCERT VENUE

Map p244 (www.march.es; Calle de Castelló 77; Ⓜ Núñez de Balboa) FREE A foundation dedicated to promoting music and culture (as well as exhibitions), the Juan March Foundation stages free concerts throughout the year. Performances range from solo recitals to themed concerts dedicated to a single style or composer.

 SHOPPING

Salamanca is the ideal place to take the pulse of the Spanish fashion scene and you'll likely find it in top shape. Here you'll discover that there's so much more to Spanish fashion than Zara and Mango. Fashions range from classically elegant to cool and cutting edge, from both leading and upcoming Spanish designers and the big names in international fashion. Shopping here is a social event, where people put on their finest and service is often impeccable, if a little stuffy. Throw in a sprinkling of gourmet food shops and you could easily spend days doing little else but shopping.

★**AGATHA RUIZ DE LA PRADA** FASHION
Map p244 (☎91 319 05 01; www.agatharuizdelaprada.com; Calle de Serrano 27; ⊙10am-8.30pm Mon-Sat; ⓂSerrano) This boutique has to be seen to be believed, with pinks, yellows and oranges everywhere you turn. It's fun and exuberant, but not just for kids. It also has serious and highly original fashion. Agatha Ruiz de la Prada is one of the enduring icons of *la movida,* Madrid's 1980s outpouring of creativity.

CAMPER SHOES
Map p244 (☎91 578 25 60; www.camper.com; Calle de Serrano 24; ⊙10am-9pm Mon-Sat, noon-8pm Sun; ⓂSerrano) Spanish fashion is not all haute couture, and this world-famous cool and quirky shoe brand from Mallorca offers bowling-shoe chic with colourful, fun designs that are all about quality coupled with comfort. There are other outlets throughout the city, including a **Malasaña shop** (☎91 531 23 47; Calle de Fuencarral 42; ⊙10am-8pm Mon-Sat; ⓂGran Vía, Tribunal) – check out the website for locations.

GALLERY CLOTHING, ACCESSORIES
Map p244 (☎91 576 79 31; www.gallerymadrid.com; Calle de Jorge Juan 38; ⊙10.30am-8.30pm Mon-Sat; ⓂPríncipe de Vergara, Velázquez) This stunning showpiece of men's and women's fashions and accessories (shoes, bags, belts and the like) is the new Madrid in a nutshell – stylish, brand conscious and all about having the right look. There are creams and fragrances, as well as quirkier items such as designer crash helmets. With an interior designed by Tomas Alia, it's one of the city's coolest shops.

MANOLO BLAHNIK SHOES
Map p244 (☎91 575 96 48; www.manoloblahnik.com; Calle de Serrano 58; ⊙10am-2pm & 4-8pm Mon-Sat; ⓂSerrano) Nothing to wear to the Oscars? Do what many Hollywood celebrities do and head for Manolo Blahnik. The showroom is exclusive and each shoe is displayed like a work of art.

ORIOL BALAGUER FOOD
Map p244 (www.oriolbalaguer.com; Calle de José Ortega y Gasset 44; ⊙9am-8pm Mon-Fri, 10am-8pm Sat, 10am-2.30pm Sun; ⓂNúñez de Balboa) Catalan pastry chef Oriol Balaguer has a formidable CV – he worked in the kitchens of Ferran Adrià in Catalonia and won the prize for the World's Best Dessert (the 'Seven Textures of Chocolate') in 2001. More recently, his croissants won the title of Spain's best in 2014. His chocolate boutique is presented like a small art gallery dedicated to exquisite chocolate collections and cakes. You'll never be able to buy ordinary chocolate again.

BOMBONERÍAS SANTA FOOD, WINE
Map p244 (☎91 576 76 25; www.bomboneriassanta.com; Calle de Serrano 56; ⊙10am-2pm & 5-8.30pm Mon, 10am-8.30pm Tue-Sat, shorter hours in Jul & Aug; ⓂSerrano) If your style is as refined as your palate, the exquisite chocolates in this tiny shop will satisfy. The packaging is every bit as pretty as the *bombones* within, but they're not cheap – count on paying around €60 per kilo of chocolate.

MADRID'S INTERNATIONAL DESIGNER STREET

The world's most prestigious international designers occupy what is known as *la milla del oro* (the golden mile) along **Calle de José Ortega y Gasset**, close to the corner with Calle de Serrano. On the south side of the street, you'll find Dolce & Gabbana, Chanel, Tiffany & Co, Hermès, Valentino and Dior, with Balenciaga just around the corner. Just across the road is Jimmy Choo and Cartier, with Gucci not far away.

LAVINIA
WINE

Map p244 (☑91 650 33 92; www.lavinia.es; Calle de José Ortega y Gasset 16; ☺10am-9pm Mon-Sat; ⓂNúñez de Balboa) 🍴 Although we love the intimacy of old-style Spanish wine shops, they can't match the selection of Spanish and international wines available at Lavinia, which has more than 4000 bottles to choose from. It also organises wine courses, tastings and excursions to nearby bodegas (wineries). The 1st-floor restaurant is a fine gastronomic space.

EKSEPTION & EKS
CLOTHING, ACCESSORIES

Map p244 (☑91 361 97 76; www.ekseption.es; Calle de Velázquez 28; ☺10.30am-2.30pm & 4.30-8.30pm Mon-Sat; ⓂVelázquez) This elegant showroom store consistently leads the way with the latest trends, spanning catwalk designs alongside a look that is more informal, though always sophisticated. The unifying theme is urban chic and its list of designer brands includes Balenciaga, Givenchy, Marc Jacobs and Dries van Noten. Next door is the preserve of younger, more casual lines, including a fantastic selection of jeans.

Victoria Beckham was a regular customer here in her Madrid days; make of that what you will.

CUARTO DE JUEGOS
TOYS

Map p244 (☑91 435 00 99; www.cuartodejuegos.es; Calle de Jorge Juan 42; ☺10am-8.30pm Mon-Fri, 10.30am-2pm & 5-8pm Sat; ⓂVelázquez, Príncipe de Vergara) We're not sure if it's an official rule, but batteries seem to be outlawed at this traditional toy shop, where all kinds of old-fashioned board games and puzzles are still sold. Yes, there's Ludo, Chinese checkers and backgammon, but there's so much more here and it's not just for kids.

MANTEQUERÍA BRAVO
FOOD, WINE

Map p244 (www.bravo1931.com; Calle de Ayala 24; ☺9.30am-2.30pm & 5.30-8.30pm Mon-Fri, 9.30am-2.30pm Sat; ⓂSerrano) Behind the attractive old facade lies a connoisseur's paradise, filled with local cheeses, sausages, wines and coffees. The products here are great for a gift, but everything's so good that you won't want to share. Not that long ago, Mantequería Bravo won the prize for Madrid's best gourmet food shop or delicatessen – it's as simple as that.

DE VIAJE
BOOKS

Map p244 (☑91 577 98 99; www.deviaje.com; Calle de Serrano 41; ☺10am-8.30pm Mon-Fri, 10.30am-2.30pm & 5-8pm Sat; ⓂSerrano) Whether you're after a guidebook, a coffee-table tome or travel literature, De Viaje, Madrid's largest travel bookshop, probably has it. Covering every region of the world, it has mostly Spanish titles, but plenty in English as well. Staff are helpful, there's also a travel agency and it sells North Face, Columbia and Helly Hansen clothing.

PURIFICACIÓN GARCÍA
FASHION

Map p244 (☑91 435 80 13; www.purificaciongarcia.com; Calle de Serrano 28; ☺10am-8.30pm Mon-Sat; ⓂSerrano) Fashions may come and go but Puri consistently manages to keep ahead of the pack. Her signature style for men and women is elegant and mature designs that are just as at home in the workplace as at a wedding.

🏃 SPORTS & ACTIVITIES

LAB ROOM SPA
SPA

Map p244 (☑91 431 21 98; www.thelabroom.com; Calle de Claudio Coello 13; ☺11am-8.30pm Mon-Fri, 11am-8pm Sat; ⓂRetiro) An exclusive spa and beauty parlour whose past clients include Penélope Cruz, Jennifer Lopez, Gwyneth Paltrow and Gael García Bernal, the Lab Room is close to the ultimate in pampering for both men and women. It offers a range of make-up sessions, massages and facial and body treatments; prices can be surprisingly reasonable.

Manicures start at €25, massages start from €35 and it has a range of well-priced, all-inclusive package deals. There's even a complete 'change of image' costing €300 – you won't believe the results they promise.

CHI SPA
SPA

Map p244 (☑91 578 13 40; www.thechispa.com; Calle del Conde de Aranda 6; ☺10am-8pm Mon-Sat; ⓂRetiro) Wrap up in a robe and slippers and prepare to be pampered in one of Spain's best day spas. There are separate areas for men and women, and services include a wide range of massages, facials, manicures and pedicures. Now, what was it you were stressed about?

Malasaña & Chueca

MALASAÑA | CHUECA

Neighbourhood Top Five

1 Passing under the fabulous doorway and spending an hour or two delving into Madrid's past at the **Museo de Historia** (p130).

2 Shopping for retro fashions in the true rebellious spirit of Malasaña at the **Mercado de Fuencarral** (p144).

3 Taking your pick for lunch along one of Madrid's best culinary streets, starting perhaps with **Bazaar** (p134).

4 Kicking back in true Malasaña style in one of the terrific restaurants along Calle de Manuela Malasaña, such as **Albur** (p132).

5 Following the footsteps of Hemingway and other *famosos* (celebrities) by ordering a mojito at the legendary **Museo Chicote** (p140).

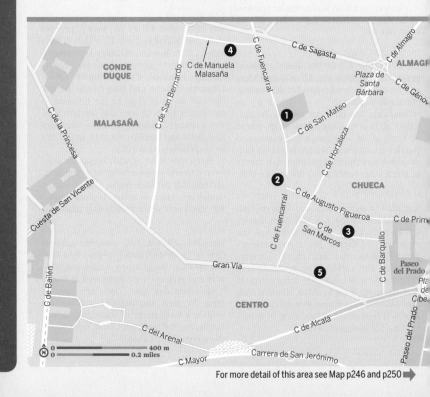

For more detail of this area see Map p246 and p250

Explore: Malasaña & Chueca

Malasaña and Chueca are at their best in the evening and into the night – other than a flurry of activity around lunchtime as people hurry to and from their favourite tapas bar or restaurant, these *barrios* (districts) mostly live for the night. That said, the daytime shopping is fantastic in both *barrios*.

Calle de Fuencarral is the dividing line between the two, a narrow but nonetheless major city thoroughfare that has been pedestrianised for much of its length. West of that line in Malasaña, shopfronts announce names such as 'True Love Tattoo' and 'Retro City' alongside graffiti and posters of heavy-rocking bands that have become an integral part of its gritty urban charm. Slightly more refined and less clamorous, the sub-*barrio* of Conde Duque, to the west, has the best of Malasaña without quite the same grit and noise.

If Malasaña holds fast to its roots, Chueca, east of Calle de Fuencarral, wears its heart on its sleeve, a *barrio* that the gay and lesbian community has transformed into one of the coolest places in Spain. Sometimes it's in your face, but more often it's what locals like to call 'hetero-friendly'. The further east you go, the more sophisticated Chueca becomes.

Local Life

➜ **Neighbourhood hub** Plaza del Dos de Mayo is Malasaña's epicentre, at its best late afternoon when children pour out of nearby schools to play while their parents order beer and wine at adjacent outdoor tables.

➜ **Hang out** Antigua Casa Ángel Sierra (p141), right on Plaza de Chueca, has seen it all in almost a century of Chueca life and the crowds here stand six or seven deep on a busy Saturday night.

Getting There & Away

➜ **Metro** Chueca metro station (line 5) sits right in the heart of Chueca, while Tribunal (lines 1 and 10) serves a similar purpose in Malasaña. Noviciado (lines 2 and 10) is good for Conde Duque.

➜ **Metro** Other convenient metro stations around these neighbourhoods' perimeters include San Bernardo, Bilbao, Alonso Martínez, Gran Vía and Santo Domingo.

Lonely Planet's Top Tip

In order to make the most of their popularity, some restaurants in Malasaña and elsewhere offer two sittings on Friday and Saturday nights, usually around 9pm and 11pm. Unless you can't wait (yes, we know that eating at 11pm and finishing dinner after midnight takes some getting used to), we recommend reserving a table for the second sitting – otherwise you'll often get the feeling that they're trying to hurry you along.

 Best Places to Eat

➜ Bazaar (p134)

➜ Albur (p132)

➜ Yakitoro by Chicote (p135)

➜ Casa Julio (p132)

For reviews, see p131

 Best Places to Drink

➜ Museo Chicote (p140)

➜ Le Cabrera (p140)

➜ Del Diego (p141)

➜ Café Belén (p140)

For reviews, see p137 ➡

Best Architecture

➜ Sociedad General de Autores y Editores (p130)

➜ Antiguo Cuartel del Conde Duque (p130)

➜ Museo de Historia (p130)

➜ Casa de las Siete Chimeneas (p131)

For reviews, see p130

◉ SIGHTS

SOCIEDAD GENERAL DE AUTORES Y EDITORES ARCHITECTURE

Map p250 (General Society of Authors & Editors; Calle de Fernando VI 4; MAlonso Martínez) This swirling, melting wedding cake of a building is as close as Madrid comes to the work of Antoni Gaudí, which so illuminates Barcelona. It's a joyously self-indulgent ode to Modernisme and is virtually one of a kind in Madrid. Casual visitors are actively discouraged, although what you see from the street is impressive enough. The only exceptions are on the first Monday of October, International Architecture Day, when its interior staircase alone is reason enough to come.

MUSEO DEL ROMANTICISMO MUSEUM

Map p250 (☏91 448 10 45; museoromanticismo. mcu.es; Calle de San Mateo 13; adult/child/ student €3/free/1.50, Sat after 2.30pm free; ☺9.30am-8.30pm Tue-Sat & 10am-3pm Sun May-Oct, 9.30am-6.30pm Tue-Sat & 10am-3pm Sun Nov-Apr; MTribunal) This intriguing museum is devoted to the Romantic period of the 19th century. It houses a minor treasure trove of mostly 19th-century paintings, furniture, porcelain, books, photos and other bits and bobs from a bygone age and offers an insight into what upper-class houses were like in the 19th century. The best-known work in the collection is Goya's *San Gregorio Magno, Papa*.

The museum occupies a late 18th-century mansion which was converted into a museum in 1924 by the Marqués de la Vega-Inclán (who was involved in the creation of the chain of luxury hotels known as the *paradores*). There's a limit of 100 visitors inside the museum at any one time.

SMALL PRIVATE GALLERIES

For those with an interest in contemporary art that extends beyond what you'll find at the Centro de Arte Reina Sofía (p108), central Madrid is studded with small galleries showcasing both up-and-coming and longer-established painters, sculptors and photographers. For a near-complete list, check out **Arte Madrid** (www.artemadrid. com); its brochure of the same name, available online in PDF format, contains a map and program of upcoming exhibitions.

MUSEO DE HISTORIA MUSEUM

Map p246 (☏91 701 16 86; www.madrid.es/museo dehistoria; Calle de Fuencarral 78; ☺11am-2pm & 4-7pm Tue-Fri, 10am-2pm & 4-7pm Sat & Sun; MTribunal) FREE The fine Museo de Historia (formerly the Museo Municipal) has an elaborate and restored baroque entrance, raised in 1721 by Pedro de Ribera. Behind this facade, the collection is dominated by paintings and other memorabilia charting the historical evolution of Madrid. The highlights are Goya's *Allegory of the City of Madrid* (on the 1st floor), the caricatures lampooning Napoleon and the early 19th-century French occupation of Madrid (1st floor), and the expansive model of Madrid as it was in 1830 (basement).

MUSEO MUNICIPAL DE ARTE CONTEMPORÁNEO MUSEUM

Map p246 (☏91 588 59 28; www.madrid.es/museo artecontemporaneo/; Calle del Conde Duque 9-11; MPlaza de España, Ventura Rodríguez, San Bernardo) FREE Closed for major renovation works at the time of research, this rich collection of modern Spanish art includes mostly paintings and graphic art with a smattering of photography, sculpture and drawings. Highlights include Eduardo Arroyo and Basque sculptor Jorge Oteiza. Running throughout the collection are creative interpretations of Madrid's cityscape – avant-garde splodges and almost old-fashioned visions of modern Madrid side by side, among them a typically fantastical representation of the Cibeles fountain by one-time icon of *la movida madrileña* (the Madrid scene), Ouka Leele.

The museum is inside the Antiguo Cuartel del Conde Duque.

ANTIGUO CUARTEL DEL CONDE DUQUE NOTABLE BUILDING

Map p246 (Calle del Conde Duque 9; MPlaza de España, Ventura Rodríguez, San Bernardo) This grand former barracks dominates Conde Duque on the western fringe of Malasaña with its imposing facade stretching 228m down the hill. Built in 1717 under the auspices of architect Pedro de Ribera, its highlight is the extravagant 18th-century doorway, a masterpiece of the baroque churrigueresque style. These days it's home to a cultural centre, which hosts government archives, libraries, the Hemeroteca Municipal (Spain's biggest collection of newspapers and magazines), temporary exhibitions and, when it reopens, the Museo Municipal de Arte Contemporáneo.

By night, in summer, one of the two large patios becomes an atmospheric venue for concerts; programs for exhibitions and concerts are posted outside.

GALERÍA MORIARTY
GALLERY

Map p250 (☑91 531 43 65; www.galeriamoriarty.com; Calle de Tamayo y Baus 6; ☺11am-7pm Tue-Fri, 11am-2pm Sat; MChueca, Colón) **FREE** During *la movida madrileña* in the 1980s, Galería Moriarty (then in Calle del Almirante) was one of Madrid's most important meeting places of culture and counterculture, drawing the iconic Agatha Ruiz de la Prada, film-maker Pedro Almodóvar and photographer García-Alix, among others, to attend its exhibitions and parties. It has moved a number of times since, but it remains one of the most important small galleries in Madrid, with all manner of interesting contemporary exhibitions.

PALACIO DE LIRIA
NOTABLE BUILDING

Map p246 (☑91 548 15 50; www.fundacioncasadealba.com; Calle de la Princesa 20; ☺10am, 11am & noon Fri; MVentura Rodríguez) This 18th-century mansion, rebuilt after a fire in 1936, nestles amid the modern architecture just north of Plaza de España as a reminder of the days when Madrid's streets were lined with mansions like these. It holds an impressive collection of art, period furniture and objets d'art. Fill in the online form to join a guided visit.

PALACIO BUENAVISTA
NOTABLE BUILDING

Map p250 (Plaza de la Cibeles; MBanco de España) Set back amid gardens on the northwest edge of Plaza de la Cibeles stands the Palacio Buenavista, now occupied by the army. It once belonged to the Alba family, and the young Duchess of Alba, Cayetana, who was widely rumoured to have had an affair with the artist Goya in the 18th century, lived here for a time.

CASA DE LAS SIETE CHIMENEAS
ARCHITECTURE

Map p250 (Plaza del Rey; MBanco de España) A block northwest of the Plaza de la Cibeles is the Casa de las Siete Chimeneas, a 16th-century mansion that takes its name from the seven chimneys it still boasts. They say that the ghost of one of Felipe II's lovers still runs about here in distress on certain evenings. Nowadays, it's home to the Ministry of Education, Culture and Sport.

LOCAL KNOWLEDGE

CHILDREN'S PLAYGROUNDS

The richest pickings for children's playgrounds are on Plaza del Dos de Mayo, where you'll find three. Dog walkers also love to let their animals off the leash here so stick to the fenced playgrounds and watch for dog droppings.

There's a handkerchief-sized playground with play equipment at the southwestern end of Calle del Conde Duque, where it meets Calle de San Bernardino, with another, slightly larger play area in the Plaza de las Comendadoras, which gets busy after school and on weekends.

MUSEO DE CERA
MUSEUM

Map p250 (☑91 319 93 30; www.museoceramadrid.com; Paseo de los Recoletos 41; adult/child €17/12; ☺10am-2.30pm & 4.30-8.30pm Mon-Fri, 10am-8.30pm Sat & Sun; MColón) This wax museum, with more than 450 characters, is a fairly standard version of the genre. Models range from the Beatles to Bart Simpson, and from Cristiano Ronaldo to Cervantes, Dalí and Picasso – it's a typically broad-ranging collection of international and Spanish figures down through the centuries. If you're drawn to the darker side of life, there's everything from the Inquisition to Freddy Krueger, while the Tren del Terror is not for the faint hearted.

✖ EATING

Cool *barrios*. Cool places to eat. Chueca and Malasaña may be radically different, one newly modern, the other firmly rooted in the past, but their restaurants are remarkably similar. Blending old *tabernas* (taverns) with laid-back temples to Spanish nouvelle cuisine, the eating scene here revolves around an agreeable buzz, innovative cooking and casual but stylish surrounds. Some streets stand out, especially Calle de Manuela Malasaña in Malasaña and Calle de la Libertad in Chueca. For cheap but decent international cuisine (eg Asian, Indian, Thai, Persian), head down to Calle de San Bernardino at the lower end of Calle del Conde Duque in Malasaña.

✖ Malasaña

★ CASA JULIO   SPANISH €

Map p246 (☎91 522 72 74; Calle de la Madera 37; 6/12 croquetas €5/10; ☺1-3.30pm & 6.30-11pm Mon-Sat Sep-Jul; ⓂTribunal) A city-wide poll for the best *croquetas* (croquettes) in Madrid would see half of those polled voting for Casa Julio and the remainder not doing so only because they haven't been yet. They're that good that celebrities and mere mortals from all over Madrid come here, along with the crusty old locals.

They come to sample the traditional *jamón* (cured ham) variety or more creative versions such as spinach with gorgonzola. Strangely, the place acquired a certain celebrity when U2 chose the bar for a photo shoot a few years back.

BODEGA DE LA ARDOSA   TAPAS €

Map p246 (☎91 521 49 79; www.laardosa.es; Calle de Colón 13; tapas & raciónes €4-11; ☺8.30am-2am Mon-Fri, 12.45pm-2.30am Sat & Sun; ⓂTribunal) Going strong since 1892, the charming, wood-panelled bar of Bodega de la Ardosa is brimful of charm. To come here and not try the *salmorejo* (cold tomato soup made with bread, oil, garlic and vinegar), *croquetas* or *tortilla de patatas* (potato and onion omelette) would be a crime. On weekend nights there's scarcely room to move.

TRIBALL – THE NEW MALASAÑA

Malasaña is unlikely to shed its carefully cultivated retro image any time soon, but a project run by local businesses is seeking to change the way people think about the *barrio* (district). Entitled **Triángulo Ballesta** (www.triballmadrid. com), it's named after the famously seedy Calle de Ballesta, close to Gran Vía, and includes streets such as Calle del Desengaño (where prostitutes linger in full view), Calle de Valverde, Calle de la Corredera Baja de San Pablo and surrounds. The project is one of regeneration and involves cleaning up the streets, as well as encouraging new businesses and the avant-garde arts community to make it their *barrio* of choice. These businesses have promised not to stop until they've transformed Malasaña into the new Soho.

BAR PALENTINO   TAPAS €

Map p246 (☎91 532 30 58; Calle del Pez 8; bocadillos €1.80-2.50; ☺7am-2pm Mon-Sat; ⓂNoviciado) Formica tables, not a single attention to decor detail, and yet... This ageless Malasaña bar is a reminder of an important lesson in eating Spanish style: don't be fooled by appearances. Wildly popular with young and old alike, Bar Palentino has an irresistible charm, thanks in large part to its owners María Dolores (who claims to be 'the house speciality') and Casto. And the food? Simple traditional tapas and *bocadillos* (filled rolls) that have acquired city-wide fame, not least for their price.

BEHER DE GUIJELO   SPANISH, FAST FOOD €

Map p246 (☎91 521 27 41; www.beher.com; Calle de Fuencarral 106; bocadillos €3.60; ☺10am-11pm Sun-Thu, 10am-midnight Fri & Sat; ⓂBilbao) Part of the wave of Spanish fast food sweeping the capital, Beher follows the same, winning formula as other, longer-established examples of the genre – cured meats in vacuum-sealed packs and takeaway options such as paper cones and *bocadillos* filled with *jamón*.

CON OLIVA   SPANISH, FAST FOOD €

Map p246 (☎91 521 12 67; www.conoliva.com; Calle del Barco 45; mains from €4; ☺1-4pm & 8pm-midnight; ⓂTribunal) It sounds like a simple idea but Con Oliva builds its offering around extra-virgin olive oil and uses it to cook excellent Spanish staples such as *tortilla de patatas*, *bocadillo de calamares* (roll filled with calamari), croquettes, lightly fried seafood, or churros, or to accompany *jamón serrano*, salads and other carefully chosen stars of the Spanish kitchen.

PEGGY SUE'S AMERICAN DINER   AMERICAN €

Map p246 (☎91 521 85 60; www.peggysues.es; Calle de Santa Cruz de Marcenado 13; mains €5-18; ☺1.30-4.30pm & 8.30-11.30pm Mon-Fri, 2-5pm & 8.30pm-12.30am Sat & Sun; ⓂSan Bernardo) American-style burgers have developed something of a cult following in Madrid in recent years and this place has been at the forefront of the trend. The decor re-creates 1950s America and the jukebox belts out Aretha Franklin and Chuck Berry at regular intervals. The burgers are the genuine article and as good as you'll find in town.

★ ALBUR   TAPAS, SPANISH €€

Map p246 (☎91 594 27 33; www.restaurantealbur. com; Calle de Manuela Malasaña 15; mains €11-16; ☺1-5pm & 8pm-12.30am Mon-Fri, 1pm-1am Sat &

Sun; MBilbao) One of Malasaña's best deals, this place has a wildly popular tapas bar and a classy but casual restaurant out the back. The restaurant waiters never seem to lose their cool, and their extremely well-priced rice dishes are the stars of the show, although in truth you could order anything here and leave well satisfied.

LA MUCCA DE PEZ
SPANISH, TAPAS €€

Map p246 (☎91 521 00 00; www.lamucca.es; Plaza Carlos Cambronero 4; mains €9-16; ☺1pm-1am Mon-Fri, 1pm-2am Sat & Sun; MCallao) The only problem with this place is that it's such an agreeable spot to spend an afternoon, it can be impossible to snaffle a table. An ample wine list complements the great salads, creative pizzas and a good mix of meat and seafood mains, while the atmosphere makes it all taste even better.

MARICASTAÑA
SPANISH €€

Map p246 (☎91 082 71 42; www.maricastanamadrid.com; Corredera Baja de San Pablo 12; mains €9-19; ☺9am-2am Mon-Thu, 9am-2.30am Fri & Sat, 10am-2am Sun; MCallao) This fabulous find sits in the increasingly cool corner of Malasaña that is flourishing just off the back of Gran Vía. The decor is quite lovely, all potted plants, creative lighting, iron pillars and rustic brickwork. The food is simple but excellent – try the pumpkin croquettes or the tuna pieces with bean shoots and strawberries.

LA T GASTROBAR
TAPAS, MODERN SPANISH €€

Map p246 (☎91 531 14 06; www.latgastrobar.es; Calle del Molino de Viento 4; mains €14-19; ☺1-4pm & 9pm-midnight Tue-Sat; MCallao) This slick split-level place does variations on Spanish classics, such as thin layers of bull's tail with pastrami and baked apple, or lamb ribs with chestnuts, pine nuts and potatoes. The atmosphere is classy yet casual in the finest Madrid tradition.

LA GASTROCROQUETERÍA
DE CHEMA
TAPAS €€

Map p246 (☎91 364 22 63; www.gastrocroqueteria.com; Calle del Barco 7; tapas €3-13, set menus €16-28; ☺9pm-midnight Mon-Fri, 2-4.30pm & 9pm-midnight Sat & Sun; MTribunal) *Croquetas* in all their glory are what this place is all about. Try the classic version (made with *jamón* or cod) or any number of riffs on the croquette theme (with *sobrasada* – spreadable cured meat – and chocolate, for example). It also does other tapas, with a couple of set menus to guide your way.

LA MUSA
SPANISH, FUSION €€

Map p246 (☎91 448 75 58; www.grupolamusa.com; Calle de Manuela Malasaña 18; cold/hot tapas from €4/6, mains €11-16; ☺9am-midnight Mon-Wed, 9am-1am Fri, 1pm-2am Sat, 1pm-midnight Sun; MSan Bernardo) Snug, loud and unpretentious, La Musa is all about designer decor, lounge music and memorably fun food. The menu is divided into three types of tapas – hot, cold and barbecue. Among the hot varieties is the fantastic *jabalí con ali-oli de miel y sobrasada* (wild boar with honey mayonnaise and *sobrasada*).

CASA PERICO
SPANISH €€

Map p246 (☎91 532 81 76; www.casapericomadrid.es; Calle de la Ballesta 18; mains €6-17; ☺1.30-4pm & 8.30pm-midnight Mon-Sat, 1.30-4pm Sun Sep-Jul; MGran Vía) Going strong since the 1940s, Casa Perico does everything from legume-based stews to ribs, but its signature dish is *arroz a lo cutre* (literally 'coarse rice', actually a delicious creamy rice dish). Lunchtime specials include *cocido a la madrileña* (meat-and-chickpea stew; €19) on Mondays. A great, quirky place to eat.

CONACHE
SPANISH €€

Map p246 (☎91 522 95 00; www.restauranteconache.com; Plaza de San Ildefonso; mains €8-15; ☺9.30am-1.30am Mon-Thu, 9.30am-2.30am Fri & Sat; MTribunal) With Asian and African decoration, creative Mediterranean cooking and a noisy Spanish clientele, Conache is a hub of *barrio* life and is as good for breakfast as for dinner. The food is outstanding; the *salmorejo* is among the best we've tasted this far from Córdoba. It's difficult to snaffle a table on the outdoor terrace but worth the wait.

HOME BURGER BAR
AMERICAN €€

Map p246 (☎91 522 97 28; www.homeburgerbar.com; Calle del Espíritu Santo 12; mains €10-14; ☺1.30-4pm & 8.30pm-midnight Mon-Thu, 2-5pm & 8.30pm-midnight Fri & Sat, 2-5pm & 8.30-11pm Sun; MTribunal) There are times when you just need a burger. One of Madrid's longest-running and most authentic burger bars, Home Burger Bar is terrific, with an interesting mix of vegetarian, gourmet and classic hamburgers served by friendly waiters in an American-diner-style setting. The meat is 'ecologically sound' and, in the Spanish style, medium-rare (the chef will cook it more if you ask).

There is another, larger **restaurant** (Map p246; ☎91 115 12 79; Calle de Silva 25; ☺1.30-4pm & 8.30pm-midnight Mon-Thu, 1.30-5pm &

MALASAÑA & CHUECA EATING

8.30pm-midnight Fri & Sat, 1.30-5pm & 8.30-11pm Sun; Ⓜ Callao) close to Gran Vía, and another in **Chueca** (🖉91 521 85 31; Calle de San Marcos 26; 🕙1.30-4pm & 8.30pm-midnight Mon-Thu, 2-5pm & 8.30pm-midnight Fri & Sat, 2-5pm & 8.30-11pm Sun; Ⓜ Chueca).

CASA HORTENSIA   ASTURIAN €€
Map p246 (🖉91 539 00 90; www.casahortensia. com; 2nd fl, Calle de la Farmacia 2; mains €16-25; 🕙1-4.30pm & 8.30-11.30pm Tue-Sat, 1.30-4pm Sun Sep-Jul; Ⓜ Tribunal, Gran Vía) With all the innovations happening elsewhere in Madrid, it's good to know that some things don't change. Casa Hortensia doesn't bother much with decoration, allowing you to concentrate on the Asturian specialities, such as *fabada asturiana* (white-bean stew with pork and blood sausage). *Sidra* (cider) is, of course, obligatory.

BAR AMOR   SPANISH, TAPAS €€
Map p246 (🖉91 594 48 29; www.baramor.es; Calle de Manuela Malasaña 22; mains €13-16; 🕙1.30-4pm & 8.30pm-12.30am Tue-Sat; Ⓜ Bilbao, San Bernardo) An engaging little corner bar that's good for lunch and often full. There's nothing too fancy about the cooking but that's the point – it's all about well-presented Spanish home cooking using top-notch ingredients, such as *anchoas de Santoña* (anchovies from the Cantabrian port of Santoña).

A DOS VELAS   SPANISH, INTERNATIONAL €€
Map p246 (🖉91 446 18 63; www.adosvelas.net; Calle de San Vicente Ferrer 16; mains €10-18, set menus €10-25; 🕙1.15-5pm & 8.30pm-12.15am Sun-Thu, 1.15-5pm & 8.30pm-2am Fri & Sat; Ⓜ Tribunal) We're fans of this place – the food is creative, with Mediterranean cooking fused with occasional Indian or even Argentine flavours, there's a lovely dining area with soft lighting and exposed brick, and the service is attentive without being intrusive.

★ LA TASQUITA DE ENFRENTE   MODERN SPANISH €€€
Map p246 (🖉91 532 54 49; www.latasquitadenfrente.com; Calle de la Ballesta 6; mains €17-32, set menus €45-69; 🕙1.30-4.30pm & 8.30pm-midnight Mon-Sat; Ⓜ Gran Vía) It's difficult to overstate how popular this place is among people in the know in Madrid's food scene. The seasonal menu prepared by chef Juanjo López never ceases to surprise while also combining simple Spanish staples to stunning effect. His *menú de degustación* (tasting menu; €50) or *menú de Juanjo* (€65) would be our choice if this is your first time. Reservations are essential.

🍴 Chueca

★ BAZAAR   MODERN SPANISH €
Map p250 (🖉91 523 39 05; www.restaurant bazaar.com; Calle de la Libertad 21; mains €6.50-10; 🕙1.15-4pm & 8.30-11.30pm Sun-Wed, 1.15-4pm & 8.15pm-midnight Thu-Sat; Ⓜ Chueca) Bazaar's popularity among the well-heeled Chueca set shows no sign of abating. Its pristine white interior design, with theatre-style lighting and wall-length windows, may draw a crowd that looks like it's stepped out of the pages of *¡Hola!* magazine, but the food is extremely well priced and innovative, and the atmosphere is casual.

It doesn't take reservations, so get there early or be prepared to wait, regardless of whether you're famous or not.

BACO Y BETO   TAPAS €
Map p250 (🖉91 522 84 41; Calle de Pelayo 24; tapas from €4; 🕙8pm-1am Mon-Fri, 2-4.30pm & 8.30pm-1am Sat; Ⓜ Chueca) Friends of ours in Madrid begged us not to include this place in our reviews and we must admit that we were tempted to keep this secret all to ourselves. Some of the tastiest tapas in Madrid are what you'll find here. The clientele is predominantly gay, and they, like our friends, can't have it all to themselves.

Tapas might include quail's eggs with *salmorejo*, or *raciónes* (larger tapas servings), such as aubergine with parmesan. The *croquetas* are wonderful and the chefs are not averse to bringing international influences into their dishes.

TIENDA DE VINOS   SPANISH €
Map p250 (El Comunista; 🖉91 521 70 12; Calle de Augusto Figueroa 35; mains €6.50-12; 🕙1pm-12.30am; Ⓜ Chueca) This place with a wonderful old facade opposite the Mercado de San Antón earned its name as a bastion of left-wing sympathies (hence its better-known name of 'El Comunista') and for no-nonsense Spanish cooking. The latter still holds sway, with lamb, lentils and other homemade specialities for very reasonable prices.

MAGASAND   SANDWICHES €
Map p250 (🖉91 319 68 25; www.magasand.com; Travesía de San Mateo 16; sandwiches €4.50-7, salads €5-8; 🕙9.30am-10pm Mon-Fri, noon-8pm

SPANISH COOKING COURSES

There are plenty of places in Madrid to learn Spanish cooking. In most cases, you'll need at least passable Spanish, but some run special classes for English speakers.

Alambique (☑91 547 42 20; www.alambique.com; Plaza de la Encarnación 2; per person from €45; Ⓜ Ópera, Santo Domingo) Cooking classes in Spanish, with a handful of English- and French-speaking courses.

Apunto – Centro Cultural del Gusto (☑91 702 10 41; www.apuntolibreria.com; Calle de Hortaleza 64; per person from €40; Ⓜ Chueca) This engaging little bookstore runs cooking classes across a range of cuisines.

Cooking Club (☑91 323 29 58; www.club-cooking.com; Calle de Veza 33; per person from €51; Ⓜ Valdeacederas) The regular, respected program of classes encompasses a vast range of cooking styles.

Kitchen Club (☑91 522 62 63; www.kitchenclub.es; Calle de Ballesta 8; Ⓜ Gran Vía, Callao) Offers a top-notch range of courses just off the back of Gran Vía in the city centre.

Sat; 🛜; Ⓜ Alonso Martínez) Comfy sofas, bar stools, free wi-fi and designer magazines elevate this above your average sandwich bar. It does creative sandwiches and bagels, as well as salads and hot soups.

⭐ **YAKITORO BY CHICOTE**   JAPANESE, SPANISH €€

Map p250 (☑91 737 14 41; www.yakitoro.com; Calle de la Reina 41; tapas €3-8; ⊙1pm-midnight; Ⓜ Banco de España) Based on the idea of a Japanese tavern, driven by a spirit of innovation and a desire to combine the best in Spanish and Japanese flavours, Yakitoro is a hit. Apart from salads, it's all built on brochettes cooked over a wood fire, with wonderful combinations of vegetable, seafood and meat.

Just as importantly, Yakitoro is a hugely appealing space – waiters dressed in army khaki circulate among wooden tables to create the perfect mix of classy and casual. It's all overseen by the restless talent that is Alberto Chicote, one of Spain's more innovative restaurateurs.

BOCAITO   TAPAS €€

Map p250 (☑91 532 12 19; www.bocaito.com; Calle de la Libertad 4-6; tapas €2-8, mains €10-29; ⊙1-4pm & 8.30pm-midnight Mon-Sat; Ⓜ Chueca, Sevilla) Film-maker Pedro Almodóvar once described this traditional bar and restaurant as 'the best antidepressant'. Forget about the sit-down restaurant (which is nonetheless well regarded) and jam into the bar, shoulder-to-shoulder with the casual crowd, order a few Andalucian *raciónes* from the menu and slosh them down with some gritty red or a *caña* (small glass of beer).

Enjoy the theatre in which the busy bar staff excel. Specialities include the *tostas* (open sandwiches on toasted bread), *bocaitos* (small filled rolls) and the mussels with bechamel, canapés and fried fish.

BON VIVANT & CO   SPANISH, INTERNATIONAL €€

Map p250 (☑91 704 82 86; www.bonvivantco.es; Calle de San Gregorio 8; mains €9-15; ⊙9am-1am Mon-Fri, 10am-2am Sat & Sun; Ⓜ Chueca) What a lovely little spot this is. Set on a tiny square, its wooden tables flooded with natural light through the big windows, Bon Vivant & Co is ideal for a casual meal, a quietly intimate encounter or simply an afternoon spent reading the papers. Food is simple but tasty – tapas, focaccias, salads, brunch...

OLIVIA TE CUIDA   CAFE €€

Map p250 (☑91 702 00 66; Calle de Santa Teresa 8; mains €9-14; ⊙9am-6pm Mon-Sat; Ⓜ Alonso Martínez) One of Chueca's most agreeably intimate little spaces, 'Olivia Looks After You' serves up a constantly changing seasonal menu at its communal wooden tables. Typical are the light meals (such as couscous with mint, or the carrot-and-mango salad) from mostly organic produce. A gorgeous little spot.

LE CABRERA   TAPAS €€

Map p250 (☑91 319 94 57; www.lecabrera.com; Calle de Bárbara de Braganza 2; tapas €3.50-22; ⊙8pm-midnight Wed, Thu & Sun, 8pm-2.30am Fri & Sat; Ⓜ Colón, Alonso Martínez) They describe this slick new tapas bar as a 'Cocktail and Gastrobar' and as much thought has gone into the decoration (with mirrors that resemble shattered glass) as the cooking. The emphasis here is on quality rather than experimentation, though some well-known

Spanish dishes do head off in surprising directions. The downstairs cocktail bar (p140) is one of the coolest spots in town.

MERCADO DE SAN ANTÓN TAPAS €€

Map p250 (☑91 330 07 30; www.mercadosananton.com; Calle de Augusto Figueroa 24; mains €5-20; ◷10am-midnight Mon-Thu, to 1.30am Fri-Sun; MChueca) Spain's fresh food markets make for an interesting alternative to bars and restaurants. Many have been transformed to meet all of your food needs at once. Downstairs is all about fresh produce, but upstairs there's all manner of appealing tapas varieties from Japan, the Canary Islands and other corners of the country/globe.

RIBEIRA DO MIÑO SEAFOOD €€

Map p250 (☑91 521 98 54; www.marisqueriaribeiradomino.com; Calle de la Santa Brígida 1; mains €7-15; ◷1-4pm & 8pm-midnight Tue-Sun Sep-Jul; MTribunal) This riotously popular seafood bar and restaurant is where *madrileños* (people from Madrid) with a love for seafood indulge their fantasy. The *mariscada de la casa* (€35 for two) is a platter of seafood so large that even the hungriest of visitors will be satisfied. Leave your name with the waiter and be prepared to wait up to an hour for a table on weekends.

LA PAELLA DE LA REINA MEDITERRANEAN €€

Map p250 (☑91 531 18 85; www.lapaelladelareina.com; Calle de la Reina 39; mains €14-21; ◷1-4pm & 7.30-11.30pm; MBanco de España) Madrid is not renowned for its paella (Valencia is king in that regard), but *valencianos* (people from Valencia) who can't make it home are known to frequent La Paella de la Reina. Like any decent paella restaurant, you need two people to make an order but, that requirement satisfied, you've plenty of choice. The typical Valencia paella is cooked with beans, chicken and rabbit.

There are also plenty of seafood varieties on offer, including *arroz negro* (black rice), whose colour derives from squid ink).

RESTAURANTE MOMO SPANISH €€

Map p250 (☑91 532 73 48; Calle de la Libertad 8; mains €7.50-11, lunch/dinner set menu €12/16; ◷1-4pm & 9pm-midnight Mon-Sat; MChueca) Momo is a Chueca beacon of reasonably priced home cooking for a casual crowd. It has an artsy vibe and is ideal for those who want a hearty meal without too much elaboration. Unusually, the well-priced three-course set menus spill over into the evening. It's a mostly gay crowd, but everyone's welcome.

LA MORDIDA MEXICAN €€

Map p250 (☑91 308 20 89; www.lamordida.com; Calle de Belén 13; mains €10-16; ◷1.30-5pm & 8pm-1am Sun-Thu, 1.30pm-1.30am Fri & Sat; MChueca) If your idea of Mexican food was born in Taco Bell, La Mordida, owned by singer-songwriter Joaquín Sabina, will show you a whole new world. This is homestyle Mexican cooking, the sort of place where most of the names on the menu will

---

ⓘ SPANISH FAST FOOD & WHERE TO EAT BETWEEN MEALS

If your stomach is struggling to adjust to Spain's notoriously late eating hours, and/or you're looking for a quick meal without resorting to junk food, there are plenty of options in Malasaña and Chueca.

➡ **Bodega de La Ardosa** (p132) Great tapas.

➡ **Bar Palentino** (p132) Old-style bar food.

➡ **Beher de Guijelo** (p132) *Jamón* (cured ham) rolls.

➡ **Con Oliva** (p132) Spanish staples.

➡ **La Mucca de Pez** (p133) Tapas and more.

➡ **Maricastaña** (p133) Modern Spanish meals.

➡ **La Musa** (p133) Creative tapas.

➡ **Yakitoro by Chicote** (p135) Mini-brochettes.

➡ **Magasand** (p134) All-day sandwiches.

➡ **Conache** (p133) Outdoor bar food.

➡ **Bon Vivant & Co** (p135) Chueca comfort food.

➡ **Olivia Te Cuida** (p135) Light fusion meals.

➡ **Mercado de San Antón** (p136) International market food.

need explanation from the waiters. There's Mexican cantina-style decor, and Coronitas and margaritas in abundance.

RESTAURANTE EXTREMADURA
EXTREMADURAN €€

Map p250 (📞91 531 88 22; www.restaurante extremadura.com; Calle de la Libertad 13; mains €14-17; ☺2-4pm & 9pm-midnight; Ⓜ Chueca, Banco de España) Hearty, meat-dominated cooking from the Spanish interior is what you'll find here; *jamón* is a key fixture (some of the best *jamón* comes from Extremadura). The quality of the products is unimpeachable, and the cooks thankfully let the ingredients breathe without too many elaborations. There's live piano in the background.

TEPIC
MEXICAN €€

Map p250 (📞91 522 08 50; www.tepic.es; Calle de Pelayo 4; mains €12-18; ☺1.15-4.30pm & 9pm-midnight; Ⓜ Chueca) Chic dining rooms, gay-friendly service and international flavours here come with the label of 'Urban Mexican Food'. Tepic's signature dish is the Acapulco Tropical, a cheese taco with meat and pineapple, but it's all good and leaves you with none of that heavy after-dinner feel that can spoil the aftermath of many Mexican meals. Its *menú de degustación* (€26) is outstanding, there are lots of Mexican beers to choose from and the margaritas are spectacular.

JANATOMO
JAPANESE €€

Map p250 (📞91 521 55 66; Calle de la Reina 27; mains €12-18; ☺1.30-4pm & 8.30pm-midnight Tue-Sun Sep-Jul; Ⓜ Gran Vía) Restaurateurs Tomoyuki and Eiko Ikenaga arrived in Spain in the 1950s and have watched Spaniards slowly become accustomed to foreign cuisines – sushi bars are now all the rage here. Their patience has paid off and now their restaurant, Janatomo, has undergone a style overhaul, adding a Zen ambience to its splendid Japanese cooking.

LA CARMENCITA
SPANISH €€

Map p250 (📞91 531 09 11; www.tabernalacarmencita.es; Calle de la Libertad 16; mains €14-20; ☺9am-2am; Ⓜ Chueca) La Carmencita has been around since 1854 and is the bar where legendary poet Pablo Neruda was once a regular. The folk of La Carmencita have taken 75 of their favourite traditional Spanish recipes and brought them to the table, sometimes with a little updating but more often safe in the knowledge that nothing needs changing.

Backed up by what they call 'wines with soul', it's hard to resist this place.

⭐ LA BUENA VIDA
SPANISH €€€

Map p250 (📞91 531 31 49; www.restaurantelabuenavida.com; Calle del Conde de Xiquena 8; mains €23-28; ☺1-4pm & 9-11.30pm Tue-Thu, 1.30-4pm & 9pm-12.30am Fri & Sat; Ⓜ Chueca, Colón) A cross between a Parisian bistro and an old-school upmarket Madrid restaurant, this prestigious Chueca place is popular with a well-heeled, knowledgable crowd. The menu is seasonal and leans towards classic Spanish tastes, although dishes such as the red tuna sirloin with guacamole and sesame seeds suggest that they're not averse to the odd playful interpretation.

DRINKING & NIGHTLIFE

Although it's a close-run thing, if you had to choose just one area in Madrid for the complete night out, we'd make it Malasaña and Chueca (Huertas and, to a lesser extent, La Latina are the other prime candidates). Spending a night exploring these two *barrios* is like taking a journey through Madrid's multifaceted past. As close as Madrid came to the intellectual cafes of Paris' Left Bank, the cafes of the Glorieta de Bilbao were in the 1950s and 1960s a centre of coffee-house intellectualism with their *tertulias* (literary discussions) and intrigues – a few gems remain. Throughout Malasaña, *rockeros* (rock fans) nostalgic for the hedonistic Madrid of the 1970s and 1980s will find ample bars in which to indulge their memories. At the same time all across the *barrios*, especially in gay Chueca and away to the west in Conde Duque, modern Madrid is very much on show, with chill-out spaces and swanky, sophisticated bars. Small and intimate live venues are here in numbers, Madrid's best cocktail bars are to be found in Chueca, along Calle de la Reina and Gran Vía, and nightclubs that reflect the *barrios'* split personalities keep things moving until dawn. In short, going out at night in Malasaña and Chueca is the stuff of Madrid legend, whatever your era, whatever your drink, whatever your sexual preference, whatever your look.

🍷 Malasaña

CAFÉ DE MAHÓN
CAFE

Map p246 (☎91 532 47 56; Plaza del Dos de Mayo 4; ⊗noon-1.30am Mon-Thu, to 3am Fri-Sun; ⓂBilbao) If we had to choose our favourite slice of Malasaña life, this engaging little cafe, whose outdoor tables watch out over Plaza del Dos de Mayo, would be a prime candidate. It's beloved by *famosos* (celebrities) as much as by the locals catching up for a quiet drink with friends. Their official opening times notwithstanding, they have a habit of opening and closing whenever the whim takes them.

CAFÉ MANUELA
CAFE

Map p246 (☎91 531 70 37; Calle de San Vicente Ferrer 29; ⊗4pm-2am Sun-Thu, 4pm-2.30am Fri & Sat; ⓂTribunal) Stumbling into this graciously restored throwback to the 1950s along one of Malasaña's grittier streets is akin to discovering hidden treasure. There's a luminous quality to it when you come in out of the night and, like so many Madrid cafes, it's a surprisingly multifaceted space, serving cocktails, delicious milkshakes and offering board games atop the marble tables.

LOLINA VINTAGE CAFÉ
CAFE

Map p246 (☎91 523 58 59; www.lolinacafe.com; Calle del Espíritu Santo 9; ⊗10am-12.30am Sun-Thu, 10am-2am Fri & Sat; ⓂTribunal) Lolina Vintage Café seems to have captured the essence of the *barrio* in one small space, with its studied retro look (comfy old-style chairs and sofas, gilded mirrors and 1970s-era wallpaper). It's low-key, full from the first breakfast to closing time and caters to every taste with salads and cocktails.

1862 DRY BAR
COCKTAIL BAR

Map p246 (☎609 531151; Calle del Pez 27; ⊗3.30pm-2am Mon-Thu, 3.30pm-2.30am Fri & Sat, 3.30-10.30pm Sun; ⓂNoviciado) Fab cocktails, muted early-20th-century decor and a refined air make this one of our favourite bars down Malasaña's southern end. Prices are reasonable, the cocktail list extensive and new cocktails appear every month.

EL JARDÍN SECRETO
BAR

Map p246 (☎91 541 80 23; www.eljardinsecreto madrid; Calle del Conde Duque 2; ⊗5.30pm-12.30am Sun-Wed, 6.30pm-1.30am Thu, 6.30pm-2.30am Fri & Sat; ⓂPlaza de España) 'The Secret Garden' is intimate and romantic in a *barrio* that's one of Madrid's best-kept secrets. Lit by Spanish designer candles, draped in organza from India and serving up chocolates from the Caribbean, El Jardín Secreto ranks among our most favoured drinking corners in Conde Duque. It serves milkshakes, cocktails and everything in between.

CAFÉ AJENJO
CAFE

Map p246 (☎91 447 70 76; Calle de la Galería de Robles 4; ⊗3.30pm-2am Mon-Fri, 3.30pm-2.30am Fri & Sat; ⓂBilbao) Malasaña's old cafes don't come any better than this one, with beguiling old-world decor, a vaguely intellectual air and some of the best cakes and coffees in the *barrio*. It's the sort of place to retreat to if Malasaña gets too much, although it does get lively here without getting out of hand.

LA VÍA LÁCTEA
BAR, CLUB

Map p246 (☎91 446 75 81; Calle de Velarde 18; ⊗8pm-3am Sun-Thu, 8pm-3.30am Fri & Sat; ⓂTribunal) A living, breathing and delightfully grungy relic of *la movida*, La Vía Láctea remains a Malasaña favourite for a mixed, informal crowd who seems to live for the 1980s. The music ranges across rock, pop, garage, rockabilly and indie. There are plenty of drinks to choose from and by late Saturday night anything goes. Expect long queues to get in on weekends.

TUPPERWARE
BAR, CLUB

Map p246 (☎91 446 42 04; www.tupperwareclub. com; Calle de la Corredera Alta de San Pablo 26; ⊗9pm-3am Mon-Wed, 8pm-3.30am Thu-Sat, 8pm-3am Sun; ⓂTribunal) A Malasaña stalwart and prime candidate for the bar that best catches the enduring *rockero* spirit of Malasaña, Tupperware draws a thirtysomething crowd, spins indie rock with a bit of soul and classics from the '60s and '70s, and generally revels in its kitsch (eyeballs stuck to the ceiling, and plastic TVs with action-figure dioramas lined up behind the bar). By the way, locals pronounce it 'Tupper-warry'.

MOLOKO
BAR, CLUB

Map p246 (☎626 529967; Calle de Quiñones 12; ⊗10pm-3.30am Tue-Sat; ⓂSan Bernardo) Its walls plastered with old concert flyers and the odd art-house movie poster (*A Clockwork Orange*, for example), Moloko remains an excellent middle-of-the-night option in the Conde Duque area of western Malasaña. The music – indie, rock, soul, garage and '60s – is consistently good, which is why people return here again and again.

CAFÉ DE RUIZ
CAFE

Map p246 (☑91 446 12 32; cafederuiz.com; Calle de Ruiz 11; ⊙3.30pm-2am Mon-Thu, 3.30pm-2.30am Fri & Sat, 3.30-11.30pm Sun; Ⓜ Bilbao) Another of the old Malasaña cafes that so distinguish the northern end of the *barrio*, Café de Ruiz has all-wooden furniture and columns, draws a mature crowd and offers everything from creative teas and coffees to milkshakes and cocktails.

EL PARNASILLO
CAFE

Map p246 (☑91 447 00 79; Calle de San Andrés 33; ⊙4pm-3am Sun-Thu, 4pm-3.30am Fri & Sat; Ⓜ Bilbao) Another of the grand old literary cafes to have survived close to the Glorieta de Bilbao, El Parnasillo has seigneurial decor with muted art-nouveau frescoes and stained glass adorning the walls, but it's a preferred drinking hole for the diverse crowd drawn to the Malasaña night for reasons other than the heavy rock scene.

LA PALMERA
BAR

Map p246 (☑630 884470; Calle de la Palma 67; ⊙7.30pm-2am Mon-Sat, noon-4pm Sun; Ⓜ Noviciado) Tucked away in the quiet-by-day laneways of Conde Duque, this tiny, unprepossessing place is covered in blue and yellow tiles and has an antique bar that looks like a huge bathtub. La Palmera draws an artsy crowd who come to sit at the small wooden tables and nurse a drink or two. The atmosphere is very low key. In summer the outdoor tables are the place to be.

PICNIC
BAR, CLUB

Map p246 (☑91 521 08 89; Calle de las Minas 1; ⊙6pm-1.30am Tue-Thu, 5pm-2.30am Fri & Sat, 4pm-1.30am Sun Sep-Jul; Ⓜ Noviciado) The quieter little brother to the more-famous Tupperware, Picnic is another die-hard bar that gives the *barrio* its indie soul. The look is retro, as you'd expect in this Malasaña subculture, and there are concerts most Sundays.

BAR EL 2D
BAR

Map p246 (☑91 445 88 39; Calle de Velarde 24; ⊙noon-2am; Ⓜ Tribunal) An enduring symbols of *la movida madrileña,* El 2D's fluted columns, 1970s-brown walls and 1980s music suggest that it hasn't quite arrived in the 21st century yet. No one seems to care.

JOSÉ ALFREDO
COCKTAIL BAR

Map p246 (☑91 521 49 60; www.josealfredobar. com; Calle de Silva 22; ⊙7pm-3am Sun-Thu, 7pm-

CLANDESTINE BARS

A small but growing trend of the Madrid night is that of *bares clandestinos* (clandestine bars). While it may sound vaguely illicit, it's all above board and involves places that are shops by day morphing effortlessly into cool bars after dark. Our favourite is **Kikekeller** (Map p246; ☑91 522 87 67; www.kikekeller.com; Calle de la Corredera Baja de San Pablo 17; ⊙shop 5-9pm Mon, noon-3pm & 5-9pm Tue-Fri, 12.30-9.30pm Sat, bar 7pm-2.30am Thu-Sat; Ⓜ Callao), an avant-garde furniture and interior-decoration shop a short distance north of Gran Vía, where they can't even wait for the shop to close on Saturday before opening the bar. It's one of the more original places to enjoy the Madrid night.

3.30am Fri & Sat; Ⓜ Callao) This American-style cocktail bar is an institution, just off Gran Vía. It plays indie music and does fabulous cocktails – try the 'Lazy Bitch' (rum, banana liqueur, cinnamon liqueur and lime juice) or the 'José Alfredo' (tequila, curaçao, grenadine, lime and juice of pineapple and orange).

THE PASSENGER
BAR

Map p246 (☑91 169 49 76; Calle del Pez 16; ⊙4pm-4am; Ⓜ Noviciado) Quietly sophisticated coffee shop by day, hipster rock bar by night, the Passenger has the appearance of a train in motion (cabin interior, screens with moving images for the windows) and great drinks. Live music sometimes livens things up in the evenings – check its Facebook page for upcoming gigs.

MARTÍNEZ BAR
COCKTAIL BAR

Map p246 (☑91 080 26 83; Calle del Barco 4; ⊙5pm-2.30am Mon-Fri, 1pm-2.30am Sat, 1pm-1am Sun; Ⓜ Gran Vía) This fine old cocktail bar recreates a 1920s-era ambience with plenty of wood panelling. The gin and tonics are excellent and the mojito-with-a-free-tapa for €5 from Monday to Thursday is outrageous value.

SALA BASH/OHM
GAY, CLUB

Map p246 (www.ohmclub.es; Plaza de Callao 4; admission €12; ⊙midnight-6am Fri; Ⓜ Callao) The DJs who get you waving your hands in the air like you just don't care have made

LOCAL KNOWLEDGE

LITERARY CAFES

For a tour of Madrid's grand old literary cafes (a Malasaña speciality), begin down on Paseo de los Recoletos at Gran Café de Gijón (p142), followed by Café-Restaurante El Espejo (p142). Having ticked off the big ones, try El Parnasillo (p139) and Café de Ruiz (p139) – they also capture the spirit of another age. Café Manuela (p138) is another fine old place.

this club, as have its sessions that go by the name of 'Ohm', arguably the number-one nightspot for Madrid's gay community. The music never strays far from techno-house.

SIROCO   CLUB
Map p246 (☑91 593 30 70; www.siroco.es; Calle de San Dimas 3; admission €8; ⊙9pm-6am Thu-Sat; ⓂNoviciado) One of the most popular and eclectic nightclubs in Madrid, Siroco does everything from reggae to drum and bass, funk, soul and danceable disco tunes. The one unifying theme is the commitment to Spanish music (there are often upcoming local rock bands at 10pm before the action really kicks off). It's a good place to hear local music before it becomes too mainstream.

MOROCCO   CLUB
Map p246 (☑91 531 51 67; www.morocco-madrid. com; Calle del Marqués de Leganés 7; admission €10; ⊙midnight-6am Fri & Sat; ⓂSanto Domingo, Noviciado) Owned by the zany Alaska, the standout musical personality of *la movida*, Morocco has decor that's so kitsch it's cool, and a mix of musical styles that never strays too far from 1980s Spanish and international tunes, with electronica another recurring theme. The bouncers have been known to show a bit of attitude, but then that kind of comes with the profession.

LA BICICLETA   CAFE
Map p246 (☑91 532 97 42; www.labicicletacafe. com; Plaza de San Ildefonso 9; ⊙10am-1am Mon-Wed, 10am-2am Thu, 10am-2.30am Fri, 11am-2.30am Sat, 11am-midnight Sun; ⓦ; ⓂTribunal) Combining a slew of hipster passions – bicycles, urban art and good coffee – this trendy place won't be for everyone, but it has become one of the hottest places in Malasaña. It exhibits street art, there's room to park your bicycle, and they also describe the cafe

as a workplace – there's free wi-fi, accessible plugs and a cast of regulars who pass the day here 'working'.

FÁBRICA MARAVILLAS   BAR, BREWERY
Map p246 (☑915 21 87 53; www.fabricamaravillas. com; Calle de Valverde 29; ⊙6pm-midnight Mon-Fri, 12.30pm-midnight Sat & Sun; ⓂTribunal, Gran Vía) Spain has taken its time in getting behind the worldwide trend of boutique or artisan beers, but it's finally starting to happen. The finest example of this in Madrid is Fábrica Maravillas, a microbrewery known for its 'Malasaña Ale'.

YA'STA   CLUB
Map p246 (☑91 521 88 33; www.yastaclub.net; Calle de Valverde 10; admission €10; ⊙11.45pm-6am Wed-Sat; ⓂGran Vía) Going strong since 1985 and the height of *la movida madrileña*, Ya'sta is a stalwart of the Malasaña night. Everything gets a run here, from techno, psychedelic trance and electronica to indie pop. Check the website for upcoming sessions.

🍸 Chueca

★MUSEO CHICOTE   COCKTAIL BAR
Map p250 (☑91 532 67 37; grupomercadodelareina.com/en/museo-chicote-en/; Gran Vía 12; ⊙5pm-3am Mon-Thu, to 3.30am Fri & Sat; ⓂGran Vía) This place is a Madrid landmark, complete with its 1930s-era interior, and its founder is said to have invented more than 100 cocktails, which the likes of Hemingway, Ava Gardner, Grace Kelly, Sophia Loren and Frank Sinatra have all enjoyed at one time or another. It's at its best after midnight, when a lounge atmosphere takes over, couples cuddle on the curved benches and some of the city's best DJs do their stuff.

★CAFÉ BELÉN   BAR
Map p250 (☑91 308 27 47; elcafebelen.com; Calle de Belén 5; ⊙3.30pm-3am Tue-Thu, 3.30pm-3.30am Fri, 1pm-3.30am Sat, 1-10pm Sun; ⓂChueca) Café Belén is cool in all the right places – lounge and chill-out music, dim lighting, a great range of drinks (the mojitos are especially good) and a low-key crowd that's the height of casual sophistication. It's one of our preferred Chueca watering holes.

LE CABRERA   COCKTAIL BAR
Map p250 (☑91 319 94 57; www.lecabrera.com; Calle de Bárbara de Braganza 2; ⊙7pm-2am Sun, Wed & Thu, 7pm-2.30am Fri & Sat; ⓂColón, Alonso

Martínez) In the basement below the exciting tapas bar (p135) of the same name, this cocktail bar is every bit as appealing. The 60-plus different cocktail varieties are the work of Diego Cabrera, the long-standing bartender of renowned master chef Sergi Arola.

LA TERRAZA DE ARRIBA LOUNGE
Map p250 (Splash Óscar; Plaza de Vázquez de Mella 12; ⏱6.30pm-2.30am Wed & Thu, 4.30pm-2.30am Fri-Sun mid-May–mid-Sep; MGran Vía) Another of the stunning rooftop terraces (although this one has a small swimming pool), this chilled space atop Hotel Óscar (p178) with gorgeous skyline views has become something of a retreat among A-list celebrities.

DEL DIEGO COCKTAIL BAR
Map p250 (☎91 523 31 06; www.deldiego.com; Calle de la Reina 12; ⏱7pm-3am Mon-Thu, 7pm-3.30am Fri & Sat; MGran Vía) Del Diego is one of the city's most celebrated cocktail bars. The decor blends old-world cafe with New York style, and it's the sort of place where the music rarely drowns out the conversation. Even with around 75 cocktails to choose from, we'd still order the signature 'El Diego' (vodka, advocaat, apricot brandy and lime).

BAR COCK COCKTAIL BAR
Map p250 (☎91 532 28 26; www.barcock.com; Calle de la Reina 16; ⏱4pm-3am Mon-Fri, 7pm-3am Sat & Sun; MGran Vía) With a name like this, Bar Cock could go either way, but it's definitely cock as in 'rooster', so the atmosphere is elegant and classic rather than risqué. The decor evokes an old gentlemen's club, but it is beloved by A-list celebrities and A-list wannabes, and a refined thirty-something crowd who come here for the lively atmosphere and great cocktails.

On weekends all the tables seem to be reserved, so be prepared to hover on the fringes of fame.

AREIA LOUNGE
Map p250 (☎91 310 03 07; www.areiachillout.com; Calle de Hortaleza 92; ⏱2pm-3am Mon-Fri, 1pm-3am Sat & Sun; MChueca, Alonso Martínez) The ultimate lounge bar by day (cushions, chill-out music and dark secluded corners, where you can hear yourself talk or even snog quietly), this place is equally enjoyable by night. That's when groovy DJs take over (from 11pm Sunday to Wednesday, and from 9pm the rest of the week).

BRISTOL BAR CAFE, BAR
Map p250 (☎91 522 45 68; www.bristolbar.es; Calle del Almirante 20; ⏱10am-1am Mon-Wed, 10am-2am Thu & Fri, 11am-2am Sat; MChueca) You could come here for the English breakfast or the brunch, but we like this place for its 75-plus different types of gin. By day, the atmosphere is that of a quiet cafe; after work, a busy gathering place; and, as the evening wears on, a sophisticated gin parlour.

MAMÁ INÉS CAFE
Map p250 (☎91 523 23 33; www.mamaines.com; Calle de Hortaleza 22; ⏱9am-1.30am Sun-Thu, 9am-2.30am Fri & Sat; MChueca) A gay meeting place, this cafe-bar is never sleazy and has a laid-back ambience by day and a romantic air by night. You can get breakfast, yummy pastries and the word on where that night's hot spot will be. There's a steady stream of people coming and going throughout the day and they turn the lights down low as evening turns into night.

CAFÉ ACUARELA CAFE
Map p250 (☎91 522 21 43; www.cafeacuarela.es; Calle de Gravina 10; ⏱11am-2am Sun-Thu, 11am-3am Fri & Sat; MChueca) A few steps up the hill from Plaza de Chueca and long a centrepiece of gay Madrid – a huge statue of a nude male angel guards the doorway – this is an agreeable, dimly lit salon decorated with, among other things, religious icons. It's ideal for quiet conversation and catching the weekend buzz as people plan their forays into the more clamorous clubs in the vicinity.

ANTIGUA CASA ÁNGEL SIERRA TAVERNA
Map p250 (☎91 531 01 26; Calle de Gravina 11; ⏱noon-1am; MChueca) This historic old *taberna* is the antithesis of modern Chueca chic – it has hardly changed since it opened in 1917. As Spaniards like to say, the beer on tap is very 'well poured' here and it also has vermouth on tap. Fronting onto Plaza de Chueca, it can get pretty lively of a weekend evening when it spills over onto the plaza.

STOP MADRID BAR
Map p250 (☎91 521 88 87; www.stopmadrid.es/en/; Calle de Hortaleza 11; ⏱12.30pm-2am; MGran Vía) The name may not be Madrid's most evocative but this terrific old *taberna* is friendly, invariably packed and wins the vote of at least one Lonely Planet author for the best sangria in Madrid. The tapas are also outstanding and there's always a buzz here in the evenings.

ℹ GAY CHUECA

If you're eager to tap into the gay networks of Chueca, Mamá Inés (p141) is the place to start – apart from being a gay meeting place par excellence, its bar staff have their finger on the pulse. Also outstanding is **Librería Berkana** (☑91 522 55 99; www.libreriaberkana. com; Calle de Hortaleza 62; ◷10.30am-9pm Mon-Fri, 11.30am-9pm Sat, noon-2pm & 5-9pm Sun; Ⓜ Chueca), where you'll find the biweekly *Shanguide* (jammed with listings and contact ads), *Shangay Express* (better for articles) and possibly the *Mapa Gaya de Madrid,* which lists gay bars, discos and saunas.

BLACK & WHITE
GAY, CLUB

Map p250 (☑91 521 24 92; Calle de la Libertad 34; ◷10pm-6.30am; Ⓜ Chueca) People *still* talk about the opening party of Black & White way back in 1982, and ever since it's been a pioneer of Chueca's gay nights. This place is extravagantly gay with drag acts, male strippers and a refreshingly no-holds-barred approach to life.

WHY NOT?
CLUB

Map p250 (☑91 521 80 34; www.whynotmadrid. com; Calle de San Bartolomé 7; ◷10.30pm-6am; Ⓜ Chueca) Underground, narrow and packed with bodies, gay-friendly Why Not? is the sort of place where nothing's left to the imagination (the gay and straight crowd who come here are pretty amorous) and it's full nearly every night of the week. Pop and top-40 music are the standard here, and the dancing crowd is mixed and serious about having a good time. We're not huge fans of the bouncers here, but once you get past them it's all good fun. Admission is €10.

DIURNO
CAFE

Map p250 (☑91 522 00 09; grupomercadodelareina.com/en/diurno-en/; Calle de San Marcos 37; ◷10am-1am Sun-Thu, 10am-2am Fri & Sat; Ⓜ Chueca) One of the most important hubs of *barrio* life in Chueca, this cafe (with DVD store attached) has become to modern Chueca what the grand literary cafes were to another age. It's always full with a fun Chueca crowd relaxing amid the greenery. It also serves well-priced meals and snacks if you can't bear to give up your seat.

LIQUID MADRID
GAY, CLUB

Map p250 (☑91 523 28 08; www.liquid.es; Calle de Barbieri 7; ◷8pm-3am Mon-Thu, to 3.30am Fri & Sat; Ⓜ Chueca) An essential stop on any gay itinerary through Chueca, although Liquid is a little overwhelming with its multiple video screens and endless movement of people.

CLUB 54 STUDIO
CLUB

Map p250 (www.studio54madrid.com; Calle de Barbieri 7; ◷11am-3.30am Wed-Sun; Ⓜ Chueca) Modelled on the famous New York club Studio 54, this nightclub draws a predominantly gay crowd, but its target market is more upmarket than many in the *barrio.* Unlike other Madrid nightclubs where paid dancers up on stage try to get things moving, here they let the punters set the pace.

CAFÉ-RESTAURANTE EL ESPEJO
CAFE

Map p250 (☑91 308 23 47; www.restauranteelespejo.com; Paseo de los Recoletos 31; ◷8am-midnight; Ⓜ Colón) Once a haunt of writers and intellectuals, this architectural gem blends Modernista and art-deco styles and its interior could well overwhelm you with all the mirrors, chandeliers and bow-tied service of another era. The atmosphere is suitably quiet and refined, although our favourite corner is the elegant glass pavilion out on the Paseo de los Recoletos.

GRAN CAFÉ DE GIJÓN
CAFE

Map p250 (☑91 521 54 25; www.cafegijon.com; Paseo de los Recoletos 21; ◷7am-1.30am; Ⓜ Chueca, Banco de España) This graceful old cafe has been serving coffee and meals since 1888 and has long been favoured by Madrid's literati for a drink or a meal – *all* of Spain's great 20th-century literary figures came here for coffee and *tertulias.* You'll find yourself among intellectuals, conservative Franco die-hards and young *madrileños* looking for a quiet drink.

☆ ENTERTAINMENT

In addition to the places listed here, some of Malasaña's nightclubs begin the night with live music acts, among them Siroco (p140).

CAFÉ LA PALMA
LIVE MUSIC, DANCE

Map p246 (☑91 522 50 31; www.cafelapalma. com; Calle de la Palma 62; ◷5pm-3am Sun, Wed & Thu, 5pm-3.30am Fri & Sat; Ⓜ Noviciado) It's amazing how much variety Café La Palma has packed into its labyrinth of rooms. Live shows featuring hot local bands are held at the back, while DJs mix it up at the front. Admission ranges from free to €12.

BARCO
LIVE MUSIC

Map p246 (☏91 521 24 47; www.barcobar.com; Calle del Barco 34; ⏰10pm-5.30am Sun-Thu, to 6am Fri & Sat; MTribunal) Located just before Malasaña spills over into the seedy back end of Gran Vía, BarCo is an outstanding live venue with jazz, flamenco (Sunday at 9pm), Latin music, funk, rock and blues. Admission varies from free to €12. It's also the headquarters for Madrid's School of Creative Music. Concerts start at 11pm and there's room to dance if the mood takes you.

EL JUNCO JAZZ CLUB
JAZZ

Map p250 (☏91 319 20 81; www.eljunco.com; Plaza de Santa Bárbara 10; ⏰10.30pm-5.30am Tue-Thu & Sun, 9pm-6am Fri & Sat, concerts 11pm Tue-Sun; MAlonso Martínez) El Junco has established itself on the Madrid nightlife scene by appealing as much to jazz aficionados as to clubbers. Its secret is high-quality live jazz gigs from Spain and around the world, followed by DJs spinning funk, soul, nu jazz, blues and innovative groove beats. There are also jam sessions at 11pm in jazz (Tuesday) and blues (Sunday). Concerts cost from €6 to €9; free on Sunday. The emphasis is on music from the American South and the crowd is classy and casual.

BOGUI JAZZ
JAZZ

Map p250 (☏91 521 15 68; www.boguijazz.com; Calle de Barquillo 29; ⏰10pm-6am Wed-Sat; MChueca) One of Madrid's best-loved jazz clubs has finally reopened its doors after years of being closed (it fell foul of a council crackdown on licensing laws). It has picked up right where it left off, with 10.30pm live jazz shows from Thursday to Saturday, followed by rock DJs until dawn – an intoxicating mix. Admission from €5 to €12.

EL BÚHO REAL
LIVE MUSIC

Map p250 (☏91 319 10 88; www.buhoreal.com; Calle de Regueros 5; ⏰8pm-3am Wed-Sun; MAlonso Martínez, Chueca) It looks like your average Madrid *bar de copas* (bar serving spirits and mixed drinks), but El Búho Real (The Royal Owl) is all about acoustic music. It interprets the term pretty widely to include flamenco, rock and singer-songwriter solo acts, and it's been around long enough

to have drawn a loyal following. Admission from €5 to €10; concerts start at 9.30pm.

LIBERTAD 8
LIVE MUSIC

Map p250 (☏91 532 11 50; www.libertad8cafe.com; Calle de la Libertad 8; ⏰4pm-2.30am; MChueca) One of the most enduring live venues in Chueca, this small-stage bar attracts storytellers, poets and local and international singer-songwriters and a whole range of other acts; it also often has exhibitions. Admission ranges from free to €6. We like the mix, and it is intimate venues like these that add depth to the Madrid night.

TABOÓ
LIVE MUSIC

Map p246 (☏91 524 11 89; www.taboo-madrid.com; Calle de San Vicente Ferrer 23; ⏰10pm-6am Fri & Sat; MTribunal) With everything from pop to hard-core punk and a whole lot of house music in between, Taboó likes to keep its options open. Admission is from €5 to €10; check out the website to see which way it's leaning, and spend as little time as possible talking to the bouncers while you wait in the queue.

THUNDERCAT
LIVE MUSIC

Map p250 (☏654 511457; www.thundercatclub.com; Calle de Campoamor 11; ⏰10pm-6am Thu-Sat; MAlonso Martínez) They keep it simple at Thundercat – it's rock, as classic as they can find it, with live gigs beginning after midnight and rolling on through the night.

 # SHOPPING

Malasaña is one of Madrid's quirkiest *barrios* in which to shop, home to edgy clothing stores and shops where mainstream designers show off their street cred. Shop staff here won't look down their noses at you no matter what you wear – they've seen it all before. Chueca, on the other hand, can be zany or elegant and caters as much for gay clubbers as for a refined gay sensibility. Where Chueca eases gently down the hill towards the Paseo de los Recoletos and beyond to Salamanca, especially in Calle de Piamonte, Calle del Conde de Xiquena and Calle del Almirante, niche designers take over with exclusive boutiques and the latest individual fashions. In short, it's Madrid in microcosm and ideal for those style-

conscious shoppers who value an alternative look at life.

🔒 Malasaña

★ **MERCADO DE FUENCARRAL**　CLOTHING
Map p246 (www.mdf.es; Calle de Fuencarral 45; ⊙11am-9pm Mon-Sat; MTribunal) Madrid's home of alternative club cool is still going strong, revelling in its reverse snobbery. With shops such as Fuck, Ugly Shop and Black Kiss, it's funky, grungy and filled to the rafters with torn T-shirts and more black leather and silver studs than you'll ever need. This is a Madrid icon and when it was threatened with closure in 2008 there was nearly an uprising.

NEST　GIFTS
Map p246 (☑91 523 10 61; www.nest-boutique.com; Plaza de San Ildefonso 3; ⊙11am-2.30pm & 4-8.30pm Mon-Fri, 11am-3pm & 4-8.30pm Sat; MTribunal) Small offerings of lamps, Japanese dolls, wrapping paper, jewellery and so much more fills this intimate little British-run boutique. It's difficult to describe the secret of its success, but it unmistakably has what Spaniards call *encanto* (charm) and is a welcome recent addition to Malasaña's shopping portfolio.

POPLAND　GIFTS
Map p246 (☑91 591 21 20; www.popland.es; Calle de Manuela Malasaña 24; ⊙11am-2pm & 5-8.30pm Mon-Sat; MSan Bernardo) 'Curiosity and Retro' are the buzzwords here and Popland has both by the vinyl-suitcase load. 'Go Eighties' T-shirts, Pink Panther dolls, Elvis card games, candy handcuffs, mirrored disco balls, Space Invaders handbags… If you can't find it here, it simply didn't exist in the world of street pop art.

CURIOSITE　GIFTS
Map p246 (☑91 287 21 77; www.curiosite.es; Calle de la Corredera Alta de San Pablo 28; ⊙11am-9pm Mon-Sat; @; MTribunal) Some of Madrid's more original gifts are on offer in this quirky shop that combines old favourites (eg Star Wars Lego, voodoo dolls) and a sideways glance at mundane household items. It's fun and modern and retro all at once, which makes it a perfect fit for Malasaña.

ZOOM EDITION　ARTS
Map p246 (☑91 083 71 89; www.zoomedition.com; Calle del Pez 1; ⊙11am-2.30pm & 5-9pm Mon-Sat; MCallo, Noviciado) Stunning photographic prints by mostly Spanish photographers, including a growing portfolio of Madrid images, catch the eye at this new little gallery. All are framed or unframed and ready to ship around the world. Prices start from around €35 and the quality is excellent.

KLING　FASHION
Map p246 (☑91 522 51 45; www.kling.es; Calle de la Ballesta 6; ⊙11am-9pm Mon-Sat; MGran Vía) Like a classy version of Zara but with just a hint of attitude, Kling is housed in a reconceived former sex club (prostitutes still scout for clients outside) and is one of Madrid's best-kept secrets. It's ideal for fashion-conscious women who can't afford Salamanca's prices.

CUSTO BARCELONA　FASHION
Map p246 (☑91 360 46 36; www.custo.com; Calle de Fuencarral 29; ⊙10am-9pm Mon-Sat, noon-8pm Sun; MGran Vía) The chic shop of Barcelona designer Custo Dalmau wears its Calle de Fuencarral address well, because the now-iconic T-shirts are at once edgy, awash in attitude and artfully displayed. It's not to everyone's taste, but always worth a look.

DIVINA PROVIDENCIA　FASHION
Map p246 (☑91 521 10 95; www.divinaprovidencia.com; Calle de Fuencarral 42; ⊙10am-2.30pm & 5-8pm Mon-Sat; MTribunal, Gran Vía) Divina Providencia has moved seamlessly from fresh new face on the Madrid fashion scene to almost mainstream stylishness, with fun clothes for women and strong retro and Asian influences.

ADOLFO DOMÍNGUEZ　FASHION
Map p246 (☑91 523 39 38; www.adolfodominguez.com; Calle de Fuencarral 5; ⊙10am-9pm Mon-Sat; MGran Vía) The stylish shop of this inventive Spanish designer is where you'll find utterly casual and colourful designs for the consciously cool among us.

SNAPO　CLOTHING, ACCESSORIES
Map p246 (☑91 017 16 72; www.snaposhoponline.com; Calle del Espíritu Santo 6; ⊙11am-2pm & 5-8.30pm Mon-Sat; MTribunal) Snapo is rebellious Malasaña to its core, thumbing its nose at the niceties of fashion respectability – hardly surprising given that one of its lines of clothing is called Fucking Bastardz Inc. It does jeans, caps and jackets, but its T-shirts are the Snapo trademark; there are even kids' T-shirts for *really* cool parents.

Down through the years, we've seen everything from a mocked-up cover of 'National Pornographic' to Pope John Paul II with fist raised and 'Vatican 666' emblazoned across the front. Need we say more?

RETRO CITY CLOTHING
Map p246 (Calle de Corredera Alta de San Pablo 4; ☉noon-2.30pm & 5.30-9pm Mon-Sat; ⓂTribunal) Malasaña down to its Dr Martens, Retro City lives for the colourful '70s and '80s and proclaims its philosophy to be all about 'vintage for the masses'. Whereas other such stores in the *barrio* have gone for an angry, thumb-your-nose-at-society aesthetic, Retro City just looks back with nostalgia.

EL TEMPLO DE SUSU CLOTHING, ACCESSORIES
Map p246 (⌨91 523 31 22; Calle del Espíritu Santo 1; ☉10am-2.30pm & 5.30-9pm Mon-Sat; ⓂTribunal) They won't appeal to everyone, but El Templo de Susu's second-hand clothes from the 1960s and 1970s have clearly found a market among Malasaña's too-cool-for-the-latest-fashions types. It's kind of like charity shop meets vintage, which is either truly awful or retro cool, depending on your perspective.

KARIBU MALASAÑA GIFTS
Map p246 (⌨91 115 36 74; www.tiendakaribu.com; Calle de Manuela Malasaña 29; ☉11am-2.30pm & 4.30-8.30pm Mon-Sat; ⓂSan Bernardo, Bilbao) Quirky gift items dominate this lovely little boutique, which spans the full range of pop art, retro, vintage and the tastefully modern. There are must-have gadgets (magnetic key holders, a boxing glove to aim at snorers), kitchen items (retro toasters) and the purely decorative.

POLAR SHOP CLOTHING, ACCESORIES
Map p246 (⌨91 559 46 49; Calle del Conde Duque 5; ☉11am-2pm & 5-8.30pm Mon-Fri, 11am-3pm & 5-8.30pm Mon-Sat; ⓂPlaza de España) Mostly men's fashions and accessories dominate this Conde Duque store that has been around since 2003. Hawaiian shirts and more sedate looks bookend a range that hovers close to the mainstream without losing its alternative slant.

LE TRIP CLOTHING
Map p246 (⌨91 447 17 16; www.letrip.es; Calle de Manuela Malasaña 24; ☉11am-2pm & 5-8.30pm Mon-Thu, 11am-2pm & 5-9pm Fri & Sat; ⓂSan Bernardo, Bilbao) Fun T-shirts with a message are all this shop does and its motto is 'cool living under difficult circumstances'. The T-shirts have Spanish-language slogans (often in-jokes non-Spaniards may struggle to catch) and drawings of famous people.

EL MERCADO DE LA CORREDERA FOOD & DRINK
Map p246 (⌨91 532 21 52; Calle de la Puebla 15; ☉9am-3pm & 5-8.30pm Mon-Fri, 9am-2.30am Sat; ⓂCallao, Tribunal) This little community market has all that's good about Spanish produce, from deli items and cured meats to fruit, organic produce and even Spanish craft beers.

LA JUGUETERÍA ADULT SHOP
Map p246 (⌨91 308 72 69; www.lajugueteria.com; Calle del Pez 13; ☉11am-10pm Mon-Sat; ⓂNoviciado) We don't normally include sex shops in our reviews but this softly lit one tickled our fancy. Home to sultry staff and carefully chosen feathers and erotic toys, there's nothing 'brown paper bag and men in anoraks' about this place; you won't feel guilty by stepping across the threshold.

🛍 Chueca

LOEWE FASHION
Map p250 (⌨91 522 68 15; www.loewe.com; Gran Vía 8; ☉10am-8.30pm Mon-Sat, 11am-8pm Sun; ⓂGran Vía) Born in 1846 in Madrid, Loewe is arguably Spain's signature line in high-end fashion and its landmark store on Gran Vía is one of the most famous and elegant stores in the capital. Classy handbags and accessories are the mainstays and prices can be jaw-droppingly high, but it's worth stopping by here, even if you don't plan to buy.

There's another branch in **Salamanca** (Map p244; ⌨91 426 35 88; Calle de Serrano 26 & 34; ☉10am-8.30pm Mon-Sat; ⓂSerrano).

LURDES BERGADA FASHION
Map p250 (⌨91 531 99 58; www.lurdesbergada.es; Calle del Conde de Xiquena 8; ☉10am-2.30pm & 4.30-8.30pm Mon-Sat; ⓂChueca, Colón) Lurdes Bergada and Syngman Cucala, a mother-and-son designer team from Barcelona, offer classy and original men's and women's fashions using neutral colours and all-natural fibres. They've developed something of a cult following and it's difficult to leave without finding something that you just have to have. They have another branch in

Malasaña (Map p250; Calle de Fuencarral 70; ⊘10.30am-8.30pm Mon-Sat; ⓜTribunal).

MALABABA
ACCESSORIES, FASHION

(☎91 203 59 51; www.malababa.com; Calle de Santa Teresa 5; ⊘10.30am-8.30pm Mon-Thu, 10.30am-9pm Fri & Sat; ⓜAlonso Martínez) This corner of Chueca is one of Madrid's happiest hunting grounds for the style-conscious shopper who favours individual boutiques with personality above larger stores. Classy Spanish-made accessories here at Malababa, one such place, include jewellery, handbags, shoes, purses and belts, and they're all beautifully arranged in this light-filled store.

PATRIMONIO COMUNAL OLIVARERO
FOOD

Map p250 (☎91 308 05 05; www.pco.es; Calle de Mejía Lequerica 1; ⊘10am-2pm & 5-8pm Mon-Fri, 10am-2pm Sat Sep-Jun, 9am-3pm Mon-Sat Jul; ⓜAlonso Martínez) For picking up some of the country's olive-oil varieties (Spain is the world's largest producer), Patrimonio Comunal Olivarero is perfect. With examples of the extra-virgin variety (and nothing else) from all over Spain, you could spend ages agonising over the choices. The staff know their oil and are happy to help out if you speak a little Spanish.

PONCELET
FOOD

Map p250 (☎91 308 02 21; www.poncelet.es; Calle de Argensola 27; ⊘10.30am-8.30pm Mon-Sat; ⓜAlonso Martínez) For 80 Spanish and another 240 European cheese varieties, this fine cheese shop is the best of its kind in Madrid. The range is outstanding and the staff really know their cheese.

CACAO SAMPAKA
FOOD

Map p250 (☎91 319 58 40; www.cacaosampaka.com; Calle de Orellana 4; ⊘10am-9.30pm; ⓜAlonso Martínez) If you thought chocolate was about fruit 'n' nut, think again. This gourmet chocolate shop is a chocoholic's dream come true, with more combinations to go with humble cocoa than you ever imagined possible. It also has a cafe that's good for lunch.

RESERVA Y CATA
WINE

Map p250 (☎91 319 04 01; www.reservaycata.com; Calle del Conde de Xiquena 13; ⊘11am-2.30pm & 5-9pm Mon-Fri, 11am-2.30pm Sat; ⓜColón, Chueca) This old-style shop stocks an excellent range of local wines, and the knowledgable staff can help you pick out

a great one for your next dinner party or a gift for a friend back home. It specialises in quality Spanish wines that you just don't find in El Corte Inglés. There's often a bottle open so you can try before you buy.

ISOLÉE
FOOD, FASHION

Map p250 (☎902 876 136; www.isolee.com; Calle de las Infantas 19; ⊘11am-9pm Mon-Sat; ⓜGran Vía, Chueca) Multipurpose lifestyle stores were late in coming to Madrid, but they're now all the rage and there's none more stylish than Isolée. It sells a select range of everything from clothes (Andy Warhol to Adidas) and shoes to CDs and food. It has another branch in **Salamanca** (☎902 876 136; Calle de Claudio Coello 55; ⊘11am-8.30pm Mon-Fri, 11am-9pm Sat; ⓜSerrano).

ELISA BRACCI
FASHION

Map p250 (☎91 435 03 05; www.elisabracci.es; Calle de Bárbara de Braganza 2; ⊘10.30am-2.30pm & 5.30-8.30pm Mon-Sat; ⓜAlonso Martínez, Colón) One of the most enduring and respected names of Spanish catwalk fashion and a key figure of the 1980s' outpouring of cultural creativity that was *la movida madrileña,* Elisa Bracci is the place to find that evening dress for a special occasion. The mix of colours and unrestrained elegance suggests a confident designer who long ago reached the pinnacle of her profession.

FUTURAMIC
VINTAGE

Map p250 (☎91 531 63 57; www.futuramics.com; Calle de Válgame Dios 5; ⊘11.30am-3pm & 5.30-8.30pm Mon-Fri, 11am-2.30pm Sat; ⓜChueca) Looking for that 1960s jukebox? Or a real-life parking meter? Just about anything you can imagine in memorabilia (either original or in replica) from the 1930s to the 1980s is available here. Not everything is for sale (the life-size London phone booth, for example), as many of the items are in demand for movie sets, but much of it is. Ring before you head here as the staff are often out on location.

OBJETOLOGY
HOMEWARES

Map p250 (☎91 531 55 31; objetology.eu; Calle de Colmenares 7; ⊘4-8pm Mon-Thu; ⓜChueca, Banco de España) This is the sort of shop that was once the preserve of Barcelona, but now sits very comfortably in Chueca's cool surrounds. The home furnishings here – chairs, lamps, tables and a suite of decorative homewares – have a mostly vintage, mid-20th-century look to them but there are older and newer pieces as well.

CASA POSTAL
ANTIQUES

Map p250 (📞91 532 70 37; www.casapostal.net; Calle de la Libertad 37; ⊙10am-2pm & 5-7.45pm Mon-Fri, 11am-2pm Sat; Ⓜ Chueca) Old postcards, posters, books and other period knick-knacks fill this treasure cave to the rafters. It's a wonderful slice of old Madrid in which to lose yourself.

ALDABA
HOMEWARES

Map p250 (📞91 310 10 45; Calle de Belén 4; ⊙10am-8.30pm Mon-Sat; Ⓜ Chueca) You never quite know what you'll find in this densely packed designer homewares store on a quiet street towards the northern end of Chueca. There's a specialist kitchen section but every corner of your house is catered for, as is your every mood – products range from Alessi to 'ex-lover's voodoo dolls'.

EL TINTERO
CLOTHING

Map p250 (📞91 308 14 18; www.eltintero.es; Calle de Gravina 5; ⊙11am-2pm & 5-9pm Mon-Fri, 11am-2.30pm & 5-9pm Sat; Ⓜ Chueca) Terrific T-shirts are all that El Tintero sells. So if you're looking for a colourful *camiseta* (T-shirt) with Spanish-language slogans that translate as 'I'm maturing – apologies for any inconvenience' or 'Does anyone have an instruction manual?', this is your place. It's all good, clean fun and it also takes a similar approach with kids' wear, from newborns to 10-year-olds.

MACCHININE
CHILDREN

Map p250 (📞91 701 05 18; www.macchinine.es; Calle de Barquillo 7; ⊙10am-2pm & 4.30-8.30pm Mon-Sat; Ⓜ Banco de España) Collectors and children will love this small shop in equal

measure, packed as it is with perfectly created replica model cars and wooden and metal figures. There are also games, toys without batteries and all manner of perfectly proportioned knick-knacks.

L'HABILLEUR
FASHION

Map p250 (📞91 531 32 22; Plaza de Chueca 8; ⊙11am-2pm & 5-9pm Mon-Sat; Ⓜ Chueca) This popular Paris boutique now has a branch on Plaza de Chueca and the deal is the same: designer names at discounted prices, especially downstairs. For women, top names include Forte-Forte, Dr Fango, Marlota and Sofie Doore, while men are served by Hartford, Ganesh and Vintage.

LOMOGRAPHY
GIFTS

Map p250 (📞91 310 44 18; www.lomography.es; Calle de Argensola 1; ⊙11am-8.30pm Mon-Sat; Ⓜ Alonso Martínez, Chueca) Dedicated to the Lomo LC-A, a 1980s-era Russian Kompakt camera that has acquired cult status for its zany colours, fisheye lenses and anticool clunkiness, this eclectic shop sells the cameras (an original will set you back €295) and offbeat design items, from bags and mugs to retro memorabilia loved by adherents of 'lomography'. You can even develop your Lomo photos here.

COORLEONE'S COMPANY
FASHION

Map p250 (📞91 521 47 46; www.coorleonecompany.com; Calle de Hortaleza 37; ⊙11am-9pm Mon-Sat, noon-8pm Sun; Ⓜ Gran Vía, Chueca) This stunning shop has been used to film TV series, advertisements and movies, but you come here primarily for designer clothing, belts and handbags from international designers with a few big local names thrown in, among them Davidelfín and Locking Shocking.

Parque del Oeste & Northern Madrid

CHAMBERÍ | ARGÜELLES | NORTHERN MADRID

Neighbourhood Top Five

1 Visiting the **Ermita de San Antonio de la Florida** (p150), a stunning collection of frescoes that remain exactly where Goya painted them.

2 Surrounding yourself with paintings infused with the clear light of the Mediterranean at the **Museo Sorolla** (p151).

3 Propping up the bar and ordering *patatas bravas* (fried potatoes with a spicy tomato sauce) and a vermouth at the ageless **Bodega de la Ardosa** (p153).

4 Discovering the weird-and-wonderful world of Spanish nouvelle cuisine by dining at **Sergi Arola Gastro** (p155).

5 Watching Real Madrid play in front of 80,000 passionate fans at the **Estadio Santiago Bernabéu** (p154).

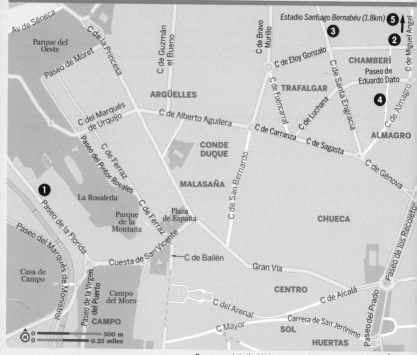

For more detail of this area see Map p252 and p255 ➡

Explore: Parque del Oeste & Northern Madrid

Ranged around central Madrid to the north and west, these neighbourhoods cover a vast area and visiting here requires careful planning. Chamberí is worth visiting in its own right, a reasonably self-contained *barrio* (district) with enough sights, shops and restaurants to warrant at least half a day. Chamberí is good at any time of the day or night, but to understand its appeal as one of the more accessible slices of Madrid life away from the tourist crowds, late afternoon is our favourite time of the day.

The rest of the attractions are thinly spread. Catch the metro to Moncloa metro station, and then follow Parque del Oeste roughly south and then on down to Templo de Debod on the cusp of the city centre. Ermita de San Antonio de la Florida is more of a dedicated (though easily made) excursion – catch the metro to Príncipe Pío and walk to the hermitage, before returning via the same route.

Northern Madrid follows the path of that great Madrid artery, known for much of its length as Paseo de la Castellana. Again, you're more likely to come here as part of a surgical strike on a particular sight or restaurant, but metro connections are good.

Local Life

→ **Meeting point** Plaza de Olavide is the heart and soul of Chamberí, from the old timers watching the world go by from park benches and children in the playgrounds to the outdoor tables that encircle the plaza.

→ **Hang out** Bodega de la Ardosa (p153) is one of the best places in Madrid to understand the appeal of the neighbourhood bar – utterly unpretentious, serving great food and drawing a cast of regulars; it's Madrid in microcosm.

→ **Traditional shops** A Chamberí speciality are the shops that have been serving the *barrio* for decades, places such as Calzados Cantero (p158), Papelería Salazar (p158) and Relojería Santolaya (p158).

Getting There & Away

→ **Metro** The most convenient metro stations for Chamberí are Bilbao (lines 1 and 4), Quevedo (line 2) and Iglesia (line 1).

→ **Metro** Other useful stations include Príncipe Pío (lines 6 and 10) for Ermita de San Antonio de la Florida, and Moncloa (lines 3 and 6), Argüelles (lines 3 and 4) and Plaza de España (lines 2, 3 and 10). Metro line 10 connects northern Madrid to the rest of Madrid.

Lonely Planet's Top Tip

From 8am to around 2pm on Sundays, Calle de Fuencarral between the Glorieta de Quevedo and Glorieta de Bilbao is closed to traffic and all the *barrio* comes out to play. It's a nice alternative to touristy Madrid and you'll mingle with kids on bicycles and rollerblades, and see occasional jumping castles, puppet shows and the like. This has been a *barrio* tradition for over four decades, and also occurs on public holidays.

 Best Places to Eat

→ DiverXo (p155)

→ Santceloni (p155)

→ Sergi Arola Gastro (p155)

→ Mama Campo (p153)

→ Costa Blanca Arrocería (p154)

For reviews, see p153 →

 Best Places to Drink

→ Bodega de la Ardosa (p153)

→ Real Café Bernabéu (p157)

→ Honky Tonk (p157)

→ Sala Clamores (p157)

For reviews, see p157 →

 Best Museums

→ Ermita de San Antonio de la Florida (p150)

→ Museo Sorolla (p151)

→ Museo de América (p151)

→ Templo de Debod (p152)

For reviews, see p151 →

PARQUE DEL OESTE & NORTHERN MADRID

This humble hermitage ranks alongside Madrid's finest art galleries. Recently restored and also known as the Panteón de Goya, the chapel has frescoed ceilings as painted by Goya in 1798 on the request of Carlos IV. As such, it's one of the few places to see Goya masterworks in their original setting.

The Miracle of St Anthony

Figures on the dome depict the miracle of St Anthony. The saint heard word from his native Lisbon that his father had been unjustly accused of murder. St Anthony was whisked miraculously to his hometown from northern Italy, where he tried in vain to convince the judges of his father's innocence. He then demanded that the corpse of the murder victim be placed before the judges. Goya's painting depicts the moment in which St Anthony calls on the corpse (a young man) to rise up and absolve his father.

An 18th-Century Madrid Crowd

As interesting as the miracle that forms the fresco's centrepiece, a typical Madrid crowd swarms around the saint. It was customary in such works that angels and cherubs appear in the cupola, above all the terrestrial activity, but Goya, never one to let himself be confined within the mores of the day, places the human above the divine.

Goya's Tomb

The painter is buried in front of the altar. His remains were transferred in 1919 from Bordeaux (France), where he had died in self-imposed exile in 1828. Oddly, the skeleton that was exhumed in Bordeaux was missing one important item – the head.

Fiesta de San Antonio

Young women (traditionally seamstresses) flock to the hermitage on 13 June to petition for a partner. Whether spiritually inclined or not, the attitude seems to be 'why take a chance?'

DON'T MISS...

➡ Miracle of St Anthony
➡ An 18th-century Madrid crowd
➡ Goya's Tomb
➡ Fiesta de San Antonio

PRACTICALITIES

➡ Map p255
➡ ☎ 91 542 07 22
➡ www.sanantoniodela florida.es
➡ Glorieta de San Antonio de la Florida 5
➡ ⊙10am-8pm Tue-Sun, hours vary Jul & Aug
➡ Ⓜ Príncipe Pío

⦿ SIGHTS

ERMITA DE SAN ANTONIO
DE LA FLORIDA   GALLERY
See p150.

MUSEO SOROLLA   GALLERY
Map p252 (☏91 310 15 84; http://museoso-rolla.mcu.es; Paseo del General Martínez Campos 37; adult/child €3/free, Sun & 2-8pm Sat free; ☺9.30am-8pm Tue-Sat, 10am-3pm Sun; Ⓜ Iglesia, Gregorio Marañón) The Valencian artist Joaquín Sorolla immortalised the clear Mediterranean light of the Valencian coast. His Madrid house, a quiet mansion surrounded by lush gardens that he designed himself, was inspired by what he had seen in Andalucía and now contains the most complete collection of the artist's works.

On the ground floor there's a cool *patio cordobés*, an Andalucian courtyard off which is a room containing collections of Sorolla's drawings. The 1st floor, with the main salon and dining areas, was mostly decorated by the artist himself. On the same floor are three separate rooms that Sorolla used as studios. In the second one is a collection of his Valencian beach scenes. The third was where he usually worked. Upstairs, works spanning Sorolla's career are organised across four adjoining rooms.

MUSEO DE CERRALBO   MUSEUM
Map p255 (☏91 547 36 46; http://en.museocerralbo.mcu.es; Calle de Ventura Rodríguez 17; adult/concession €3/free, Sun, 2-3pm Sat & 5-8pm Thu free; ☺9.30am-3pm Tue, Wed, Fri & Sat, 9.30am-3pm & 5-8pm Thu, 10am-3pm Sun; Ⓜ Ventura Rodríguez) Huddled beneath the modern apartment buildings northwest of Plaza de España, this noble old mansion is a reminder of how wealthy *madrileños* (people from Madrid) once lived. The former home of the 17th Marqués de Cerralbo (1845–1922) – politician, poet and archaeologist – is a study in 19th-century opulence. The upper floor boasts a gala dining hall and a grand ballroom. The mansion is jammed with the fruits of the collector's eclectic meanderings – from Oriental pieces to religious paintings and clocks.

On the main floor are suits of armour from around the world, while the Oriental room is full of carpets, Moroccan kilims, tapestries, musical instruments and 18th-century Japanese suits of armour, much of it obtained at auction in Paris in the 1870s. The music room is dominated by a gon-

PLAZA DE OLAVIDE

Plaza de Olavide (Map p252; Ⓜ Bilbao, Iglesia, Quevedo) hasn't always had its current form. From 1934, the entire plaza was occupied by a covered, octagonal market. In November 1974, the market was demolished in a spectacular controlled explosion, opening up the plaza as one of Madrid's most agreeable public spaces. To see the plaza's history told in pictures, step into Bar Méntrida at No 3 for a drink and admire the photos on the wall.

dola of Murano glass and pieces of Bohemian crystal. The house is also replete with porcelain, including Sèvres, Wedgwood, Meissen and local ceramics.

Clearly the *marqués* was a man of diverse tastes and it can be a little overwhelming, especially once you factor in artworks by Zurbarán, Ribera, Van Dyck and El Greco.

CEMENTERIO DE LA FLORIDA   CEMETERY
Map p255 (Calle de Francisco Jacinto y Alcantara; Ⓜ Príncipe Pío) Across the train tracks east of the Ermita de San Antonio de la Florida is the cemetery where 43 rebels executed by Napoleon's troops lie buried. They were killed on the nearby Montaña del Príncipe Pío in the predawn of 3 May 1808, after the Dos de Mayo uprising. The event was immortalised by Goya in his *Dos de mayo* and *Tres de mayo* paintings, which hang in the Museo del Prado (p99). The forlorn cemetery, established in 1796, is often closed.

MUSEO DE AMÉRICA   MUSEUM
Map p255 (☏91 549 26 41; www.mecd.gob.es/museodeamerica; Avenida de los Reyes Católicos 6; adult/concession €3/1.50, Sun free; ☺9.30am-3pm Tue, Wed, Fri & Sat, 9.30am-7pm Thu, 10am-3pm Sun; Ⓜ Moncloa) Empire may have become a dirty word but it defined how Spain saw itself for centuries. Spanish vessels crossed the Atlantic to the Spanish colonies in Latin America, carrying adventurers one way and gold and other looted artefacts from indigenous cultures on the return journey. These latter pieces – at once the heritage of another continent and a fascinating insight into imperial Spain – are the subject of this excellent museum.

The two levels of the museum show off a representative display of ceramics, statuary,

TOP SIGHT
TEMPLO DE DEBOD

Yes, that *is* an Egyptian temple in downtown Madrid. No matter which way you look at it, there's something incongruous about finding the Templo de Debod in the Parque de la Montaña northwest of Plaza de España. The temple was saved from the rising waters of Lake Nasser in southern Egypt when Egyptian president Gamal Abdel Nasser built the Aswan High Dam. After 1968 it was sent block by block to Spain as a gesture of thanks to Spanish archaeologists in the Unesco team that worked to save the monuments that would otherwise have disappeared forever.

Begun in 2200 BC and completed over many centuries, the temple was dedicated to the god Amon of Thebes, about 20km south of Philae in the Nubian desert of southern Egypt. According to some authors of myth and legend, the goddess Isis gave birth to Horus in this very temple, although obviously not in Madrid.

Rather than treating the temple as a sight on its own, consider a stroll in the surrounding parkland from where the views towards the Palacio Real are some of Madrid's prettiest.

DON'T MISS...

➡ Temple interior
➡ Parque de la Montaña

PRACTICALITIES

➡ Map p255
➡ www.madrid.es
➡ Paseo del Pintor Rosales
➡ ⊙10am-2pm & 6-8pm Tue-Fri, 9.30am-8pm Sat & Sun Apr-Sep, 9.45am-1.45pm & 4.15-6.15pm Tue-Fri & 9.30am-8pm Sat & Sun Oct-Mar
➡ Ⓜ Ventura Rodríguez

---

jewellery and instruments of hunting, fishing and war, along with some of the paraphernalia of the colonisers. The display is divided into five thematic zones: **El Conocimiento de América** (which traces the discovery and exploration of the Americas), **La Realidad de América** (a big-screen summary of how South America wound up as it has today), and others on society, religion and language, which each explore tribal issues, the clash with the Spanish newcomers and its results. The Colombian gold collection, dating as far back as the 2nd century AD, is particularly eye-catching.

FARO DE MADRID   VIEWPOINT
Map p255 (☎91 544 81 04; Avenida de los Reyes Católicos; adult/child/concession €3/free/1.50; ⊙9.30am-8.30pm; ⓂMoncloa) After a decade closed, this supremely ugly Madrid landmark just in front of the Museo de América reopened in April 2015. It looks out over the northern corner of the Parque del Oeste and has sweeping views of western Madrid. It was built in 1992 to commemorate the 500th anniversary of the discovery of America and to celebrate Madrid's role that year as the European Capital of Culture. Sunset is the perfect time to visit.

Entry is every half-hour from 9.30am to 1.30pm, whereafter it's less restrictive.

PARQUE DEL OESTE   GARDENS
Map p255 (Avenida del Arco de la Victoria; ⓂMoncloa) Sloping down the hill behind the Moncloa metro station, Parque del Oeste (Park of the West) is quite beautiful, with plenty of shady corners where you can recline under a tree in the heat of the day and enjoy fine views out to the west towards Casa de Campo. It has been a *madrileño* favourite ever since its creation in 1906. Until a few years ago, the Paseo de Camoens, a main thoroughfare running through the park, was lined with prostitutes by night. To deprive them of clients, the city authorities now close the park to wheeled traffic from 11pm on Friday until 6am on Monday.

TELEFÉRICO   CABLE CAR
Map p255 (☎91 541 11 18; www.teleferico.com; cnr Paseo del Pintor Rosales & Calle de Marqués de Urquijo; one-way/return €4.20/5.90; ⊙noon-9pm May-Aug, reduced hours Sep-Apr; ⓂArgüelles) One of the world's most horizontal cable cars (it never hangs more than 40m above the ground), the Teleférico putters out from the slopes of Parque del Oeste. The 2.5km journey takes you into the depths of the Casa de Campo (p156), Madrid's enormous green open space (more a dry olive hue in summer), to the west of the city centre. Views on the way are splendid and there's a decent chil-

dren's playground near Casa de Campo station. Time it so you can settle in for a cool lunch or evening tipple on one of the *terrazas* (terraces) along Paseo del Pintor Rosales.

ESTACIÓN DE CHAMBERÍ   MUSEUM

Map p252 (Andén 0; http://museomadrid.com/ tag/anden-0-horario; cnr Calles de Santa Engracia & de Luchana; ⊙11am-1pm & 5-7pm Fri, 10am-2pm Sat & Sun; Iglesia, Bilbao) FREE Estación de Chamberí, the long-lost ghost station of Madrid's metro, is now a museum piece that re-creates the era of the station's inauguration in 1919 with advertisements from the time (including Madrid's then-four-digit phone numbers), ticket offices and other memorabilia almost a century old. It's an engaging journey down memory lane.

For years, *madrileños* wondered what happened to the Chamberí metro station – they knew it existed, yet it appeared on no maps and no trains ever stopped there. The answer was that Chamberí station lay along line 1, between the stops of Bilbao and Iglesia, until 1966 when Madrid's trains (and, where possible, platforms) were lengthened. Logistical difficulties meant that Chamberí could not be extended and the station was abandoned. In 2008 the Estación de Chamberí finally reopened to the public, if not for trains.

EATING

Chamberí & Argüelles

BODEGA DE LA ARDOSA   TAPAS €

Map p252 (91 446 58 94; Calle de Santa Engracia 70; raciónes from €7; ⊙9am-3pm & 6-11.30pm Thu-Tue; Iglesia) Tucked away in a fairly modern corner of Chamberí, this fine old relic has an extravagantly tiled facade complete with shrapnel holes dating back to the Spanish Civil War. For decades locals have been coming here for their morning tipple and for some of the best traditional Spanish *patatas bravas* (fried potatoes with a spicy tomato sauce) in town. It also has vermouth on tap.

VIANDAS DE SALAMANCA   SPANISH €

Map p252 (91 593 40 77; museosorolla.mcu. es museosorolla.mcu.es viandasdesalamanca. es; Calle de Fuencarral 156; bocadillos €3.60; ⊙9.30am-9.30pm Mon-Sat, 11.30am-9.30pm Sun; Quevedo) Across Madrid you'll find delis

from Spain's *jamón*-producing regions selling *jamón* (cured ham), chorizo and the like. But Viandas de Salamanca was one of the first to see their potential as simple but filling and quintessentially Spanish fast food. A few steps off the Glorieta de Quevedo, this shop sells *bocadillos de jamón* (rolls with ham), little paper cones filled with *jamón* and *jamón*-filled pastries. Vacuum-sealed cured meats are also available.

CASA MINGO   ASTURIAN €

Map p255 (91 547 79 18; www.casamingo.es; Paseo de la Florida 34; raciónes €3-11; ⊙11am-midnight; Príncipe Pío) Opened in 1888, Casa Mingo is a well-known and vaguely cavernous Asturian cider house. It's kept simple here, focusing primarily on the signature dish of *pollo asado* (roast chicken, cut in quarters; €11) accompanied by a bottle of cider. Combine with a visit to the neighbouring Ermita de San Antonio de la Florida (p150). It also serves up *chorizo a la sidra* (chorizo cooked with cider) and *queso cabrales* (a blue cheese from Asturias).

CERVECERÍA 100 MONTADITOS   FAST FOOD €

Map p252 (www.100montaditos.com; Calle de Fuencarral 145; mini-rolls €0.50-3; ⊙noon-midnight; Quevedo) This bar with outlets all across the city serves up no fewer than 100 different varieties of mini-*bocadillos* (filled rolls) that span the full range of Spanish staples, such as chorizo, *jamón*, tortilla and a variety of cheeses and seafood, in more combinations than you could imagine. You order at the counter and your name is called in no time. Menus are available in English.

⭐MAMA CAMPO   SPANISH €€

Map p252 (91 447 41 38; www.mamacampo. es; Plaza de Olavide; mains €6-12; ⊙1.30-5.30pm & 8.30pm-1.30am Tue-Sat, 1.30-5.30pm Sun;

ⓘ METRO LINE 10

Two of the neighbourhood's top sights – the Ermita de San Antonio de la Florida (p150) and the Estadio Santiago Bernabéu (p154) – may seem far flung but they're actually connected by metro line 10. En route between the two, the line also has stops at Plaza de España and Tribunal, which are handy stations for the rest of the *barrio* (district).

TOP SIGHT
ESTADIO SANTIAGO BERNABÉU

Football fans and budding Madridistas (Real Madrid supporters) will want to make a pilgrimage to the Estadio Santiago Bernabéu, a temple to all that's extravagant and successful in football. For a tour of the stadium, buy your ticket at window 10 (next to gate 7). The self-guided tours take you up into the stands for a panoramic view of the stadium, then pass through the presidential box, press room, dressing rooms, players' tunnel and even onto the pitch itself. The tour ends in the extraordinary Exposición de Trofeos (trophy exhibit).

Better still, attend a game alongside 80,000 delirious fans. For bigger games, tickets are difficult to find unless you're willing to take the risk with scalpers. For less important matches, you shouldn't have too many problems. Tickets can be purchased online, by phone or in person from the ticket office at gate 42 on Av de Concha Espina; for the last option, turn up early in the week before a scheduled game (eg a Monday morning for a Sunday game).

The football season runs from September (or the last weekend in August) until May, with a two-week break just before Christmas until early in the New Year.

DON'T MISS...

➔ Live game

➔ Guided tour

➔ Tienda Real Madrid (p158)

➔ Exposición de Trofeos

PRACTICALITIES

➔ 91 398 43 00, tickets 902 324 324

➔ www.realmadrid.com

➔ Av de Concha Espina 1

➔ tour adult/child €19/13

➔ tours 10am-7pm Mon-Sat, 10.30am-6.30pm Sun, except match days

➔ Santiago Bernabéu

Bilbao, Iglesia, Quevedo) There's a certain sameness to the bars that surround the Plaza de Olavide, but this new place changes everything. Positioning itself as an eco-friendly take on the Spanish *taberna* (tavern), it's gone for a winning white decor within and a fresh approach to Spanish staples, always with an emphasis on fresh, organic ingredients. It also has tables on the plaza, one of our favourites.

Just around the corner in Calle de Trafalgar, it also has a health food store, and even a cooking school/workshop for kids (where the Mama Campo empire began).

LAS TORTILLAS DE GABINO   SPANISH €€

Map p252 (91 319 75 05; www.lastortillasdegabino.com; Calle de Rafael Calvo 20; tortillas €9-15, mains €12-20; 1.30-4pm & 9-11.30pm Mon-Sat; Iglesia) It's a brave Spanish chef that fiddles with the iconic *tortilla de patatas* (potato omelette), but the results here are delicious – such as tortilla with octopus, and with all manner of surprising combinations. This place also gets rave reviews for its *croquetas* (croquettes). The service is excellent and the bright yet classy dining area adds to the sense of a most agreeable eating experience. Reservations highly recommended.

COSTA BLANCA ARROCERÍA   SPANISH €€

Map p252 (91 448 58 32; Calle de Bravo Murillo 3; mains €12-22; 1.30-4pm Mon, 1.30-4pm & 8.30-11.30pm Tue-Fri, 2-4pm & 8.30-11.30pm Sat & Sun; Quevedo) Even if you don't have plans to be in Chamberí, it's worth a trip across town to this casual bar-restaurant that offers outstanding rice dishes, including paella. The quality is high and prices are among the cheapest in town. Start with *almejas a la marinera* (baby clams) and follow it up with *paella de marisco* (seafood paella) for the full experience. As always in such places, you'll need two people to make up an order.

SAGARETXE   TAPAS €€

Map p252 (91 446 25 88; www.sagaretxe.com; Calle de Eloy Gonzalo 26; tapas from €2; noon-5pm & 7pm-midnight; Iglesia) One of the best Basque *pintxos* (Basque tapas) bars in Madrid, Sagaretxe takes the stress out of eating tapas, with around 20 varieties lined up along the bar (and more than 100 that can be prepared in the kitchen upon request). Simply point and any of the wonderful selection will be plated up for you. There's a more expensive but equally good Basque restaurant downstairs.

LA FAVORITA
SPANISH €€

Map p252 (☎91 448 38 10; www.restaurantelafavorita.com; Calle de Covarrubias 25; mains €12-25, set menus from €25; ⊙1.30-4pm & 9pm-midnight Mon-Fri, 9pm-midnight Sat; ⊠Alonso Martínez) Set in a delightful old mansion, La Favorita is famous for its opera arias throughout the night, sung by professional opera singers masquerading as waiters. The outdoor garden courtyard is delightful on a summer's evening, while the music and food are top drawer.

IL CASONE
ITALIAN €€

Map p252 (☎91 591 62 66; Calle de Trafalgar 25; mains €8-15; ⊙1-4pm & 8.30-11pm; ⊠Quevedo, Iglesia, Bilbao) With its outdoor tables on the lovely Plaza de Olavide in summer, reasonable prices and fresh and inventive Italian cooking, Il Casone is excellent. There are flashes of creativity in the pasta, such as *fagottini* (dumplings) with black truffles and cream of foie gras and mushroom, while the salads, carpaccios and grilled provolone are great starters.

★SERGI AROLA GASTRO
MODERN SPANISH €€€

Map p252 (☎91 310 21 69; www.sergiarola.es; Calle de Zurbano 31; mains €49-58, set menus €49-195; ⊙2-3.30pm & 9-11.30pm Tue-Sat Sep-May; ⊠Alonso Martínez) Sergi Arola, a stellar Catalan celebrity chef who has adopted Madrid as his own, runs this highly personalised temple to all that's innovative in Spanish gastronomy. The menus change with the seasons but this is culinary indulgence at its finest, the sort of place where creativity, presentation and taste are everything. And oh, what tastes... Booking well in advance is necessary. Check the website for opening hours – there was talk of it closing not just in summer, but in winter, too, as Arola attends to his other projects around the world.

EL PEDRUSCO
SPANISH €€€

Map p252 (☎91 446 88 33; www.elpedruscodealcorvo.com; Calle de Juan de Austria 27; mains €19-44; ⊙1.30-4pm Tue-Sun; ⊠Iglesia) If you haven't time to visit one of the *asadores* (restaurants specialising in roasted meats) of Segovia, head to this fine restaurant where the *cochinillo asado* (roast suckling pig) and quarter *lechazo* (quarter roast lamb) are succulent and as good as any in Madrid. It's the sort of place where a salad is a must to counterbalance all that meat and you'll be delighted to see a vegetable.

✖ Northern Madrid

The business and well-to-do clientele who eat in the restaurants of northern Madrid know their food and they're happy to pay for it. These restaurants are often a fair metro, taxi or chauffeur-driven limousine ride north of the centre, but they're well worth it for a touch of class.

★DIVERXO
MODERN SPANISH €€€

(☎915 70 07 66; diverxo.com; Calle de Padre Damián, 23; mains €70-90, set menus €95-200; ⊙2-3.30pm & 9-10.30pm Tue-Sat, closed 3 weeks Aug; ⊠Cuzco) Madrid's only three-Michelin-starred restaurant, DiverXo in northern Madrid is one of Spain's most unusual culinary experiences. Chef David Muñoz is something of the enfant terrible of Spain's cooking scene. Still in his 30s, he favours what he has described as a 'brutal' approach to cooking – his team of chefs appear in mid bite to add surprising new ingredients.

The carefully choreographed experience centres on the short (2½-hour, seven-course) or long (four-hour, 11-course) menus, or the 'Wow' and 'Glutton Wow' menus, and is utterly unlike the more formal upmarket dining options elsewhere. The nondescript suburban setting and small premises (chefs sometimes end up putting the finishing touches to dishes in the hallway) only add to the whole street-smart atmosphere. Bookings up to six months in advance are required.

★SANTCELONI
CATALAN €€€

Map p252 (☎91 210 88 40; www.restaurantesantceloni.com; Paseo de la Castellana 57; mains €44-71, set menus €150-180; ⊙2-4pm & 9-11pm Mon-Fri, 9-11pm Sat Sep-Jul; ⊠Gregorio Marañón) The Michelin-starred Santceloni is one of Madrid's best restaurants, with luxury decor, faultless service, fabulous wines and nouvelle cuisine from the kitchen of chef Óscar Velasco. Each dish is a work of art and the menu changes with the seasons, but we'd recommend one of the *menús gastronómicos* to really sample the breadth of surprising tastes.

ZALACAÍN
BASQUE, NAVARRAN €€€

Map p252 (☎91 561 48 40; www.restaurantezalacain.com; Calle de Álvarez de Baena 4; mains €30-50, set menu €106; ⊙1.15-4pm & 9pm-midnight Mon-Fri, 9pm-midnight Sat, closed

CASA DE CAMPO

Sometimes called the 'lungs of Madrid', **Casa de Campo** (Map p255; M Batán) is a 17-sq-km expanse of greenery stretching west of the Río Manzanares. There are prettier and more central parks in Madrid but it's less manicured and has numerous walking trails, lakeside restaurants and other attractions. And visit the *madrileños* (people from Madrid) do, nearly half a million of them every weekend.

Zoo Aquarium de Madrid (902 345 014; www.zoomadrid.com; Casa de Campo; adult/child €22.95/18.60, purchased online €19.95/16.90; 10.30am-10pm Sun-Thu, 10.30am-midnight Fri & Sat Jul & Aug, shorter hours Sep-Jun; 37 from Intercambiador de Príncipe Pío, M Casa de Campo), Madrid's zoo, is a fairly standard European city zoo and is home to about 3000 animals. Exhibits range from white Siberian tigers to mambas, Atlas lions, zebras, giraffes, rhinoceroses, flamingos, koalas and celebrity pandas. There's also an aquarium with shows; however, animal welfare groups suggest interaction with dolphins and other sea mammals held in captivity creates stress for these complex creatures.

The 3000-sq-metre **Aviario** (Aviary) contains some 60 species of eagle, condor and vulture. Spend long enough here, however, and the Disneyfication of the zoo will start to grate.

Arriving by bus is the best option as it leaves you right at the door; if you take the metro to Casa de Campo, you've a 15-minute walk from the station, or you can take bus 37 from the station for one stop.

Weekends can be busy, so try and visit during the week, although check the opening hours online before setting out. It might also be worth checking online the program for the day (for shows) and planning your visit accordingly. And it's considerably cheaper if you book online.

Parque de Atracciones (91 463 29 00; www.parquedeatracciones.es; Casa de Campo; adult/child €31.90/24.90; noon-midnight Jul & Aug, shorter hours Sep-Jun; 37 from Intercambiador de Príncipe Pío, M Batán) is an amusement park that has the usual collection of high-adrenaline rides, shows for the kids and kitsch at every turn. In the **Zona de Máquinas** are most of the bigger rides, such as classic roller-coasters, the Lanzadera (which takes you up 63m and then drops you in a simulated bungee jump), La Máquina (a giant wheel that spins on its axis) and the favourite, the Tornado, a kind of upside-down roller-coaster that zips along at up to 80km/h.

After all that gut-churning stuff, you'll be grateful for the **Zona de Tranquilidad**, where you can climb aboard a gentle Ferris wheel, take a theme ride through the jungle or just sit back for a snack. Of course, tranquillity is relative – El Viejo Caserón (haunted house) is not for the nervous among you (in our experience, it's the adults who get spooked). **La Zona de la Naturaleza** (Nature Zone) offers, among other things, dodgems and various water rides.

Finally, in the **Zona Infantil**, younger kids can get their own thrills on less hair-raising rides, such as a Ford-T, the Barón Rojo (Red Baron) and Caballos del Oeste (Horses of the Wild West).

The park has all sorts of timetable variations, so it is always a good idea to check before committing yourself, and it's always cheaper to buy your entrance ticket online. Long queues form on weekends, both at the rides and to get in, so either get here early or come another day if you can.

Aug & Easter; M Gregorio Marañón) Where most other fine-dining experiences centre on innovation, Zalacaín is a bastion of tradition, with a refined air and a loyal following. The pig's trotters filled with mushrooms and lamb is a house speciality, as is the lobster salad. The wine list is purported to be one of the city's best (with an estimated 35,000 bottles and 1200 different varieties).

Everyone who's anyone in Madrid, from the king down, has eaten here since the doors opened in 1973; it was the first restaurant in Spain to receive three Michelin stars – it now has one. You should certainly dress to impress (men will need a tie and a jacket).

PUERTA 57
SPANISH €€€

(☎91 457 33 61; www.grupolamaquina.es; Gate 57, Estadio Santiago Bernabéu, Calle de Padre Damián; mains €20-38; ⊙1-4pm & 8.30pm-midnight; Ⓜ Santiago Bernabéu) There are many reasons to recommend this place, but the greatest novelty lies in its location – inside the home stadium of Real Madrid; its Salón Madrid (one of a number of dining rooms) looks out over the playing field. Needless to say, you'll need to book a long time in advance for a meal during a game.

The cuisine is traditional Spanish with an emphasis on seafood and it gets rave reviews from its predominantly business clientele.

DRINKING & NIGHTLIFE

REAL CAFÉ BERNABÉU
BAR

(☎91 458 36 67; www.realcafebernabeu.es; Gate 30, Estadio Santiago Bernabéu, Av de Concha Espina; ⊙9pm-1am; Ⓜ Santiago Bernabéu) Overlooking one of the most famous football fields on earth, this trendy cocktail bar will appeal to those who live and breathe football or those who simply enjoy mixing with the beautiful people. Views of the stadium are exceptional, although it closes two hours before a game and doesn't open until an hour after. There's also a good restaurant.

ENTERTAINMENT

SALA CLAMORES
LIVE MUSIC

Map p252 (☎91 445 79 38; www.clamores.es; Calle de Alburquerque 14; ⊙6.30pm-2am Sun-Thu, 6.30pm-5.30am Fri & Sat; Ⓜ Bilbao) Clamores is a one-time classic jazz cafe that has morphed into one of the most diverse live music stages in Madrid. Jazz is still a staple, but flamenco, blues, world music, singer-songwriters, pop and rock all make regular appearances. Live shows can begin as early as 7pm on weekends but sometimes really only get going after 1am!

On the rare nights when there's nothing live, a DJ takes over, spinning pop, indie and funk. Admission varies from free to €15.

GALILEO GALILEI
LIVE MUSIC

Map p252 (☎91 534 75 57; www.salagalileogalilei.com; Calle de Galileo 100; ⊙6pm-4.30am; Ⓜ Islas Filipinas) There's no telling what will be staged here next, but it's sure to be good, as the list of past performers attests: Jackson Browne, El Cigala, Kiko Veneno, Niña Pastori and Brazilian songstress Cibelle among others. The program changes nightly, with singer-songwriters, jazz, flamenco, folk, fusion, indie, world music and even comedians. Admission ranges from free to €18; most performances start at 10.30pm.

HONKY TONK
LIVE MUSIC

Map p252 (☎91 445 61 91; www.clubhonky.com; Calle de Covarrubias 24; ⊙9.30pm-5am Sun-Thu, 9.30pm-6am Fri & Sat; Ⓜ Alonso Martínez) Despite the name, this is a great place to see blues or local rock, though many acts have a little country, jazz or R & B thrown into the mix, too. It's a fun vibe in a smallish club that's been around since the heady 1980s. Admission varies from free to €5; it opens 365 days a year.

It's a reliable late-night option in a *barrio* of few, and the range of malt whiskies is impressive. Arrive early as it fills up fast.

TEATROS DEL CANAL
THEATRE

Map p252 (☎91 308 99 99; www.teatroscanal.com; Calle de Cea Bermúdez 1; Ⓜ Canal) A state-of-the-art theatre complex, Teatros del Canal does major theatre performances, as well as musical and dance concerts, and it's a popular festival venue.

MOBY DICK
LIVE MUSIC

(☎91 555 76 71; www.mobydickclub.com; Avenida del Brasil 5; ⊙9pm-3am Mon-Wed, to 6am Thu-Sat; Ⓜ Santiago Bernabéu) In a corner of Madrid that works hard by day and parties even harder on weekends, Moby Dick is an institution on the live music circuit. It's

> ### ℹ SPANISH FAST FOOD & WHERE TO EAT BETWEEN MEALS
>
> If you just can't wait until restaurants open, try the following:
>
> ➡ **Plaza de Olavide** Most bars and restaurants around the square don't close their kitchens between lunch and dinner.
>
> ➡ **Viandas de Salamanca** (p153) Rolls filled with *jamón* (cured ham).
>
> ➡ **Cervecería 100 Montaditos** (p153) Mini-rolls with all manner of fillings.

mostly well-known rock bands who can't quite fill the 25,000-seater venues, and there are plenty of dance bars alongside if the music's not to your liking. Admission is anything from free to €20.

AUDITORIO NACIONAL
DE MÚSICA
CLASSICAL MUSIC

(☏91 337 01 40; www.auditorionacional.mcu. es; Calle del Príncipe de Vergara 146; MCruz del Rayo) When it's not playing the Teatro Real, Madrid's Orquesta Sinfónica plays at this modern venue, which also attracts famous conductors from all across the world. It's usually fairly easy to get your hands on tickets at the box office.

 SHOPPING

CALZADOS CANTERO
SHOES

Map p252 (☏91 447 07 35; Plaza de Olavide 12; ◷9.45am-2pm & 4.45-8.30pm Mon-Fri, 9.45am-2pm Sat; MQuevedo, Iglesia, Bilbao) A charming old-world shoe store, Calzados Cantero sells a range of shoes at rock-bottom prices. But it's most famous for its rope-soled *alpargatas* (espadrilles), which start from €7. This is a *barrio* classic, the sort of store to which parents bring their children as their own parents did a generation before.

BAZAR MATEY
GIFTS

Map p252 (☏91 446 93 11; www.matey.com; Calle de la Santísima Trinidad 1; ◷9.30am-1.30pm & 4.30-8pm Mon-Sat; MIglesia, Quevedo) A wonderful store, Bazar Matey caters for collectors of model trains, aeroplanes and cars, and all sorts of accessories. The items here are the real deal, with near-perfect models of everything from old Renfe trains to obscure international airlines. Prices can be sky high, but that doesn't deter the legions of collectors who stream in from all over Madrid on Saturdays. The kids will love it, too.

RELOJERÍA SANTOLAYA
ANTIQUES

Map p252 (☏91 447 25 64; www.relojeriasantolaya.com; Calle Murillo 8; ◷10am-1pm & 5-8pm Mon-Fri; MQuevedo, Iglesia, Bilbao) Founded in 1867, this timeless old clock repairer just off Plaza de Olavide is the official watch repairer to Spain's royalty and heritage properties. There's not much that's for sale here, but stop by the tiny shopfront/workshop to admire the dying art of timepiece repairs, with not a digital watch in sight.

PAPELERÍA SALAZAR
BOOKS, STATIONERY

Map p252 (☏91 446 18 48; www.papeleriasalazar.es; Calle Luchana 7-9; ◷9.30am-1.30pm & 4.30-8pm Mon-Fri, 9.30am-1.30pm Sat; MBilbao) Opened in 1905, Papelería Salazar is Madrid's oldest stationery store and is now run by the fourth generation of the Salazar family. It's a treasure trove that combines items of interest only to locals (old-style Spanish bookplates, First Communion invitations) with useful items such as Faber-Castell pens and pencils, maps, notebooks and drawing supplies. It's a priceless relic of the kind that is slowly disappearing in Madrid.

PASAJES LIBRERÍA
INTERNACIONAL
BOOKS

Map p252 (☏91 310 12 45; www.pasajeslibros. com; Calle de Génova 3; ◷9.30am-9.30pm Mon-Sat; MAlonso Martínez) One of the best bookshops in Madrid, Pasajes Librería Internacional has an extensive English section (downstairs at the back), which includes high-quality fiction (if it's a new release, it'll be the first bookshop in town to have it), as well as history, Spanish subject matter and travel, and a few literary magazines. There are also French, German, Italian and Portuguese books, children's books and DVDs, and a useful noticeboard.

EL DRAGÓN LECTOR
CHILDREN'S BOOKS

Map p252 (☏91 448 60 15; www.eldragonlector.com; Calle de Sagunto 20; ◷10am-2pm & 5-8.30pm Mon-Fri, 10.30am-2pm & 5.30-8pm Sat; MIglesia) Tucked away in a quiet corner of Chamberí, this fab little bookstore for little people has mostly Spanish titles, but some English-language ones as well.

MERCADILLO MARQUÉS DE VIANA
MARKET

(El Rastrillo; Calle del Marqués de Viana; ◷9am-2pm Sun; MTetuán) This calmer version of the rowdy El Rastro (p72) is located in northern Madrid.

TIENDA REAL MADRID
SPORTS

(☏91 458 72 59; www.realmadrid.com; Gate 55, Estadio Santiago Bernabéu, Av de Concha Espina 1; ◷10am-9pm Mon-Sat, 11am-7.30pm Sun; MSantiago Bernabéu) The club shop of Real Madrid sells replica shirts, posters, caps and just about everything else under the sun to which it could attach a club logo. From the shop window, you can see down onto the stadium itself.

Day Trips from Madrid

San Lorenzo de El Escorial p160
One of Spain's grandest monuments, this Unesco World Heritage–listed palace-monastery complex combines a cool mountain setting with the imposing grandeur of imperial Spain.

Toledo p161
Toledo is a beautifully sited, architecturally distinguished city with sign-posts to its glory days as a crossroads of civilisation.

Segovia p164
A Roman aqueduct, a castle that inspired Disney and a colour scheme of sandstone and warm terracotta make Segovia one of the most agreeable towns close to Madrid.

Ávila p165
Surrounded by the finest medieval walls in Spain, Ávila is an evocative Castilian city that's the spiritual home to the cult of Santa Teresa.

Aranjuez p167
A royal getaway down through the centuries, Aranjuez has an extraordinary palace and expansive gardens grafted onto a delightfully small-town canvas.

Chinchón p167
Home to one of the prettiest town squares in Spain, Chinchón is a world away from downtown Madrid, with fabulous food thrown in.

Home to the majestic monastery and palace complex of San Lorenzo de El Escorial, this one-time royal getaway rises up from the foothills of the mountains that shelter Madrid. The prim little town is overflowing with quaint shops, restaurants and hotels and the fresh, cool air, among other things, has been drawing city dwellers here since the complex was built on the orders of King Felipe II in the 16th century as both a royal palace and as a mausoleum for Felipe's parents, Carlos I and Isabel.

DON'T MISS...

➡ Patio de los Reyes
➡ Basílica
➡ Museums
➡ Salas Capitulares
➡ Jardín del Príncipe

PRACTICALITIES

➡ ☏91 890 78 18
➡ www.patrimonio
nacional.es
➡ adult/concession
€10/5, guide/audioguide
€4/4, EU citizens free last
3 hours Wed & Thu
➡ ⊙10am-8pm Apr-Sep,
10am-6pm Oct-Mar,
closed Mon

Patio de los Reyes

At the monastery's main entrance on the west side of the complex, note the statue of St Lawrence holding a symbolic gridiron, the instrument of his martyrdom (he was roasted alive on one). After passing St Lawrence, you'll enter the Patio de los Reyes (Patio of the Kings), which houses statues of the six kings of Judah.

Basílica

Directly ahead of the Patio de los Reyes lies the sombre basilica. Once inside the church proper, turn left to view Benvenuto Cellini's white Carrara marble statue of Christ crucified (1576). Nearby there's an El Greco painting, although it's a far cry from the artist's dream of decorating the whole complex.

Two Museums

As you head downstairs to the northeastern corner of the complex you pass through the Museo de Arquitectura and the Museo de Pintura. The former tells (in Spanish) the story of how the complex was built, the latter contains 16th- and 17th-century Italian, Spanish and Flemish art.

The Crypts

The route through the monastery takes you down into the 17th-century Panteón de los Reyes (Crypt of the Kings), where almost all Spain's monarchs since Carlos I are interred. Nearby is the Panteón de los Infantes (Crypt of the Princesses).

Salas Capitulares

Stairs lead up from the Patio de los Evangelistas (Patio of the Gospels) to the Salas Capitulares (Chapter Houses) in the southeastern corner of the monastery. These bright, airy rooms, whose ceilings are richly frescoed, contain a treasure chest of works by El Greco, Titian, Tintoretto, José de Ribera and Hieronymus Bosch.

Jardín del Príncipe

The Prince's Garden, which leads down to the town of El Escorial, is a lovely monumental garden and contains the Casita del Príncipe, a little neoclassical gem built in 1772 by Juan de Villanueva under Carlos III for his heir, Carlos IV.

Transport

Buses 661 and 664 leave every 15 minutes (every half-hour on weekends; €4.20) from Madrid's Moncloa Intercambiador de Autobuses station. A few dozen Renfe C8 *cercanías* (local train network) trains make the one-hour trip (€3.40) daily from Madrid's Atocha or Chamartín stations to El Escorial.

Toledo

Explore

Toledo's charms, and its proximity to Madrid, mean that it can get choked with tour groups. If you're arriving on the fast train from Madrid, try to make it an early one to arrive before the buses, then try to stay till dusk when the city returns to the locals and the streets take on a moody, other-worldly air.

It's a steep climb up into the old town, but buses 61 and 62 connect the train station with Plaza de Zocodover in the old town, while bus 5 runs a similar service from the bus station.

The Best...

➡ **Sight** Catedral
➡ **Place to Eat** Kumera (p163)
➡ **Place to Shop** Casa Cuatero (p163)

Top Tip

If you don't feel like taking the bus up into the old town from down below and feel like walking, the worst of the climb can be avoided by taking the *remonte peatonal* (escalator), which starts near the Puerta de Alfonso VI and ends near the Monasterio de Santo Domingo El Antiguo.

Getting There & Away

➡ **Bus** Buses (€5.43) make the one-hour trip from Madrid's Estación Sur (ticket windows 12 and 13) to Toledo every half-hour.
➡ **Train** Renfe's high-speed AVANT Rail Link is the best way to get to Toledo, with around 11 trains daily. The trip takes 30 minutes.

Need to Know

➡ **Area Code** ☑925
➡ **Location** 71km southwest of Madrid
➡ **Tourist Office** Main Tourist Office (☑925 25 40 30; www.toledo-turismo.com; Plaza del Ayuntamiento; ☺10am-6pm), Regional Tourist Office (☑925 22 08 43; Puerta de Bisagra; ☺9am-6pm Mon-Fri, 9am-7pm Sat, 9am-3pm Sun)

◉ SIGHTS

The old city and the most important sights are stacked stone upon stone in a crook of the Río Tajo. For a relaxing view of the old city, hop on the Zoco Tren, a small train that does a 45-minute loop up the hill and through Toledo. The train leaves hourly into the early evening and tickets are available from the tourist office.

CATEDRAL   CATHEDRAL
(www.catedralprimada.es; Plaza del Ayuntamiento; adult/child €11/free; ☺10.30am-6.30pm Mon-Sat, 2-6.30pm Sun) Toledo's cathedral reflects the city's historical significance as the heart of Catholic Spain and it's one of the most extravagant cathedrals in the country. The heavy interior, with sturdy columns dividing the space into five naves, is on a monumental scale. Every one of the numerous side chapels has artistic treasures, with the other main highlights being the Capilla Mayor, Transparente, *coro* (choir stalls), *sacristia* (sacristy) and bell tower.

From the earliest days of the Visigothic occupation, the current site of the cathedral has been a centre of worship. During Muslim rule, it contained Toledo's central mosque, destroyed in 1085. Dating from the 13th century and essentially a Gothic structure, the cathedral is nevertheless a melting pot of styles, including Mudéjar and Renaissance. The Visigothic influence continues today in the unique celebration of the Mozarabic Rite, a 6th-century liturgy that was allowed to endure after Cardinal Cisneros put its legitimacy to the test by burning missals in a fire of faith; they survived more or less intact. The rite is celebrated in the Capilla Mozarabe at 9am Monday to Saturday, and at 9.45am on Sunday.

The high altar sits in the extravagant **Capilla Mayor**, whose masterpiece is the *retablo* (altarpiece), with painted wooden sculptures depicting scenes from the lives of Christ and the Virgin Mary; it's flanked by royal tombs. The oldest of the cathedral's magnificent stained-glass pieces is the **rose window** above the Puerta del Reloj. Behind the main altar lies a mesmerising piece of 18th-century churrigueresque (lavish baroque ornamentation), the **Transparente**, which is illuminated by a light well carved into the dome above.

In the centre of things, the **coro** is a feast of sculpture and carved wooden stalls. The

EL GRECO IN TOLEDO

Few artists are as closely associated with a city as El Greco is with Toledo. Born in Crete in 1541, Domenikos Theotokopoulos (El Greco; the Greek) moved to Venice in 1567 to be schooled as a Renaissance artist. Under the tutelage of masters such as Tintoretto, he learned to express dramatic scenes with few colours, concentrating the observer's interest in the faces of his portraits and leaving the rest in relative obscurity, a characteristic that remained one of his hallmarks.

El Greco came to Spain in 1577 hoping to get a job decorating El Escorial, but Felipe II rejected him as a court artist. In Toledo, the painter managed to cultivate a healthy clientele and command good prices. He had to do without the patronage of the cathedral administrators, who were the first of many clients to haul him to court for his high fees.

As Toledo's fortunes declined, so did El Greco's personal finances, and although the works of his final years are among his best, he often found himself unable to pay the rent. He died in 1614, leaving his works scattered about the city.

15th-century lower tier depicts the various stages of the conquest of Granada.

The **tesoro** (treasury, however, deals in treasure of the glittery kind. It's dominated by the extraordinary **Custodia de Arfe**: with 18kg of pure gold and 183kg of silver, this 16th-century processional monstrance bristles with some 260 statuettes. Its big day out is the Feast of Corpus Christi, when it is paraded around Toledo's streets.

Other noteworthy features include the sober **cloister**, off which is the 14th-century **Capilla de San Blas**, with Gothic tombs and stunning frescoes; the gilded **Capilla de Reyes Nuevos**; and the **sala capitular** (chapter house), with its remarkable 500-year-old *artesonado* (wooden Mudéjar ceiling) and portraits of all the archbishops of Toledo.

The highlight of all, however, is the **sacristía**, which contains a gallery with paintings by such masters as El Greco, Zurbarán, Caravaggio, Titian, Raphael and Velázquez. It can be difficult to appreciate the packed-together, poorly lit artworks, but it's a stunning assemblage in a small space. In an adjacent chamber, don't miss the spectacular Moorish standard captured in the Battle of Salado in 1340.

An extra €3 gets you entrance to the upper level of the cloister, and the **bell tower**, which offers wonderful views over the centre of historic Toledo.

ALCÁZAR
FORTRESS, MUSEUM

(Museo del Ejército; Calle Alféreces Provisionales; adult/child €5/free, Sun free; ⊙11am-5pm Thu-Tue) At the highest point in the city looms the foreboding Alcázar. Rebuilt under Fran-

co, it has been reopened as a vast military museum. The usual displays of uniforms and medals are here, but the best part is the exhaustive historical section, with an in-depth overview of the nation's history in Spanish and English.

MONASTERIO SAN JUAN
DE LOS REYES
MONASTERY

(www.sanjuandelosreyes.org; Calle San Juan de los Reyes 2; admission €2.50; ⊙10am-6.30pm Jun-Sep, 10am-5.30pm Oct-May) This imposing 15th-century Franciscan monastery and church was provocatively founded in the heart of the Jewish quarter by the Catholic monarchs Isabel and Fernando to demonstrate the supremacy of their faith. The rulers had planned to be buried here but eventually ended up in their prize conquest, Granada. The highlight is the amazing two-level cloister, a harmonious fusion of late (flamboyant) Gothic downstairs and Mudéjar architecture upstairs, with superb statuary, arches, vaulting, elaborate pinnacles and gargoyles surrounding a lush garden with orange trees and roses.

IGLESIA DE SANTO TOMÉ
CHURCH

(www.santotome.org; Plaza del Conde; admission €2.50; ⊙10am-6pm mid-Oct–mid-Mar, 10am-7pm mid-Mar–mid-Oct) Iglesia de Santo Tomé contains El Greco's masterpiece *El entierro del conde de Orgaz* (The Burial of the Count of Orgaz). When the count was buried in 1322, Saints Augustine and Stephen supposedly descended from heaven to attend the funeral. El Greco's work depicts the event, complete with miracle guests including himself, his son and Cervantes.

MUSEO DE SANTA CRUZ   MUSEUM

(Calle de Cervantes 3; ⊗10am-8pm Mon-Sat, 10am-2.30pm Sun) `FREE` The 16th-century Museo de Santa Cruz is a beguiling combination of Gothic and plateresque styles. The cloisters and carved wooden ceilings are superb, as is the collection of Spanish ceramics. Also upstairs is an atmospheric cruciform gallery that contains an archaeological display, some fine Flemish religious art, a number of El Grecos, a crucifixion attributed to Goya, a flag from the Battle of Lepanto, and the wonderful 15th-century *Tapestry of the Astrolabes*.

SINAGOGA DEL TRÁNSITO   SYNAGOGUE

(☑925 22 36 65; museosefardi.mcu.es; Calle Samuel Leví; adult/child €3/1.50, after 2pm Sat & all day Sun free; ⊗9.30am-7.30pm Tue-Sat Mar-Oct, 9.30am-6pm Tue-Sat Nov-Feb, 10am-3pm Sun year-round) This magnificent synagogue was built in 1355 by special permission from Pedro I. The synagogue now houses the Museo Sefardí. The vast main prayer hall has been expertly restored and the Mudéjar decoration and intricately carved pine ceiling are striking. Exhibits provide an insight into the history of Jewish culture in Spain, and include archaeological finds, a memorial garden, costumes and ceremonial artefacts.

MEZQUITA DEL CRISTO DE LA LUZ   MOSQUE

(Calle Cristo de la Luz; admission €2.50; ⊗10am-2pm & 3.30-5.45pm Mon-Fri, 10am-5.45pm Sat & Sun) On the northern slopes of town you'll find a modest, yet beautiful, mosque (the only one remaining of Toledo's 10) where architectural traces of Toledo's medieval Muslim conquerors are still in evidence. Built around AD 1000, it suffered the usual fate of being converted into a church (hence the religious frescoes), but the original vaulting and arches survived.

MUSEO DEL GRECO   MUSEUM, GALLERY

(☑925 22 44 05; museodelgreco.mcu.es; Paseo del Tránsito; adult/child €3/1.50, after 2pm Sat & all day Sun free; ⊗9.30am-8pm Tue-Sat Apr-Sep, to 6.30pm Oct-Mar, 10am-3pm Sun) In the early 20th century, an aristocrat bought what he thought was El Greco's house and did a stunning job of returning it to period style. He was wrong, but the museum remains worthwhile. As well as the house itself, with its lovely patio and informative details on the painter's life, there are excavated cellars from a Jewish-quarter palace and a good selection of paintings, including a Zurbarán, a set of the apostles by El Greco and works by his son and followers.

EATING & DRINKING

Of Toledo's specialities, *cuchifritos* (a potpourri of lamb, tomato and egg cooked in white wine with saffron) is especially good, while *carcamusa* (a pork dish) is also popular. Otherwise, it's good, hearty Castilian fare.

★KUMERA   MODERN SPANISH €

(☑925 25 75 53; www.restaurantekumera.com; Calle Alfonso X El Sabio 2; meals €9-10, set menus €20-35; ⊗8am-2.30am Mon-Fri, 11am-2.30am Sat & Sun) With arguably the best price-to-quality ratio in town, this place serves up innovative takes on local traditional dishes such as *cochinillo* (suckling pig), *rabo de toro* (bull's tail) or *croquetas* (croquettes, filled with *jamón,* squid, cod or wild mushrooms), alongside gigantic toasts and other creatively conceived dishes. The dishes with foie gras as the centrepiece are especially memorable.

LA ABADÍA   CASTILIAN, TAPAS €€

(www.abadiatoledo.com; Plaza de San Nicolás 3; raciónes €4-15; ⊗bar 8am-midnight, restaurant 1-4pm & 8.30pm-midnight) In a former 16th-century palace, this atmospheric bar and restaurant has arches, niches and subtle lighting spread over a warren of brick-and-stone-clad rooms. The menu includes lightweight dishes and tapas, but the 'Menú de Montes de Toledo' (€19) is a fabulous collection of tastes from the nearby mountains.

SHOPPING

CASA CUATERO   FOOD & DRINK

(☑925 22 26 14; www.casacuartero.com; Calle Hombre de Palo 5; ⊗10am-2pm & 5-8pm Mon-Fri, 10am-3pm & 4-8pm Sat) Just north of the cathedral, this fabulous food shop (here since 1920) sells marzipan, cured meats, wines, cheeses and all manner of local delicacies from around Castilla-La Mancha. It's ideal for gifts to take back home or for a picnic.

Segovia

Explore

Amid the rolling hills of Castilla, Segovia is a year-round, 24-hour destination. In the mornings and afternoons, Segovia goes quietly about its business with a steady stream of visitors animating the city's beautiful (and largely pedestrianised) streets. One time not to miss is the last couple of hours before sunset, best enjoyed from the gardens close to the Alcázar entrance. And if you're here after dark, the winking lights of the old town framed by the aqueduct (sometimes floodlit, sometimes not) are rather lovely.

One other issue of timing to remember is that the city's restaurants are frequently booked out on winter weekends for lunch when people flock from all over the region (including Madrid) in search of *cochinillo asado* (roast suckling pig). If you plan to join them, you'll need a reservation.

The Best...

→ **Sight** Alcázar

→ **Place to Eat** Casa Duque

→ **Place to Drink** La Tasquina

Top Tip

Unless you're in a hurry to get back, consider taking the slow train to Madrid. From Segovia it climbs up through the quiet villages of the Sierra de Guadarrama foothills, before dropping down to Madrid.

Getting There & Away

→ **Bus** Buses run by **La Sepulvedana** (☑902 119699; www.lasepulvedana.es) leave every half-hour from Madrid's Intercambiador de Príncipe Pío (platforms 6 and 7) and arrive in Segovia's central bus station 1¼ hours later. Tickets cost €7.96.

→ **Train** There are two options by train, both operated by **Renfe** (☑902 240202; www.renfe.es). Up to nine normal trains run daily from Madrid to Segovia (one way €8.25, two hours), leaving you at the main train station 2.5km from the aqueduct. The faster option is the high-speed AVE (one way €12.90, 28 minutes), which deposits you at the new Segovia-Guiomar station, 5km from the aqueduct.

Need to Know

→ **Area Code** ☑921

→ **Location** 90km northwest of Madrid

→ **Tourist Office** Centro de Recepción de Visitantes (☑921 46 67 20; www.turismodesegovia.com; Plaza del Azoguejo 1; ☺10am-7pm Sun-Fri, 10am-8pm Sat); Regional Tourist Office (www.segoviaturismo.es; Plaza Mayor 10; ☺9am-8pm Sun-Thu, 9am-9pm Fri & Sat)

 SIGHTS

ALCÁZAR
CASTLE

(☑921 46 07 59; www.alcazardesegovia.com; Plaza de la Reina Victoria Eugenia; adult/child/concession under 6yr €5/free/3, tower €2, 3rd Tue of month EU citizens free; ☺10am-6pm Oct-Mar, 10am-7pm Apr-Sep; ⊕) Rapunzel towers, turrets topped with slate witches' hats and a deep moat at its base make the Alcázar a prototype fairy-tale castle, so much so that its design inspired Walt Disney's vision of Sleeping Beauty's castle. Fortified since Roman days, the site takes its name from the Arabic *al-qasr* (fortress). It was rebuilt in the 13th and 14th centuries, but the whole lot burned down in 1862. What you see today is an evocative, over-the-top reconstruction of the original.

Highlights include the **Sala de las Piñas**, with its ceiling of 392 pineapple-shaped 'stalactites', and the **Sala de Reyes**, featuring a three-dimensional frieze of 52 sculptures of kings who fought during the Reconquista. The views from the summit of the Torre de Juan II are truly exceptional.

ACUEDUCTO
AQUEDUCT

Segovia's most recognisable symbol is El Acueducto (Roman Aqueduct), an 894m-long engineering wonder that looks like an enormous comb plunged into Segovia. First raised here by the Romans in the 1st century AD, the aqueduct was built with not a drop of mortar to hold the more than 20,000 uneven granite blocks together. It's made up of 163 arches and, at its highest point in Plaza del Azoguejo, rises 28m high.

CATEDRAL
CATHEDRAL

(☑921 46 22 05; Plaza Mayor; adult/concession €3/2, Sun morning free, tower €5; ☺9.30am-5.30pm Oct-Mar, 9.30am-6.30pm Apr-Sep) Started in 1525 on the site of a former chapel, Segovia's cathedral is a powerful expression of Gothic architecture that took almost 200 years to complete. The austere three-nave interior is anchored by an imposing choir stall and enlivened by 20-odd chapels, including the **Capilla del Cristo del Consuelo**, which houses a magnificent Romanesque doorway, and the **Capilla de la Piedad**, containing an important altarpiece by Juan de Juni.

PLAZA MAYOR SQUARE

The shady Plaza Mayor is the nerve centre of old Segovia, lined by an eclectic assortment of buildings, arcades and cafes and an open pavilion in its centre. It's also the site of the *catedral* and the tourist office. The road connecting Plaza Mayor and the aqueduct is a pedestrian thoroughfare that locals know simply as Calle Real.

PLAZA DE SAN MARTÍN SQUARE

This is one of the most captivating small plazas in Segovia. The square is presided over by a statue of Juan Bravo; the 14th-century **Torreón de Lozoya** (⊙5-9pm Tue-Fri, noon-2pm & 5-9pm Sat & Sun) **FREE**, a tower that now houses exhibitions; and the **Iglesia de San Martín** (⊙before & after Mass), a pièce de Romanesque résistance with its Mudéjar tower and arched gallery. The interior boasts a Flemish Gothic chapel.

IGLESIA DE VERA CRUZ CHURCH

(☑921 43 14 75; Carretera de Zamarramala; admission €1.75; ⊙10.30am-1.30pm & 4-7pm Tue-Sun Dec-Oct) This 12-sided church is one of the best preserved of its kind in Europe. Built in the early 13th century by the Knights Templar and based on Jerusalem's Church of the Holy Sepulchre, it once housed a piece of the *Vera Cruz* (True Cross), now in the nearby village church of Zamarramala (on view only at Easter).

✖ EATING & DRINKING

If you love your meat, you'll love Segovia. People come here from all over Spain to try delicious *cochinillo asado* (roast suckling pig) and *asado de cordero* (roasted lamb). Reservations are highly recommended, especially on weekends.

★LA ALMUZARA ITALIAN €

(☑921 46 06 22; Calle Marqués del Arco 3; mains €7.50-10; ⊙noon-4pm & 8pm-midnight Wed-Sun, 8pm-midnight Tue; 🖉🐾) If you're a vegetarian, you don't need to feel like an outcast in this resolutely carnivorous city. La Almuzara offers a dedicated vegetarian menu, as well as pizzas, pastas and around 18 innovative salads. It's not too pious to scrimp on desserts either, with some decadent daily-changing choices. The ambience is warm and artsy.

★RESTAURANTE EL FOGÓN SEFARDÍ SEPHARDIC €€

(☑921 46 62 50; www.lacasamudejar.com; Calle de Isabel la Católica 8; mains €15-25, tapas from €2.50; ⊙1.30-4.30pm & 5.30-11.30pm) Located within the Hospedería La Gran Casa Mudéjar, this is one of the most original places in town. Sephardic and Jewish cuisine is served either on the intimate patio or in the splendid dining hall with original, 15th-century Mudéjar flourishes. The theme in the bar is equally diverse. Stop here for a taste of the award-winning tapas. Reservations recommended.

CASA DUQUE GRILL €€

(☑921 46 24 87; www.restauranteduque.es; Calle de Cervantes 12; mains €9-21, set menus €36-39; ⊙12.30-4.30pm & 8.30-11.30pm) *Cochinillo asado* has been served at this atmospheric *mesón* (tavern) since the 1890s. For the uninitiated, try the *menú segoviano* (€32), which includes *cochinillo,* or the *menú gastronómico* (€39). Downstairs is the informal *cueva* (cave), where you can get tapas and full-bodied *cazuelas* (stews). Reservations recommended.

LA TASQUINA WINE BAR

(Calle de Valdeláguila 3; ⊙9pm-late) This wine bar draws crowds large enough to spill out onto the pavement, nursing their good wines, *cavas* (sparkling wines) and cheeses.

Ávila

Explore

You wouldn't come here for the nightlife, but the view of Ávila's floodlit walls is worth waiting around for before catching the train or bus back to Madrid. The eerily quiet, lamp-lit streets within the walls after dark also speak strongly of magic.

By day, the sense of a somnambulant provincial town is palpable – head outside the walls to Plaza de Santa Teresa for a more animated slice of local life.

Ávila is one of the best places in Castilla y León to watch the solemn processions of Easter, so it's worth planning to be here at this time if you're in the area. It all begins on Holy Thursday and the most evocative event is the early morning (around 5am) Good Friday procession which circles the city wall.

The Best...

→ **Sight** Murallas

→ **Place to Eat** Soul Kitchen (p168)

→ **Place to Drink** La Bodeguita de San Segundo (p168)

Top Tip

Ávila is one of the coldest and windiest cities in Spain and winter snow is always a possibility. If you're coming in winter, come prepared.

Getting There & Away

→ **Bus** Up to nine buses (fewer on weekends) connect Madrid's Estación Sur and Ávila (€8.76, 1½ hours). Contact Ávila's **bus station** (☑920 256505; Av de Madrid 2) for more information.

→ **Train** The company **Renfe** (☑902 240202; www.renfe.es) has up to 30 trains to Ávila daily. The trip takes up to two hours (one way from €8.95).

Need to Know

→ **Area Code** ☑920

→ **Location** 101km west of Madrid

→ **Tourist Office** (☑920 35 40 00, ext 790; www.avilaturismo.com; Av de Madrid 39; ⊙9am-8pm)

 ## SIGHTS

MURALLAS WALLS

(muralladeavila.com; adult/child under 12yr €5/ free; ⊙10am-8pm Tue-Sun; 🖫) Ávila's splendid 12th-century walls stretch for 2.5km atop the remains of earlier Roman and Muslim battlements and rank among the world's best-preserved medieval defensive perimeters. Two sections of the walls can be climbed – a 300m stretch that can be accessed from just inside the **Puerta del Alcázar**, and a longer 1300m stretch that runs the length of the old city's northern perimeter. The admission price includes a multilingual audioguide.

CATEDRAL DEL SALVADOR CATHEDRAL

(Plaza de la Catedral; admission €4; ⊙10am-7.30pm Mon-Fri, 10am-8pm Sat, noon-6.30pm Sun) Ávila's 12th-century cathedral is both a house of worship and an ingenious fortress: its stout granite apse forms the central bulwark in the historic city walls. The sombre Gothic-style facade conceals a magnificent interior with an exquisite early 16th-century altar frieze showing the life of Jesus, plus Renaissance-era carved choir stalls and a museum with an El Greco painting and a splendid silver monstrance by Juan de Arfe. Push the buttons to illuminate the altar and the choir stalls.

The cathedral was the first Gothic church in Spain; the famous altar frieze of 24 paintings was completed by Juan de Borgoña in 1515, the year of Santa Teresa's

---

IN THE FOOTSTEPS OF SANTA TERESA

Probably the most important woman in the history of the Catholic church in Spain, Santa Teresa spent most of her life in Ávila.

Teresa de Cepeda y Ahumada – a Catholic mystic and reformer – was born in Ávila on 28 March 1515, one of 10 children of a merchant family. Raised by Augustinian nuns after her mother's death, she joined the Carmelite order at age 20. After her early, undistinguished years as a nun, she was shaken by a vision of Hell in 1560, which crystallised her true vocation: she would reform her order.

With the help of many supporters Teresa founded convents of the Carmelitas Descalzas (Shoeless Carmelites) all over Spain. Santa Teresa's writings were first published in 1588 and proved enormously popular, perhaps partly for their earthy style. She died in 1582 in Alba de Tormes, where she is buried. She was canonised by Pope Gregory XV in 1622.

ARANJUEZ & CHINCHÓN

Aranjuez was founded as a royal pleasure retreat, away from the riff-raff of Madrid, and it remains a place to escape the rigours of city life. The **Palacio Real** (☎91 891 07 40; www.patrimonionacional.es; palace adult/concession €9/4, guide/audioguide €6/4, last 3 hours Wed & Thu EU citizens free, gardens free; ☺palace 10am-8pm Apr-Sep, 10am-6pm Oct-Mar, gardens 8am-9.30pm mid-Jun–mid-Aug, reduced hours mid-Aug–mid-Jun) started as one of Felipe II's modest summer palaces but took on a life of its own as a succession of royals lavished money upon it. The obligatory guided tour (in Spanish) provides insight into the palace's art and history. In the lush gardens, you'll find the Casa de Marinos, which contains the **Museo de Falúas** (admission €3; ☺10am-4pm Oct-Mar, to 6.15pm Apr-Sep), a museum of royal pleasure boats from days gone by. The 18th-century neoclassical **Casa del Labrador** (☎91 891 03 05; adult/child, senior or student €5/2.50; ☺10am-6pm Tue-Sun Apr-Sep, to 5pm Tue-Sun Oct-Mar) is also worth a visit. If you're here for lunch, try the Michelin-starred **Casa José** (☎91 891 14 88; www.casajose.es; Calle de Abastos 32; mains €14-29, set menu €75; ☺1.45-3.30pm & 9-11.30pm Tue-Sat, 1.45-3.30pm Sun Sep-Jul). Aranjuez is accessible from Madrid aboard C3 _cercanías_ (local train serving suburbs and nearby towns) that leaves every 15 or 20 minutes from Madrid's Atocha station (€3.40).

Another fine day trip is to Chinchón, just 45km from Madrid yet worlds away. Visiting Chinchón is like stepping back into a charming, ramshackle past, with most of the appeal concentrated around the glorious **Plaza Mayor**. **Café de la Iberia** (☎91 894 08 47; www.cafedelaiberia.com; Plaza Mayor 17; mains €13-22; ☺12.30-4.30pm & 8-10.30pm) is the pick of the restaurants serving roasted meats surrounding the square. To get here, the La Veloz bus 337 leaves half-hourly to Chinchón from Avenida del Mediterráneo in Madrid, 100m west of Plaza del Conde de Casal. The 50-minute ride costs €3.65.

birth. Above, the stunning ochre-stained limestone columns and cantilevered ceilings in the side aisles produce an effect unlike any other cathedral in the country.

EL MONASTERIO DE
SANTO TOMÁS   MONASTERY
(☎920 35 22 37; www.monasteriosantotomas.com; Plaza de Granada 1; admission €3; ☺10am-1pm & 4-8pm) Commissioned by the Reyes Católicos (Catholic Monarchs), Fernando and Isabel, and completed in 1492, this monastery is an exquisite example of Isabelline architecture and is rich in historical resonance. Three interconnected cloisters lead up to the church that contains the alabaster tomb of Don Juan, the monarchs' only son. It's backed by an altarpiece by Pedro de Berruguete depicting scenes from the life of St Thomas Aquinas.

The magnificent choir stalls, in Flemish Gothic style, are accessible from the upper level of the third cloister, the Claustro de los Reyes, so called because Fernando and Isabel often attended Mass here. It's thought that the Grand Inquisitor Torquemada is buried in the sacristy.

MONASTERIO DE LA
ENCARNACIÓN   MONASTERY
(Calle de la Encarnación; admission €2; ☺9.30am-1.30pm & 3.30-6pm Mon-Fri, 10am-1pm & 4-6pm Sat & Sun) North of the city walls, this unadorned Renaissance monastery is where Santa Teresa fully took on the monastic life and lived for 27 years. One of the three main rooms open to the public is where the saint is said to have had a vision of the baby Jesus. Also on display are relics such as the piece of wood used by Teresa as a pillow (ouch!) and the chair upon which St John of the Cross made his confessions.

BASÍLICA DE SAN VICENTE   CHURCH
(Plaza de San Vicente; admission €2; ☺10am-6.30pm Mon-Sat, 4-6pm Sun) This graceful church is a masterpiece of Romanesque simplicity: a series of largely Gothic modifications in sober granite contrasted with the warm sandstone of the Romanesque original. Work started in the 11th century, supposedly on the site where three martyrs – San Vicente and his sisters – were slaughtered by the Romans in the early 4th century. Their canopied cenotaph is an outstanding piece of Romanesque style with nods to the Gothic.

CONVENTO DE SANTA TERESA
MUSEUM

(☑920 21 10 30; Plaza de la Santa; ⊙8.45am-1.30pm & 3.30-9pm Tue-Sun) **FREE** Built in 1636 around the room where the saint was born in 1515, this is the epicentre of the cult surrounding Teresa. There are three attractions in one here: the church, a relics room and a museum. Highlights include the gold-adorned chapel (built over the room where she was born), the baroque altar and the (albeit macabre) relic of the saint's ring finger, complete with ring. Apparently Franco kept it beside his bedside throughout his rule.

LOS CUATRO POSTES
VIEWPOINT

Northwest of the city, on the road to Salamanca, Los Cuatro Postes provides the best views of Ávila's walls. It also marks the place where Santa Teresa and her brother were caught by their uncle as they tried to run away from home (they were hoping to achieve martyrdom at the hands of the Muslims). The best views are at night.

 EATING & DRINKING

Ávila is famous for its *chuleton de avileño* (T-bone-steak) and *judias del barco de Ávila* (white beans, usually with chorizo, in a thick sauce).

★SOUL KITCHEN
MODERN CASTILIAN €€

(www.soulkitchen.es; Calle de Caballeros 13; mains €9-19; ⊙10am-midnight Mon-Fri, 11am-2am Sat, 11am-midnight Sun) Opened in 2013, this restaurant has the kind of contemporary energy that can seem lacking in Ávila's staider restaurants. The eclectic menu changes regularly and ranges from salads, with dressings such as chestnut and fig, to hamburgers with cream of *setas* (oyster mushrooms). Lighter eats include bruschetta with tasty toppings. Live music, poetry readings (and similar) take place in summer.

HOSTERÍA LAS CANCELAS
CASTILIAN €€

(☑920 21 22 49; www.lascancelas.com; Calle de la Cruz Vieja 6; mains €16-25; ⊙1-4pm & 7.30-11pm) This courtyard restaurant occupies a delightful interior patio dating back to the 15th century. Renowned for being a mainstay of Ávila cuisine, traditional meals are prepared with a salutary attention to detail; the *solomillo con salsa al ron y nueces* (sirloin in a rum-and-walnut sauce) is a rare deviation from tradition. Reservations recommended.

POSADA DE LA FRUTA
CASTILIAN, INTERNATIONAL €€

(www.posadadelafruta.com; Plaza de Pedro Dávila 8; bar mains €8-10, restaurant mains €12-20; ⊙1-4pm & 7.30pm-midnight) Simple tasty bar-style meals can be had in a light-filled, covered courtyard, while the traditional *comedor* (dining room) is typically all about hearty meat dishes offset by simple fresh salads. The unusual international meat dishes, which include gazelle and kangaroo, are the standouts here.

★LA BODEGUITA DE SAN SEGUNDO
WINE BAR

(Calle de San Segundo 19; ⊙11am-midnight Thu-Tue) Situated in the 16th-century Casa de la Misericordia, this superb wine bar is standing-room only most nights and more tranquil in the quieter afternoon hours. Its wine list is renowned throughout Spain, with over 1000 wines to choose from, with tapas-sized servings of cheeses and cured meats the perfect accompaniment.

Sleeping

Madrid has high-quality accommodation at prices that haven't been seen in the centre of other European capitals in decades. Five-star temples to good taste and a handful of buzzing hostels bookend a fabulous collection of midrange hotels; most of the midrangers are creative originals, blending high levels of comfort with an often-quirky sense of style.

Hotels

Madrid's accommodation scene keeps getting better. The best of the old have survived, upgrading their facilities while adhering to old-style values of discretion and hospitality, but they have been joined by modern designer hotels that capture the essence of Spain's style revolution.

Many of these newcomers have taken the shells of charming traditional architecture and converted their interiors into chic, high-tech accommodation that blends the casual and the classy – two essential elements in the irresistible personality of contemporary Spain. These *hoteles con encanto* (hotels with charm) share the market with stylish, modern monuments to 21st-century fashions that seem to push the boundaries of design in ways that were once the preserve of Barcelona, that eternal rival up the road.

It's in the midrange price category that you'll find the best examples of this revolution. At surprisingly reasonable prices and devoid of stuffiness, hotels in this category enable you to feel pampered without the price tag of a five-star hotel – the choice can be seemingly endless and examples are to be found in every Madrid neighbourhood. And if the top end is your end of the market, you'll be able to choose between the grand old dames that are counted among Europe's elite of luxury hotels and newly minted boutique hotels.

Hostales

The Spanish *hostal* is a cross between a cheap hotel and a hostel and usually represents outstanding value. The better ones can be bright and spotless, with private rooms featuring full en suite bathroom (*baño completo;* most often with a shower – *ducha* – rather than a bathtub), usually a TV and air-conditioning and/or heating. Some are new and slick, but the overwhelming majority are family run, adhering to traditional, old-style decor and old-style warmth.

Hostels

At the budget end of the market, Madrid has its share of hostel-style accommodation with multibed (usually bunk) dorms and busy communal areas. They're cheap, usually plugged in to the local nightlife scene and are terrific places to meet other travellers.

Useful Websites & Resources

➡ **Reserva Madrid** (☑91 000 69 19; www. reservamadrid.com) Good for finding well-priced apartments.

➡ **Centro de Turismo de Madrid** (p208) Good for an overview of the accommodaton scene.

➡ **Lonely Planet** (www.lonelyplanet.com/ spain/madrid/hotels) For more reviews and bookings online.

NEED TO KNOW

Room Rates & Reservations

Some places have separate prices for *temporada alta* (high season), *temporada media* (midseason) or *temporada baja* (low season), but in Madrid prices are more likely to vary on a daily basis according to occupancy, trade fairs and other major events.

Taxes

All accommodation prices are subject to 10% IVA (*impuesto sobre el valor anadido;* value-added tax). When quoted a price, always ask: *¿Está incluido el IVA?* ('Is IVA included?').

Price Ranges

The following price ranges refer to the cost for a double room per night:

€	under €75
€€	€75 to €200
€€€	over €200

Terminology

A *habitación doble* (double room) usually indicates a room with two single beds; cuddly couples should request a *cama de matrimonio* (literally, a 'marriage bed').

Lonely Planet's Top Choices

Hostal Central Palace Madrid (p172) Palace views and gorgeous rooms.

Posada del León de Oro (p173) Stunningly converted old inn along Madrid's best tapas street.

Hotel Silken Puerta América (p178) Landmark hotel with rooms designed by world-famous architects.

Praktik Metropol (p174) New hotel with quirky decor, fine views and high levels of comfort.

Hotel Orfila (p178) Arguably Madrid's top address and best service.

Best by Budget

€

Madrid City Rooms (p174) Outstanding service and excellent rooms in the centre.

Lapepa Chic B&B (p176) Fabulous budget B&B with attention to detail.

Hostal Main Street Madrid (p177) Central and very cool *hostal*.

Flat 5 Madrid (p177) One of Madrid's best deals away from the tourist hordes.

€€

Hostal Central Palace Madrid (p172) Some of the best views in Madrid, whatever the price.

Posada del León de Oro (p173) La Latina at its most atmospheric.

Catalonia Las Cortes (p174) Great rooms, service and Huertas location.

NH Collection Palacio de Tepa (p175) Palace on the outside, stylish rooms within.

€€€

Hotel Orfila (p178) Unquestionable luxury with service to match.

Hotel Ritz (p176) Quite simply one of Europe's grandest hotels.

Villa Magna (p176) Refined Salamanca address for the well heeled.

Westin Palace (p176) Near faultless five-star address close to Paseo del Prado.

Best for Contemporary Cool

Only You Hotel (p178) Designer rooms with unexpected extras.

Innside Madrid Luchana (p178) Converted Chamberí palace in a modern style.

Artrip (p173) Artsy location with stylish contemporary rooms.

VP El Madroño (p176) Salamanca's swishest address in a quiet setting.

Best Hotel Chains

AC (www.ac-hoteles.com) Business-oriented but well regarded.

Hi Tech (www.hthoteles.com) Mostly converted mansions with hi-tech rooms.

NH (www.nh-hotels.com) Consistently good modern rooms.

Room Mate (www.roommatehoteles.com) So personalised you'll forget it's a chain.

Best Apartments

Apartamentos Mayor Centro (Hostal Madrid) (p172) Rambling collection of apartments, old and new.

ApartoSuites Jardines de Sabatini (p172) Fabulous palace views and modern apartments.

Where to Stay

Neighbourhood	For	Against
Plaza Mayor & Royal Madrid	Walking distance to most attractions, as well as shopping and restaurants; good metro connections elsewhere	Can be noisy, although generally from night-time revellers rather than traffic
La Latina & Lavapiés	Excellent central location, combining medieval architecture with terrific restaurants and tapas bars	Uphill walk from the art galleries; can be noisy in the evening (less so later at night)
Sol, Santa Ana & Huertas	Close to most attractions and excellent eating, drinking and entertainment options	Possibly Madrid's noisiest neighbourhood, with all-night revellers, especially on weekends; steep hills can test weary legs
El Retiro & the Art Museums	You're right next door (or just around the corner) from Madrid's big three art galleries	Traffic noise can be a problem; most restaurants at least a 10-minute walk away
Salamanca	Puts you in the heart of fantastic shopping and close to good eating options; quieter by night than most other Madrid neighbourhoods	A decent walk from the rest of the city
Malasaña & Chueca	Lively streets and wonderful places to eat and drink; sense of Madrid beyond the tourist crowds; gay friendly (Chueca)	Another noisy night-time neighbourhood
Parque del Oeste & Northern Madrid	Removed from the clamour of downtown but a short metro ride away; immersion in local Madrid life	Attractions more thinly spread

🛏 Plaza Mayor & Royal Madrid

HOSTAL MADRID
HOSTAL, APARTMENT €

Map p232 (☑91 522 00 60; www.hostal-madrid. info; Calle de Esparteros 6; s €35-62, d €45-78, d apt €45-150; ❋🛜; Ⓜ Sol) The 24 rooms at this well-run *hostal* have been wonderfully renovated with exposed brickwork, brand-new bathrooms and a look that puts many three-star hotels to shame. It also has terrific apartments (some recently renovated, others ageing in varying stages of gracefulness and ranging in size from 33 sq metres to 200 sq metres). The apartments have a separate website – www.apartamentos mayorcentro.com.

The apartments come with fully equipped kitchens, their own sitting area, bathroom and, in the case of the larger ones (room 51 on the 5th floor is one of the best), an expansive terrace with good views over the rooftops of central Madrid. It's a favoured haunt of writers (Günter Grass wrote one of his novels in room 53). Fabulous value all round.

HOSTAL PATRIA
HOSTAL €

Map p232 (☑91 366 21 87; www.hostalpatria.com; 4th fl, Calle Mayor 10; s/d €32/42; ❋🛜; Ⓜ Sol) Simple rooms with parquetry floor, helpful staff and rooms that are a cut above your *hostal* average – it's a winning combination. The location, a few steps from the Puerta del Sol, is terrific. Noise can be an issue, but that can be said about most cheaper places in the centre.

LOS AMIGOS SOL BACKPACKERS' HOSTEL
HOSTEL €

Map p232 (☑91 559 24 72; www.losamigoshostel. com; 4th fl, Calle de Arenal 26; dm incl breakfast €28-33; @🛜; Ⓜ Ópera, Sol) If you arrive in Madrid keen for company, this could be the place for you – lots of students stay here, the staff are savvy (and speak English) and there are bright dorm-style rooms (with free lockers) that sleep from two to four people. There's also a kitchen for guests. A steady stream of repeat visitors is the best recommendation we can give.

★HOSTAL CENTRAL PALACE MADRID
HOSTAL, HOTEL €€

Map p232 (☑91 548 20 18; centralpalacemadrid. com; Plaza de Oriente 2; d without/with view €99/119; ❋🛜; Ⓜ Ópera) Now here's something special. The views alone here would be reason enough to come and definitely worth paying extra for – rooms with balcony look out over the Palacio Real and Plaza de Oriente. But the rooms themselves are lovely and light filled, with tasteful, subtle faux-antique furnishings, comfortable beds, light-wood floors and plenty of space.

APARTOSUITES JARDINES DE SABATINI
APARTMENT €€

Map p255 (☑91 198 32 90; www.jardinesdesabati-ni.com; Cuesta de San Vicente 16; studio without/with views from €85/110, ste without/with views from €125/150; ❋🛜; Ⓜ Plaza de España, Príncipe Pío) Modern, spacious studios and suites are only half the story at this terrific property just down the hill from Plaza de España. Definitely pay extra for a room with a view. The studios, with a balcony and uninterrupted views over the lovely Jardines de Sabatini to the Palacio Real are simply brilliant. The Campo del Moro is just across the road.

HOTEL MENINAS
BOUTIQUE HOTEL €€

Map p232 (☑91 541 28 05; www.hotelmeninas. com; Calle de Campomanes 7; s/d from €75/95; ❋🛜; Ⓜ Ópera) This is a classy, cool choice. The colour scheme is blacks, whites and greys, with dark-wood floors and splashes of fuchsia and lime green. Flat-screen TVs in every room, modern bathroom fittings, and even a laptop in some rooms, round out the clean lines and latest innovations. Past guests include Viggo Mortensen and Natalie Portman. Some rooms are on the small side.

HOTEL PRECIADOS
BUSINESS HOTEL €€

Map p232 (☑91 454 44 00; www.preciadoshotel. com; Calle de Preciados 37; s/d from €78/115; ❋🛜; Ⓜ Santo Domingo, Callao) With a classier feel than many of the other business options around town, the Preciados gets rave reviews for its service. Soft lighting, light shades and plentiful glass personalise the rooms and provide an intimate feel.

HOTEL VINCCI CAPITOL
HOTEL €€

Map p232 (☑91 521 83 91; www.vinccihoteles. com; Gran Vía 41; d €120-190; ❋🛜❄; Ⓜ Callao) Opened in 2007 in the landmark Carrión building, this modern hotel has large rooms with muted tones, and some even have the novelty of circular beds. But what makes the hotel stand out are the views – straight down Gran Vía, with its life and grandeur. Not all rooms have views, but there's a 9th-floor viewing area for guests.

One local newspaper gave the hotel a '9' for architecture, a '4' for decoration and a '6' for the comfort of the rooms; they're being a little harsh, but we know what they mean.

MARIO ROOM MATE
BOUTIQUE HOTEL €€

Map p232 (☑91 548 85 48; www.room-matehotels.com; Calle de Campomanes 4; s €80-125, d €100-175; ❄☎; MÓpera) Entering this swanky boutique hotel is like crossing the threshold of Madrid's latest nightclub, with staff dressed all in black, black walls and swirls of red lighting in the lobby. Rooms can be small, but have high ceilings, simple furniture and light tones contrasting smoothly with muted colours and dark surfaces. Some rooms are pristine white; others have splashes of colour with zany murals.

PETIT PALACE POSADA DEL PEINE
BOUTIQUE HOTEL €€

Map p232 (☑91 523 81 51; www.hthoteles.com; Calle de Postas 17; r from €120; ❄☎; MSol) This hotel combines a splendid historic building (dating to 1610), brilliant location (just 50m from the Plaza Mayor) and modern hi-tech rooms. The bathrooms sparkle with stunning fittings and hydromassage showers, and the rooms are beautifully appointed; many historical architectural features remain in situ in the public areas. It's just a pity some of the rooms aren't larger.

CASA DE MADRID
HOTEL €€€

Map p232 (☑91 559 57 91; www.casademadrid.com; 2nd fl, Calle de Arrieta 2; r from €120-350, ste from €370; ☎; MÓpera) Refined, extravagantly decorated rooms make Casa de Madrid a luxurious choice overlooking the Teatro Real. The rooms, in an 18th-century building, are awash in antique furnishings and marble busts, with each built around a theme (eg Japan, India). It's a little like staying at the Ritz, but more discreet.

It's also without the service – there's rarely anyone on hand and rooms are cleaned only upon request.

🛏 La Latina & Lavapiés

HOSTAL HORIZONTE
HOSTEL €

Map p235 (☑91 369 09 96; www.hostalhorizonte.com; 2nd fl, Calle de Atocha 28; s with/without bathroom €44/32, d €60/48; ☎; MAntón Martín) Billing itself as a hostel run by travellers for travellers, Hostal Horizonte is a well-run place. The rooms have far more character

than your average hostel, with high ceilings, deliberately old-world furnishings and modern bathrooms. The King Alfonso XII room is especially well presented.

CAT'S HOSTEL
HOSTEL €

Map p235 (☑91 369 28 07; www.catshostel.com; Calle de Cañizares 6; dm €17-29; ❄@☎; MAntón Martín) Forming part of a 17th-century palace, the internal courtyard here is one of Madrid's finest – lavish Andalucian tilework, a fountain, a spectacular glass ceiling and stunning Islamic decoration, surrounded on four sides by an open balcony. There's a supercool basement bar with free internet and fiestas, often with live music. The rooms are functional.

MAD HOSTEL
HOSTEL €

Map p235 (☑91 506 48 40; www.madhostel.com; Calle de la Cabeza 24; dm €20-24; ❄@☎; MAntón Martín) From the people who brought you Cat's Hostel, Mad Hostel is similarly filled with life. The 1st-floor courtyard – with retractable roof – re-creates an old Madrid *corrala* (traditional internal or communal patio) and is a wonderful place to chill, while the four- to eight-bed rooms are smallish but clean. There's a small, rooftop gym.

★ POSADA DEL LEÓN DE ORO
BOUTIQUE HOTEL €€

Map p236(☑91 119 14 94; www.posadadelleondeoro.com; Calle de la Cava Baja 12; r from €105; ❄☎; MLa Latina) This rehabilitated inn has muted colour schemes and generally large rooms. There's a *corrala* in its core, and thoroughly modern rooms (some on the small side) along one of Madrid's best-loved streets. The downstairs bar is terrific.

POSADA DEL DRAGÓN
BOUTIQUE HOTEL €€

Map p236 (☑91 119 14 24; www.posadadeldragon.com; Calle de la Cava Baja 14; r from €80; ❄☎; MLa Latina) At last, a boutique hotel in the heart of La Latina. This restored 19th-century inn sits on one of our favourite Madrid streets, and rooms either look out over the street or over the pretty internal patio. Some of the rooms are on the small side, but they've extremely comfortable beds, and bold, brassy colour schemes and designer everything. There's a terrific bar-restaurant downstairs.

ARTRIP
BOUTIQUE HOTEL €€

Map p235 (☑91 539 32 82; www.artriphotel.com; Calle de Valencia 11; d/ste from €100/120; ❄☎; MLavapiés) For an alternative but supremely comfortable take on Madrid life, Artrip is close to the big-three art museums and surrounded by plenty of private art galleries in the heart of multicultural Lavapiés. Rooms are dazzling white offset by strong splashes of colour and artful use of wooden beams.

🛏 Sol, Santa Ana & Huertas

MADRID CITY ROOMS   HOSTAL €

Map p238 (📞91 360 44 44; www.madridcityrooms.com; 2nd fl, Calle de la Cruz 6; s/d from €39/54; ❄🛜; Ⓜ Sol) Don't let the exterior fool you because within, the simple yet colourful rooms, all with balconies and double-glazing, make for an excellent downtown budget bolt-hole. The friendly service, too, is a plus and the overall look is a touch more polished than your average *hostal*.

HOSTAL LUIS XV   HOSTAL €

Map p238 (📞91 522 10 21; www.hrluisxv.net; 8th fl, Calle de la Montera 47; s/d/tr from €44/58/74; ❄🛜; Ⓜ Gran Vía) Everything here – especially the spacious rooms and attention to detail – makes this family-run place feel pricier than it is. You'll find it hard to tear yourself away from the rooms with balconies, from where the views are superb (especially from the triple in room 820) and you're so high up that noise is rarely a problem.

HOSTAL ADRIANO   HOSTAL €

Map p238 (📞91 521 13 39; www.hostaladriano.com; 4th fl, Calle de la Cruz 26; s/d from €51/59; ❄🛜; Ⓜ Sol) They don't come any better than this bright and friendly *hostal* wedged in the streets that mark the boundary between Sol and Huertas. Most rooms are well sized and each has its own colour scheme. Indeed, more thought has gone into the decoration than in your average *hostal,* from the bed covers to the pictures on the walls.

On the same floor, the owners run the **Hostal Adria Santa Ana** (Map p238; www.hostaladriasantaana.com; s/d €62/70; ❄🛜; Ⓜ Sol), which is a step up in price, style and comfort. Both *hostales* drop their prices in summer.

HOSTAL ACAPULCO   HOSTAL €

Map p238 (📞91 531 19 45; www.hostalacapulco.com; 4th fl, Calle de la Salud 13; s/d €58/68; ❄🛜; Ⓜ Gran Vía, Callao) A cut above many other *hostales* in Madrid, this immaculate little *hostal* has marble floors, recently renovated

bathrooms (with bathtubs), double-glazed windows and comfortable beds. Street-facing rooms have balconies overlooking a sunny plaza and are flooded with natural light. The staff are also friendly and always more than happy to help you plan your day in Madrid. There's also a coffee machine.

HOSTAL SARDINERO   HOSTAL €

Map p238 (📞91 429 57 56; www.hostalsardinero.com; Calle del Prado 16; d/tr from €59/69; ❄@; Ⓜ Sol, Antón Martín) The cheerful rooms here have high ceilings, air-conditioning, safes, hairdryers, comfortable mattresses and renovated bathrooms, and are complemented nicely by the owners who are attentive without being in your face. We especially like the light-filled room 5 (a triple), but all the rooms are well turned out.

★ PRAKTIK METROPOL   BOUTIQUE HOTEL €€

Map p238 (📞91 521 29 35; www.hotelpraktikmetropol.com; Calle de la Montera 47; s/d from €89/99; ❄🛜; Ⓜ Gran Vía) You'd be hard-pressed to find better value anywhere in Europe than here in this recently overhauled hotel. The rooms have a fresh, contemporary look with white wood furnishings, and some (especially the corner rooms) have brilliant views down to Gran Vía and out over the city. It's spread over six floors and there's a roof terrace if you don't have a room with a view.

★ HOTEL ALICIA   BOUTIQUE HOTEL €€

Map p238 (📞91 389 60 95; www.room-matehoteles.com; Calle del Prado 2; d €100-175, ste from €200; ❄🛜; Ⓜ Sol, Sevilla, Antón Martín) One of the landmark properties of the designer Room Mate chain of hotels, Hotel Alicia overlooks Plaza de Santa Ana with beautiful, spacious rooms. The style (the work of designer Pascua Ortega) is more muted than in other Room Mate hotels, but the supermodern look remains intact, the downstairs bar is oh-so-cool, and the service is young and switched on.

CATALONIA LAS CORTES   HOTEL €€

Map p238 (📞91 389 60 51; www.hoteles-catalonia.es; Calle del Prado 6; s/d from €150/180; ❄🛜; Ⓜ Antón Martín) Occupying an 18th-century palace and renovated in a style faithful to the era, this elegant hotel is a terrific choice right in the heart of Huertas. It's something of an oasis surrounded by the nonstop energy of the streets in this *barrio* (district), and the service is discreet and attentive. It gets plenty of return visitors, which is just about the best recommendation we can give.

NH COLLECTION PALACIO DE TEPA
HOTEL €€

Map p238 (☑91 389 64 90; www.nh-collection.com; Calle de San Sebastián 2; d from €175; ❄ 🛜; Ⓜ Antón Martín) Inhabiting a 19th-century palace a stone's throw from Plaza de Santa Ana, this flagship property of the respected NH chain has modern designer rooms with hardwood floors and soothing colours. Service is also professional and the location is outstanding. The Premium Rooms and Junior Suites in particular have real class.

HOTEL SENATOR
HOTEL €€

Map p238 (☑91 531 41 51; www.playasenator.com; Gran Vía 21; s/d from €98/114; ❄ 🛜; Ⓜ Gran Vía) One of central Madrid's prettiest facades conceals some of the most attractive four-star accommodation in the city centre. Unusually, only one room on each floor doesn't face onto the street and the views down Gran Vía from the corner rooms are brilliant. Rooms are sophisticated and come with armchairs and, wait for it, reclinable beds.

Room rates vary daily and when they drop they're Madrid's best bargain.

HOTEL PLAZA MAYOR
HOTEL €€

Map p238 (☑91 360 06 06; www.h-plazamayor.com; Calle de Atocha 2; s/d from €37/47; ❄ 🛜; Ⓜ Sol, Tirso de Molina) We love this place. Sitting just across from the Plaza Mayor, here you'll find stylish decor, helpful staff and charming original elements of this 150-year-old building. The rooms are attractive, some with a light colour scheme and wrought-iron furniture. The pricier attic rooms boast dark wood and designer lamps, and have lovely little terraces with wonderful rooftop views of central Madrid.

HOTEL VINCCI SOHO
HOTEL €€

Map p238 (☑91 141 41 00; www.vinccihoteles.com; Calle del Prado 18; d from €150; ❄ 🛜; Ⓜ Sevilla, Antón Martín) A refined sense of style permeates everything about this hotel, from the subtly lit public areas to the rooms that combine vaguely Zen aesthetics with blood-red bathrooms. As ideal a base for the museums along the Paseo del Prado as for the clamour of central Madrid, it gets most things right.

HOTEL EUROPA
HOTEL €€

Map p238 (☑91 521 29 00; www.hoteleuropa.es; Calle del Carmen 4; s/d from €79/99; ❄ 🛜; Ⓜ Sol) Around since 1917 but with tastefully renovated rooms, Hotel Europa combines excellent service with modern midrange comforts just a few steps from Puerta del Sol. Here you'll find all the benefits of the central location with few of its drawbacks – windows are double-glazed. You pay more for the rooms that overlook the square.

SUITE PRADO HOTEL
HOTEL €€

Map p238 (☑91 420 23 18; www.suiteprado.com; Calle de Manuel Fernández y González 10; ste €85-190; ❄ 🛜; Ⓜ Sevilla) The spacious modern suites at this centrally located hotel have plenty of space and are semiluxurious. All have sitting rooms and good bathrooms and kitchenettes.

APARTASOL
APARTMENT €€

(☑91 828 95 11; www.apartasol.com; apt €50-115) If you'll be in Madrid for more than a few days and you'd like the comfort and space of your own apartment, consider Apartasol. This traveller-friendly agency has well-equipped modern apartments scattered around the vicinity of the Puerta del Sol and Gran Vía. Prices are first rate and there are discounts available for longer stays.

HOTEL URBAN
LUXURY HOTEL €€€

Map p238 (☑91 787 77 70; www.derbyhotels.com; Carrera de San Jerónimo 34; r from €225; ❄ 🛜 🏊; Ⓜ Sevilla) This towering glass edifice is the epitome of art-inspired designer cool. It boasts original artworks from Africa and Asia, dark-wood floors and dark walls are offset by plenty of light, while the dazzling bathrooms have wonderful designer fittings – the washbasins are sublime. The rooftop swimming pool is one of Madrid's best and the gorgeous terrace is heaven on a candlelit summer's evening.

ME MELIÁ REINA VICTORIA
LUXURY HOTEL €€€

Map p238 (☑91 701 60 00; www.memadrid.com; Plaza de Santa Ana 14; r from €175; ❄ 🛜; Ⓜ Sol, Antón Martín) Once the landmark Gran Victoria Hotel, the Madrid home of many a famous bullfighter, this audacious new hotel is a landmark of a different kind. Overlooking the western end of Plaza de Santa Ana, this luxury hotel is decked out in minimalist white with curves and comfort in all the right places.

This is one place where it's definitely worth paying extra for the view, quite apart from the additional space that you'll have in the plaza-facing Supreme rooms.

🛏 El Retiro & the Art Museums

⭐ LAPEPA CHIC B&B
B&B €

Map p242 (📞648 474742; lapepa-bnb.com; 7th fl, Plaza de las Cortes 4; s/d from €63/69; ❊🛜; 🅜Banco de España) A short step off the Paseo del Prado and on a floor with an art nouveau interior, this fine little B&B has lovely rooms with a contemporary, clean-lined look so different from the dour *hostal* furnishings you'll find elsewhere – modern art or even a bed-head lined with flamenco shoes give this place personality in bucketloads. It's worth paying extra for rooms with a view.

HOTEL MORA
HOTEL €€

Map p242 (📞91 420 15 69; www.hotelmora.com; Paseo del Prado 32; s/d from €67/86; ❊🛜; 🅜Atocha) Alongside the landmark Caixa Forum, close to the main museums and a short (up-hill) walk from the city centre, this simple, friendly hotel is a conveniently located and extremely well-priced option. Rooms are a little sparse and the furnishings a tad tired, but they're spacious and clean, and some look out across the Paseo del Prado.

⭐ HOTEL RITZ
LUXURY HOTEL €€€

Map p242 (📞91 701 67 67; www.ritzmadrid.com; Plaza de la Lealtad 5; d from €325, ste €850-5000; ❊🛜; 🅜Banco de España) The grand old lady of Madrid, the Hotel Ritz is the height of exclusivity. One of the most lavish buildings in the city, it has classic style and impeccable service that is second to none. Unsurprisingly it's the favoured hotel of presidents, kings and celebrities. The public areas are palatial and awash with antiques, while rooms are extravagantly large, opulent and supremely comfortable. In the Royal Suite, the walls are covered with raw silk and there's a personal butler to wait upon you. We challenge you to find a more indulgent hotel experience anywhere in Spain.

WESTIN PALACE
LUXURY HOTEL €€€

Map p242 (📞91 360 80 00; www.westinpalace-madrid.com; Plaza de las Cortes 7; d/ste from €275/600; ❊🛜; 🅜Banco de España, Antón Martín) An old Madrid classic, this former palace of the Duque de Lerma opened as a hotel in 1911 and was Spain's second luxury hotel. Ever since, it has looked out across Plaza de Neptuno at its rival, the Ritz, like a lover unjustly scorned. It may not have the world-famous cachet of the Ritz, but it's not called the Palace for nothing.

After the snooty Ritz banned actors and other public performers in the early 20th century, the Palace became the hotel of choice for celebrities – Mata Hari lived here during WWI and her ghost reportedly occupies the corridors, while Hemingway, Dalí and Lorca were all regulars in the cocktail bar. The 1999 renovations cost €144,000 per room...

🛏 Salamanca

VP EL MADROÑO
BOUTIQUE HOTEL €€

Map p244 (📞91 198 30 92; www.madrono-hotel.com; Calle del General Diaz Porlier 101; r €79-144; ❊🛜; 🅜Diego de León) You're a long way from touristy Madrid out here not far from the bullring, but therein lies part of this swish place's appeal. All of the rooms have been renovated, either in a vaguely classic style or with more contemporary designer flair. It also has family rooms and there's even a lovely garden out back.

HOTEL JARDÍN DE RECOLETOS
HOTEL €€

Map p244 (📞91 781 16 40; www.recoletos-hotel.com; Calle de Gil de Santivanes 6; d/tr from €185/212; ❊🛜; 🅜Retiro, Serrano) Attractive rooms are a given here, although decor varies from a more classic, understated look to wall-length modern photos and abundant use of wood. The overall feel is that of a downtown oasis, sheltered from the worst of Madrid's notorious noise and with a lovely terrace, garden area. The location is within walking distance of just about anywhere downtown.

VILLA MAGNA
HOTEL €€€

Map p244 (📞91 587 12 34; www.villamagna.es; Paseo de la Castellana 22; d €300-380, ste from €460; ❊🛜; 🅜Rubén Dario) This is a very Salamanca address, infused as it is with elegance and impeccable service. The look is brighter than you might imagine with the use of Empire chairs, Bauhaus ideas and even Chinese screens. The rooms are studiously classic in look with supremely comfortable furnishings and plenty of space. No expense has been spared in the rooftop suites.

ADLER HOTEL
BOUTIQUE HOTEL €€€

Map p244 (📞91 426 32 20; www.adlermadrid.com; Calle de Velázquez 33; d/ste from €200/475; ❊🛜; 🅜Velázquez) A five-star boutique hotel at the intersection of two of Salamanca's iconic streets, the Adler combines classy and supremely comfortable rooms with near-faultless service. Room decor subscribes to a vaguely old-world elegance, but is light-filled and never stuffy.

⌂ Malasaña

★HOSTAL MAIN STREET MADRID
HOSTAL €

Map p246 (☎91 548 18 78; www.mainstreetmadrid. com; 5th fl, Gran Vía 50; r from €61; 🌂🛜; MCallao, Santo Domingo) Excellent service is what travellers rave about here, but the rooms – modern and cool in soothing greys – are also some of the best *hostal* rooms you'll find anywhere in central Madrid. It's an excellent package and not surprisingly often full. Book in advance.

FLAT 5 MADRID
HOSTAL €

Map p246 (☎91 127 24 00; www.flat5madrid.com; 5th fl, Calle de San Bernardo 55; r €65-110, without bathroom from €40; 🌂🛜; MNoviciado) Unlike so many other *hostales* in Madrid where the charm depends on a time-worn air, Flat 5 Madrid has a fresh, clean-lined look with bright colours, flat-screen TVs and flower boxes on the window sills. Even the rooms that face onto a patio have partial views over the rooftops. If the rooms and bathrooms were a little bigger, we'd consider moving in.

HOSTAL LA ZONA
HOSTAL €

Map p246 (☎91 521 99 04; www.hostallazona. com; 1st fl, Calle de Valverde 7; s incl breakfast €38-58, d incl breakfast €50-70; 🌂🛜; MGran Vía) Catering primarily to a gay clientele, the stylish Hostal La Zona has exposed brickwork, subtle colour shades and wooden pillars. We like a place where a sleep-in is encouraged – breakfast is served from 9am to noon, which shows understanding of Madrid's nightlife merits. Arnaldo and Vincent are friendly hosts.

HOSTAL AMÉRICA
HOSTAL €

Map p246 (☎91 522 64 48; www.hostalamerica. net; 5th fl, Calle de Hortaleza 19; s/d €45/55; 🌂🛜; MGran Vía) Run by a lovely mother-and-son team, the América has superclean, spacious and Ikea-dominated rooms. As most rooms face onto the usual interior 'patio' of the building, you should get a good night's sleep despite the busy area. For the rest of the time, there's a roof terrace – quite a luxury for a *hostal* in downtown Madrid – with tables, chairs and a coffee machine.

HOSPEDAJE ROMERO
HOSTAL €

Map p246 (☎91 198 32 41; www.hospedajeromero-granvia.com; 6th fl, Gran Vía 64; r from €60; 🌂🛜; MSanto Domingo, Plaza de España) Simple but pleasant rooms in the heart of town are here watched over by a friendly mother-and-son team. Noise can be an issue, but most travellers agree that the location and warmth of the welcome more than compensate.

HOTEL ATLANTICO
HOTEL €€

Map p246 (☎91 198 01 15; www.hotelatlantico.es; Gran Vía 38; s/d from €160/195; 🌂🛜; MCallao) The rooms here have a classy look with a predominantly white colour scheme and dark-wood floors; some have balconies overlooking Gran Vía. The hotel's repeat visitors rave about the helpfulness of the staff and the continental breakfast. And, of course, it would be difficult to be any more central.

HOTEL ABALÚ
BOUTIQUE HOTEL €€

Map p246 (☎91 531 47 44; www.hotelabalu.com; Calle del Pez 19; d/ste from €75/119; 🌂🛜; MNoviciado) Malasaña's very own boutique hotel is starting to age and the word on the street is that it's not what it was. Even so, it's located on cool Calle del Pez and each room (some on the small side) has its own design drawn from the imagination of designer Luis Delgado, from retro chintz to Zen, baroque and pure white. It also has some suites across the road and you're close to Gran Vía, but away from the tourist scrum.

⌂ Chueca

HOSTAL DON JUAN
HOSTAL €

Map p250 (☎91 522 31 01; www.hostaldonjuan. net; 2nd fl, Plaza de Vázquez de Mella 1; s/d/tr €38/53/71; 🌂🛜; MGran Vía) Paying cheap rates for your room doesn't mean you can't be treated like royalty. This elegant two-storey *hostal* is filled with original artworks and antique furniture that could grace a palace. Rooms are large and simple but luminous; most have a street-facing balcony. The location is good, close to where Chueca meets Gran Vía.

ALBERGUE JUVENIL
HOSTEL €

Map p250 (☎91 593 96 88; www.ajmadrid.es; Calle de Mejía Lequerica 21; dm incl breakfast €19-23; 🌂@🛜; MBilbao, Alonso Martínez) If you're looking for dormitory-style accommodation, you'd need a good reason to stay anywhere other than here while you're in

Madrid. The Albergue has spotless rooms, no dorm houses more than six beds (each has its own bathroom), and facilities include a pool table, a gymnasium, wheelchair access, free internet, laundry and a TV/DVD room with a choice of movies. Breakfast is included in the price. Yes, there are places with more character or a more central location, but we'd still rate this as one of Madrid's best hostels for backpackers.

CASA CHUECA HOSTAL €

Map p250 (☏91 523 81 27; www.casachueca.com; 2nd fl, Calle de San Bartolomé 4; s/d from €44/59; ☂; Ⓜ Gran Vía) If you don't mind lugging your baggage up to the 2nd floor, Casa Chueca is outstanding. The rooms are modern, colourful and a cut above your average *hostal;* in keeping with the *barrio* that it calls home, Casa Chueca places a premium on style. Add casual, friendly service and you'd be hard pressed to find a better price-to-quality ratio anywhere in central Madrid.

★ ONLY YOU HOTEL BOUTIQUE HOTEL €€

Map p250 (☏91 005 22 22; www.onlyyouhotels. com; Calle de Barquillo 21; d €158-260; ☀@☂; Ⓜ Chueca) This stunning new boutique hotel makes perfect use of a 19th-century Chueca mansion. The look is classy and contemporary and is the latest project by respected interior designer Lázaro Rosa-Violán. Nice touches include all-day à la carte breakfasts and a portable router that you can carry out into the city to stay connected.

HOTEL ÓSCAR BOUTIQUE HOTEL €€

Map p250 (☏91 701 11 73; www.room-matehoteles.com; Plaza de Vázquez de Mella 12; d €90-225, ste €150-280; ☀☂; Ⓜ Gran Vía) Hotel Óscar belongs to the highly original Room Mate chain of hotels, and the designer rooms ooze style and sophistication. Some have floor-to-ceiling murals, the lighting is always funky, and the colour scheme has splashes of pinks, lime greens, oranges or more-minimalist black and white.

🛏 Parque del Oeste & Northern Madrid

★ INNSIDE MADRID LUCHANA HOTEL €€

Map p252 (☏91 292 29 40; www.melia.com; Calle de Luchana 22; d €119-179, ste from €221; ☀☂; Ⓜ Bilbao) Classy, contemporary rooms in an early-20th-century, neoclassical palace close to Plaza de Olavide in Chamberí make for a pleasant alternative to staying downtown. The wrap-around Innside Loft with views has abundant light and a modern four-poster bed.

★ HOTEL SILKEN PUERTA AMÉRICA LUXURY HOTEL €€

(☏91 744 54 00; www.hoteles-silken.com; Av de América 41; d/ste from €125/250; ☀☂; Ⓜ Cartagena) Given the location of their hotel (halfway between the city and the airport) the owners knew they had to do something special – to build a self-contained world so innovative and luxurious that you'd never want to leave. Their idea? Give 22 of architecture's most creative names (eg Zaha Hadid, Norman Foster, Ron Arad, David Chipperfield, Jean Nouvel) a floor each to design. The result? An extravagant pastiche of styles, from zany montages of 1980s chic to bright-red bathrooms that feel like a movie star's dressing room. Even the bar ('a temple to the liturgy of pleasure'), restaurant, facade, gardens, public lighting and car park had their own architects. It's an extraordinary, astonishing place.

★ HOTEL ORFILA HOTEL €€€

Map p252 (☏91 702 77 70; www.hotelorfila.com; Calle de Orfila 6; r from €222; ☀☂; Ⓜ Alonso Martínez) One of Madrid's best hotels, Hotel Orfila has all the luxuries of any five-star hotel – supremely comfortable rooms, for a start – but it's the personal service that elevates it into the upper echelon; regular guests get bathrobes embroidered with their own initials. An old-world elegance dominates the decor, and the quiet location and sheltered garden make it the perfect retreat at day's end.

HOTEL AC SANTO MAURO HOTEL €€€

Map p252 (☏91 319 69 00; www.ac-hotels.com; Calle de Zurbano 36; d/ste from €225/450; ☀☂☒; Ⓜ Alonso Martínez) Everything about this place oozes exclusivity and class, from the address – one of the elite patches of Madrid real estate – to the 19th-century mansion that's the finest in a *barrio* of many. It's a place of discreet elegance and warm service, and rooms are suitably lavish.

There's a predominantly modern aesthetic in some rooms and a more old-world look (with Persian carpets) in others; the Arabian-styled indoor pool isn't bad either. David Beckham, Madonna and Richard Gere have been guests here.

Understand Madrid

Madrid Today

It takes more than nearly a decade of economic crisis to shake Madrid from its stride. Yes, the city has suffered from Spain's dire economic numbers. But it was in Madrid where the fightback began, first with the *indignados* (those who are indignant) and their sit-in protest that served as an inspiration to the worldwide Occupy phenomenon. Then came an electoral storm that in 2015 swept away Madrid's old political order.

Best on Film

Pepi, Luci, Bom y otras chicas del montón (1980) Early Almodóvar film showcasing 1980s Madrid in all its madness.
La colmena (1982) Faithful rendering of Camilo José Cela's Madrid during the grim 1950s.
La comunidad (2000) Cheerfully off-the-wall tale of greed in a Madrid apartment block.
Los fantasmas de Goya (2006) Goya, the Spanish Inquisition and the painter's many scandals.
Volver (2006) Heart-warming Almodóvar film starring Penélope Cruz.

Best in Print

A Heart So White (Javier Marías) A tale of subtle family intrigue.
Madrid: A Cultural and Literary History (Elizabeth Nash) Joyfully written account of the city's past and present.
Winter in Madrid (CJ Sansom) Easy-to-read spy thriller set in post–Spanish Civil War Madrid.
Historias del Kronen (José Ángel Mañas) Cult novel about alienated urban Madrid youth.
A Load of Bull: An Englishman's Adventures in Madrid (Tim Parfitt) Humorous love letter to Madrid in the 1980s and beyond.

Boom to Bust

It can be difficult to remember now, but Spain was, not so long ago, the envy of Europe. Its economy was booming and the whole country seemed brimful of optimism. Then things fell apart. In 2008, unemployment stood at around 6%. Seven years later, one out of every four Spaniards (over 5.5 million people) can't find work. Old-timers you speak to can't remember a time this bad, with businesses closing their doors forever, including many that weathered civil war and dictatorship down through the decades.

Madrid is doing slightly better than the rest of the country (in 2015, the capital's unemployment rate stood at 17.79%, still stubbornly high but better than the 23% country-wide). But with nearly one in five *madrileños* (people from Madrid) looking for work, no one is celebrating.

Where did it all go wrong? Spain's (and to a large extent Madrid's) economy was heavily reliant on construction and tourism, two industries that are exceptionally susceptible to economic downturns. Spain's property market also spiralled out of control for far too long – prices rose exponentially, prompting banks to hand out money to those who simply couldn't afford to pay it back. What began in 2008 shows only tentative signs of abating, but those signs are nonetheless important. Business owners report a slow but steady rise in consumer confidence and restaurant owners state that the number of those eating out is growing. Yes, it's slow, but the economy may finally have bottomed out and be once again on the rise.

Young People

If Spain's economic numbers make for depressing reading, those relating to the country's younger generation can seem catastrophic. More than half of young Spaniards are out of work, and there is talk of an entire generation being lost to the economic downturn. The disparity between salaries – the *mileuristas* (those earning no more than €1000 a month) became a cause célèbre in the Spanish media – and still-high house prices means that young Spaniards are taking ever longer to move out of home. And for the first time in decades, young people are leaving the country in search of opportunity in greater numbers than there are immigrants wanting to come to Spain.

Striking Back

What began in May 2011 with the *indignados* taking over the Plaza de la Puerta del Sol in central Madrid in a peaceful sit-in protest, would turn into a political revolution. In regional elections throughout 2015, the two major parties – the conservative Partido Popular (PP; Popular Party) and the Socialists – who had dominated Spanish politics for decades, saw their power bases eroded by newcomers to the political stage. Two parties in particular – Ciudadanos (Citizens) and Podemos (We Can) – began winning seats in regional parliaments across the country. At times populist, just as often nationalist, these parties came to speak for the deep dissatisfaction that many Spaniards felt towards the two major parties, who were tainted by corruption scandals and their perceived inability to understand the suffering of ordinary Spaniards.

In Madrid region, the ruling PP won the largest number of seats in the regional election, but their vote collapsed (48 seats, down from 72 in 2011). The Socialists came second (with 37 seats). However, the tide was with Podemos (27 seats) and Ciudadanos (17 seats). At the time of research, the shape of the future government in the 129-seat regional parliament remained uncertain.

When it came to Madrid's city council, the results were clearer, bringing to an end 24 years of conservative rule. Although the PP's Esperanza Aguirre (a former leader of Madrid's regional government) won the highest number of seats (21 out of 57), retired judge, Podemos-backed Manuela Carmena came from nowhere to win 20 seats for her Ahora Madrid (Now Madrid) party. With the votes of minor parties, she became mayor on 13 June 2015, promising a new left-leaning politics that included an end to the evictions of those unable to pay their mortgages, job creation and plans to cut inequality between Madrid's neighbourhoods. Carmena also promised to cut her mayoral salary in half. On her first day as mayor, she rode to work on the metro.

if Madrid were 100 people

84 would be Spanish 1 would be Colombian
3 would be Ecuadorian 1 would be Peruvian
1 would be Bolivian 10 would be Other

belief systems
(% of population)

Roman Catholic Other Muslim

population per sq km

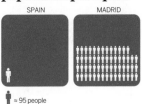

SPAIN MADRID

≈ 95 people

History

Founded as a Muslim garrison town in the 9th century, Madrid took centre stage in 1561 when it was unexpectedly chosen as Spain's capital. As the centre of a global empire and the seat of the Spanish royal court, Madrid was transformed from a cultural backwater into Spain's most important city. In the centuries that followed, it accumulated prestige, people from all across Spain and beyond, and the trappings of power and wealth. The end result is the most Spanish of all Spain's major cities.

Muslim Mayrit

The remains of Roman villas and inns have been found in the Madrid region. The small Roman outpost known as Miacum, close to modern Madrid, was an obscure way-station on the important Roman road that crossed the Iberian Peninsula.

When the Muslim army of Tariq ibn Ziyad crossed the Strait of Gibraltar in the 8th century, it sparked an upheaval that would convulse the Iberian Peninsula for more than 700 years. In 756 the emirate of Córdoba was established in the south in what the Muslims called Al-Andalus and its soldiers and administrators would occupy much of the peninsula until the beginning of the 9th century.

As Iberia's Christians began the Reconquista (Reconquest) – the centuries-long campaign by Christian forces to reclaim the peninsula – the Muslims of Al-Andalus constructed a chain of fortified positions through the heart of Iberia. One of these forts was built by Muhammad I, emir of Córdoba, in 854, on the site of what would become Madrid. They called the new settlement Mayrit (or Magerit), which comes from the Arabic word *majira,* meaning water channel. As the Reconquista gathered strength, forts such as Mayrit grew in significance as part of a defensive line against Christian incursion. Recognising that Mayrit lacked natural fortifications to the east, Muhammad I constructed a defensive wall within whose boundaries only Muslims could live; Mayrit's small Christian community lived outside, near what is now the Iglesia de San Andrés. The last remaining fragment of the Muralla Árabe sits below the modern Catedral de Nuestra Señora de la Almudena.

Mayrit's strategic location in the centre of the peninsula drew an increasing number of soldiers and traders. To accommodate the many newcomers, Mayrit grew into a town. The main mosque was built on

TIMELINE	1st–5th centuries AD	854	end 9th century
	The Roman Empire subdues the Celtiberian tribes. The Roman road that connects Mérida with Toledo (Toletum), Segovia, Alcalá de Henares and Zaragoza (Cesaraugusta) runs close to Madrid.	Muhammad I, emir of Córdoba, establishes the fortress of Mayrit (Magerit), one of many across the so-called Middle March, a frontier land connecting Al-Andalus with the Christian kingdoms of the north.	Muhammad I orders the construction of a wall along the ridgeline, enclosing the current Catedral de Nuestra Señora de la Almudena and what is now the Plaza de Oriente.

BEAR NECESSITIES

Madrid's emblem – a bear nuzzling a *madroño*, or strawberry tree (so named because its fruit looks like strawberries), framed by seven five-point stars and topped by a crown – is one of the most photographed corners of the Plaza de la Puerta del Sol (p86). When Alfonso VI accepted Mayrit from the Muslims in 1083, it was seen as an example of things to come for Christian forces hoping to sweep across Spain from the north. Taking the theme further, a group of seven stars that lies close to the North Star in the northern hemisphere forms a shape known as the Ursa Minor, or small she-bear. Thus the bear (once a common sight in El Pardo north of the city) and seven stars came to symbolise Madrid. The five points of the stars later came to represent the five provinces that surround Madrid (Segovia, Ávila, Toledo, Cuenca and Guadalajara).

what is now the corner of Calle Mayor and Calle de Bailén, although only the smallest fragment remains. Even so, Mayrit was dispensable to its far-off Muslim rulers. As the armies of Muslim and Christian Spain battled for supremacy elsewhere, Mayrit was not considered one of the great prizes and ultimately passed into Christian hands without a fight. In 1083 Toledo's ruler gave Mayrit to King Alfonso VI of Castilla during a period of rare Muslim-Christian entente.

A Medieval Christian Outpost

Madrid never again passed into Muslim hands, although the city was often besieged by Muslim forces. As the frontline gradually pushed south, Christian veterans from the Reconquista and clerics and their orders flooded into Madrid and forever changed the city's character. A small Muslim community remained and to this day the warren of streets around Las Vistillas, where they lived, is known as La Morería – the Moorish quarter. Nearby, the Plaza de la Paja was the site of the city's main market. By the end of the 13th century, a new city wall, bordered by what are now Calle Arenal, Cava de San Miguel, Calle de la Cava Baja, Plaza de la Puerta de Moros and Calle de Bailén, was built. Where the Plaza Mayor, Plaza de España and the Plaza de la Puerta del Sol all stand then lay beyond the walls.

Madrid may have been growing, but its power was negligible and the city existed in the shadow of the more established cities of Segovia and Toledo. Left largely to their own devices, a small number of local families set about governing themselves, forming Madrid's first town council, the Consejo de Madrid. The travelling Cortes (royal court and parliament) sat in Madrid for the first time in 1309. This first sign of

Books on Madrid History

A Traveller's Companion to Madrid (Hugh Thomas)

Hidden Madrid: A Walking Guide (Mark and Peter Besas)

Madrid: The History (Jules Stewart)

c 1070	1083	1110	1222
Madrid's patron saint, San Isidro Labrador, is born among the small community of Christians clustered around the Iglesia de San Andrés (where he is buried in 1130) in Muslim Mayrit.	Mayrit passes into the hands of King Alfonso VI of Castilla without a fight, ending Muslim rule over Mayrit, in return for the king's assistance in capturing Valencia.	Almoravid Muslims attack Madrid in an attempt to wrest the city back from Christian rule. They succeed in destroying Madrid's walls but are unable to seize the *alcázar* (fortress).	Madrid's emblem of seven stars and a bear nuzzling a *madroño* (strawberry tree) appears for the first time in historical records. A statue of it now stands in the Plaza de la Puerta del Sol.

royal favour was followed by others – Madrid was an increasingly popular residence with the Castilian monarchs, particularly Enrique IV (r 1454–74). They found it a relaxing base from which to set off on hunting expeditions, especially for bears in the district of El Pardo.

Despite growing evidence of royal attention, medieval Madrid remained dirt-poor and small-scale. In 1348 the horrors of the Black Death struck, devastating the population, and a handful of local families ran a feudal system of government, lording it over the peasants who worked the surrounding *tierra* (land). As one 15th-century writer observed, 'in Madrid there is nothing except what you bring with you'. It simply bore no comparison with other major Spanish, let alone European, cities.

A Tale of Two Cities

When Carlos I's son and successor, Felipe II, ascended the Spanish throne in 1556, Madrid was surrounded by walls that boasted 130 towers and six stone gates. Although it sounds impressive, these fortifications were largely built of mud and were designed more to impress than provide any meaningful defence of the city. Such modest claims to significance notwithstanding, Madrid was chosen by Felipe II as the capital of Spain in 1561.

Felipe II was more concerned with the business of empire and building his monastic retreat, the Real Monasterio de San Lorenzo at San Lorenzo de El Escorial than he was in developing Madrid. Despite a handful of elegant churches, the imposing *alcázar* and a smattering of noble residences, Madrid consisted, for the most part, of precarious, whitewashed houses that were little more than mud huts. They lined chaotic, ill-defined and largely unpaved lanes and alleys. The monumental Paseo del Prado, which now provides Madrid with so much of its grandeur, was nothing more than a small creek. Even so, Madrid went from having just 2000 homes in 1563 to more than 7000 just 40 years later as opportunists, impoverished rural migrants, would-be princes and fortune-seekers flocked to the city hoping for a share of the glamour and wealth that came from being close to royalty.

The sumptuous Palacio del Buen Retiro was completed in 1630 and replaced the *alcázar* as the prime royal residence (the former Museo del Ejército building and Casón del Buen Retiro are all that remain). Countless grand churches, convents and mansions were also built and, thanks to royal patronage, this was the golden age of art in Spain: Velázquez, El Greco, José de Ribera, Zurbarán, Murillo and Coello were all active in Madrid in the 17th century. For the first time, Madrid began to take on the aspect of a city.

For medieval travellers to Madrid, the impression was of streets 'which would be beautiful if it were not for the mud and filth'. Houses were 'bad and ugly and almost all made of mud'. Rubbish and human excrement were thrown from balconies, 'a thing which afterwards creates an insupportable odour'.

1309	1348	1426	1478
The Cortes sits for the first time in Madrid. During the sitting, the royals declare war on Granada; the Reconquista's demands ensure that the royal court often travels throughout Spain.	The Black Death sweeps across Spain, killing King Alfonso XI and many of his compatriots. Estimates suggest that the plague kills anywhere between 20% and 50% of Madrid's population.	In the midst of a devastating drought, devout *madrileños* (people from Madrid) take the body of San Isidro, Madrid's patron saint, out onto the streets, whereupon it begins to rain.	Isabel and Fernando, the Reyes Católicos (Catholic Monarchs), stir up religious bigotry and establish the Spanish Inquisition; thousands will be killed up until its abolition in 1834.

A CAPITAL CHOICE

When Felipe II decided to make Madrid Spain's capital in 1561, you could almost hear the collective gasp of disbelief from Spain's great and good, few of whom lived in Madrid. Madrid was home to just 30,000 people, whereas Toledo and Seville each boasted more than 80,000. Even Valladolid, the capital of choice for Isabel and Fernando, had 50,000 inhabitants. What's more, in the 250 years since 1309, Madrid had hosted Spain's travelling road show of royalty just 10 times, far fewer than Spain's other large cities.

Madrid's apparent obscurity may, however, explain precisely why Felipe II chose it as his capital. Valladolid was considered to be of questionable loyalty. Toledo, which like Madrid stands close to the geographical heart of Spain, was known for its opinionated nobles and powerful clergy who had shown an annoying tendency to oppose the king's whims and wishes. In contrast, more than one king had described Madrid as 'very noble and very loyal'. By choosing Madrid Felipe II was choosing the path of least resistance. Felipe II also wanted the capital to be 'a city fulfilling the function of a heart located in the middle of the body'.

In 1601 Felipe III, tired of Madrid, moved the court to Valladolid. Within five years, the population of Madrid halved. The move was so unpopular, however, that the king, realising the error of his ways, returned to Madrid. *'Sólo Madrid es corte'* (roughly, 'Only Madrid can be home to the court') became the catchcry and thus it has been ever since.

By the middle of the 17th century Madrid had completely outgrown its capacity to cope: it was home to 175,000 people, making it the fifth-largest city in Europe. But if you took away the court, the city amounted to nothing and when Pedro Teixeira drew the first map of the city in 1656, the place was still largely a cesspit of narrow, squalid lanes.

The Bourbons Leave Their Mark

After King Carlos II died in 1700 without leaving an heir, the 12-year War of the Spanish Succession convulsed Europe. While Europe squabbled over the Spanish colonial carcass, Felipe V (grandson of Louis XIV of France and Maria Teresa, a daughter of Felipe IV) ascended the throne in 1702 as the first member of the Bourbon dynasty, which remains at the head of the Spanish state today. Felipe's centralisation of state control and attempts at land reform are viewed by some historians as the first steps in making Spain a modern European nation, and the former clearly cemented Madrid's claims to being Spain's pre-eminent city. He preferred to live outside the noisy and filthy capital, but when

1479–81	1492	1520	1561
Isabel, Queen of Castilla, marries Fernando, King of Aragón. An edict by Madrid's authorities forces Muslims to wear signs identifying their religion,	The last Muslim rulers of Al-Andalus are defeated by Christian armies in Granada, uniting the peninsula for the first time in seven centuries. Jews are expelled from the peninsula.	Madrid joins Toledo in the rebellion of the Comuneros against Carlos I, a disastrous decision that prompts the victorious king to rein in Madrid's growing independence.	Against all the odds, Felipe II establishes his permanent court at Madrid, which was, in Felipe II's words, 'a city fulfilling the function of a heart located in the middle of the body'.

in 1734 the *alcázar* was destroyed in a fire, the king laid down plans for a magnificent new royal palace, the Palacio Real, to take its place.

His immediate successors, especially Carlos III (r 1759–88), also gave Madrid and Spain a period of comparatively commonsense governance. Carlos (his equestrian statue dominates the Puerta del Sol) came to be known as the best 'mayor' Madrid had ever had. By introducing Madrid's first program of sanitation and public hygiene, he cleaned up a city that was, by all accounts, the filthiest in Europe. Carlos III was so successful that, near the end of his reign, France's ambassador in Madrid described the city as one of the cleanest capitals in Europe. Mindful of his legacy, Carlos III also completed the Palacio Real, inaugurated the city's botanical gardens, the Real Jardín Botánico, and carried out numerous other public works. His stamp upon Madrid's essential character was also evident in his sponsorship of local and foreign artists, among them Goya and Tiepolo. Carlos III also embarked on a major road-building program.

Napoleon & El Dos de Mayo

Within a year of Carlos III's death Europe was again in uproar, this time as the French Revolution threatened to sweep away the old order of privileged royals and inherited nobility. Through the machinations of Carlos IV, the successor to Carlos III, and his self-serving minister, Manuel Godoy, Spain incurred the wrath of both the French and the British. The consequences were devastating. First, Nelson crushed the Spanish fleet in the Battle of Trafalgar in 1805. Next, Napoleon convinced a gullible Godoy to let French troops enter Spain on the pretext of a joint attack on Portugal, whereby General Murat's French detachment took control of Madrid. By 1808 the French presence had become an occupation and Napoleon's brother, Joseph Bonaparte, was crowned king of Spain.

Madrid did not take kindly to foreign rule and, on the morning of 2 May 1808 *madrileños* (people from Madrid), showing more courage than their leaders, attacked French troops around the Palacio Real and what is now Plaza del Dos de Mayo in Malasaña. Murat moved quickly and by the end of the day the rebels were defeated. Goya's masterpieces, *El dos de mayo* and *El tres de mayo,* on display in the Museo del Prado, poignantly evoke the hope and anguish of the ill-fated rebellion.

Although reviled by much of Madrid's population, Joseph Bonaparte's contribution to Madrid in five short years should not be underestimated. Working hard to win popular support, Bonaparte staged numerous free *espectáculos* – bullfights, festivals of food and drink, and religious processions. He also transformed Madrid with a host of

When, in the 17th century, all home owners were ordered to reserve the second storey of their homes for government bureaucrats and clergy newly arrived in the city, *madrileños* instead built homes with just a single-storey facade at street level, building additional storeys out the back, away from prying eyes.

1601	1622	mid-17th century	1702
In the last serious challenge to Madrid's position as capital, Felipe III moves Spain's capital to Valladolid, but popular discontent convinces him to return the royal court to Madrid.	Seville-born Diego Rodríguez de Silva Velázquez moves to Madrid, takes up a position as a painter in the royal court and becomes synonymous with the golden age of Spanish art.	Madrid's population swells to 175,000 people, up from just 30,000 a century before. Only London, Paris, Constantinople and Naples can boast larger populations in Europe.	Felipe V is crowned king, beginning the Bourbon dynasty that still rules Spain and, save for four decades of the 20th century, has done so from Madrid.

measures necessary in a city that had grown up without any discernible sense of town planning. These measures included widening streets and the destruction of various churches and convents to create public squares (such as the Plaza de Oriente, Plaza de Santa Ana, Plaza de San Miguel, Plaza de Santa Bárbara, Plaza de Tirso de Molina and Plaza de Callao). He also conceived the viaduct that still spans Calle de Segovia. Under Bonaparte sanitation was also improved and cemeteries were moved to the outskirts of the city.

The French were finally evicted from Spanish territory in 1813 as a result of the Guerra de la Independencia (War of Independence, or Peninsular War). But when the autocratic King Fernando VII returned in 1814, Spain was in disarray. Though far from Spain's most distinguished ruler, Fernando was responsible for opening to the public the Parque del Buen Retiro, which had been largely destroyed during the war, and founding an art gallery in the Prado.

Capital of a Country Divided

For much of the 19th century, Spain and Madrid were in turmoil, with no less than three civil wars (the Carlist Wars between liberals and conservatives as the royal family squabbled over the spoils of succession), and a series of coups and counter coups. At the heart of it all, Madrid was incredibly backward, although the *desmortización* (disentailment) of Church property in 1837, the emergence of a middle class and growing entrepreneurial activity finally enabled Madrid's ordinary inhabitants to emerge from the shadow of royalty and powerful clergy.

In 1851 the city's first railway line, operating between Madrid and Aranjuez, opened. Seven years later the Canal de Isabel II, which still supplies the city with water from the Sierra de Guadarrama, was inaugurated. Street paving, the sewage system and rubbish collection were improved and gas lighting was introduced. More importantly, foreign (mostly French) capital was beginning to fill the investment vacuum. In the years that followed, a national road network radiating from the capital was built and public works, ranging from the reorganisation of the Puerta del Sol to the building of the Teatro Real, Biblioteca Nacional and Congreso de los Diputados (lower house of parliament), were carried out. In the 1860s the first timid moves to create an Ensanche, or extension of the city, were undertaken. The initial spurt of building took place around Calle de Serrano, where the enterprising Marqués de Salamanca bought up land and built high-class housing.

In 1873 Spain was declared a republic, but the army soon intervened to restore the Bourbon monarchy. Alfonso XII, Isabel II's son, assumed

Madrileños never forgave Bonaparte his foreign origins and the brutality with which he suppressed uprisings against his rule, mocking his yearning for legitimacy by calling him names that included the Cucumber King, Pepe Botella and King of the Small Squares.

HISTORY CAPITAL OF A COUNTRY DIVIDED

1734	1759–88	1808	1812
Medieval Madrid's most enduring symbol, the *alcázar* (fortress), is destroyed by fire. Plans begin almost immediately for a lavish royal palace to take its place.	Carlos III, King of Spain and patron of Madrid, cleans up the city, lays out the Real Jardín Botánico and sponsors Goya, transforming Madrid into a sophisticated European capital.	Napoleon's troops under General Murat march into Madrid and Joseph Bonaparte, Napoleon's brother, is crowned King of Spain; citizens rise up to protest against foreign rule.	Thirty thousand *madrileños* die of hunger caused by fighting the French in the lead-up to the War of Independence (Peninsular War). The French are expelled a year later.

power. In the period of relative tranquillity that ensued, the expansion of the Ensanche gathered momentum, the city's big train stations were constructed and the foundation stones of a cathedral were laid. Another kind of 'cathedral', the Banco de España, was completed and opened its doors in 1891. By 1898 the first city tramlines were electrified and in 1910 work began on the Gran Vía. Nine years later the first metro line started operating.

The 1920s were a period of frenzied activity, not just in urban construction but in intellectual life. As many as 20 newspapers circulated on the streets of Madrid, and writers and artists (including Lorca, Dalí and Buñuel) converged on the capital, which hopped to the sounds of American jazz and whose grand cafes resounded with the clamour of lively *tertulias* (literary discussions). The '20s roared as much in Madrid as elsewhere in Europe.

In the Eye of the Storm

In 1923 the captain-general of Catalonia and soon-to-be dictator, General Miguel Primo de Rivera, seized power and held it until Alfonso XIII had him removed in 1930. Madrid erupted in joyful celebration, but it would prove to be a false dawn. By now, the Spanish capital, home to more than one million people, had become the seething centre of Spain's increasingly radical politics, and the rise of the socialists in Madrid, as well as anarchists in Barcelona and Andalucía, sharpened tensions throughout the country.

Municipal elections in Madrid in April 1931 brought a coalition of republicans and socialists to power. Three days later a second republic was proclaimed and Alfonso XIII fled. The republican government opened up to the public the Casa de Campo – until then serving as a private royal playground – and passed numerous reformist laws, but divisions within the government enabled a right-wing coalition to assume power in 1933. Again the pendulum swung and in February 1936 the left-wing Frente Popular (Popular Front) barely defeated the right's Frente Nacional (National Front) to power. General Francisco Franco was exiled, supposedly out of harm's way, to the Canary Islands, but with the army supporting the right-wing parties and the extreme left clamouring for revolution, the stage was set for a showdown. In July 1936 garrisons in North Africa revolted, quickly followed by others on the mainland. The Spanish Civil War had begun.

Having stopped Franco's nationalist troops advancing from the north, Madrid found itself in the sights of Franco's forces moving up from the south. Take Madrid, Franco reasoned, and Spain would be his. By early November 1936 Franco was in the Casa de Campo. The republi-

During the Madrid siege, Francoist general Emilio Mola assured a journalist that he would take Madrid with his four columns of soldiers massed on the city's outskirts and with the help of his 'fifth column', a phrase that has since remained in the popular lexicon and referred to Franco's right-wing sympathisers in Madrid.

1819	1833	1873	1881
Fernando VII opens the Museo del Prado. Originally conceived as a storehouse for royal art accumulated down through the centuries, it later becomes one of the most important art galleries in Europe.	King Fernando VII dies, leaving three-year-old Isabel II as heir-apparent. Her mother, María Cristina rules as regent and Spain descends into the Carlist civil wars, devastating Madrid in the process.	Spain's first, short-lived republic is declared in February, although the Bourbon monarchy returns to power in Madrid's Palacio Real with help from the army in December of the following year.	The Partido Socialista Obrero Español (PSOE; Spanish Socialist Workers' Party) is founded in a backroom of Casa Labra, still one of Madrid's most prestigious tapas bars.

can government escaped to Valencia, but the resolve of the city's defenders, a mix of hastily assembled and poorly trained recruits, sympathisers from the ranks of the army and air force, the International Brigades and Soviet advisers, held firm. Madrid became an international cause célèbre, drawing luminaries as diverse as Ernest Hemingway and Willy Brandt in defence of the city. For all the fame of the brigades, the fact remains, however, that of the 40,000 soldiers and irregulars defending Madrid, more than 90% were Spaniards.

Madrid's defenders held off a fierce nationalist assault in November 1936, with the fighting heaviest in the northwest of the city, around Argüelles and the Ciudad Universitaria. Soldiers loyal to Franco inside Madrid were overpowered by local militias and 20,000 Franco supporters sought protection inside the walls of foreign embassies. Faced with republican intransigence – symbolised by the catchphrase *'No pasarán!'* ('They shall not pass!') coined by the communist leader Dolores Ibárruri – Franco besieged Madrid, bombarded the city from the air and waited for the capital to surrender. It didn't.

German bombers strafed Madrid, one of the first such campaigns of its kind in the history of warfare, although the Salamanca district was spared, allegedly because it was home to a high proportion of Franco supporters. The Museo del Prado was not so fortunate and most of its paintings were evacuated to Valencia. As many as 10,000 people died in the Battle of Madrid; Franco's approach was summed up by his promise that 'I will destroy Madrid rather than leave it to the Marxists'.

By 1938 Madrid was in a state of near famine, with food, clothes and ammunition in short supply. As republican strongholds fell elsewhere across Spain, Madrid's republican defenders were divided over whether to continue the resistance. After a brief internal power struggle, those favouring negotiations won. On 28 March 1939 an exhausted Madrid finally surrendered.

Franco's Madrid

Mindful that he was occupying a city that had hardly welcomed him with open arms, Franco considered shifting the capital south to the more amenable Seville. As if to punish Madrid for its resistance, he opted instead to remake Madrid in his own image and transform the city into a capital worthy of its new master. Franco and his right-wing Falangist Party maintained a heavy-handed repression, and Madrid in the early 1940s was impoverished and battle scarred, a 'city of a million cadavers', according to one observer.

In the Francoist propaganda of the day, the 1940s and 1950s were the years of *autarquía* (economic self-reliance), a policy that owed more to

The grandiose folly of Franco's Valle de los Caídos monument northwest of Madrid was largely constructed through the forced labour of republican prisoners of war.

1898	1919	1920s	1931
Spain loses its remaining colonies of Cuba, Puerto Rico and the Philippines to the USA, setting off a period of national angst. In the same year, Madrid's tramlines are electrified.	Madrid's first metro line starts running, crossing the city from north to south, with eight stations and a total length of 3.5km from Puerta del Sol to Cuatro Caminos.	Madrid enjoys a cultural revival with Salvador Dalí, Federico García Lorca and Luis Buñuel bringing both high culture and mayhem to a city in love with jazz and *tertulias* (literary discussions).	After a period of right-wing dictatorship, Spain's Second Republic is proclaimed and King Alfonso XIII flees, leaving Spain in political turmoil and planting the seeds for civil war.

Spain's international isolation post-WWII due to its perceived support for Hitler than any principled philosophy. For most Spaniards, however, these were the *años de hambre* (years of hunger). Throughout the 1940s, tens of thousands of suspected republican sympathisers were harassed, imprisoned, tortured and shot. Thousands of political prisoners were shipped off to Nazi concentration camps. Many who remained were put to work in deplorable conditions.

The dire state of the Spanish economy forced hundreds of thousands of starving *campesinos* (peasants) to flock to Madrid, increasing the already enormous pressure for housing. Most contented themselves with erecting *chabolas* (shanty towns) in the increasingly ugly satellite suburbs that began to ring the city.

By the early 1960s, known as the *años de desarrollo* (years of development), industry was taking off in and around Madrid. Foreign investment poured in and the services and banking sector blossomed. Factories of the American Chrysler motor company were Madrid's single biggest employers in the 1960s. In 1960 fewer than 70,000 cars were on the road in Madrid; 10 years later more than half a million clogged the capital's streets.

For all the signs of development in Madrid, Franco was never popular in his own capital and an increased standard of living did little to diminish *madrileños'* disdain for a man who held the capital in an iron grip. In the Basque Country the terrorist group Euskadi Ta Askatasuna (ETA; Basque Homeland and Freedom) began to fight for Basque independence. Their first important action outside the Basque Country was the assassination in Madrid in 1973 of Admiral Carrero Blanco, Franco's prime minister and designated successor.

Franco fell ill in 1974 and died on 20 November 1975.

The Transition to Democracy

After the death of Franco, Spaniards began to reclaim their country and Madrid took centre stage.

King Juan Carlos I, of the Bourbon family that had left the Spanish political stage with the flight of Alfonso XIII in 1931, had been groomed as head of state by Franco. But the king confounded the sceptics by entrusting Adolfo Suárez, a former moderate Francoist with whom he had long been in secret contact, with government in July 1976. With the king's approval Suárez quickly rammed a raft of changes through parliament while Franco loyalists and generals, suddenly rudderless without their leader, struggled to regroup.

Suárez and his centre-right coalition won elections in 1977 and set about writing a new constitution in collaboration with the now-legal

Madrid's first democratically elected conservative mayor, José María Álvarez del Manzano of the Partido Popular (Popular Party; PP), ruled from 1991 until 2003 and became known as 'The Tunnelator' for beginning the ongoing mania of Madrid governments for semipermanent roadworks and large-scale infrastructure projects.

1936–39	1960s	1973	1975–78
The Spanish Civil War breaks out. Nationalist forces bombard Madrid from the air and with artillery, besieging it for three years, before the exhausted city surrenders on 28 March 1939.	After two decades of extreme economic hardship, the decade becomes known as the *años de desarollo* (years of development), with investment and rural immigrants flooding into Madrid.	Admiral Carrero Blanco, Franco's prime minister and designated successor, is assassinated by ETA in a car-bomb attack in Salamanca after leaving Mass at the Iglesia de San Francisco de Borga.	Franco dies in Madrid on 20 November 1975, after 39 years in power. Without an obvious successor to Franco, Spain returns to democratic rule three years later.

opposition. It provided for a parliamentary monarchy with no state religion, and guaranteed a large degree of devolution to the 17 regions (including the Comunidad de Madrid) into which the country was now divided.

Spaniards got the fright of their lives in February 1981 when a pistol-brandishing, low-ranking Guardia Civil (Civil Guard) officer, Antonio Tejero Molina, marched into the Cortes in Madrid with an armed detachment and held parliament captive for 24 hours. Throughout a day of high drama the country held its breath as Spaniards waited to see whether Spain would be thrust back into the dark days of dictatorship or if the fledgling democracy would prevail. With the nation glued to their TV sets, King Juan Carlos I made a live broadcast denouncing Tejero and calling on the soldiers to return to their barracks. The coup fizzled out.

A year later Felipe González' Partido Socialista Obrero Español (PSOE; Spanish Socialist Workers' Party) won national elections. Spain's economic problems were legion – incomes were on a par with those of Iraq, ETA terrorism was claiming dozens of lives every year and unemployment was above 20%. But one thing Spaniards had in abundance was optimism and when, in 1986, Spain joined the European Community (EC), as it was then called, the country had well and truly returned to the fold of modern European nations.

La Movida Madrileña

Madrid's spirits could not be dampened and, with grand events taking place on the national stage, the city had become one of the most exciting places on earth. What London was to the swinging '60s and Paris to 1968, Madrid was to the 1980s. After the long, dark years of dictatorship and conservative Catholicism, Spaniards, especially *madrileños*, emerged onto the streets with all the zeal of ex-convent schoolgirls. Nothing was taboo in a phenomenon known as *'la movida madrileña'* (the Madrid scene), as young *madrileños* discovered the '60s, '70s and early '80s all at once. Drinking, drugs and sex suddenly were OK. All-night partying was the norm, drug taking in public was not a criminal offence (that changed in 1992) and the city howled. All across Madrid, summer terraces roared to the drinking, carousing crowds and young people from all over Europe flocked here to take part in the revelry.

What was remarkable about *la movida* is that it was presided over by Enrique Tierno Galván, an ageing former university professor who had been a leading opposition figure under Franco and was affectionately known throughout Spain as 'the old teacher'. A Socialist, he became mayor in 1979 and, for many, launched *la movida* by telling a public

The Popular Party's Esperanza Aguirre became the country's first-ever woman regional president in close-run elections for the Comunidad de Madrid in 2003, a position she held until 2012. In 2015, the leftist coalition Ahora Madrid, backed by the nationwide Podemos, won municipal elections, and retired judge Manuela Carmena became Madrid's first female mayor.

1980s	1981	1986	1991
La movida madrileña (the Madrid scene) takes over the city, and becomes a byword for hedonism. The era produces such talents as Pedro Almodóvar, Agatha Ruiz de la Prada and Alaska.	On 23 February a group of armed Guardia Civil led by Antonio Tejero Molina attempt a coup; the king denounces them and the coup collapses.	Spain joins the European Community (EC), later the European Union (EU). EU subsidies and other assistance will later be credited with building the foundations of the modern Spanish economy.	Madrid elects a conservative mayor, José María Álvarez del Manzano of the Partido Popular (PP; Popular Party), for the first time, bringing an end to *la movida*.

A CITY OF IMMIGRANTS

In a country where regional nationalisms abound – even Barcelona, that most European of cities, is fiercely and parochially Catalan – Madrid is notable for its absence of regional sentiment. If you quiz madrileños as to why this is so, they often reply, 'but we're all from somewhere else'. It has always been thus in Madrid. In the century after the city became the national capital in 1561, the population swelled by more than 500%, from 30,000 to 175,000. Most were Spaniards (peasants and would-be nobles) who left behind the impoverished countryside and were drawn by the opportunities that existed on the periphery of the royal court.

During the first three decades of the 20th century Madrid's population doubled from half a million to around one million; in 1930 a study found that less than 40% of the capital's population was from Madrid. The process continued in the aftermath of the civil war, and in the 1950s alone more than 600,000 arrived from elsewhere in Spain. In the late 20th century the process of immigration took on a new form, as Spain became the EU's largest annual recipient of immigrants. Between 15% and 20% of Madrid's population are foreigners, more than double the national average.

Unsurprisingly, true madrileños are something of a rare breed. Those who can claim four grandparents born in the city are dignified with the name gatos (cats). The term dates from when one of Alfonso VI's soldiers artfully scaled Muslim Mayrit's formidable walls in 1083. 'Look,' cried his comrades, 'he moves like a cat!'

gathering 'a colocarse y ponerse al loro', which loosely translates as 'get stoned and do what's cool'. Unsurprisingly he was Madrid's most popular mayor ever and when he died in 1986 a million madrileños turned out for his funeral.

But la movida was not just about rediscovering the Spanish art of salir de copas (going out for a drink). It was also accompanied by an explosion of creativity among the country's musicians, designers and filmmakers keen to shake off the shackles of the repressive Franco years. The most famous of these was film director Pedro Almodóvar. Still one of Europe's most creative directors, his riotously colourful films captured the spirit of la movida, featuring larger-than-life characters who pushed the limits of sex and drugs. Although his later films became internationally renowned, his first films, Pepi, Luci, Bom y otras chicas del montón (Pepi, Luci, Bom and the Other Girls; 1980) and Laberinto de pasiones (Labyrinth of Passion; 1982), are where the spirit of the movement really comes alive. When he wasn't making films, Almodóvar immersed himself in the spirit of la movida, doing drag acts in smoky bars that people-in-the-know would frequent.

1992	11 March 2004	2007	2007
In the same year that Barcelona hosts the Summer Olympics, Madrid is designated a European Capital of Culture. Drug taking in public is finally outlawed in the capital.	Terrorist bombings on Madrid commuter trains kill 191 people and injure 1755. The next day three million take to the streets in protest. The PSOE wins national elections on 14 March.	The PP's Alberto Ruiz-Gallardón, who first won election in 2003, wins an absolute majority in municipal elections, cementing the conservatives hold over Madrid's Ayuntamiento (town hall).	Twenty-one people are convicted of involvement in the March 2004 terrorist attacks, although the trial uncovers no evidence of Al-Qaeda involvement in the planning or execution of the bombings.

So what happened to *la movida*? Many say that it died in 1991 with the election of José María Álvarez del Manzano of the Partido Popular (PP; Popular Party) as mayor. In the following years rolling spliffs in public became increasingly dangerous and creeping clamps (ie closing hours) were imposed on the almost-lawless bars. Pedro Almodóvar was even heard to say that Madrid had become 'as boring as Oslo'. Things have indeed quietened down a little, but you'll only notice if you were here during the 1980s. If only all cities were this 'boring'.

Madrid Sobers Up

After 12 years of Socialist rule, the conservative PP won mayoral elections in 1991 (they would hold the town hall until 2015) and from 1996 until 2004 the three levels of government in Madrid (local, regional and national) remained the preserve of the PP. Throughout this period, observers from other regions claimed that the PP overtly favoured development of the capital at the expense of Spain's other regions. Whatever the truth of such accusations, the city moved ahead in leaps and bounds, and as the national economy took off in the late 1990s, Madrid reaped the benefits. Extraordinary expansion programs for the metro, highways, airport, outer suburbs and for inner-city renewal were unmistakable signs of confidence. By one reckoning, up to 75% of inward foreign investment into Spain was directed at the capital.

On 11 March 2004, just three days before the country was due to vote in national elections, Madrid was rocked by 10 bombs on four rush-hour commuter trains heading into the capital's Atocha station. When the dust cleared, 191 people had died and 1755 were wounded, many of them seriously. It was the biggest such terror attack in the nation's history.

If this attack united the city, political division lay ahead. On 15 May 2011, at the height of the economic crisis and with dissatisfaction with Spain's political class at an all-time high, *indignados* (those who are indignant) took over the Plaza de la Puerta del Sol in the centre of Madrid in a peaceful sit-in protest. Their popularity maintained by social media networks, they stayed for months, and were the forerunners to numerous such movements around the world, including Occupy Wall Street and its offshoots. It was the start of a movement that would transform Spanish politics.

Madrid was a candidate for the 2012 and 2016 Olympics, coming third and second respectively. Madrid's bid for the 2020 Olympics was a familiar story, as it came in third behind Istanbul and eventual winners Tokyo, leaving it as the only major European capital never to have hosted the Games.

2011	2011	2014	2015
Protesters known as *indignados* (those who are indignant) occupy the Plaza de la Puerta del Sol, a forerunner to the worldwide Occupy protests.	The PP win municipal and national elections. After the latter, Mayor Gallardón is drafted into the national government as Justice Minister. Ana Botella is the new mayor.	Real Madrid football team wins a record 10th European Champions League, defeating cross-city rivals Atlético de Madrid 4-1 in Lisbon.	Despite finishing second in municipal elections, Manuela Carmena of the leftist Ahora Madrid becomes mayor, a post held by the conservative Popular Party since 1991.

City of Painters

Spanish kings down through the centuries were a pretty vain and decadent lot, and loved to pose for portraits or compete with other European royals for the prestige that came from lavishing money on the great artists of the day. This marriage of royal money and personal patronage transformed Madrid into one of the world's richest producers and storehouses of paintings. Since the early 20th century, Spain's finest artistic academies have drawn Spain's most creative talents.

The Early Days

With royal patronage of the arts kicking off in the 16th century, it was difficult for local artists to get a look in. Felipe II – the monarch who made Madrid the permanent seat of the royal court – preferred the work of Italian artists such as Titian (Tiziano in Spanish) ahead of home-grown talent. Even some foreign artists who would later become masters were given short shrift. One of these was the Cretanborn Domenikos Theotokopoulos (1541–1614), known as El Greco (the Greek), who was perhaps the most extraordinary and temperamental 'Spanish' artist of the 16th century, but whom Felipe II rejected as a court artist. The Museo del Prado is the place to see works by Titian and El Greco.

Velázquez & the Golden Age

As Spain's monarchs sought refuge from the creeping national malaise of the 17th century by promoting the arts, they fostered an artist who would rise above all others: Diego Rodríguez de Silva Velázquez (1599–1660). Born in Seville, Velázquez later moved to Madrid as court painter and stayed to make the city his own. He composed scenes (landscapes, royal portraits, religious subjects, snapshots of everyday life) that owe their vitality not only to his photographic eye for light and contrast but also to a compulsive interest in the humanity of his subjects, who seem to breathe on the canvas. His masterpieces include *Las meninas* (The Maids of Honour) and *La rendición de Breda* (The Surrender of Breda), both on view in the Museo del Prado.

Francisco de Zurbarán (1598–1664), a friend and contemporary of Velázquez, ended his life in poverty in Madrid; it was only after his death that he received the acclaim that his masterpieces deserved. He is best remembered for the startling clarity and light in his portraits of monks, a series of which hangs in the Real Academia de Bellas Artes de San Fernando.

Other masters of the era whose works hang in the Prado, though their connection to Madrid was limited, include José (Jusepe) de Ribera (1591–1652), who was influenced by Caravaggio and produced fine chiaroscuro works, and Bartolomé Esteban Murillo (1617–82).

The 20th Century & Beyond

The 17th century may have been Spain's golden age, but the 20th century was easily its rival.

Sorolla & Solana

Valencian native Joaquín Sorolla (1863–1923) flew in the face of the French Impressionist style, preferring the blinding sunlight of the Mediterranean coast to the muted tones favoured in Paris. He lived and worked in Madrid and his work can be studied in Madrid's Museo Sorolla, where he once lived.

Leading the way into the 20th century was Madrid-born José Gutiérrez Solana (1886–1945), whose disturbing, avant-garde approach to painting revels in low lighting, sombre colours and deathly pale figures. His work is emblematic of what historians now refer to as *España negra* (black Spain). A selection of his canvases is on display in the Centro de Arte Reina Sofía.

Picasso, Dalí & Juan Gris

Málaga-born Pablo Ruiz Picasso (1881–1973) is one of the greatest and most original Spanish painters of all time. Although he spent much of his working life in Paris, he arrived in Madrid from Barcelona in 1897 at the behest of his father for a year's study at the Escuela de Bellas Artes de San Fernando. Never one to allow himself to be confined within formal structures, the precocious Picasso instead took himself to the Prado to learn from the masters, and to the streets to depict life as he saw it. Picasso went on to become the master of cubism, which was

GOYA – A CLASS OF HIS OWN

Francisco José de Goya y Lucientes (1746–1828), who was born in the village of Fuendetodos in Aragón, started his career as a cartoonist in the Real Fábrica de Tapices in Madrid. In 1776 Goya began designing for the tapestry factory, but illness in 1792 left him deaf; many critics speculate that this condition was largely responsible for his wild, often merciless style that would become increasingly unshackled from convention. By 1799 Goya was appointed Carlos IV's court painter.

Several distinct series and individual paintings mark his progress. In the last years of the 18th century he painted enigmatic masterpieces, such as *La maja vestida* (The Young Lady Dressed) and *La maja desnuda* (The Young Lady Undressed), identical portraits but for the lack of clothes in the latter. The rumour mill suggests the subject was none other than the Duchess of Alba, with whom he allegedly had an affair. Whatever the truth of Goya's sex life, the Inquisition was not amused by the artworks, and covered them up. Nowadays all is bared in the Museo del Prado.

At about the same time as his enigmatic *Majas*, the prolific Goya executed the playful frescoes in Madrid's Ermita de San Antonio de la Florida, which have recently been restored to stunning effect. He also produced *Los Caprichos* (The Caprices), a biting series of 80 etchings lambasting the follies of court life and ignorant clergy.

The arrival of the French and war in 1808 had a profound impact on Goya and inspired his unforgiving portrayals of the brutality of war: *El dos de mayo* (The Second of May) and, more dramatically, *El tres de mayo* (The Third of May). The latter depicts the execution of Madrid rebels by French troops.

After he retired to the Quinta del Sordo (Deaf Man's House) west of the Río Manzanares in Madrid, he created his nightmarish *Pinturas negras* (Black Paintings). Executed on the walls of the house, they were later removed and now hang in the Prado.

Goya spent the last years of his life in voluntary exile in France, where he continued to paint until his death.

inspired by his fascination with primitivism, primarily African masks and early Iberian sculpture. This highly complex form reached its high point in *Guernica,* which hangs in the Centro de Arte Reina Sofía.

Picasso was not the only artist who found the Escuela de Bellas Artes de San Fernando too traditional for his liking. In 1922 Salvador Dalí (1904–89) arrived in Madrid from Catalonia, but decided that the eminent professors of the renowned fine-arts school were not fit to judge him. He spent four years living in the 'Resi', the renowned students' residence (which still functions today) where he met poet Federico García Lorca and future film director Luis Buñuel. The three self-styled anarchists and bohemians romped through the cafes and music halls of 1920s Madrid, frequenting brothels, engaging in pranks, immersing themselves in jazz and taking part in endless *tertulias* (literary discussions). Dalí, a true original and master of the surrealist form, was finally expelled from art school and left Madrid, never to return. The only remaining link with Madrid is a handful of his hallucinatory works in the Centro de Arte Reina Sofía.

In the same gallery is a fine selection of the cubist creations of Madrid's Juan Gris (1887–1927), who was turning out his best work in Paris while Dalí and his cohorts were up to no good in Madrid. Along with Picasso and Georges Braque, he was a principal exponent of the cubist style and his paintings can also be seen in the Museo Thyssen-Bornemisza and Real Academia de Bellas Artes de San Fernando.

Contemporary Art

The death of Franco in 1975 unleashed a frenzy of activity and artistic creativity that was central to *la movida madrileña* (the Madrid scene). The Galería Moriarty became a focal point of exuberantly artistic reference. A parade of artists marched through the gallery, including leading *movida* lights such as Ceesepe (b 1958; real name Carlos Sánchez Pérez), who captures the spirit of 1980s Madrid with his eight short films and busy paintings full of people and activity (but recently veering towards surrealism). Another Moriarty protégé was Ouka Leele (b 1957, whose real name is Bárbara Allende), a self-taught photographer whose sometimes weird works stand out for her tangy treatment of colour. Her photos can be seen at the Centro de Arte Reina Sofía, Museo de Historia and, when it reopens, the Museo Municipal de Arte Contemporáneo. Another *movida* photographer who still exhibits around town is Alberto García-Alix (b 1956).

The rebellious, effervescent activity in the 1980s tends to cloud the fact that the visual arts in the Franco years were far from dead, although many artists spent years in exile. The art of Eduardo Arroyo (b 1937) in particular is steeped in the radical spirit that kept him in exile for 15 years from 1962. His paintings tend in part towards pop art, brimming with ironic sociopolitical comment. Of the other exiles, one of Spain's greatest 20th-century sculptors, Toledo-born Alberto Sánchez (1895–1962), whose works can be seen at the open-air Museo al Aire Libre, lived his last years in Moscow. The work of Benjamín Palencia (1894–1980) shows striking similarities with some of Sánchez' sculptures.

Antonio López García (b 1936) takes a photographer's eye to his hyper-realistic paintings. Settings as simple as *Lavabo y espejo* (Wash Basin and Mirror, 1967) convert the most banal everyday objects into scenes of extraordinary depth, and the same applies to his Madrid street scenes, which are equally loaded with detail, light play and subtle colour, especially *La Gran Vía* (1981) and *Vallecas* (1980). He won the coveted Premio Príncipe de Asturias for art in 1985 and a couple of his works are in the Centro de Arte Reina Sofía.

For paintings whose subject matter is Madrid (although she also paints other cities), Málaga-born Paula Varona (www.paulavarona.com) has few peers. The Madrid section of her website (which also lists upcoming exhibitions) has a stunning overview of her work.

Architecture

Madrid's architecture spans the centuries and tells the broad sweep of Spain's history: the grandeur of Spain's imperial past sits alongside *barroco madrileño* (Madrid baroque), belle-époque buildings and innovative contemporary architecture. It all comes together in the grand historical buildings that have been transformed by stunning modern projects of regeneration.

Madrid to the 16th Century

Madrid's origins as a Muslim garrison town yielded few architectural treasures, or at least few that remain. The only reminder of the Muslim presence is a modest stretch of the town wall, known as the Muralla Árabe below the Catedral de Nuestra Señora de la Almudena. The bell towers of the Iglesia de San Pedro El Viejo and Iglesia de San Nicolás de los Servitas are the only modest representatives of the rich Mudéjar style (developed by the Moors who remained behind in reconquered Christian territory) that once adorned Madrid.

International Architecture Day, which usually falls in early October, offers a chance to visit otherwise-closed architectural landmarks, including the Sociedad General de Autores y Editores.

Madrid Baroque & Beyond

Architect Juan de Herrera (1530–97) was perhaps the greatest figure of the Spanish Renaissance and he bequeathed to the city an architectural style all of its own. Herrera's trademark was to fuse the sternness of the Renaissance style with a timid approach to its successor, the more voluptuous, ornamental baroque. The result was an architectural style known as *barroco madrileño* (Madrid baroque). Herrera's austere masterpiece was the palace-monastery complex of San Lorenzo de El Escorial, but the nine-arched Puente de Segovia, down the southern end of Calle de Segovia, is also his.

The most successful proponent of this style was Juan Gómez de Mora (1586–1648), who was responsible for laying out the Plaza Mayor, as well as the Convento de la Encarnación and the Palacio de Santa Cruz. Gómez de Mora's uncle, Francisco de Mora (1553–1610), added to an impressive family portfolio with the Palacio del Duque de Uceda on Calle Mayor. Other exceptional examples of the style are the Real Casa de la Panadería on Plaza Mayor and the main entrance of what is now the Museo de Historia.

Ventura Rodríguez (1717–85) dominated the architectural scene in 18th-century Madrid. He redesigned the interior of the Convento de la Encarnación. He also sidelined in spectacular fountains, and it is Rodríguez whom we have to thank for the goddess Cybele in the Plaza de la Cibeles and the Fuente de las Conchas in the Campo del Moro.

Where Ventura Rodríguez leaned towards a neoclassical style, Juan de Villanueva (1739–1811) embraced it wholeheartedly, most notably in the Palacio de Villanueva that would eventually house the Museo del Prado. Villanueva also oversaw the rebuilding of the Plaza Mayor after it was destroyed by fire in 1790 and designed numerous outbuildings of the royal residences, such as San Lorenzo de El Escorial.

Belle Époque

As Madrid emerged from the chaos of the first half of the 19th century, a building boom began. The use of iron and glass, a revolution in building aesthetics that symbolised the embracing of modernity, became all the rage. The gorgeous Palacio de Cristal was built at this time.

By the dawn of the 20th century, known to many as the belle époque, Madrid was abuzz with construction. Headed by the prolific Antonio Palacios (1874–1945), architects from all over Spain began to transform Madrid into the airy city you see today. Many looked to the past for their inspiration. Neo-Mudéjar was especially favoured for bullrings. The ring at Las Ventas, finished in 1934, is a classic example of the neo-Mudéjar style. A more bombastic (and perhaps the most spectacular) interpretation of the belle-époque style is Palacios' Palacio de Comunicaciones, with its plethora of pinnacles and prancing ornaments, which was finished in 1917.

Contemporary Architecture

Madrid's contribution to the revolution taking place in Spanish architecture circles has been muted, although there are some standout buildings.

Designed by Richard Rogers, Terminal 4 (T4) of Madrid's Barajas International Airport is a stunning, curvaceous work of art, which deservedly won Rogers the prestigious Stirling Prize in October 2006.

Another significant transformation on a grand scale is to Madrid's once-low-rise skyline, with four skyscrapers rising up above the Paseo de la Castellana in northern Madrid. Of these, the Torre Caja Madrid (250m, designed by Sir Norman Foster) is Spain's tallest building, just surpassing its neighbour, the Torre de Cristal (249.5m, designed by César Pelli). The Torre Espacio (236m, designed by Henry Cobb) has also won plaudits for its abundant use of glass.

Among the architectural innovations that travellers to Madrid are more likely to experience up close and at greater depth, the most exciting is perhaps the extension of the Museo del Prado, which opened in October 2007. The work of one of Spain's premier architects, the Pritzker-prize-winning Rafael Moneo, the extension links the main gallery with what remains of the cloisters of the Iglesia de San Jerónimo El Real. Moneo won plaudits for his use of traditional building materials such as granite, red brick and oak, while the Prado's director, Miguel Zugaza, lauded the final effect as being 'like placing a still life by Juan Gris next to one by Zurbarán...discreet, elegant and profoundly modern'. Moneo met two other major Madrid challenges with his acclaimed remodelling of the Antigua Estación de Atocha and his conversion of the Palacio de Villahermosa into the Museo Thyssen-Bornemisza, both in the early 1990s.

Another landmark project in recent years has been the extension of the Centro de Arte Reina Sofía by the French architect Jean Nouvel. It's a stunning red glass-and-steel complement to the old-world Antigua Estación de Atocha across the Plaza del Emperador Carlos V and to the austerity of the remainder of the museum's 18th-century structure.

Between the Reina Sofía and the Prado and opposite the Real Jardín Botánico, the Caixa Forum, completed in 2008, is one of Madrid's most striking buildings. Designed by Swiss architects Jacques Herzog and Pierre de Meuron, its aesthetic seems to owe more to the world of sculpture than of architecture with its unusual iron-and-brick form. It's a worthy, surprising addition to the Paseo del Prado's grandeur.

And one final thing for those who love architecture: while in Madrid you really must stay at the Hotel Silken Puerta América, where each floor has been custom designed by a world-renowned architect.

Notable Old Buildings

Palacio Real

Plaza de la Villa

Palacio de Comunicaciones

Sociedad General de Autores y Editores

Plaza de Toros Monumental de Las Ventas

Edificio Metrópolis

Notable New or Fusion Buildings

Centro de Arte Reina Sofía

Caixa Forum

Museo del Prado

Antigua Estación de Atocha

Terminal 4, Aeropuerto de Barajas

Madrid's Movie-Makers

Madrid is the uncontested capital of the Spanish film industry, which is defined by some exceptional individual talents (Pedro Almodóvar, Penélope Cruz, Antonio Banderas and Javier Bardem, for example), and a local film-making industry that turns out work of real quality but struggles for both funding and international success. Hollywood and the home-grown industry come together for the annual Goya Awards (Spain's Oscars) in Madrid in February.

Directors

The still-young Alejandro Amenábar (b 1973) is already one of Spain's most respected directors. He was born in Chile but his family moved to Madrid when he was a child. He announced his arrival with *Tesis* (1996), but it was with *Abre los ojos* (Open Your Eyes; 1997), which was later adapted for Hollywood as *Vanilla Sky,* that his name became known internationally. His first English-language film was *The Others* (2001), which received plaudits from critics, but nothing like the clamour that surrounded *Mar adentro* (The Sea Inside; 2004), his stunning portrayal of a Galician fisherman's desire to die with dignity, which starred Javier Bardem. His 2009 *Ágora* was a stunning follow-up and, with a budget of US$50 million, is the most expensive Spanish film ever made. His *Regression* (2015) starred Ethan Hawke and Emma Watson. Not content with directing, Amenábar also writes his own films.

Madrid-born Fernando Trueba (b 1955) has created some fine Spanish films, the best of which was his 1992 release *Belle Époque*. It portrays gentle romps and bed-hopping on a country estate in Spain in 1931 as four sisters pursue an ingenuous young chap against a background of growing political turbulence. *Belle Époque* took an Oscar for Best Foreign Language Film in 1993. His more recent works include *El baile de la victoria* (The Dancer & the Thief; 2009) and *El artista y la modelo* (The Artist & the Model; 2012). Trueba is equally well known for his documentary *Calle 54* (2000), which did for Latin jazz what the *Buena Vista Social Club* did for ageing Cuban musicians. Trueba was a leading personality in the craziness that was *la movida madrileña* (the Madrid scene) in the 1980s.

Actors

Of Spain's best-loved actors, few are enjoying international popularity quite like the Oscar-winning heart-throb Javier Bardem, one of the best-known faces in Spanish cinema. Having made his name alongside Penélope Cruz in *Jamón Jamón* (1992), his popular roles include those in *Before Night Falls* (2000), *Mar adentro* (The Sea Inside; 2004), *Love in the Time of Cholera* (2007) and *No Country for Old Men* (2007); remarkably his Oscar for Best Supporting Actor in 2008 was a first for Spanish actors. Like so many of Spain's best actors, Bardem has passed

Almodóvar's Madrid Locations

Plaza Mayor (*La flor de mi secreto*)

El Rastro (*Laberinto de pasiones*)

Villa Rosa (*Tacones lejanos*)

Café del Circulo de Bellas Artes (*Kika*)

Viaducto de Segovia (*Matador*)

PEDRO ALMODÓVAR

Born in 1951 in a small, impoverished village in Castilla-La Mancha, Almodóvar once remarked that in such conservative rural surrounds, 'I felt as if I'd fallen from another planet'. After he moved to Madrid in 1969 he found his spiritual home and began his career making underground Super 8 movies and by selling second-hand goods at El Rastro flea market. He soon became a symbol of Madrid's counterculture, but it was after Franco's death in 1975 that Almodóvar became a nationally renowned cult figure. His early films *Pepi, Luci, Bom y otras chicas del montón* (Pepi, Luci, Bom and the Other Girls; 1980) and *Laberinto de pasiones* (Labyrinth of Passion; 1982) – the film that brought a young Antonio Banderas to attention – announced him as the icon of *la movida madrileña,* the explosion of hedonism and creativity in the early years of post-Franco Spain. Almodóvar had both in bucketloads; he peppered his films with candy-bright colours and characters leading lives where sex and drugs were the norm. By night Almodóvar performed in Madrid's most famous *movida* bars as part of a drag act called 'Almodóvar & McNamara'. He even appears in this role in *Laberinto de pasione*s.

He went on to broaden his fan base with quirkily comic looks at modern Spain, generally set in the capital, such as *Mujeres al borde de un ataque de nervios (*Women on the Verge of a Nervous Breakdown; 1988) and *¡Átame!* (Tie Me Up! Tie Me Down!; 1990). Oscar-winning *Todo sobre mi madre* (All About My Mother; 1999) is also notable for the coming of age of the Madrid-born actress Penélope Cruz, who'd starred in a number of Almodóvar films and was considered part of a select group of the director's leading ladies long before she became a Hollywood star. Other outstanding movies in a formidable portfolio include *Hable con ella* (Talk to Her; 2002), for which he won a Best Original Screenplay Oscar; and *Volver* (2006), which reunited Almodóvar with Penélope Cruz to popular and critical acclaim.

through the finishing school that are Pedro Almodóvar's movies, appearing in *Carne trémula* (Live Flesh; 1997). Javier Bardem also comes from one of Spain's most distinguished film-making families: his uncle, Juan Antonio Bardem (1922–2002), is often considered Madrid's senior cinematic bard.

Penélope Cruz is another Hollywood actress with roots in Madrid (where she was born in 1974). In the late 1990s Penélope Cruz took a leap of faith and headed for Hollywood where she has had success in such films as *Captain Corelli's Mandolin* (2001) and *Vanilla Sky* (2001), but recognition of her acting abilities has come most powerfully for her roles in the Almodóvar classics *Carne trémula* (Live Flesh; 1997), *Todo sobre mi madre* (All About My Mother; 1999) and *Volver* (2006). The last was described by one critic as 'a raging love letter' to Cruz and earned her a Best Actress Oscar nomination, a remarkable achievement for a foreign-language film. She finally won an Oscar for Best Supporting Actress in 2009 for her role in Woody Allen's *Vicky Cristina Barcelona*.

Although not born in Madrid, Málaga-born Antonio Banderas moved to Madrid in 1981 at the age of 19 to launch his career and soon became caught up in the maelstrom of *la movida madrileña,* where he made the acquaintance of Almodóvar. After an early role in *Laberinto de pasiones* (Labyrinth of Passion; 1982), Banderas would return to the Almodóvar stable with *Mujeres al borde de un ataque de nervios* (Women on the Verge of a Nervous Breakdown; 1988), as his Hollywood career was taking off.

Flamenco

Flamenco seems to capture in musical form all the passion of this most passionate of countries. The power of flamenco is clear to anyone who has heard its melancholy strains in the background of a crowded Spanish bar and taking in a live performance can be a highlight of any visit to Madrid.

Flamenco's Roots

Flamenco's origins have been lost to time. While some experts have suggested that flamenco derives from Byzantine chants used in Visigothic churches, most musical historians speculate that it probably dates back to a fusion of songs brought to Spain by the Roma people, with music and verses from North Africa crossing into medieval Muslim Andalucía. Flamenco as we now know it first took recognisable form in the 18th and early 19th centuries among the Roma in the lower Guadalquivir valley in western Andalucía.

Flamenco in Madrid

At first the Roma and Andalucians were concentrated in the area around Calle de Toledo. The novelist Benito Pérez Galdós found no fewer than 88 Andalucian taverns along that street towards the end of the 19th century. The scene shifted in the early 20th century to the streets around Plaza de Santa Ana. As flamenco's appeal widened and became a tourist attraction, more *tablaos* (flamenco venues) sprang up throughout Madrid.

Now, Madrid claims to be Spain's capital of flamenco, which is true, but only to an extent. The Cádiz–Jerez–Seville axis in Andalucía remains the genre's spiritual home and it's still the area with the most authentic flamenco venues. But Madrid is undoubtedly flamenco's biggest stage, the place where the best performers of flamenco always turn up at one time or another. And therein lies the essence of Madrid's contribution to the development of flamenco: it has always been a stage, often a prestigious one, that has brought flamenco to a wider audience. Most Madrid venues may lack the intimate atmosphere and gritty authenticity that is an essential element of the flamenco experience, but the quality is usually excellent.

One of Spain's most prestigious flamenco festivals, Suma Flamenca (p23), happens in Madrid every June.

Flamenco Stars

Two names loom large over the world of flamenco – Paco de Lucía and El Camarón de la Isla. Both were responsible for flamenco's revival in the second half of the 20th century. Theirs is the standard by which all other flamenco artists are measured.

Paco de Lucía (1947–2014) was the doyen of flamenco guitarists with a virtuosity few could match. For many in the flamenco world, he was the personification of *duende,* that indefinable capacity to transmit the

Flamenco Resources

....

A good website for all things flamenco is www. deflamenco.com.

....

El Flamenco Vive, a store near Plaza Mayor, has a wide range of flamenco books and CDs.

Madrid Flamenco Venues

....

Villa Rosa – Plaza de Santa Ana

....

Casa Patas – Lavapiés

....

Las Tablas – Plaza de España

....

Corral de la Morería – La Latina

....

Las Carboneras – near Plaza Mayor

FLAMENCO – THE ESSENTIAL ELEMENTS

A flamenco singer is known as a *cantaor* (male) or *cantaora* (female); a dancer is a *bailaor/a*. Most of the songs and dances are performed to a blood-rush of guitar from the *tocaor/a* (male/female flamenco guitarist). Percussion is provided by tapping feet, clapping hands and sometimes castanets. Flamenco *coplas* (songs) come in many different types, from the anguished *soleá* or the intensely despairing *siguiriya* to the livelier *alegría* or the upbeat *bulería*. The first flamenco was *cante jondo* (deep song), an anguished instrument of expression for a group on the margins of society. *Jondura* (depth) is still the essence of pure flamenco.

power and passion of flamenco. Other guitar maestros include members of the Montoya family (some of whom are better known by the sobriquet of Los Habichuela), especially Juan (b 1933) and Pepe (b 1944).

In 1968 Paco de Lucía began flamenco's most exciting partnership with his friend El Camarón de la Isla (1950–92); together they recorded nine classic albums. Until his premature death, El Camarón was the leading light of contemporary *cante jondo* (deep song) and it's impossible to overstate his influence on the art; his introduction of electric bass into his songs, for example, paved the way for a generation of artists to take flamenco in hitherto unimagined directions. Although born in San Fernando in Andalucía's far south, El Camarón was the artist in residence at Madrid's Torres Bermejas for 12 years, and it was during this period that his collaboration with Paco de Lucía was at its best. In his later years El Camarón teamed up with Tomatito, one of Paco de Lucía's protégés, and the results were similarly ground-breaking. When El Camarón died in 1992 an estimated 100,000 people attended his funeral.

Another artist who reached the level of cult figure was Enrique Morente (1942–2010). Referred to by one Madrid paper as 'the last bohemian', Morente was careful not to alienate flamenco purists but through his numerous collaborations across genres he helped lay the foundations for Nuevo Flamenco and Fusion. His daughter, *cantaora* (flamenco singer) Estrella Morente (b 1980), is considered one of the genre's most exciting talents.

One of the most venerable *cantaoras* is Carmen Linares (b 1951), who has spent much of her working life in Madrid. Leading contemporary figures include the flighty, adventurous Joaquín Cortés (b 1969), and Antonio Canales (b 1962), who is more of a flamenco purist.

Top Flamenco Albums

Paco de Lucía Antología (1995)

Una Leyenda Flamenca (1993)

Blues de la Frontera (1986)

Cositas Buenas (2004)

Lágrimas Negras (2003)

Sueña la Alhambra (2005)

Nuevo Flamenco & Fusion

Two of the earliest groups to fuse flamenco with rock back in the 1980s were Ketama and Pata Negra, whose music is labelled by some as gypsy rock. In the early 1990s, Radio Tarifa emerged with a mesmerising mix of flamenco, North African and medieval sounds. A more traditional flamenco performer, Juan Peña Lebrijano, better known as El Lebrijano, has created some equally appealing combinations with classical Moroccan music. Diego El Cigala, one of modern flamenco's finest voices, relaunched his career with an exceptional collaboration with Cuban virtuoso Bebo Valdés (*Lágrimas Negras;* 2003) and has released critically acclaimed albums in the years since.

Chambao is the most popular of the Nuevo Flamenco bands doing the rounds at the moment, while Barcelona group Ojos de Brujo has won acclaim for its gritty sound. Also popular is Diego Amador (b 1973), a self-taught pianist. All of these artists perform in Madrid from time to time.

Survival Guide

Transport

ARRIVING IN MADRID

Madrid's Barajas Airport is one of Europe's busiest and is served by almost 100 airlines. Direct flights – whether with low-cost carriers or other airlines – connect the city with destinations across Europe. A smaller but nonetheless significant number of airlines also fly into Madrid direct from the Americas, Asia and Africa, and there are plenty of domestic flights to Madrid from other Spanish cities. Flight times include less than one hour to Lisbon and around two hours to London, Paris and some Moroccan cities.

Within Spain, Madrid is the hub of the country's outstanding bus and train network. Bus routes radiate into and out from the Spanish capital to all four corners of the country, and long-haul cross-border services fan out across Europe, with some also going to Morocco. The ongoing expansion of Spain's high-speed rail network has dramatically cut travel times between Madrid and the rest of the country. The rail link to Barcelona in particular has also brought Madrid that much closer to the rest of Europe and there are plans for a high-speed rail link between Paris and Madrid.

Flights, cars and tours can be booked online at lonelyplanet.com.

Aeropuerto de Barajas

Madrid's **Adolfo Suárez Madrid-Barajas Airport** ([✆]902 404704; www.aena. es; Ⓜ Aeropuerto T1, T2 & T3, Aeropuerto T4) lies 15km northeast of the city, and it's Europe's sixth-busiest hub, with almost 50 million passengers passing through here every year.

Barajas has four terminals. Terminal 4 (T4) deals mainly with flights of Iberia and its partners, while the remainder leave from the conjoined T1, T2 and (rarely) T3. To match your airline with a terminal, visit the Adolfo Suárez Madrid-Barajas section of www.aena.es and click on 'Airlines'.

Although all airlines conduct check-in (facturación) at the airport's departure areas, some also allow check-in at the Nuevos Ministerios metro stop and transport interchange in Madrid itself – ask your airline.

There are car-rental services, ATMs, money-exchange bureaux, pharmacies, tourist offices, left luggage offices and parking services at T1, T2 and T4.

Metro

The easiest way into town from the airport is line 8 of the metro to the Nuevos Ministerios transport interchange, which connects with lines 10 and 6 and the local overground cercanías (local trains serving suburbs and nearby towns). It operates from 6.05am to 1.30am. A single ticket costs €4.50 including the €3 airport supplement. If you're buying a 10-ride Metrobús ticket (€12.20), you'll need to top it up with the €3 supplement if you're travelling to/from the airport. The journey to Nuevos Ministerios takes around 15 minutes, around 25 minutes from T4.

Bus

Bus 203, the **Exprés Aeropuerto** (Airport Express; www. emtmadrid.es; €5), runs between Puerta de Atocha train station and the airport (40 minutes) 24 hours a day. From 11.30pm to 6am, departures are from the Plaza de Cibeles, not the train station. Departures take place every 13 to 20 minutes from the station or at night-time every 35 minutes from Plaza de Cibeles.

Alternatively from T1, T2 and T3 take bus 200 to/from the Intercambiador de Avenida de América (transport interchange on Avenida de América). The same ticket prices apply as for the metro. The first departures from the airport are at 5.10am (T1, T2 and T3). The last scheduled service from the airport is 11.30pm; buses leave every 12 to 20 minutes.

There's also a free bus service connecting all four terminals.

CLIMATE CHANGE & TRAVEL

Every form of transport that relies on carbon-based fuel generates CO_2, the main cause of human-induced climate change. Modern travel is dependent on aeroplanes, which might use less fuel per kilometre per person than most cars but travel much greater distances. The altitude at which aircraft emit gases (including CO_2) and particles also contributes to their climate change impact. Many websites offer 'carbon calculators' that allow people to estimate the carbon emissions generated by their journey and, for those who wish to do so, to offset the impact of the greenhouse gases emitted with contributions to portfolios of climate-friendly initiatives throughout the world. Lonely Planet offsets the carbon footprint of all staff and author travel.

Minibus

AeroCITY (☑902 151654, 91 747 75 70; www.aerocity.com; per person from €17.85, express service per minibus from €34) is a private minibus service that takes you door-to-door between central Madrid and the airport (T1 in front of arrivals gate 2, T2 between gates 5 and 6, and T4 arrivals hall). It operates 24 hours and you can book by phone or online. You can reserve a seat or the entire minibus; the latter operates like a taxi.

Taxi

A taxi to the centre (around 30 minutes, depending on traffic; 35 to 40 minutes from T4) costs a fixed €30 for anywhere inside the M-30 motorway (which includes all of downtown Madrid). There's a minimum €20, even if you're only going to an airport hotel.

Estación de Atocha

Madrid's main train station, the **Puerta de Atocha** (www.renfe.es; Ⓜ Atocha Renfe) sits at the southern end of the Paseo del Prado at the southern edge of the city centre. This is where most international, national and local cercanías trains arrive, including many high-speed AVE services.

Downstairs in the station there are ATMs, car-rental offices and a left luggage service.

Metro & Cercanías

The Atocha Renfe metro station (line 1; one-way/10-trip ticket €1.50/12.20), not to be confused with the nearby Atocha station, is inside the Renfe train station. From Atocha Renfe it's 10 to 15 minutes to Sol station, with connections elsewhere via lines 2 and 3. Buy tickets from machines at the station.

While the cercanías suburban rail network mostly services outlying suburbs, it does operate a useful service that connects Atocha Renfe with Sol, Nuevos Ministerios and Estación de Chamartín. If you have a connecting Renfe ticket, travel on the cercanías network is free. Buy your ticket by scanning your Renfe ticket bar code at one of the Renfe cercanías machines close to the platform exit.

Taxi

Taxis leave from the top floor of the station. A taxi to the centre (five to 10 minutes, depending on traffic) costs around €5 to €7.50, plus a €3 train station supplement.

Bus

Not as easy to decipher as the metro, numerous bus routes (one-way/10-trip ticket €1.50/12.20) pass close to the station. For route maps check the website of the **Empresa Municipal de Transportes de Madrid** (EMT; ☑902 507850; www.emtmadrid.es).

Estación de Chamartín

North of the city centre, **Estación de Chamartín** (☑902 432343; Ⓜ Chamartín) has numerous long-distance rail services, especially those to/from northern Spain. This is also where long-haul international trains arrive from Paris and Lisbon.

Metro & Cercanías

Chamartín station has its own metro station (lines 1 & 10; one-way/10-trip ticket €1.50/12.20). From Chamartín station to Sol takes from 15 to 20 minutes with connections elsewhere via lines 2 and 3. Buy tickets from machines at the station.

There's also a Chamartín–Nuevos Ministerios–Sol–Atocha cercanías service that's free if you have a connecting Renfe ticket. Again, there are dedicated machines for this service.

Taxi

A taxi to the centre (around 15 minutes, depending on traffic) costs around €10 plus a €3 train station supplement.

Bus

Numerous bus routes (one-way/10-trip ticket €1.50/12.20) pass close to the station. Check www.emtmadrid.es for route maps.

Estación Sur de Autobuses

Estación Sur de Autobuses (☎91 468 42 00; www.estaciondeautobuses.com; Calle de Méndez Álvaro 83; ⓜMéndez Álvaro), just south of the M-30 ring road, is the city's principal bus station. It serves most destinations to the south and many in other parts of the country. Most bus companies have a ticket office here, even if their buses depart from elsewhere.

Metro

The bus station's metro stop is Méndez Álvaro (line 6; one-way/10-trip ticket €1.50/12.20). To get to the central Sol station, take line 6 to Legazpi station and change to line 3. Buy tickets from machines at the station.

Taxi

A taxi to the centre (around 20 to 30 minutes, depending on traffic) costs around €10 to €15 plus a €3 bus station supplement.

GETTING AROUND MADRID

Madrid has an excellent public transport network. The most convenient way of getting around is via the metro, whose 11 lines criss-cross the city; no matter where you find yourself you're never far from a metro station. The bus network is equally extensive and operates under the same ticketing system, although the sheer number of routes (around 200!) makes it more difficult for first-time visitors to master. Taxis in Madrid are plentiful and relatively cheap by European standards.

Bicycle

Lots of people zip around town on *motos* (mopeds), but little has been done to encourage cyclists in Madrid and bike lanes are almost as rare as drivers who keep an eye out for cyclists.

You can transport your bicycle on the metro all day on Saturday and Sunday, and at any time from Monday to Friday except 7.30am to 9.30am, 2pm to 4pm and 6pm to 8pm. You can also take your bike aboard *cercanías* at any time.

Hire

Bike & Roll (☎91 142 77 93; www.bikeandroll.es; Av de Menédez Pelayo 2; per hr/day from €4/20; ◷10am-8pm Mon-Fri, 10am-2pm Sat; ⓘ; ⓜPríncipe de Vergara) Bike & Roll rents out bikes just off the northeastern corner of El Retiro.

Bike Spain (☎91 559 06 53; www.bikespain.info; Calle del Codo; bike rental half/full day from €12/18, tours from €35; ◷10am-2pm & 4-7pm Mon-Fri Apr-Oct, 10am-2pm & 3-6pm Mon-Fri Nov-Mar; ⓜÓpera) Bicycle hire plus English-language guided city tours by bicycle, by day or (Friday) night, as well as longer expeditions.

Trixi.com (www.trixi.com; Calle de los Jardines 12; 1/2/8/24hr €4/6/12/15, helmet €2.50; ◷10am-2pm & 4-8pm Mon-Fri, 10am-8pm Sat & Sun; ⓜGran Vía) Bicycle hire and cycling tours of central Madrid.

Bus

Buses operated by Empresa Municipal de Transportes de Madrid travel along most city routes regularly between about 6.30am and 11.30pm. Twenty-six night-bus *búhos* (owls) routes operate from 11.45pm to 5.30am, with all routes originating in Plaza de la Cibeles.

Fares for day and night trips are the same as for the metro: €1.50 for a single trip, €12.20 for a 10-trip Metrobús ticket. Single-trip tickets can be purchased on board.

Metro & Cercanías

Madrid's modern **metro** (www.metromadrid.es) is a fast, efficient and safe way to navigate Madrid, and generally easier than getting to grips with bus routes. There are 11 colour-coded lines in central Madrid, in addition to the modern southern suburban MetroSur system as well as lines heading east to the population centres of Pozuelo and Boadilla del Monte. Colour maps showing the metro system are available from any metro station or online. The metro operates from 6.05am to 1.30am.

The short-range *cercanías* regional trains operated by **Renfe** (☎902 320320; www.renfe.es/cercanias/madrid) are handy for making a quick, north–south hop between Chamartín and Atocha train stations (with stops at Nuevos Ministerios and Sol), or for the trip out to San Lorenzo de El Escorial.

Tickets

Unless you're only passing through en route elsewhere, you should buy a Metrobús ticket valid for 10 rides (bus and metro) for €12.20; single-journey tickets cost €1.50. Tickets can be purchased from machines in the metro stations, as well as most *estancos* (tobacconists) and newspaper kiosks. Metrobús tickets are not valid on *cercanías* services. Children under four travel free.

Monthly or season passes (*abonos*) only make sense if you're staying long term and use local transport frequently. You'll need to get a *carnet* (ID card) from metro stations or tobacconists – take a passport-sized photo and your passport. An **Abono Transporte Turístico** (Tourist Ticket; www.metromadrid.es; per 1/2/7 days €8.40/14.20/35.40) is also possible.

The fine for being caught without a ticket on public transport is €50, in addition to the price of the ticket.

Taxi

You can pick up a taxi at ranks throughout town or simply flag one down. Flag fall is €2.40 from 7am to 9pm daily, €2.90 from 9pm to 7am and all day Saturday and Sunday. You pay between €1.05 and €1.20 per kilometre depending on the time of day. Several supplementary charges, usually posted inside the taxi, apply; these include €5.50 to/from the airport (if you're not paying the fixed rate); €3 from taxi ranks at train and bus stations, €3 to/from the Parque Ferial Juan Carlos I; and €6.70 on New Year's Eve and Christmas Eve from 10pm to 6am. There's no charge for luggage.

Among the 24-hour taxi services are **Tele-Taxi** (☏91 371 21 31; www.tele-taxi.es) and **Radio-Teléfono Taxi** (☏91 547 82 00; www.radiotelefono-taxi.com).

A green light on the roof means the taxi is *libre* (available). Usually a sign to this effect is also placed in the lower passenger side of the windscreen.

Tipping taxi drivers is not common practice, although most travellers round fares up to the nearest euro or two.

TOURS

Bicycle tours of Madrid and surrounding areas are offered by **Bike Spain** (☏91 559 06 53; www.bikespain.info; Calle del Codo; bike rental half/full day from €12/18, tours from €35; ◷10am-2pm & 4-7pm Mon-Fri Apr-Oct, 10am-2pm & 3-6pm Mon-Fri Nov-Mar; Ⓜ Ópera) and **Trixi.com** (www.trixi.com; Calle de los Jardines 12; 1/2/8/24hr €4/6/12/15, helmet €2.50; ◷10am-2pm & 4-8pm Mon-Fri, 10am-8pm Sat & Sun; Ⓜ Gran Vía).

Insider's Madrid (☏91 447 38 66; www.insidersmadrid. com; from €70) An impressive range of tailor-made tours, including walking, shopping,

fashion, fine arts, tapas, flamenco and bullfighting tours.

Letango Tours (☏655 818740; www.letangospaintours.com; per person €135) Walking tours through Madrid with additional excursions to San Lorenzo de El Escorial, Segovia and Toledo.

Madrid City Tour (☏902 024758; www.madridcitytour. es; 1-/2-day ticket adult €21/25, child up to €10/13; ◷9am-10pm Mar-Oct, 10am-6pm Nov-Feb) Hop-on, hop-off open-topped buses that run every 10 to 20 minutes along two routes: one takes in the main highlights downtown, the other heads north along Paseo de la Castellana and returns via Salamanca. You can buy tickets online or on the bus. There are also two nocturnal departures from mid-June to mid-September.

Madrid Original (☏91 521 04 49; www.madridoriginal. com; €110-150) Privately run tours (for up to six people) in English, Spanish or French by professional guides. Tours include the major museums, historical eras, Gran Vía, the Parque del Buen Retiro and tailor-made itineraries.

Madrid Segway Tours (☏659 824499; www.madsegs. com; 3hr tour per person €65,

plus refundable deposit €15) Three-hour Segway tours.

Spanish Tapas Madrid (☏672 301231; www.spanishtapasmadrid.com; per person from €40) Local boy Luis Ortega takes you through some iconic Madrid tapas bars, as well as tours that take in Old Madrid, flamenco and the Prado.

Urban Movil (☏687 535443, 91 542 77 71; www.urbanmovil. com; Plaza Santiago 2; 1/2hr Segway tours €40/65; ◷10am-8pm; Ⓜ Ópera) Segway tours around Madrid; prices include 10 minutes' worth of training before you set out. It also organises bike tours.

Visitas Guiadas Oficiales (Official Guided Tours; ☏902 221424; www.esmadrid.com/programa-visitas-guiadas-oficiales; Plaza Mayor 27; per person €17-21; Ⓜ Sol) Over 40 highly recommended walking, cycling and roller-blade tours conducted in Spanish and English. Organised by the Centro de Turismo de Madrid. Stop by the office and pick up its *M – Visitas Guiadas/Guided Tours* catalogue.

Wellington Society (☏609 143203; www.wellsoc.org; €65-90) A handful of quirky historical tours laced with anecdotes and led by the inimitable Stephen Drake-Jones. Membership costs €65 and includes a day or evening walking tour.

Directory A–Z

Customs Regulations

People entering Spain from outside the EU are allowed to bring in duty-free one bottle of spirits, one bottle of wine, 50mL of perfume and 200 cigarettes. There are no duty-free allowances for travel between EU countries. For duty-paid items bought at normal shops in one EU country and taken into another, the allowances are 90L of wine, 10L of spirits, unlimited quantities of perfume and 800 cigarettes.

Discount Cards

➡ The **International Student Identity Card** (ISIC; www.isic.org), the **Euro<26 card** (www.euro26.org) and (sometimes) university student cards entitle you to discounts of up to 50% at many sights.

➡ If you're over 65, you may be eligible for an admission discount to some attractions. Some attractions limit discounts to those with a Seniors Card issued by an EU country or other country with which Spanish citizens enjoy reciprocal rights.

➡ If you plan to visit the Museo del Prado, Museo Thyssen-Bornemisza and Centro de Arte Reina Sofía while in Madrid, the Paseo del Arte ticket covers them all in a combined ticket for €25.60 and is valid for one visit to each gallery during a 12-month period; buying separate tickets would cost €32.

➡ If you intend to do some intensive sightseeing and travelling on public transport, consider the **Madrid Card** (☑91 360 47 72; www.madridcard.com; 1/2/3/5 days adult €47/60/67/77, child aged 6-12yr €34/42/44/47). It includes entry to over 50 museums in and around Madrid (including the Museo del Prado, Museo Thyssen-Bornemisza, Centro de Arte Reina Sofía, Estadio Santiago Bernabéu and Palacio Real), walking tours and discounts in a number of restaurants, shops and bars as well as discounts for car rental. The Madrid Card can be bought online (slightly cheaper), at the **Centro de Turismo de Madrid** (☑010, 91 454 44 10; www.esmadrid.com; Plaza Mayor 27; ⊙9.30am-8.30pm; @; MSol) or at any of the sales outlets listed on the website.

Electricity

The electric current in Madrid is 220/230V, 50Hz, as in the rest of continental Europe. Several countries outside Europe (such as the USA and Canada) use 110V, 60Hz, which means that it's safest to use a transformer.

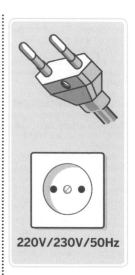

220V/230V/50Hz

Emergency

Servicio de Atención al Turista Extranjero (Foreign Tourist Assistance Service; ☑91 548 80 08, 91 548 85 37; www.esmadrid.com/informacion-turistica/sate; Calle de Leganitos 19; ⊙9am-midnight; MPlaza de España, Santo Domingo) To report thefts or other crime-related matters, your best bet is the Servicio de Atención al Turista Extranjero, which is housed in the central police station or comisaría of the National Police. Here you'll find specially trained officers working alongside representatives from the Tourism Ministry. They can also assist in cancelling credit cards, as well as contacting your embassy or your family. There's also a general number (☎902 102 112; 24-hour English and Spanish, 8am to midnight other languages) for reporting crimes.

Ambulance (☎061)

EU Standard Emergency Number (☎112) Your first port of call for most emergency situations.

Fire Brigade (Bomberos; ☎080)

Local Police (Policía Municipal; ☎092)

Military Police (Guardia Civil; ☎062) For traffic accidents.

Policía Nacional (☎091)

Teléfono de la Víctima (☎902 180995) Hotline for victims of racial or sexual violence.

Gay & Lesbian Travellers

In 2005 the Socialist president, José Luis Rodríguez Zapatero, gave the country's conservative Catholic foundations a shake with the legalisation of same-sex marriages in Spain.

Long before that, Madrid had always been one of Europe's most gay-friendly cities. The city's gay community is credited with reinvigorating the once down-at-heel inner-city *barrio* (district) of Chueca, where Madrid didn't just come out of the closet, it ripped the doors off in the process. Today the *barrio* is one of Madrid's most vibrant and it's very much the heart and soul of gay Madrid, with cafes, bars, hotels, shops and nightclubs clearly oriented to a gay clientele. But there's nothing ghetto-like about Chueca. Its extravagantly gay-and-lesbian personality is anything but exclusive and the crowd is almost always mixed gay-straight. As gay and lesbian residents like to say, Chueca isn't gay-friendly, it's hetero-friendly.

The best time of all to be in town if you're gay or lesbian is around the last Saturday in June for Madrid's gay and lesbian pride march, Orgullo Gay.

Websites

Chueca.com (www.chueca.com) Useful gay portal with extensive links.

Gay Iberia (www.gayiberia.com) Gay guides to Barcelona, Madrid, Sitges and 26 other Spanish cities.

Gay Madrid 4 U (www.gaymadrid4u.com) A good overview of Madrid's gay bars and nightclubs.

Guía Gay de España (guai.universosogay.com) A little bit of everything.

LesboNet (www.lesbonet.org) Lesbian forums, chat and news.

NightTours.com (www.nighttours.com) A reasonably good guide to gay nightlife and other attractions in Madrid, Barcelona and seven other Spanish locations.

Shangay (www.shangay.com) For news, upcoming events, reviews and contacts. It also publishes *Shanguide*, a Madrid-centric biweekly magazine jammed with listings (including saunas and hardcore clubs) and contact ads. Its companion publication *Shangay Express* is better for articles with a handful of listings and ads. They're available in gay bookshops and in gay and gay-friendly bars.

Organisations

Colectivo de Gais y Lesbianas de Madrid (Cogam; ☎91 523 00 70, 91 522 45 17; www.cogam.es; Calle de la Puebla 9; ◷10am-2pm & 5-9pm Mon-Fri; ⓂCallao, Gran Vía) Offers activities, has an information office and social centre.

Federación Estatal de Lesbianas, Gays, Transexuales & Bisexuales (☎91 360 46 05; www.felgtb.org; 4th fl, Calle de las Infantas 40; ◷8am-8pm Mon-Thu, 8am-3.30pm Fri; ⓂGran Vía) A national advocacy group, based in Madrid; it played a leading role in lobbying for the legalisation of gay marriages.

PRACTICALITIES

➡ **Currency** Euro (€)

➡ **Weights & Measures** Metric

➡ **Electric Current** 220/230V, 50Hz

➡ **Plugs** European-style, two-pin

➡ **Newspapers** Centre-left *El País* (www.elpais.com); centre-right *El Mundo* (www.elmundo.es); right-wing *ABC* (www.abc.es). The widely available *New York Times International Edition* includes an eight-page supplement of articles from *El País* translated into English (elpais.com/elpais/inenglish.html).

Fundación Triángulo
(☑91 593 05 40; www.
fundaciontriangulo.org; 1st
fl, Calle de Meléndez Valdés
52; ⊙10am-2pm & 4-8pm
Mon-Fri; Ⓜ Argüelles) One of
several sources of information
on gay issues in Madrid; it has
a separate information line,
Información LesGai (☑91 446
63 94).

Internet Access

Most of Madrid's internet
cafes have fallen by the
wayside. You'll find plenty of
small *locutorios* (small shops
selling phone cards and
cheap phone calls) all over
the city and many have a few
computers out the back, but
we don't list these as they
come and go with monoto-
nous regularity.

In the downtown area,
your best option is the Ayuntamiento's **Centro de Turismo de Madrid** (☑010, 91
454 44 10; www.esmadrid.com;
Plaza Mayor 27; ⊙9.30am-
8.30pm; @; Ⓜ Sol) on Plaza
Mayor, which offers free
internet for up to 15 minutes;
its quieter branch beneath
Plaza de Colón also offers
free access.

Medical Services

All foreigners have the
same right as Spaniards to
emergency medical treat-
ment in a public hospital.
EU citizens are entitled to
the full range of health-care
services in public hospitals

free of charge, but you'll
need to present your European Health Insurance Card
(EHIC); enquire at your national health service before
leaving home. Even if you
have no insurance, you'll be
treated in an emergency,
with costs in the public
system ranging from free to
€150 for a basic consultation. Non-EU citizens have
to pay for anything other
than emergency treatment
– one good reason among
many to have a travel-
insurance policy. If you have
a specific health complaint,
obtain the necessary in-
formation and referrals for
treatment before leaving
home.

**Hospital General Grego-
rio Marañón** (☑91 586 80
00; www.hggm.es; Calle del
Doctor Esquerdo 46; Ⓜ Sáinz
de Baranda, O'Donnell, Ibiza)
One of the city's main (and
more central) hospitals.

Unidad Medica (Anglo
American; ☑91 435 18 23;
www.unidadmedica.com; Calle
del Conde de Aranda 1; ⊙9am-
8pm Mon-Fri, 10am-1pm Sat;
Ⓜ Retiro) A private clinic with
a wide range of specialisations
and where all doctors speak
Spanish and English, with some
also speaking French and German. Each consultation costs
around €125.

Pharmacies

For minor health problems,
you can try your local *farmacia* (pharmacy), where phar-
maceuticals tend to be sold
more freely without prescrip-
tion than in other countries

such as the US, Australia or
the UK.

At least one pharmacy
is open 24 hours per day in
each district of Madrid. They
mostly operate on a rota and
details appear daily in *El País*
and other newspapers. Otherwise call ☑010. Most pharmacies have a list in their
windows indicating the location of nearby after-hours
pharmacies – if it says 'Dia y
noche', it's open 24 hours.

Farmacia Mayor (☑91 366
46 16; Calle Mayor 13; ⊙24hr;
Ⓜ Sol) Open around the clock
and couldn't be more central.

Farmacia Velázquez 70
(☑91 575 60 28; Calle de
Velázquez 70; ⊙24hr; Ⓜ Velázquez) Pharmacy in the
Salamanca neighbourhood.

Money

The easiest way to travel is
to take a small amount of
cash and withdraw money
from ATMs as you go along.

Changing Money

You can change cash or
travellers cheques in cur-
rencies of the developed
world without problems at
virtually any bank or bureau
de change (usually indicated
by the word *cambio*). Central
Madrid also abounds with
banks – most have ATMs

Exchange offices are open
for longer hours than banks
but generally offer poorer
rates. Also, keep a sharp eye
open for commissions at
bureaux de change.

Credit Cards & ATMs

Major cards, such as Visa,
MasterCard, Maestro,
Cirrus and, to a lesser extent, Amex, are accepted
throughout Spain. They
can be used in many hotels,
restaurants and shops; in
doing so you'll need to show
some form of photo ID (eg
passport) or, increasingly,
you'll be asked to key in your
PIN. Credit cards can also be

WI-FI ACCESS

Most midrange and top-end hotels have either wi-fi or
cable ADSL in-room connections; however, even some
of the better hotels can run out of cables for the latter,
so ask for one as soon as you arrive.

You can also get online at some cafes and restaurants around the city.

Alternatively, check out www.madridmemata.es/
madrid-wifi for a reasonable list of wi-fi hot spots.

used in ATMs displaying the appropriate sign (if there's no sign, don't risk it), or, if you have no PIN, you can obtain cash advances over the counter in many banks. Check charges with your bank.

If your card is lost, stolen or swallowed by an ATM, you can call the following numbers toll-free to have an immediate stop put on its use:

Amex (☑902 814500)

Diners Club (☑900 801331, 91 211 43 00)

MasterCard (☑900 971231)

Visa (☑900 991124)

Opening Hours

➡ **Banks** 8.30am to 2pm Monday to Friday; some also open 4pm to 7pm Thursday

➡ **Central post offices** 8.30am to 9.30pm Monday to Friday, 8.30am to 2pm Saturday

➡ **Nightclubs** midnight or 1am to 5am or 6am

➡ **Restaurants** 1pm to 4pm and 8.30pm to midnight or later

➡ **Shops** 10am to 2pm & 4.30pm to 7.30pm or 5pm to 8pm Monday to Saturday; some bigger shops don't close for lunch and many shops open on some Sundays, usually from 11am or noon to 7pm or 8pm

Post

Correos (☑902 197197; www.correos.es), the national postal service, has its **main office** (☑91 523 06 94; Paseo del Prado 1; ☺8.30am-9.30pm Mon-Fri, 8.30am-2pm Sat; Ⓜ Banco de España) in the ornate Palacio de Comunicaciones.

Public Holidays

Madrid's 14 public holidays are as follows:

Año Nuevo (New Year's Day) 1 January

Reyes (Epiphany or Three Kings' Day) 6 January

Jueves Santo (Holy Thursday) March/April

Viernes Santo (Good Friday) March/April

Labour Day (Fiesta del Trabajo) 1 May

Fiesta de la Comunidad de Madrid 2 May

Fiestas de San Isidro Labrador 15 May

La Asunción (Feast of the Assumption) 15 August

Día de la Hispanidad (Spanish National Day) 12 October – a fairly sober occasion with a military parade along the Paseo de la Castellana

Todos los Santos (All Saints' Day) 1 November

Día de la Virgen de la Almudena 9 November

Día de la Constitución (Constitution Day) 6 December

La Inmaculada Concepción (Feast of the Immaculate Conception) 8 December

Navidad (Christmas) 25 December

Safe Travel

Madrid is a generally safe city, although you should, as in most European cities, be wary of pickpockets on transport and around major tourist sights. Although you should be careful, don't be paranoid; remember that the overwhelming majority of travellers to Madrid rarely encounter any problems.

You're most likely to fall foul of pickpockets in the most heavily touristed parts of town, notably the Plaza Mayor and surrounding streets, the Puerta del Sol, El Rastro and around the Museo del Prado. Tricks abound. They usually involve a team of two or more (sometimes one of them an attractive woman to distract male victims). While one attracts your attention, the other empties your pockets. Be wary of jostling on crowded buses and the metro and, as a general rule, dark, empty streets are to be avoided; luckily, Madrid's most lively nocturnal areas are generally busy with crowds having a good time.

Telephone

Mobile (cell) phone numbers start with ☑6. Numbers starting with ☑900 are national toll-free numbers, while those starting ☑901 to ☑905 come with varying conditions. A common one is ☑902, which is a national standard-rate number, but which can only be dialled from within Spain. In a similar category are numbers starting with ☑800, ☑803, ☑806 and ☑807.

Mobile Phones

You can buy SIM cards and prepaid time in Spain for your mobile phone (provided you own a GSM, dual- or tri-band cellular phone). This only works if your national phone hasn't been code-blocked; check before leaving home. Only consider a full contract if you plan to live in Spain for a while.

All the Spanish mobile phone companies (Telefónica's MoviStar, Orange, Vodafone and Amena) offer *prepagado* (prepaid) accounts for mobiles. The SIM card costs from €50, which includes some prepaid phone time. Phone outlets are scattered across the city. You can then top up in their shops or by buying cards in outlets, such as *estancos* (tobacconists) and news-stands.

You can rent a mobile phone through the Madrid-based **OnSpanishTime.com** (www.onspanishtime.com/web). Delivery and pick-up start from US$5. The basic service costs US$6/32/99 per day/

week/month for the phone. You pay a US$100 deposit and the whole operation is done over the internet.

Phonecards

For international calls you have two cut-price options. Most internet cafes are Skype enabled, allowing you to call (with your Skype user ID and password) for no more than the cost of your internet time. The other option is an international phonecard, which can be bought from *estancos*, some small convenience stores and newsstands in central Madrid. Most outlets display the call rates for each card. For calls to Australia, the US or Western Europe, some €6 phonecards give you more than 600 minutes of call time (plus the cost of the local call) or more than 200 minutes calling a toll-free local number.

Phone Codes

➡ International access code (⌨00)

➡ Spain country code (⌨34)

Useful Numbers

➡ International directory enquiries (⌨11825)

➡ International operator and reverse charges (collect) – Europe (⌨1008)

➡ International operator and reverse charges (collect) – rest of the world (⌨1005)

Time

Like most of Western Europe, Madrid is one hour ahead of Greenwich Mean Time/Coordinated Universal Time (GMT/UTC) during winter, two hours during the daylight-saving period from the last Sunday in March to the last Sunday in October. Spaniards use the 24-hour clock for official business (timetables etc), but often in daily conversation switch to the 12-hour version.

Toilets

Public toilets are almost nonexistent in Madrid and it's not really the done thing to go into a bar or cafe solely to use the toilet; ordering a quick coffee is a small price to pay for relieving the problem. Otherwise you can usually get away with it in a larger, crowded place where they can't really keep track of who's coming and going. Another option is the department stores of El Corte Inglés that are dotted around the city.

Tourist Information

Ayuntamiento de Madrid

Centro de Turismo de Madrid (⌨010, 91 454 44 10; www.esmadrid.com; Plaza Mayor 27; ☺9.30am-8.30pm; @; Ⓜ Sol) The Madrid government's Centro de Turismo is terrific. Housed in the Real Casa de la Panadería on the north side of the Plaza Mayor, it allows free access to its outstanding website and city database, and offers free downloads of the metro map to your mobile; staff are helpful.

Centro de Turismo Colón (www.esmadrid.com; Plaza de Colón 1; ☺9.30am-8.30pm; Ⓜ Colón) A small, subterranean tourist office, accessible via the underground stairs on the corner of Calle de Goya and the Paseo de la Castellana.

Punto de Información Turística de Cibeles (www. esmadrid.com; Plaza de la Cibeles; ☺9.30am-8.30pm; Ⓜ Banco de España)

Punto de Información Turística CentroCentro (www.esmadrid.com; Plaza de la Cibeles 1; ☺10am-8pm Tue-Sun; Ⓜ Banco de España)

Punto de Información Turística del Paseo del Arte (www.esmadrid.com; cnr Calle de Santa Isabel & Plaza del Emperador Carlos V; ☺9.30am-8.30pm; Ⓜ Atocha)

Punto de Información Turística Adolfo Suárez Madrid-Barajas T2 (www. esmadrid.com; between salas 5 & 6; ☺9am-8pm)

Punto de Información Turística Adolfo Suárez Madrid-Barajas T4 (www. esmadrid.com; salas 10 & 11; ☺9am-8pm)

Comunidad de Madrid

The regional Comunidad de Madrid government chips in with a helpful website (www. turismomadrid.es) covering the city and surrounding region.

Travellers with Disabilities

Although things are slowly changing, Madrid remains something of an obstacle course for travellers with a disability. Audio loops for the hearing impaired in cinemas are almost nonexistent, although most Spanish TV channels allow you to turn on subtitles.

Accessibility

Your first stop for more information on accessibility for travellers should be the Madrid tourist office website section known as **Accessible Madrid** (www.esmadrid. com/en/madrid-accesible), where you can download a PDF of its excellent, 421-page *Guia de Turismo Accesible* in English or Spanish. It has an exhaustive list of the city's attractions and transport and a detailed assessment of their accessibility, as well as a list of accessible restaurants.

For hotels and *hostales* (budget hotels) go to 'Alojamientos Accesibles' to download its similarly excellent *Guía de Alojamiento Accesible*.

Museo Tiflológico (Museum for the Blind; ☑91 589 42 19; museo.once.es; Calle de la Coruña 18; ☺10am-2pm & 5-8pm Tue-Fri, 10am-2pm Sat 1st half of Aug, closed 2nd half of Aug; ⓜEstrecho) One attraction specifically for visually impaired travellers and Spaniards is the Museo Tiflológico. Run by the Organización Nacional de Ciegos Españoles (ONCE; National Organisation for the Blind), its exhibits (all of which may be touched) include paintings, sculptures and tapestries, as well as more than 40 scale models of world monuments, including Madrid's Palacio Real and Cibeles fountain, as well as La Alhambra in Granada and the aqueduct in Segovia. It also provides leaflets in Braille and audioguides to the museum.

Guided Tours

The tourist office's program of guided tours includes tours for blind, deaf and wheelchair-bound travellers, as well as travellers with an intellectual disability. On the 'Madrid Accesible' section of www.esmadrid.com click on 'Visitas Guiadas Oficiales Adaptadas' for a PDF of upcoming tours.

Transport

When it comes to transport, metro lines built (or upgraded) since the late 1990s generally have elevators for wheelchair access, but the older lines can be ill equipped; the updated metro maps available from any metro station (or at www.metromadrid.es) show stations with wheelchair access. Remember, however, that not all platforms will necessarily have functioning escalators or elevators, even in supposedly wheelchair-accessible stations. On board the metro the name of the next station is usually announced (if the broadcast system is working...).

The single-deck *piso bajo* (low floor) buses have no steps inside and in some cases have ramps that can be used by people in wheelchairs. In the long term, there are plans to make at least 50 of the buses on all routes accessible to people with a disability.

Radio-Teléfono Taxi (☑91 547 82 00; www.radio-telefono-taxi.com) runs taxis for people with a disability in addition to standard taxis. Generally, if you call any taxi company and ask for a 'eurotaxi' you should be sent one adapted for wheelchair users.

Further Information

Accessible Travel & Leisure (www.accessibletravel.co.uk) Outside Spain, Accessible Travel & Leisure claims to be the biggest UK travel agent dealing with travel for people with a disability and encourages independent travel. Might be able to offer Madrid-specific advice.

Fesorcam (Federación de Personas Sordas de la Comunidad de Madrid; ☑91 725 37 57; www.fesorcam.org; Calle de Florestan Aguilar, 11 Bajo D; ⓜManuel Becerra, Ventas) Hearing-impaired travellers can contact the Comunidad de Madrid's Federation for the Deaf, Fesorcam. It also runs guided tours of Madrid for the hearing impaired.

FEAPS Madrid (Federación de Organizaciones en favor de Personas con Discapacidad Intelectual; ☑91 501 83 35; www.feapsmadrid.org; Av de la Ciudad de Barcelona 108; ⓜMenéndez Pelayo) Travellers with an intellectual disability may wish to contact FEAPS Madrid.

ONCE (Organización Nacional de Ciegos Españoles; ☑91 532 50 00, 91 577 37 56; www.once.es; Calle de Prim 3; ⓜChueca, Colón) The Spanish association for the blind. You may be able to get hold of guides in Braille to Madrid, although they're not published every year.

Visas

Spain is one of 26 member countries of the Schengen Convention, under which EU member countries (except the UK and Ireland) plus Switzerland, Iceland and Norway have abolished checks at common borders. Legal residents of one Schengen country do not require a visa for another Schengen country. Citizens of the UK and Ireland are also exempt. Nationals of many other countries, including Australia, Canada, Israel, Japan, New Zealand and the US, do not require visas for tourist visits of up to 90 days every six calendar months. All non-EU nationals entering Spain for any reason other than tourism (such as study or work) should contact a Spanish consulate, as they may need a specific visa.

If you're a citizen of a non-Schengen country, check with a Spanish consulate about whether you need a visa. The standard tourist visa issued by Spanish consulates (and usually valid for all Schengen countries unless conditions are attached) is valid for up to 90 days and is not renewable inside Spain.

Language

Spanish (*español*) – or Castilian (*castellano*), as it's also called – belongs to the Romance language family, with Portuguese, Italian and French as its close relatives. It has more than 390 million speakers worldwide.

Most Spanish sounds are pronounced the same as their English counterparts. If you read our coloured pronunciation guides as if they were English, you won't have problems being understood. Note that the kh is a guttural sound (like the 'ch' in the Scottish *loch*), r is strongly rolled, ly is pronounced as the 'lli' in 'million' and ny as the 'ni' in 'onion'. In our pronunciation guides, the stressed syllables are in italics.

Where necessary in this chapter, masculine and feminine forms are marked as 'm/f', while polite and informal options are indicated by the abbreviations 'pol' and 'inf'.

BASICS

Hello.	Hola.	o·la
Goodbye.	Adiós.	a·dyos
How are you?	¿Qué tal?	ke tal
Fine, thanks.	Bien, gracias.	byen gra·thyas
Excuse me.	Perdón.	per·don
Sorry.	Lo siento.	lo syen·to
Yes./No.	Sí./No.	see/no
Please.	Por favor.	por fa·vor
Thank you.	Gracias.	gra·thyas
You're welcome.	De nada.	de na·da

WANT MORE?

For in-depth language information and handy phrases, check out Lonely Planet's *Spanish phrasebook*. You'll find it at **shop. lonelyplanet.com**, or you can buy Lonely Planet's iPhone phrasebooks at the Apple App Store.

My name is ...

Me llamo ...	me *lya*·mo ...

What's your name?

¿Cómo se llama Usted?	ko·mo se *lya*·ma oo·*ste* (pol)
¿Cómo te llamas?	ko·mo te *lya*·mas (inf)

Do you speak English?

¿Habla inglés?	a·bla een·*gles* (pol)
¿Hablas inglés?	a·blas een·*gles* (inf)

I don't understand.

No entiendo.	no en·*tyen*·do

ACCOMMODATION

guesthouse	pensión	pen·*syon*
hotel	hotel	o·*tel*
youth hostel	albergue juvenil	al·*ber*·ge khoo·ve·*neel*
I'd like a ... room.	Quisiera una habitación ...	kee·*sye*·ra oo·na a·bee·ta·*thyon* ...
double	doble	*do*·ble
single	individual	een·dee·vee·*dwal*
air-con	aire acondicionado	*ai*·re a·kon·dee·thyo·*na*·do
bathroom	baño	*ba*·nyo
bed	cama	*ka*·ma
window	ventana	ven·*ta*·na

How much is it per night/person?

¿Cuánto cuesta por noche/persona?	*kwan*·to *kwes*·ta por *no*·che/per·*so*·na

Does it include breakfast?

¿Incluye el desayuno?	een·*kloo*·ye el de·sa·*yoo*·no

DIRECTIONS

Where's ...?

¿Dónde está ...?	*don*·de es·*ta* ...

What's the address?

¿Cuál es la dirección?	kwal es la dee·rek·*thyon*

Can you please write it down?
¿Puede escribirlo, pwe·de es·kree·*beer*·lo
por favor? por fa·*vor*

Can you show me (on the map)?
¿Me lo puede indicar me lo pwe·de een·dee·*kar*
(en el mapa)? (en el *ma*·pa)

at the corner	*en la esquina*	en la es·*kee*·na
at the traffic lights	*en el semáforo*	en el se·*ma*·fo·ro
behind ...	*detrás de ...*	de·*tras* de ...
far away	*lejos*	*le*·khos
in front of ...	*enfrente de ...*	en·*fren*·te de ...
left	*izquierda*	eeth·*kyer*·da
near	*cerca*	*ther*·ka
next to ...	*al lado de ...*	al *la*·do de ...
opposite ...	*frente a ...*	*fren*·te a ...
right	*derecha*	de·re·cha
straight ahead	*todo recto*	*to*·do rek·to

EATING & DRINKING

What would you recommend?
¿Qué recomienda? ke re·ko·*myen*·da

What's in that dish?
¿Que lleva ese plato? ke *lye*·va e·se *pla*·to

I don't eat ...
No como ... no *ko*·mo ...

Cheers!
¡Salud! sa·*loo*

That was delicious!
¡Estaba buenísimo! es·*ta*·ba bwe·*nee*·see·mo

Please bring us the bill.
Por favor, nos trae por fa·*vor* nos *tra*·e
la cuenta. la *kwen*·ta

I'd like to book a table for ...	*Quisiera reservar una mesa para ...*	kee·*sye*·ra re·ser·*var* oo·na *me*·sa *pa*·ra ...
(eight) o'clock	*las (ocho)*	las (*o*·cho)
(two) people	*(dos) personas*	(dos) per·*so*·nas

Key Words

appetisers	*aperitivos*	a·pe·ree·*tee*·vos
bar	*bar*	bar
bottle	*botella*	bo·*te*·lya
bowl	*bol*	bol
breakfast	*desayuno*	de·sa·*yoo*·no
cafe	*café*	ka·*fe*
(too) cold	*(muy) frío*	(mooy) *free*·o
dinner	*cena*	*the*·na

KEY PATTERNS

To get by in Spanish, mix and match these simple patterns with words of your choice:

When's (the next flight)?
¿Cuándo sale kwan·do sa·le
(el próximo vuelo)? (el prok·see·mo vwe·lo)

Where's (the station)?
¿Dónde está don·de es·*ta*
(la estación)? (la es·ta·*thyon*)

Where can I (buy a ticket)?
¿Dónde puedo don·de pwe·do
(comprar (kom·prar
un billete)? oon bee·*lye*·te)

Do you have (a map)?
¿Tiene (un mapa)? tye·ne (oon *ma*·pa)

Is there (a toilet)?
¿Hay (servicios)? ai (ser·*vee*·thyos)

I'd like (a coffee).
Quisiera (un café). kee·*sye*·ra (oon ka·*fe*)

I'd like (to hire a car).
Quisiera (alquilar kee·*sye*·ra (al·kee·*lar*
un coche). oon *ko*·che)

Can I (enter)?
¿Se puede (entrar)? se pwe·de (en·*trar*)

Can you please (help me)?
¿Puede (ayudarme), pwe·de (a·yoo·*dar*·me)
por favor? por fa·*vor*

Do I have to (get a visa)?
¿Necesito ne·the·*see*·to
(obtener (ob·te·*ner*
un visado)? oon vee·*sa*·do)

food	*comida*	ko·*mee*·da
fork	*tenedor*	te·ne·*dor*
glass	*vaso*	*va*·so
highchair	*trona*	*tro*·na
hot (warm)	*caliente*	ka·*lyen*·te
knife	*cuchillo*	koo·*chee*·lyo
lunch	*comida*	ko·*mee*·da
main course	*segundo plato*	se·*goon*·do *pla*·to
market	*mercado*	mer·*ka*·do
(children's) menu	*menú (infantil)*	me·*noo* (een·fan·*teel*)
plate	*plato*	*pla*·to
restaurant	*restaurante*	res·tow·*ran*·te
spoon	*cuchara*	koo·*cha*·ra
supermarket	*supermercado*	soo·per·mer·*ka*·do
vegetarian food	*comida vegetariana*	ko·*mee*·da ve·khe·ta·*rya*·na
with/without	*con/sin*	kon/sin

Meat & Fish

beef	carne de vaca	kar·ne de va·ka
chicken	pollo	po·lyo
cod	bacalao	ba·ka·la·o
duck	pato	pa·to
lamb	cordero	kor·de·ro
lobster	langosta	lan·gos·ta
pork	cerdo	ther·do
prawns	camarones	ka·ma·ro·nes
salmon	salmón	sal·mon
tuna	atún	a·toon
turkey	pavo	pa·vo
veal	ternera	ter·ne·ra

Fruit & Vegetables

apple	manzana	man·tha·na
apricot	albaricoque	al·ba·ree·ko·ke
artichoke	alcachofa	al·ka·cho·fa
asparagus	espárragos	es·pa·ra·gos
banana	plátano	pla·ta·no
beans	judías	khoo·dee·as
beetroot	remolacha	re·mo·la·cha
cabbage	col	kol
(red/green) capsicum	pimiento (rojo/verde)	pee·myen·to (ro·kho/ver·de)
carrot	zanahoria	tha·na·o·rya
celery	apio	a·pyo
cherry	cereza	the·re·tha
corn	maíz	ma·eeth
cucumber	pepino	pe·pee·no
fruit	fruta	froo·ta
grape	uvas	oo·vas
lemon	limón	lee·mon
lentils	lentejas	len·te·khas
lettuce	lechuga	le·choo·ga
mushroom	champiñón	cham·pee·nyon
nuts	nueces	nwe·thes
onion	cebolla	the·bo·lya
orange	naranja	na·ran·kha
peach	melocotón	me·lo·ko·ton
peas	guisantes	gee·san·tes
pineapple	piña	pee·nya
plum	ciruela	theer·we·la
potato	patata	pa·ta·ta
pumpkin	calabaza	ka·la·ba·sa
spinach	espinacas	es·pee·na·kas

strawberry	fresa	fre·sa
tomato	tomate	to·ma·te
vegetable	verdura	ver·doo·ra
watermelon	sandía	san·dee·a

Other

bread	pan	pan
butter	mantequilla	man·te·kee·lya
cheese	queso	ke·so
egg	huevo	we·vo
honey	miel	myel
jam	mermelada	mer·me·la·da
oil	aceite	a·they·te
pepper	pimienta	pee·myen·ta
rice	arroz	a·roth
salt	sal	sal
sugar	azúcar	a·thoo·kar
vinegar	vinagre	vee·na·gre

Drinks

beer	cerveza	ther·ve·tha
coffee	café	ka·fe
(orange) juice	zumo (de naranja)	thoo·mo (de na·ran·kha)
milk	leche	le·che
red wine	vino tinto	vee·no teen·to
sparkling wine	vino espumoso	vee·no es·poo·mo·so
tea	té	te
(mineral) water	agua (mineral)	a·gwa (mee·ne·ral)
white wine	vino blanco	vee·no blan·ko

EMERGENCIES

| Help! | ¡Socorro! | so·ko·ro |
| Go away! | ¡Vete! | ve·te |

Signs

Abierto	Open
Cerrado	Closed
Entrada	Entrance
Hombres	Men
Mujeres	Women
Prohibido	Prohibited
Salida	Exit
Servicios/Aseos	Toilets

Call …!	¡Llame a …!	lya·me a …
a doctor	un médico	oon me·dee·ko
the police	la policía	la po·lee·thee·a

I'm lost.
Estoy perdido/a.   es·toy per·dee·do/a (m/f)

I'm ill.
Estoy enfermo/a.   es·toy en·fer·mo/a (m/f)

It hurts here.
Me duele aquí.   me dwe·le a·kee

I'm allergic to (antibiotics).
Soy alérgico/a a   soy a·ler·khee·ko/a a
(los antibióticos).   (los an·tee·byo·tee·kos) (m/f)

Where are the toilets?
¿Dónde están los   don·de es·tan los
servicios?   ser·vee·thyos

SHOPPING & SERVICES

I'd like to buy …
Quisiera comprar …   kee·sye·ra kom·prar …

I'm just looking.
Sólo estoy mirando.   so·lo es·toy mee·ran·do

Can I look at it?
¿Puedo verlo?   pwe·do ver·lo

I don't like it.
No me gusta.   no me goos·ta

How much is it?
¿Cuánto cuesta?   kwan·to kwes·ta

That's too expensive.
Es muy caro.   es mooy ka·ro

Can you lower the price?
¿Podría bajar un   po·dree·a ba·khar oon
poco el precio?   po·ko el pre·thyo

There's a mistake in the bill.
Hay un error en   ai oon e·ror en
la cuenta.   la kwen·ta

ATM	cajero automático	ka·khe·ro ow·to·ma·tee·ko
credit card	tarjeta de crédito	tar·khe·ta de kre·dee·to
internet cafe	cibercafé	thee·ber·ka·fe
post office	correos	ko·re·os
tourist office	oficina de turismo	o·fee·thee·na de too·rees·mo

Question Words		
How?	¿Cómo?	ko·mo
What?	¿Qué?	ke
When?	¿Cuándo?	kwan·do
Where?	¿Dónde?	don·de
Who?	¿Quién?	kyen
Why?	¿Por qué?	por ke

TIME & DATES

What time is it?
¿Qué hora es?   ke o·ra es

It's (10) o'clock.
Son (las diez).   son (las dyeth)

Half past (one).
Es (la una) y media.   es (la oo·na) ee me·dya

At what time?
¿A qué hora?   a ke o·ra

At (five) o'clock.
A las (cinco).   a las (theen·ko)

morning	mañana	ma·nya·na
afternoon	tarde	tar·de
evening	noche	no·che

yesterday	ayer	a·yer
today	hoy	oy
tomorrow	mañana	ma·nya·na

Monday	lunes	loo·nes
Tuesday	martes	mar·tes
Wednesday	miércoles	myer·ko·les
Thursday	jueves	khwe·bes
Friday	viernes	vyer·nes
Saturday	sábado	sa·ba·do
Sunday	domingo	do·meen·go

January	enero	e·ne·ro
February	febrero	fe·bre·ro
March	marzo	mar·tho
April	abril	a·breel
May	mayo	ma·yo
June	junio	khoo·nyo
July	julio	khoo·lyo
August	agosto	a·gos·to
September	septiembre	sep·tyem·bre
October	octubre	ok·too·bre
November	noviembre	no·vyem·bre
December	diciembre	dee·thyem·bre

TRANSPORT

Public Transport

boat	barco	bar·ko
bus	autobús	ow·to·boos
plane	avión	a·vyon
train	tren	tren
tram	tranvía	tran·vee·a

Numbers

1	*uno*	oo·no
2	*dos*	dos
3	*tres*	tres
4	*cuatro*	kwa·tro
5	*cinco*	theen·ko
6	*seis*	seys
7	*siete*	sye·te
8	*ocho*	o·cho
9	*nueve*	nwe·ve
10	*diez*	dyeth
20	*veinte*	veyn·te
30	*treinta*	treyn·ta
40	*cuarenta*	kwa·ren·ta
50	*cincuenta*	theen·kwen·ta
60	*sesenta*	se·sen·ta
70	*setenta*	se·ten·ta
80	*ochenta*	o·chen·ta
90	*noventa*	no·ven·ta
100	*cien*	thyen
1000	*mil*	meel

first	*primer*	pree·mer
last	*último*	ool·tee·mo
next	*próximo*	prok·see·mo

I want to go to ...
Quisiera ir a ...   kee·sye·ra eer a ...

At what time does it arrive/leave?
¿A qué hora llega/sale?   a ke o·ra lye·ga/sa·le

Is it a direct route?
¿Es un viaje directo?   es oon vya·khe dee·rek·to

Does it stop at ...?
¿Para en ...?   pa·ra en ...

Which stop is this?
¿Cuál es esta parada?   kwal es es·ta pa·ra·da

Please tell me when we get to ...
¿Puede avisarme   pwe·de a·vee·sar·me
cuando lleguemos a ...?   kwan·do lye·ge·mos a ...

I want to get off here.
Quiero bajarme aquí.   kye·ro ba·khar·me a·kee

a ... ticket	*un billete de ...*	oon bee·lye·te de ...
1st-class	*primera clase*	pree·me·ra kla·se
2nd-class	*segunda clase*	se·goon·da kla·se
one-way	*ida*	ee·da
return	*ida y vuelta*	ee·da ee vwel·ta

aisle/window seat	*asiento de pasillo/ ventana*	a·syen·to de pa·see·lyo/ ven·ta·na
bus/train station	*estación de autobuses/ trenes*	es·ta·thyon de ow·to·boo·ses/ tre·nes
cancelled	*cancelado*	kan·the·la·do
delayed	*retrasado*	re·tra·sa·do
platform	*plataforma*	pla·ta·for·ma
ticket office	*taquilla*	ta·kee·lya
timetable	*horario*	o·ra·ryo

Driving & Cycling

I'd like to hire a ...	*Quisiera alquilar ...*	kee·sye·ra al·kee·lar ...
4WD	*un todo- terreno*	oon to·do- te·re·no
bicycle	*una bicicleta*	oo·na bee·thee·kle·ta
car	*un coche*	oon ko·che
motorcycle	*una moto*	oo·na mo·to

child seat	*asiento de seguridad para niños*	a·syen·to de se·goo·ree·da pa·ra nee·nyos
diesel	*gasóleo*	ga·so·le·o
helmet	*casco*	kas·ko
mechanic	*mecánico*	me·ka·nee·ko
petrol	*gasolina*	ga·so·lee·na
service station	*gasolinera*	ga·so·lee·ne·ra

How much is it per day/hour?
¿Cuánto cuesta por   kwan·to kwes·ta por
día/hora?   dee·a/o·ra

Is this the road to ...?
¿Se va a ... por esta   se va a ... por es·ta
carretera?   ka·re·te·ra

(How long) Can I park here?
¿(Por cuánto tiempo)   (por kwan·to tyem·po)
Puedo aparcar aquí?   pwe·do a·par·kar a·kee

The car has broken down (at ...).
El coche se ha averiado   el ko·che se a a·ve·rya·do
(en ...).   (en ...)

I have a flat tyre.
Tengo un pinchazo.   ten·go oon peen·cha·tho

I've run out of petrol.
Me he quedado sin   me e ke·da·do seen
gasolina.   ga·so·lee·na

Are there cycling paths?
¿Hay carril bicicleta?   ai ka·reel bee·thee·kle·ta

Is there bicycle parking?
¿Hay aparcamiento   ai a·par·ka·myen·to
de bicicletas?   de bee·thee·kle·tas

GLOSSARY

abono – season pass

albergue juvenil – youth hostel; not to be confused with *hostal*

alcázar – Muslim-era fortress

Almoravid – Islamic Berbers who founded an empire in North Africa that spread over much of Spain in the 11th century and laid siege to Madrid in 1110

Ayuntamiento – city or town hall; city or town council

asador – restaurant specialising in roasted meats

baño completo – full bathroom, with a toilet, shower and/or bath and washbasin

barrio – district, quarter (of a town or city)

biblioteca – library

bodega – literally, 'cellar' (especially a wine cellar); also means a winery or a traditional wine bar likely to serve wine from the barrel

bomberos – fire brigade

calle – street

callejón – lane

cama – bed

cantaor/cantaora – flamenco singer (male/female)

capilla – chapel

Carnaval – carnival; a period of fancy-dress parades and merrymaking, usually ending on the Tuesday 47 days before Easter Sunday

carnet – identity card or driving licence

carretera – highway

castizo – literally 'pure'; refers to people and things distinctly from Madrid

catedral – cathedral

centro de salud – health centre

cercanías – local trains serving big cities, suburbs and nearby towns; local train network

cerrado – closed

cervecería – bar where the focus is on beer

chato – glass

churrigueresque – ornate style of baroque architecture named after the brothers Alberto and José Churriguera

comedor – dining room

Comunidad de Madrid – Madrid province

consejo – council

coro – choir stall

correos – post office

corrida (de toros) – bullfight

Cortes – national parliament

cuesta – lane (usually on a hill)

cutre – basic or rough-and-ready

discoteca – nightclub

ducha – shower

duende – an indefinable word that captures the passionate essence of flamenco

entrada – entrance; ticket for a performance

estanco – tobacconist shop

farmacia – pharmacy

feria – fair; can refer to trade fairs as well as city, town or village fairs, bullfights or festivals lasting days or weeks

ferrocarril – railway

fiesta – festival, public holiday or party

fin de semana – weekend

flamenco – traditional Spanish musical form involving any or all of guitarist, singer and dancer and sometimes accompanying musicians

gasolina – petrol (a *gasolinera* is a petrol station)

gatos – literally 'cats'; colloquial name for *madrileños*

gitanos – the Roma people (formerly known as the Gypsies)

glorieta – big roundabout

guiri – foreigner

habitación doble – twin room

hostal – hostel; not to be confused with *albergue juvenil*

iglesia – church

IVA – impuesto sobre el valor añadido (value-added tax)

judería – Jewish quarter

lavabo – washbasin; a polite term for toilet

lavandería – laundrette

librería – bookshop

locutorio – telephone centre

madrileño/a – a person from Madrid (m/f)

marcha – action, life, 'the scene'

marisquería – seafood eatery

media ración – a serving of tapas, somewhere between the size of tapas and *raciones*

menú del día – fixed-price meal available at lunchtime, sometimes evening, too; often just called a *menú*

mercado – market

meseta – the high tableland of central Spain

mezquita – mosque

monasterio – monastery

morería – former Islamic quarter in town

moro – 'Moor' or Muslim, usually in medieval context

moto – moped or motorcycle

movida madrileña – the halcyon days of the post-Franco years when the city plunged into an excess of nightlife, drugs and cultural expression

mozarab – Christians who lived in Muslim-ruled Spain; also style of architecture

Mudéjar – Muslim living under Christian rule in medieval Spain, also refers to their style of architecture

muralla – city wall

museo – museum

oficina de turismo – tourist office

panteón – pantheon (monument to a famous dead person)

parador – state-owned hotel in a historic building

pensión – guesthouse

pijo/pija – yuppie, snob, beautiful people (male/female)

plaza mayor – main plaza or square

puente – bridge

puerta – door or gate

ración – meal-sized serve of tapas

ronda – ring road

Semana Santa – Holy Week; the week leading up to Easter Sunday

servicio – toilet

sierra – mountain range

taberna – tavern

tapas – bar snacks traditionally served on a saucer or lid ('tapa' literally means a lid)

taquilla – ticket window/office

tasca – tapas bar

temporada alta/media/baja – high, mid- or low season

terraza – terrace; usually means outdoor tables of a cafe, bar or restaurant; can also mean rooftop open-air place

torero – bullfighter or matador

toro – bull

torreón – tower

turismo – means both tourism and saloon car

zarzuela – form of Spanish dance and music, usually satirical

MENU DECODER

a la parrilla – grilled

aceite de oliva – olive oil

aceite de oliva virgen extra – extra virgin olive oil

aceitunas – olives

adobo – marinade

aguacate – avocado

ajo – garlic

albóndigas – meat balls

alcachofas – artichokes

al horno – baked in the oven

almejas – clams

anchoas – anchovies

arroz – rice

asado – roasted

bacalao – dried and salted cod

bebida – drink

berenjena – aubergine, eggplant

bistec – steak

bocadillo – bread roll with filling

bonito – tuna

boquerones – anchovies marinated in wine vinegar

boquerones en vinagre – fresh anchovies marinated in white vinegar and garlic

boquerones fritos – fried fresh anchovies

butifarra – Catalan sausage

cabrito – kid, baby goat

calamares – calamari

calamares a la Romana – deep-fried calamari rings

caldo – broth, stock

callos – tripe

camarón – small prawn, shrimp

caracol – snail

carne – meat

cebolla – onion

cerdo – pork

champiñones – mushrooms

chipirones – baby squid

chipirones en su tinta – baby squid in their own ink

chorizo – cured pork sausage, sometimes spicy

chuleta – chop, cutlet

churro – long, deep-fried doughnut

cochinillo – suckling pig

cocido a la madrileña – meat, chickpea and broth stew

codorniz – quail

coliflor – cauliflower

conejo – rabbit

confitura – jam

cordero – lamb

cordero asado de lechal – roast spring lamb

croquetas – croquettes

de lata – from a can or tin

dorada – bream

empanadillas – small pie, either savoury or sweet

ensalada – salad

ensalada rusa – Russian salad

ensalada mixta – mixed salad

escabeche – pickle, marinade

espárragos – asparagus

estofado – stew

frito – fried

galleta – biscuit

gambas – prawns, either done *al ajillo*, with garlic, or *a la plancha*, grilled

garbanzos – chickpeas

garbanzos con espinacas – chickpeas and spinach

gazpacho – cold, tomato-based soup

granada – pomegranate

guarnición – side order

helado – ice cream

jamón – cured Spanish ham

judias – beans

langosta – lobster

langostino – king prawn

leche – milk

lechuga – lettuce

lenguado – sole

lentejas – lentils

lomo – loin (pork unless specified otherwise)

maíz – corn

mantequilla – butter

manzana – apple

marisco – seafood or shellfish

mejillones – mussels

merluza – hake

miel – honey

morcilla – black pudding, blood sausage

naranja – orange

ostra – oyster

pan – bread

pastel – cake

patatas bravas – roasted potato chunks bathed in spicy tomato sauce

patatas con huevos fritos – baked potatoes with eggs, also known as *huevos rotos*

patatas fritas – French fries

pato – duck

pavo – turkey

pescado – fish

pescaíto frito – fried fish

pil pil – garlic sauce spiked with chilli

pimentón –paprika

pimiento – pepper, capsicum

pimientos de Padrón – little green peppers from Galicia – some are hot and some not

plátano – banana

plato combinado – combination (or all-in-one) plate, usually with meat and vegetables on the same plate

pollo – chicken

postre – dessert

pulpo a la gallega – boiled octopus served with paprika, Galician style

queso – cheese

queso azul – blue cheese

rabo de toro – bull's tail

raciones – large tapas serving

rebozado – in bread crumbs

relleno – stuffing

repollo – cabbage

revuelto – scrambled eggs

riñón – kidney

rodaballo – turbot

salchichón – salami-like sausage

salmorejo – cold, tomato-based soup

salsa – sauce

sandía – watermelon

sardinas – sardines

sepia – squid

sesos – brains

seta – wild mushroom

solomillo – sirloin (usually of pork)

sopa – soup

sopa de ajo – garlic soup

tarta – cake

ternasco – lamb ribs

ternera – beef or veal

tortilla de patatas – potato and (sometimos) onion omelette

tostada – buttered toast

trucha – trout

verduras a la plancha – grilled vegetables

vinagre – vinegar

Behind the Scenes

SEND US YOUR FEEDBACK

We love to hear from travellers – your comments keep us on our toes and help make our books better. Our well-travelled team reads every word on what you loved or loathed about this book. Although we cannot reply individually to postal submissions, we always guarantee that your feedback goes straight to the appropriate authors, in time for the next edition. Each person who sends us information is thanked in the next edition – the most useful submissions are rewarded with a selection of digital PDF chapters.

Visit **lonelyplanet.com/contact** to submit your updates and suggestions or to ask for help. Our award-winning website also features inspirational travel stories, news and discussions.

Note: We may edit, reproduce and incorporate your comments in Lonely Planet products such as guidebooks, websites and digital products, so let us know if you don't want your comments reproduced or your name acknowledged. For a copy of our privacy policy visit lonelyplanet.com/privacy.

OUR READERS

Many thanks to the travellers who used the last edition and wrote to us with helpful hints, useful advice and interesting anecdotes: Minette Aalbers, Judith Brennan, Elisa Carbonell, Kenisha Evelyn, Carlos Gomez, Janet Iashmar, Ken Munn, Rachel Oliphant, Beau Witka, Julie Woods

ACKNOWLEDGMENTS

Cover photograph: Flamenco dancer, Grant Faint/Getty

Illustration on pp102-3 by Javier Zarracina

AUTHOR THANKS

Anthony Ham

Special thanks once again to Itziar Herrán, who brought both wisdom and an eye for detail to her contributions to this book. Thanks also to Marina and Alberto for their unwavering hospitality; to Jo Cooke and Lorna Parkes and Lonely Planet's fine team of editors. And to Marina, Carlota and Valentina – you are everything that is good about this wonderful country.

THIS BOOK

This 8th edition of Lonely Planet's *Madrid* guidebook was researched and written by Anthony Ham, who also wrote the previous four editions. This guidebook was produced by the following:

Destination Editors Joanna Cooke, Lorna Parkes

Coordinating Editor Nigel Chin
Product Editor Martine Power
Senior Cartographer Anthony Phelan
Book Designer Mazzy Prinsep
Assisting Editors Sarah Billington, Kate Evans, Catherine Naghten, Susan Paterson, Victoria Smith, Gabrielle Stefanos

Cartographer Mark Griffiths
Cover Researcher Campbell McKenzie
Thanks to Sasha Baskett, Ryan Evans, Andi Jones, Indra Kilfoyle, Claire Naylor, Karyn Noble, Diana Saengkham, Dianne Schallmeiner, Ellie Simpson, Angela Tinson, Saralinda Turner, Tony Wheeler

Index

✕ EATING

Madrid Maps

Sights

- Beach
- Bird Sanctuary
- Buddhist
- Castle/Palace
- Christian
- Confucian
- Hindu
- Islamic
- Jain
- Jewish
- Monument
- Museum/Gallery/Historic Building
- Ruin
- Shinto
- Sikh
- Taoist
- Winery/Vineyard
- Zoo/Wildlife Sanctuary
- Other Sight

Activities, Courses & Tours

- Bodysurfing
- Diving
- Canoeing/Kayaking
- Course/Tour
- Sento Hot Baths/Onsen
- Skiing
- Snorkelling
- Surfing
- Swimming/Pool
- Walking
- Windsurfing
- Other Activity

Sleeping

- Sleeping
- Camping

Eating

- Eating

Drinking & Nightlife

- Drinking & Nightlife
- Cafe

Entertainment

- Entertainment

Shopping

- Shopping

Information

- Bank
- Embassy/Consulate
- Hospital/Medical
- Internet
- Police
- Post Office
- Telephone
- Toilet
- Tourist Information
- Other Information

Geographic

- Beach
- Gate
- Hut/Shelter
- Lighthouse
- Lookout
- Mountain/Volcano
- Oasis
- Park
- Pass
- Picnic Area
- Waterfall

Population

- Capital (National)
- Capital (State/Province)
- City/Large Town
- Town/Village

Transport

- Airport
- Border crossing
- Bus
- Cable car/Funicular
- Cycling
- Ferry
- Metro station
- Monorail
- Parking
- Petrol station
- S-Bahn/Subway station
- Taxi
- T-bane/Tunnelbana station
- Train station/Railway
- Tram
- Tube station
- U-Bahn/Underground station
- Other Transport

Note: Not all symbols displayed above appear on the maps in this book

Routes

- Tollway
- Freeway
- Primary
- Secondary
- Tertiary
- Lane
- Unsealed road
- Road under construction
- Plaza/Mall
- Steps
- Tunnel
- Pedestrian overpass
- Walking Tour
- Walking Tour detour
- Path/Walking Trail

Boundaries

- International
- State/Province
- Disputed
- Regional/Suburb
- Marine Park
- Cliff
- Wall

Hydrography

- River, Creek
- Intermittent River
- Canal
- Water
- Dry/Salt/Intermittent Lake
- Reef

Areas

- Airport/Runway
- Beach/Desert
- Cemetery (Christian)
- Cemetery (Other)
- Glacier
- Mudflat
- Park/Forest
- Sight (Building)
- Sportsground
- Swamp/Mangrove

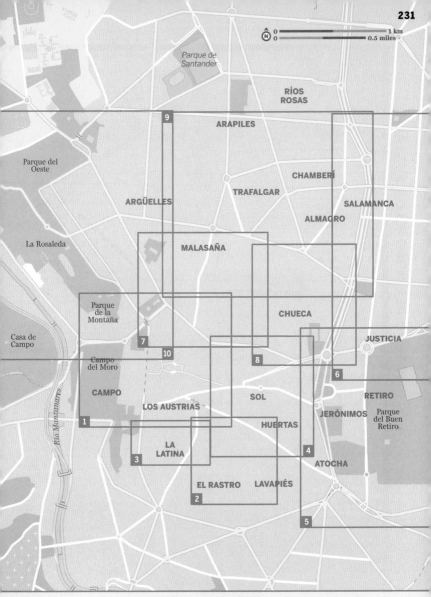

Parque de Santander

RÍOS ROSAS

ARAPILES

9

Parque del Oeste

CHAMBERÍ

TRAFALGAR

ARGÜELLES

SALAMANCA

ALMAGRO

La Rosaleda

MALASAÑA

Parque de la Montaña

CHUECA

7

Casa de Campo

JUSTICIA

10

Campo del Moro

8

6

CAMPO

SOL

RETIRO

LOS AUSTRIAS

Parque del Buen Retiro

JERÓNIMOS

Río Manzanares

HUERTAS

1

4

LA LATINA

3

ATOCHA

EL RASTRO

LAVAPIÉS

2

5

La Rosaleda

C de la Rosaleda

C de Juan Álvarez Mendizábal

C de Ferraz

Parque de la Montaña

Jardines de Ferraz

Paseo del Rey

Plaza de España

See map p255

64

Cuesta

Príncipe Pío

Cuesta de San Vicente

M Príncipe Pío

Jardines de Sabatini

C de Bailén

Cuesta de San Vicente

Paseo de la Virgen del Puerto

C de San

Jardines Cabo Naval

Park Entrance

21

Campo del Moro

CAMPO

4

Jardines de Lepanto

C de Requena

Plaza de la Armería

C de Noblejas

Palacio Real 1

C del Factor

8

27

Cuesta de la Vega

C Mayor

C de Bailén

C del

Parque del Emir Mohamed I

19

16

Parque de Atenas

Parque de Atenas

17

C de la Villa

C de Segovia

Viaduct

C de Segovia

Jardines de las Vistillas

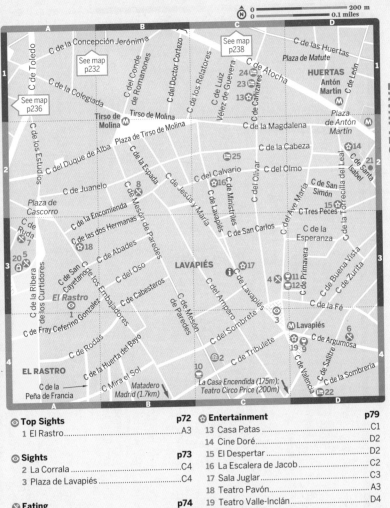

LA LATINA

200 m
0.1 miles

EL RASTRO

See map p235

See map p232

Plaza de Puerta Cerrada

Plaza de Segovia Nueva

C de los Estudios

Plaza del Duque de Alba

C del Duque de Alba

C de Juanelo

C de los Embajadores

Plaza de Cascorro

C de la Colegiada

C Salvador

C de la Concepción Jerónima

C de San Justo

C de San Milán

C de las Maldonadas

C de Ruda

C de Toledo

La Latina

Plaza de la Cebada

C de la Cebada

C del Nuncio

C de Segovia

C del Cordón

C del Almendro

LA LATINA

Plaza del Humilladero

C de Humilladero

Costanilla de San Pedro

C de la Cava Alta

C de la Cava Baja

Plaza de San Andrés

Plaza de la Paja

Costanilla de San Andrés

C del Príncipe Anglona

C de Alfonso VI

C de Oriente

C de Luciente

C de Oriente

Plaza de la Puerta de Moros

C de Granado

Plaza de Granado

C de la Morería

Cuesta de Caños Viejos

C de Bailén

Viaduct

Plaza del Alamillo

C de Segovia

Jardines de las Vistillas

Costanilla de Ramón

C de Beatriz Galindo

C de Yeseros

Plaza de Gabriel Miró

C de la Redondilla

C de Granado

C de Mancebos

C de Don Pedro

Carrera de San Francisco

C de las Aguas

Botería Julio Rodríguez (100m)

Estadio Vicente Calderón (1.6km)

C de San Isidro Labrador

Plaza de San Francisco

Basílica de San Francisco El Grande

C de San Buenaventura

C de la Morería

SOL, HUERTAS & THE CENTRE

Key on p240

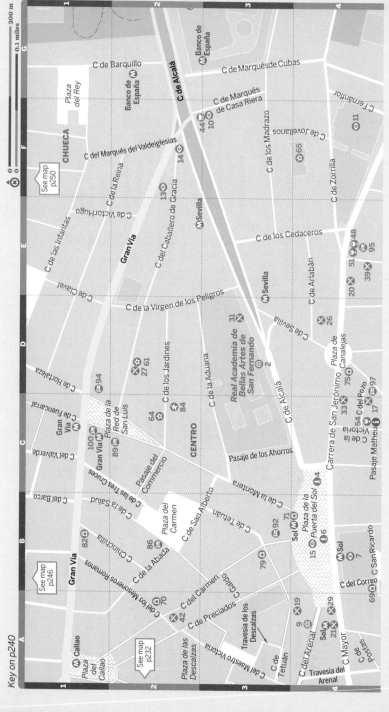

Plaza del Callao

Plaza del Rey

CHUECA

See map p250

See map p246

See map p232

CENTRO

Gran Vía

C de Alcalá

C de Barquillo

Banco de España

Banco de España

C de Marqués de Cubas

C de Marqués de Casa Riera

C de los Madrazo

C de Jovellanos

C del Marqués del Valdeiglesias

C de la Reina

C de Victor Hugo

C del Caballero de Gracia

Sevilla

C de las Infantas

C del Clavel

C de Hortaleza

C de Fuencarral

C del Valverde

C del Barco

C de Chinchilla

C de los Mesoneros Romanos

C de la Salud

C de las Tres Cruces

Plaza de la Red de San Luis

Pasaje del Commercio

C de los Jardines

C de la Aduana

C de la Virgen de los Peligros

C de los Cedaceros

C de Zorrilla

C Fernánflor

C de Arlabán

C de Sevilla

Sevilla

Real Academia de Bellas Artes de San Fernando

Plaza de Canalejas

Carrera de San Jerónimo

C de la Victoria

C del Pozo

Pasaje Matheu

C de la Montera

Pasaje de los Ahorros

Plaza del Carmen

C de San Alberto

C de San Tetuán

Plaza de la Puerta del Sol

Sol

C San Ricardo

C del Correo

C del Carmen

C de Preciados

Travesía de los Descalzos

C de Galdo

C de la Abada

Plaza de las Descalzas

C del Maestro Victoria

C de Tetuán

C del Arenal

C Mayor

Travesía del Arenal

C de Postas

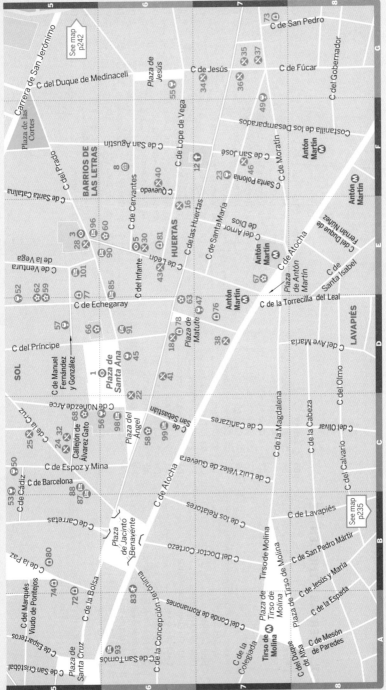

See map
p250

CHUECA

JUSTICIA

Paseo de los Recoletos

C de Salustiano

C de Villalar

C de Serrano

C de Columela

C de Lagasca

C de Alcalá

Retiro Ⓜ

Banco
de España Ⓜ Ⓜ

C de Alcalá

Plaza de la
Independencia
18 ℹ

Puerta
Independencia

Children's
Swings

Casa de
Vacas
28

Ⓜ Banco de
España

16

10

C Valenzuela

Paseo de México

ℹ ✉

C de Montalbán

Paseo de Colombia

C de los Madrazo

Paseo del Prado

14

C de Juan de Mena

13

24

Estanque

Plaza de la
Lealtad

3 Museo Thyssen-
Bornemisza

Carrera de
San Jerónimo

31

32

17

30

C de Antonio Maura

Puerta
de España

Paseo de la Argentina

RETIRO

Parque
del Buen
Retiro

4

Paseo de la República de Cuba

C de Ruiz de Alarcón

Puerta
Felipe IV

C Felipe IV

9

Madrid's
Oldest Tree

Paseo Parterre

C de Cervantes

23

11

19

12

2

Museo del
Prado

C de la Academia

C Casado del Alisal

C Alberto Bosch

Paseo San Pablo

Jerónimos

ℹ

7

See map
p238

C de las Huertas

C de Moratín

Paseo del Prado

JERÓNIMOS

Plaza de
Bravo
Murillo

C de Espalter

Puerta
Murillo

Jardín
de los
Planteles

C de Fúcar

C de Verónica

C del Gobernador

C Almadén

29

8

ATOCHA

C de Atocha

21

Real Jardín
Botánico

Jardín
de los
Planteles

C de Alfonso XII

Paseo de Fernán Núñez

C de Cenicero

25

26

C del
Doctor
Drumén

Cuesta de Claudio Moyano

Ⓜ Atocha

LAVAPIÉS

Centro de
Arte Reina
Sofía

1

22

Ⓜ
Atocha

Ⓜ
Atocha

Plaza del Emperador
Carlos V

27

Paseo de la Infanta Isabel

C de Alfonso XII

5

6

Atocha
Renfe Ⓜ

Ⓜ Atocha
Renfe

C de Julián Gayarre

Ronda de Atocha

Paseo de Santa María
de la Cabeza

Paseo de las Delicias

C de Méndez Álvaro

Av de la Ciudad de Barcelona

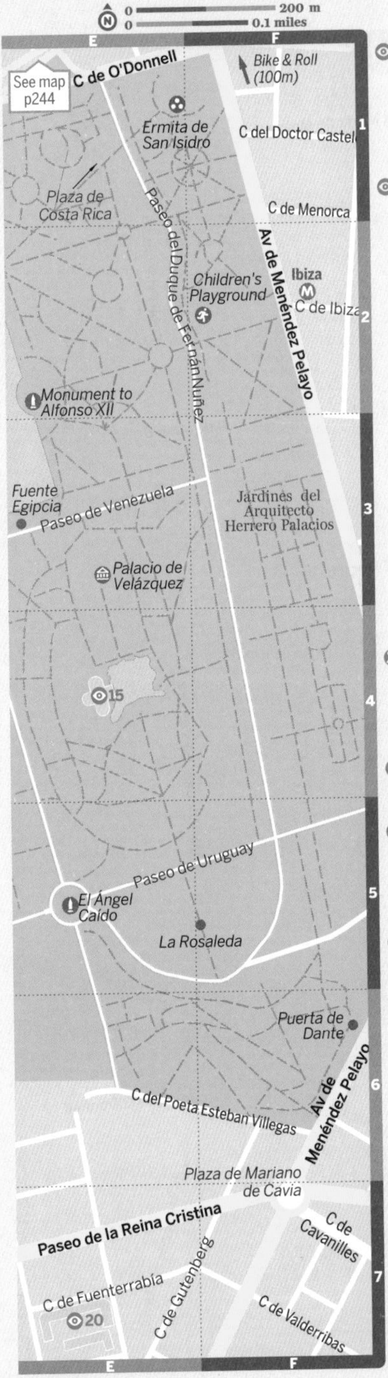

0 200 m
0 0.1 miles
E
F
See map p244
C de O'Donnell
Bike & Roll (100m)
Ermita de San Isidro
C del Doctor Castelo
Plaza de Costa Rica
Paseo del Duque de Fernán Nuñez
C de Menorca
Av de Menéndez Pelayo
Ibiza
Children's Playground
C de Ibiza
Monument to Alfonso XII
Fuente Egipcia
Paseo de Venezuela
Jardines del Arquitecto Herrero Palacios
Palacio de Velázquez
15
Paseo de Uruguay
El Ángel Caído
La Rosaleda
Puerta de Dante
Av de Menéndez Pelayo
C del Poeta Esteban Villegas
Plaza de Mariano de Cavia
Paseo de la Reina Cristina
C de Cavanilles
C de Fuenterrabía
C de Gutenberg
C de Valderribas
20
1
2
3
4
5
6
7

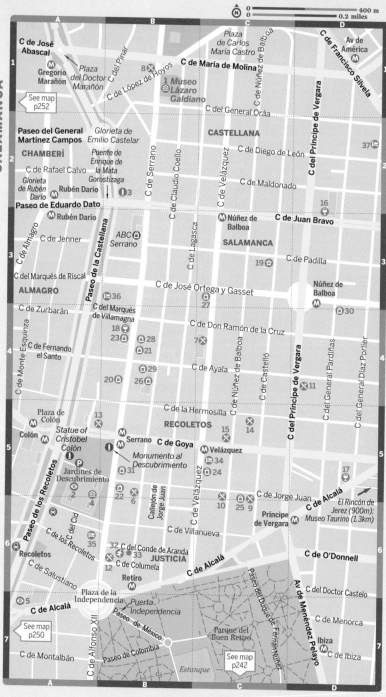

N
0   400 m
0   0.2 miles

C de José Abascal

Plaza de Carlos María Castro

C de María de Molina

C de Francisco Silvela

Av de América

Gregorio Marañón

Plaza del Doctor Marañón

C del Pinar

C de López de Hoyos

8

1 Museo Lázaro Galdiano

C de Núñez de Balboa

C del Príncipe de Vergara

See map p252

C del General Oráa

Paseo del General Martínez Campos

Glorieta de Emilio Castelar

CASTELLANA

C de Diego de León

37

CHAMBERÍ

C de Rafael Calvo

Puente de Enrique de la Mata Gorostizaga

C de Serrano

C de Velázquez

C de Maldonado

Glorieta de Rubén Darío

Rubén Darío

3

C de Claudio Coello

Paseo de Eduardo Dato

Rubén Darío

Núñez de Balboa

C de Juan Bravo

16

C de Almagro

C de Jenner

ABC Serrano

C de Lagasca

SALAMANCA

C de Padilla

19

C del Marqués de Riscal

ALMAGRO

C de José Ortega y Gasset

Núñez de Balboa

C de Zurbarán

36

C del Marqués de Villamagna

27

30

C de Monte Esquinza

C de Fernando el Santo

18

23

28

21

C de Don Ramón de la Cruz

7

C del Príncipe de Vergara

C del General Pardiñas

C del General Díaz Porlier

29

C de Ayala

C de Núñez de Balboa

C de Castelló

20

26

Plaza de Colón

13

C de la Hermosilla

RECOLETOS

15

14

11

Colón

Statue of Cristobel Colón

Serrano

C de Goya

Velázquez

Jardines de Descubrimiento

Monumento al Descubrimiento

34

31

2

4

22

6

Callejón de Jorge Juan

C de Velázquez

24

10

25

9

C de Jorge Juan

17

Príncipe de Vergara

C de Alcalá

El Rincón de Jerez (900m); Museo Taurino (1.3km)

Paseo de los Recoletos

C de Villanueva

C de los Recoletos

C del Cid

35

32

C del Conde de Aranda

33

JUSTICIA

Recoletos

12

C de Columela

C de Salustiano

Retiro

C de Alcalá

C de O'Donnell

5

Plaza de la Independencia

Puerta Independencia

Paseo del Duque de Fernán Núñez

Av de Menéndez Pelayo

C del Doctor Castelo

See map p250

C de Alcalá

Paseo de México

Parque del Buen Retiro

C de Menorca

Ibiza

C de Ibiza

C de Montalbán

C de Alfonso XII

Paseo de Colombia

See map p242

Estanque

SALAMANCA

SALAMANCA

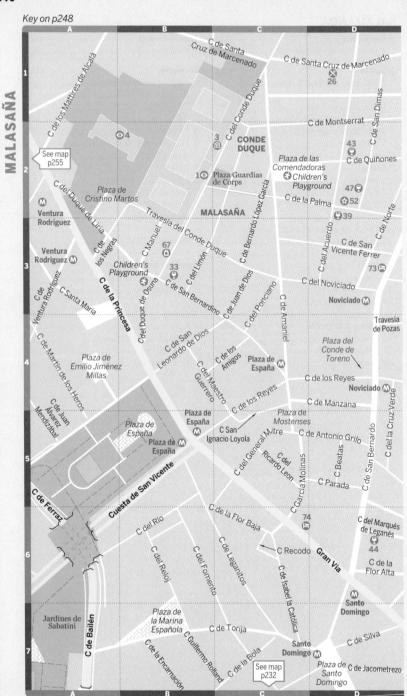

MALASAÑA

CONDE DUQUE

MALASAÑA

Plaza de las Comendadoras

Children's Playground

Plaza Guardias de Corps

Plaza de Cristino Martos

Ventura Rodríguez

Ventura Rodríguez

Children's Playground

Plaza de Emilio Jiménez Millas

Plaza del Conde de Toreno

Travesía de Pozas

Noviciado

Noviciado

Plaza de España

Plaza de España

Plaza de España

Plaza de Mostenses

Plaza de la Marina Española

Jardines de Sabatini

Santo Domingo

Santo Domingo

Plaza de Santo Domingo

See map p255

See map p232

C de Santa Cruz de Marcenado

C de Santa Cruz de Marcenado

C de los Mártires de Alcalá

C del Conde Duque

C de Montserrat

C de San Dimas

C de Quiñones

C de la Palma

C de Norte

C de San Vicente Ferrer

C de Acuerdo

C del Noviciado

C del Duque de Liria

C de Bernardo López García

Travesía del Conde Duque

C Manuel

C de los Negras

C de la Princesa

C del Duque de Osuna

C del Limón

C de San Bernardino

C de Juan de Dios

C del Ponciano

C de Amaniel

C de Santa María

C de Ventura Rodríguez

C de Martín de los Heros

C de San Leonardo de Dios

C del Maestro Guerrero

C de los Amigos

C de los Reyes

C de los Reyes

C de Manzana

C de la Cruz Verde

C de San Bernardo

C de Juan Álvarez Mendizábal

C de Ferraz

Cuesta de San Vicente

C del Río

C del Reloj

C del Fomento

C de la Flor Baja

C de Leganitos

C Recodo

Gran Vía

C del Marqués de Leganés

C de la Flor Alta

C San Ignacio Loyola

C del General Mitre

C del Ricardo Leon

C García Molinas

C Beatas

C Parada

C de Antonio Grilo

C de Bailén

Plaza de España

C de Isabel la Católica

C de Torija

C de Silva

C de la Encarnación

C Guillermo Rolland

C de la Bola

C de Jacometrezo

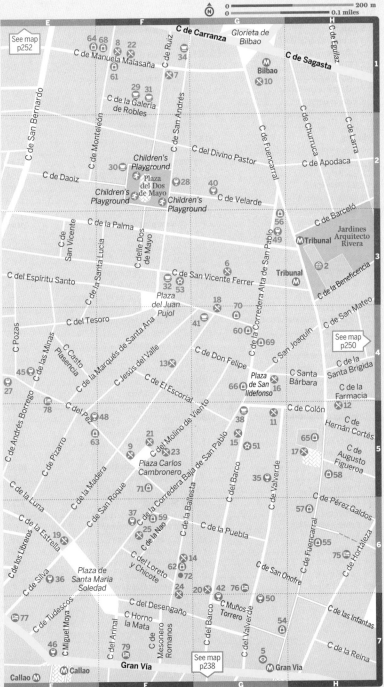

C de Carranza

Glorieta de Bilbao

C de Sagasta

See map p252

C de Manuela Malasaña

C de la Galería de Robles

C de San Bernardo

C de Montelón

C de Daoiz

Children's Playground

Plaza del Dos de Mayo

Children's Playground

Children's Playground

C de la Palma

C de San Vicente

C de la Santa Lucía

C delle Dos de Mayo

C del Espíritu Santo

C del Divino Pastor

C de Fuencarral

C de Apodaca

C de Velarde

C de Barceló

Jardines Arquitecto Rivera

Tribunal

C de la Beneficencia

C de San Mateo

C de San Vicente Ferrer

C de la Corredera Alta de San Pablo

Tribunal

Plaza del Juan Pujol

C del Tesoro

See map p250

C Pozas

C de las Minas

C Casto Plasencia

C de la Marqués de Santa Ana

C de Jesús del Valle

C de Don Felipe

C de la Corredera Alta de San Pablo

C San Joaquín

C de Andrés Borrego

C del Pez

C de El Escorial

Plaza de San Ildefonso

C Santa Bárbara

C de la Santa Brígida

C de la Farmacia

C de Colón

C de Hernán Cortés

C de Augusto Figueroa

C de la Luna

C de Pizarro

C de la Madera

C del Molino de Viento

Plaza Carlos Cambronero

C de la Corredera Baja de San Pablo

C del Barco

C de Valverde

C de Pérez Galdos

C de la Estrella

C de San Roque

C de la Nao

C de la Ballesta

C de la Puebla

C de Fuencarral

C de Hortaleza

C de los Libreros

C de Silva

Plaza de Santa María Soledad

C del Loreto y Chicote

C de San Onofre

C de Tudescos

C Miguel Moya

C del Arinal

C del Desengaño

C Horno la Mata

C de Mesonero Romanos

C del Barco

C Muñoz Torrero

C del Valverde

C de las Infantas

C de la Reina

Callao

Callao

Gran Vía

See map p238

Gran Vía

MALASAÑA *Map on p246*

CHUECA

Key on p249

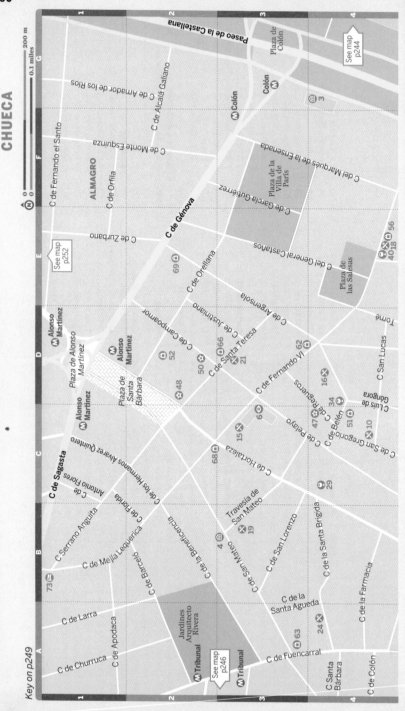

See map p252
See map p244
See map p246

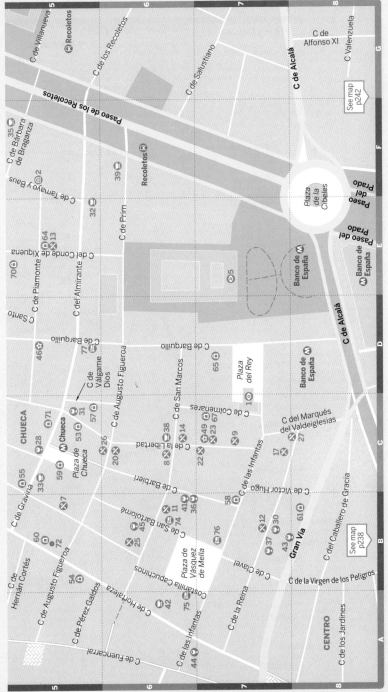

See map p242

See map p238

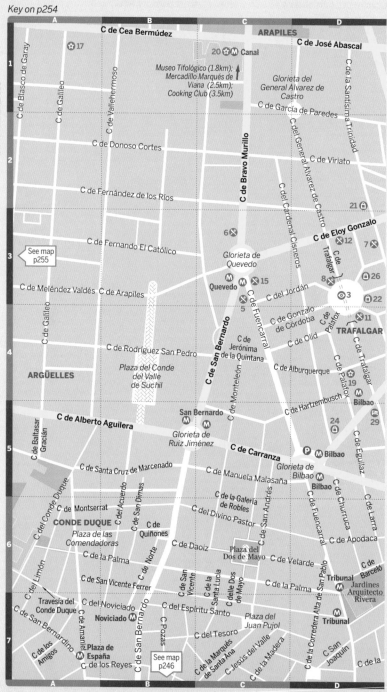

CHAMBERÍ

C de Cea Bermúdez

ARAPLES

C de José Abascal

C de Blasco de Garay

C de Galileo

C de Vallehermoso

☆17

20 ☆ Ⓜ Canal

Museo Tiflológico (1.8km);
Mercadillo Marqués de
Viana (2.5km);
Cooking Club (3.5km)

Glorieta del
General Alvarez de
Castro

C de García de Paredes

C de la Santísima Trinidad

C de Donoso Cortes

C de Bravo Murillo

C de Viriato

C de Fernández de los Ríos

C del Cardenal Cisneros

C del General Alvarez de Castro

21 🔒

C de Fernando El Católico

6 ✕

C de Eloy Gonzalo

See map
p255

Glorieta de
Quevedo

12

7 ✕

C de Meléndez Valdés C de Arapiles

Quevedo Ⓜ

Ⓜ ✕ 15

C del Jordán

C de Tratalgar

8 🔒

26 🔒

C de Galileo

5

C de Fuencarral

C de Gonzalo
de Córdoba

3 ◎

22 🔒

ARGÜELLES

C de Rodríguez San Pedro

C de San Bernardo

C de
Jerónima
de la Quintana

C de Olid

11 ✕

TRAFALGAR

C de Palafox

C de Trafalgar

Plaza del Conde
del Valle
de Suchil

C de Montelón

C de Alburquerque

C de Palafox

19 ☆

C de Alberto Aguilera

San Bernardo
Ⓜ

C de Hartzembusch

Bilbao Ⓜ

C de Baltasar
Gracián

Glorieta de
Ruiz Jiménez

C de Carranza

24 🔒

29 🛒

C de Eguilaz

C de Santa Cruz de Marcenado

C de Manuela Malasaña

Glorieta de
Bilbao Ⓜ

P 🅿 Bilbao Ⓜ

C de Conde Duque

C de Montserrat

C del Acuerdo

C de San Dimas

C de la Galería
de Robles

Bilbao Ⓜ

C de Churruca

C de Larra

CONDE DUQUE

C del Divino Pastor

C de San Andrés

C de Fuencarral

C del Conde Duque

Plaza de las
Comendadoras

C de
Quiñones

C de Daoiz

C de Apodaca

C de la Palma

C de Norte

Plaza del
Dos de Mayo

C de Velarde

C de
Barceló

C del Limón

C de San Vicente Ferrer

C de San
Vicente

C de
Santa Lucia

Calle Dos
de Mayo

C de la Palma

Tribunal Ⓜ

Jardines
Arquitecto
Rivera

Travesía del
Conde Duque

C del Noviciado

C del Espíritu Santo

Plaza del
Juan Pujol

C de la Corredera Alta de San Pablo

Tribunal Ⓜ

C de San Bernardino

Noviciado Ⓜ

C de Amaniel

C de San Bernardo

C Pozas

C del Tesoro

C San
Joaquín

C de los
Amigos

Plaza de
España Ⓜ

C de los Reyes

See map
p246

C de la Marqués
de Santa Ana

C Jesús del Valle

C de la Madera

C de la

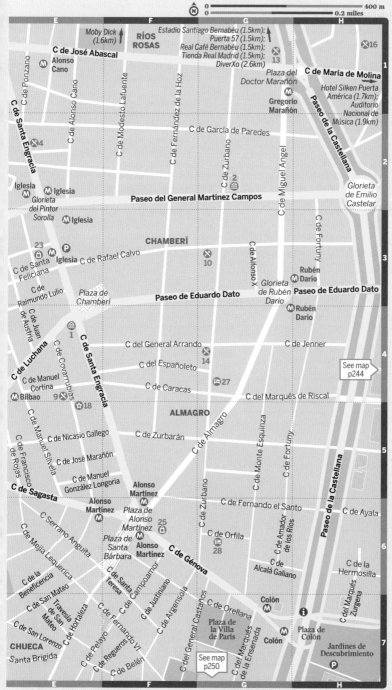

CHAMBERÍ *Map on p252*

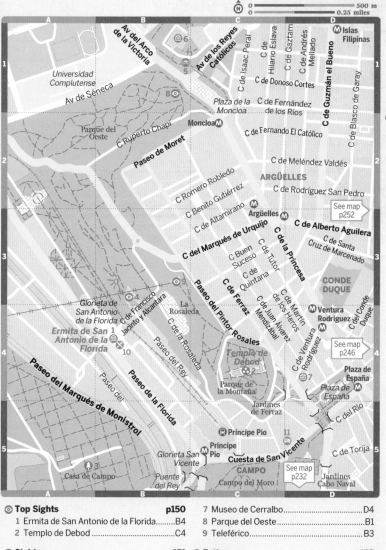

Our Story

A beat-up old car, a few dollars in the pocket and a sense of adventure. In 1972 that's all Tony and Maureen Wheeler needed for the trip of a lifetime – across Europe and Asia overland to Australia. It took several months, and at the end – broke but inspired – they sat at their kitchen table writing and stapling together their first travel guide, *Across Asia on the Cheap*. Within a week they'd sold 1500 copies. Lonely Planet was born.

Today, Lonely Planet has offices in Franklin, London, Melbourne, Oakland, Beijing and Delhi, with more than 600 staff and writers. We share Tony's belief that 'a great guidebook should do three things: inform, educate and amuse'.

Our Writer

Anthony Ham

In 2001, Anthony (www.anthonyham.com) fell in love with Madrid on his first visit to the city. Less than a year later, he arrived on a one-way ticket, with not a word of Spanish and not knowing a single person. After 10 years living in the city, he recently returned to Australia with his Spanish-born family, but he still adores his adopted country as much as the first day he arrived. When he's not writing for Lonely Planet, Anthony writes about and photographs Spain, Scandinavia, the Middle East, Australia and Africa for newspapers and magazines around the world.

31901057085419

Published by Lonely Planet Publications Pty Ltd
ABN 36 005 607 983
8th edition – Jan 2016
ISBN 978 1 74321 501 2
© Lonely Planet 2016   Photographs © as indicated 2016
10 9 8 7 6 5 4 3 2 1
Printed in China